P9-CJX-530

BY JUSTIN KAPLAN

LINCOLN STEFFENS
MARK TWAIN AND HIS WORLD
MR. CLEMENS AND MARK TWAIN

Walt Whitman

A LIFE

Justin Kaplan

SIMON AND SCHUSTER · NEW YORK

PUBLISHED BY SIMON AND SCHUSTER
A DIVISION OF GULF & WESTERN CORPORATION
SIMON & SCHUSTER BUILDING
ROCKEFELLER CENTER
1230 AVENUE OF THE AMERICAS
NEW YORK, NEW YORK 10020
SIMON AND SCHUSTER AND COLOPHON ARE TRADEMARKS
OF SIMON & SCHUSTER

DESIGNED BY EVE METZ
PHOTO EDITOR: VINCENT VIRGA

MANUFACTURED IN THE UNITED STATES OF AMERICA

1 3 5 7 9 10 8 6 4 2

LIBRARY OF CONGRESS CATALOGING IN PUBLICATION DATA

KAPLAN, JUSTIN.
WALT WHITMAN, A LIFE.
INCLUDES BIBLIOGRAPHICAL REFERENCES AND INDEX.
1. WHITMAN, WALT, 1819–1892. 2. POETS, AMERICAN—
19TH CENTURY—BIOGRAPHY. I. TITLE.
PS3231.K3   811'.3 [B]
80–16538
ISBN 0–671–22542–1

Parts of Chapter 8 appeared in different form in *Telling Lives: The Biographer's Art*, edited by Marc Pachter, published by New Republic Books in association with the National Portrait Gallery. Copyright © 1979 by the Smithsonian Institution.

A LIMITED EDITION OF THIS BOOK HAS BEEN PRIVATELY PRINTED.

ACKNOWLEDGMENTS

I thank Charles E. Feinberg, prince of Whitman collectors; Gay Wilson Allen and Edwin Haviland Miller, whose work has set the standard for all subsequent Whitman scholarship; and Gordon N. Ray and the trustees of the Guggenheim Memorial Foundation for the award of a fellowship in aid of this biography.

For help and generosity with information and materials of one sort or another I am grateful to the late Frederick Anderson, E. Digby Baltzell, John B. Blake, Stella Blum, David Cavitch, Heather Cole, James M. Cox, Julie Cummings, George Gloss, David R. Godine, David Gollaher, Edward F. Grier, Patrick D. Hazard, Howard Mumford Jones, Jerome Loving, Frank McQuilkin, Robert K. Martin, Tom Maschler, Paddington Matz, Robert F. W. Meader, Edwin Haviland Miller, Henry A. Murray, Donald Newlove, Stephen B. Oates, James Parton, Joel Porte, John H. Reed, Charlotte Sagoff, Robert J. Scholnick, Peter Shaw, Lola Sladitz, Henry Nash Smith, Irene A. Talarowski, Stanley Tamarkin, Randall Waldron, and Alden Whitman.

I could not have written this book without drawing on the resources of the Berg Collection, New York Public Library; Harvard University Library; Manuscript Division, Library of Congress (the chief repository of Whitman materials, including the Feinberg Collection); Long Island Historical Society; Special Collections, Ohio Wesleyan University.

Two mentors no longer living, F. O. Matthiessen and Louis Untermeyer, helped shape my interest in Whitman many years ago. I salute them, and for more recent counsel and encouragement I thank Daniel Aaron, Michael Korda, and, always, Anne Bernays.

J. K.

Cambridge, Massachusetts
February 29, 1980

In loving and grateful memory of Howard Kaplan 1916–1979

Contents

1

Mickle Street

I

IN THE SPRING OF 1884 the poet Walt Whitman bought a house in
the unlovely city of Camden, New Jersey, and at the age of sixty-
five slept under his own roof for the first time in his life. Eleven
years earlier, disabled by a stroke and a breakdown when his mother
died, he had been taken in by his younger brother, George Washington Whitman, a blunt, practical man, inspector in a Camden pipe
foundry. George's hospitality had been affectionately extended and
gratefully accepted, but the arrangement proved to be at best toler-
able for everyone concerned. George cared only about pipes and
money, Walt said, complaining about "the chilling atmosphere,
(both moral and meteorological) of this house." George was similarly
baffled and exasperated. "Mother thought as I did—did not know
what to make of it," he recalled, comparing his brother's *Leaves of
Grass* with another American epic published in the same year, 1855,
Professor Longfellow's tuneful *Song of Hiawatha*. "The one seemed
to us pretty much the same muddle as the other." In George's view,
Leaves of Grass was either a prank or an aberration. Moreover, Walt's
poems celebrating the love of men and women, in particular the
cluster titled "Children of Adam," were "of the whorehouse order"
and had brought him the worst kind of notoriety; some critics
branded them shameless self-revelations that were offensively explicit about sex and body functions and were incitements to public
licentiousness. "What are you up to, anyhow?" George asked.
"Nothing, George." Walt never explained his work to his family or

wrote them a letter that could be called literary. "I just did what I did because I did it—that's the whole secret." "You're as stubborn as hell," George said; "you are stubborner, Walt, than a load of bricks."

George found it difficult to reconcile such waywardness with the fact that year after year eminent, even dazzling, visitors from abroad journeyed to Camden, a place of few attractions, to call on the author of *Leaves of Grass*. Oscar Wilde—"a fine large handsome youngster," Walt said—drank elderberry wine and hot toddies in George's house and then wrote a note to "My Dear Dear Walt" to say, "There is no one in this great wide world of America whom I love and honor so much." A large photograph, inscribed "To Walt from Oscar," joined the conventional clutter of albums, Civil War mementos, things under glass bells, whatnots, and dust catchers that adorned the parlor on Stevens Street. The internationally celebrated *bon vivant* and man of letters Richard Monkton Milnes, first Baron Houghton, was delighted to eat plain baked apples here with America's chief, perhaps only, poet of universal stature, the creator of a radical book and a radical consciousness.

I know I am restless and make others so,

Whitman had written,

For I confront peace, security, and all the settled laws, to unsettle
them.

According to one visitor, the naturalist John Burroughs, Whitman was a leviathan entering a duck pond.

Accommodating themselves to the leviathan and the fish that swam with him was a trial to George and his wife, Louisa. She had had trials enough already, when her mother-in-law lived with them. Since then she had lost two children, one dead at eight months and the other stillborn. In addition to caring for Walt, whose stroke had left him partly crippled, she looked after his brother Eddy, who also lived at Stevens Street. Eddy was mentally incompetent, and until 1881, when he was finally put away in an institution, Louisa helped him bathe and dress, and supervised his meals—he would eat himself into a stupor unless stopped.

Although decrepit, Walt was radiantly and even aggressively healthy in spirit, and Louisa was as fond of him as he was of her.

Still, it graveled her that when she rang the dinner bell he acted in a way that struck her as downright contrary, as if he had chosen to respond to another set of signals altogether. He took his daily bath, and while the food on the table grew cold, she heard him splashing in the tub and singing "When Johnny Comes Marching Home," "Jim Crow," "The Star-Spangled Banner," tunes without words, popular ballads, broken arias from the Italian operas that were among the passions of his life. Leaning heavily on his cane, he went for a hobble around the block with his little yellow-and-white dog, Tip, or rode the ferry back and forth across the Delaware River. Often, acting on impulse or sudden invitation, he went away to see friends in New York and Philadelphia or to stay at a farm at nearby Laurel Springs and spend hours alone in the woods and by the pond at Timber Creek. He slept late, and he was as casual as he had always been about engagements, schedules, meals, and the regulated life that George and Louisa cherished. He found it oppressive. "He seems always to have been a sort of visitor in life," Burroughs said. "All his urgency and strenuousness he reserved for his book."

George stopped short of calling his brother shiftless, but he did not hide his disapproval. "He got offers of literary work—good offers: and we thought he had chances to make money. Yet he would refuse to do anything except at his own notion—most likely when advised would say 'We won't talk about that!' or anything else to pass the matter off . . . He would never make concessions for money—always was so . . . On literary topics Walt was the one to go to . . . But in business the rest of us were nearer the mark. We mixed up in business affairs." George was to leave an estate of over $58,000 in cash in addition to real estate; another brother, Jeff, a civil engineer in St. Louis, prospered enough to send two daughters to private school in the East. But Walt was far from being as impractical as George supposed. He scrupulously paid for his board at Stevens Street and even made loans to George over the years; he had always taken financial responsibility for Eddy, to whom he was to bequeath some six thousand dollars in savings, along with literary and real property.

When George and Louisa moved to a farmhouse in Burlington, New Jersey, about twenty miles from Camden, Walt declined their invitation to go on living with them. He saw a chance to regain his freedom and stayed behind, a decision that angered George and strained the bond between them. With $1,250 in cash, earned from a recent flurry of *Leaves of Grass* sales, and a loan from the publisher of the Philadelphia *Public Ledger,* Walt put down the purchase price of $1,750 for Number 328 Mickle Street, a raddled two-story house in a working-class neighborhood. It was not a slum, as George claimed, but it was several rungs down on the amenity ladder from the establishment on Stevens Street. Southwest breezes wafted choking exhalations from a fertilizer-processing plant on the Pennsylvania shore. Night and day trains of the Camden and Amboy Railroad puffed and rattled along about a hundred yards away from the house. It was also within earshot of factory whistles, shipping on the Delaware, and the ferry terminal. Sundays Whitman closed his windows against the bells and harsh choir of a Methodist church on the corner. A woman across the street thrummed for hours on her piano—"She can beat the devil for noise and give him odds." He was so tormented by neighborhood fife-and-drum brigades and boys with firecrackers that he came to anticipate the Fourth of July as a day of headache. Nevertheless, he was happy to be settled for good in "a little old shanty of my own."

He had taken possession expecting that the people living there, an elderly laborer and his wife, would stay on and help him manage in lieu of paying rent. But after ten months, probably because of the sort of domestic friction that had occurred at Stevens Street, they moved out and took all their furnishings with them. In his empty house he slept upstairs in a front room that had a narrow plank floor, a wood-burning stove with a pipe going up into the wall, and three windows looking north through the branches of a dying tree. He cooked his meals over a kerosene stove, ate them off the top of a packing case, and in other ways tried to make a go of it alone, even though he was lamer than ever and suffered spells of faintness and blurred vision. It was the sort of situation that gave rise to rumors, less well-founded at other times, that he had become a derelict. Eventually he invited Mary Davis, a sailor's widow living a few blocks away, to become his housekeeper in informal exchange for occupancy of an apartment in the rear. The neighbors gossiped, but Mary moved in anyway and stayed there for seven devoted years until Whitman died; then she sued his estate, claiming she had spent far more on him out of her own pocket than the one thousand dollars that he left her in his will. Perhaps she had hoped they would marry when she first moved in with her household goods, her nautical souvenirs and relics, a dog, a cat, and some birds.

John Burroughs, who had known him for about twenty years, said that it was not until old age that Whitman's presence and ambience became fully achieved. His health was failing, he was often testy and self-absorbed, but he created an overall impression of sunniness, equanimity, and contemplative leisure. He weighed two hundred pounds and was about six feet tall, had big hands and feet, a broad, strong nose, full lips, and the wild-hawk look foreigners associated with Americans. He liked buckwheat cakes, beef steak, oysters, and strong coffee. Except when he sat at the table with others, he preferred to drink directly from his water pitcher and his bottle of sherry or rum. He had the free and easy manners of someone who worked outdoors, and his closest friends were laborers, drivers, semiliterates, like Peter Doyle, a horse-car conductor and railroad hand, and Harry Stafford, a New Jersey farm boy. He greeted people with "Howdy" and said goodbye with "So long," an idiom he associated with sailors and prostitutes. "Ram a needle in his ass," he said about a Philadelphia bookbinder who was slow in delivering, "not far enough to hurt him—only far enough to wake him up." Then he *ha-ha*'d until the tears ran.

Burroughs regarded these personal traits as evidence of Whitman's "rank masculinity," but at the same time he recognized another nature—"a curious feminine undertone in him which revealed itself in the quality of his voice, the delicate texture of his skin, the gentleness of his touch and ways." The fictive hero of Whitman's poetry was the sexual athlete and swaggerer, "one of the roughs," not Whitman himself, "a great tender mother-man" who, as a soldier in the war, would have been as out of character as General Sherman would have been as a nurse. His body was rosy and soft, like a child's, and his skin smelled of soap and cologne. He liked to keep a bowl of flowers by him—pinks, mignonette, roses, lilacs, whatever was in season. His beard and hair had thinned and turned white with age, emphasizing the clear outlines of the face, the high forehead, and high-arching brows over pale gray-blue eyes, surprisingly mild and receptive. After the Quaker manner Whitman kept his hat on indoors, a soft gray felt sombrero, which he tilted all the way back. He dressed in rough homespun suits and wide-collared shirts of unbleached linen, worn without a tie, open at his neck and chest to the breastbone. For special occasions he wore a shirt that Mary Davis had trimmed with lace at the collar and wrists. He was undeniably stylish, in his own way. A young poet who met Whitman in

1887 exclaimed, "Never has such a beautiful old man appeared among men." "I have little doubt it was the finest head this age or country has seen," said Burroughs, and, judging from the visual record, photographers, painters, and sculptors too numerous to count agreed with him.

The bedroom at Mickle Street reminded visitors of a newspaper office; a cornfield at husking time, piled with shucks and stalks; the Sargasso Sea; and Professor Teufelsdröckh's study as described by Thomas Carlyle in one of Whitman's favorite books, *Sartor Resartus.* "It was a strange apartment; full of books and tattered papers, and miscellaneous shreds of all conceivable substances, 'united in a common element of dust.' " Whitman thought of his room as a ship's cabin with everything he wanted within reach and therefore shipshape, even though there was an appearance of the contrary. From boxes and bundles in the storeroom, from a big iron-banded double-hasped trunk that had been with him in Washington and now stood against the bedroom wall, he released drifts and billows of paper. He had kept every imaginable variety of written and printed matter: manuscripts, old letterheads and billheads thriftily saved and written over, faded scraps of writing paper and even wallpaper pinned, pasted, or tied together in ragged bundles that had a before-the-flood look, notebooks and diaries, many of them homemade, scrapbooks, letters received and drafts of letters sent, printer's proofs and samples, photographs, memoranda, circulars, receipts and accounts rendered, official documents, clippings from magazines and newspapers. With an occasional shoe or wad of stamps or stick of kindling mixed in haphazardly, this tide churned in a widening semicircle in front of Whitman's chair, seeped into the corners of the room and under the furniture and was tracked out into the hallway.

Year after year, Whitman stirred his archive with the crook of his cane. Relics of personal history floated to the surface. Here were documents relating to the settlement of an old debt and to his dismissal from his government clerkship in 1865. Here was a "for sale" advertisement inserted by one Asa L. Thomson in the *Natchez Free Trader* on May 11, 1848, when Whitman was living in the South. "I have just arrived from Missouri with ten Negroes, which I will sell at a bargain for cash. I have several boys about 21 years of age that are very likely, strictly No. l." ("The way Mr. Thomson expresses himself," Whitman observed, "you might think he was handling a line of reduced goods in a department store.") Casually mixed in with the other papers was the letter, still in its envelope addressed to "Walter Whitman, Esq.," that Ralph Waldo Emerson sent from Concord on July 21, 1855, a few weeks after *Leaves of Grass* first went out into an indifferent world. "I find it the most extraordinary piece of wit and wisdom that America has yet contributed," Emerson had told the thirty-six-year-old poet. "I greet you at the beginning of a great career, which yet must have had a long foreground somewhere, for such a start." The letter had been lost for years.

Whitman's floor yielded up fragments and beginnings that suggested that a great transformation had once taken place somewhere in this foreground—

> I cannot be awake, for nothing looks to me as it did before,
> Or else I am awake for the first time, and all before has been a mean
>   sleep.

—along with the birth of an overmastering purpose. Naming Homer, Shakespeare, and Sir Walter Scott, all "masters" after their own kind, the outsetting bard had declared,

> I will be also a master after my own kind, making the poems of
> emotions, as they pass or stay, the poems of freedom, and the exposé
> of personality—singing in high tones democracy and the New World
> of it through These States.

Yet there were hints that a less robust spirit had once prevailed, a spirit covert, hesitant, perturbed, lonely, and always unrequited. ("It is I you hold and who holds you," he addressed his reader, becoming his own book, "I spring from the pages into your arms.") His entire life, it seemed, may have been a demonstration of the regenerative power of personality, change and language. "The character you give me is not a true one in the main," he said in 1883 to his friend and biographer Dr. Richard Maurice Bucke. "I am by no means the benevolent, equable, happy creature you portray—but let that pass—I have left it as you wrote." ("The actual W. W. is a very plain personage," he had said on a much earlier occasion.) Even now, despite his composure, a certain "reserve and sadness" were in evidence, wrote an English admirer Edward Carpenter, "a sense of remoteness and inaccessibility," of omnivorous egotism and contrary moods. "He celebrates in his poems the fluid, all-solvent disposition, but was often himself less the river than the rock," Carpenter observed. He guessed it was this rocklike disposition that had prevented Whitman from ever being "quite what is called 'happy in love affairs,' " for he seemed to take pleasure in saying "No" for its own sake, abruptly, and with magnificent finality.

"What lies behind *Leaves of Grass*," Whitman told Carpenter in a rare confessional moment, "is something that few, very few, only one here and there, perhaps oftenest women, are at all in a position to seize. It lies behind every line; but concealed, studiedly concealed; some passages left purposely obscure. There is something in my nature *furtive* like an old hen! You see a hen wandering up and down a hedgerow, looking apparently quite unconcerned, but presently she finds a concealed spot, and furtively lays an egg, and comes away as though nothing had happened. That is how I felt in writing *Leaves of Grass*."

As a description of himself he was willing to accept "cautious" and also "artful"—"which about hits the mark," he told Carpenter, adding, "I think there are truths which it is necessary to envelop or wrap up." In what may have been his ultimate disguise he declared his belief in the existence of "the real Me," the core Walt Whitman who stood apart from the pulling and hauling of events and relationships:

> Trippers and askers surround me,
> People I meet, the effect upon me of my early life or the ward and
>   city I live in, or the nation,
> The latest dates, discoveries, inventions, societies, authors old and
>   new,
> My dinner, dress, associates, looks, compliments, dues,
> The real or fancied indifference of some man or woman I love,
> The sickness of one of my folks or of myself, or ill-doing or loss or
>   lack of money, or depressions or exaltations,
> Battles, the horrors of fratricidal war, the fever of doubtful news,
>   the fitful events;
> These come to me days and nights and go from me again,
> But they are not the Me myself.

He said there was a secret personality "lurking" behind Shakespeare's plays. Perhaps this was true of every "highest poetic nature," including his own. Something compelled the poet "to cover up and involve [his] real purpose and meaning in folded removes and far recesses," to create myths, suppress history, and reveal himself only in riddles and obliquities. ("Tell all the Truth but tell it slant," Emily Dickinson said. "Success in Circuit lies.") Sometimes Whitman was hardly conscious of reshaping his past to make it conform to the ample, serene and masterful identity he achieved long after. Sometimes he reshaped his past deliberately, just as he reshaped *Leaves of Grass* over the course of nine editions in order to give his life as well as his work a different emphasis. Ever since his stroke he had been editing his archives. "I have twice hurriedly destroyed a large mass of letters and MSS.—to be ready for what might happen," he said in 1874. Fourteen years later a visitor at Mickle Street noted, "W. had been burning some old manuscripts today. A piece had dribbled at the foot of the stove." Certain things, Whitman explained, were "too sacred—too surely and only mine—to be perpetuated." Some manuscripts he carefully altered, destroying single pages, effacing or disguising identifications, transposing genders, changing "him" to "her" or a man's initials to a number code. By the time he died scarcely a period in his life had not been "revised" in one way or another. Some periods had practically ceased to exist so far as intimate documentation was concerned. These revisions and suppressions, deepening the already profound mystery that surrounded the emergence of *Leaves of Grass* from its long foreground, appeared to be all the more remarkable because Whitman the poet avowedly adored nakedness in all its manifestations, including the naked truth, and declared that body and soul were "sacred" in their entirety and therefore indivisible.

Whitman's overflowing archives remained chaotic and unclear, except to himself. "This is not so much of a mess as it looks," he remarked, pointing to the papers on the floor and table. "You notice I find most of the things I look for, and without much trouble. The disorder is more suspected than real."

In *Specimen Days*, published in 1882, Whitman had written a random autobiography that he described as "the most wayward, spontaneous, fragmentary book ever printed." He provided a few glimpses of his family and early life, but mostly he dealt with wartime Washington and his recovery from breakdown at Timber

Creek. Perhaps thinking of his own history as well, he had warned his readers that "the real war will never get into the books . . . will never be written—perhaps must not and should not be." Now, at Mickle Street, Whitman had taken to writing articles in the same retrospective vein but further removed from intimate autobiography. He recalled the glories of the New York theater in the days of the tragedian Junius Brutus Booth, his visit to New Orleans in 1848, the military hospitals again. In contrast to these casual, even careless pieces written or merely assembled in order to earn a little cash, was the long essay, "A Backward Glance O'er Travel'd Roads," that he published in 1888 as the preface to *November Boughs*, a collection of valedictory and reflective poems. He had worked on this essay for four years, on and off, and had already published it in preliminary stages as "My Book and I," "How 'Leaves of Grass' Was Made," and "How I Made a Book." Eventually he was satisfied that "A Backward Glance," a summary and justification of his life in poetry, should be the last of his many critical declarations and farewells.

"Here I sit gossiping in the early candle-light of old age," Whitman wrote, "I and my book—casting backward glances over our travel'd road." He and his book had seen a young country, incomparably vital but bitterly divided against itself, survive a terrible bloodletting and once and for all, it seemed, vindicate the idea of democracy and union. During those unloosened decades the twelve untitled poems and 95 pages of the 1855 *Leaves of Grass* had grown to 293 poems and 382 pages in the sixth edition published in Boston by James R. Osgood and Company in 1881. Just when it seemed that *Leaves of Grass* had finally won its battle for a fair hearing, the Boston District Attorney put Osgood under notice: "We are of the opinion that this book is such a book as brings it within the provisions of the Public Statutes respecting obscene literature and suggest the propriety of withdrawing the same from circulation and suppressing the editions thereof." Osgood proposed a list of deletions, including extensive passages and three poems in their entirety, "A Woman Waits for Me," "The Dalliance of the Eagles," and "To A Common Prostitute." Whitman took the book away from Osgood. "The list whole & several is rejected by me, & will not be thought of under any circumstances." Soon after this latest defeat—*"No book on earth ever had such a history"*—he was able to find a more or less permanent home with an enterprising young publisher in Philadelphia, David McKay. Now the poems stood in their final form and sequence, not to be further altered in Whitman's lifetime except for the addition of new matter at the end as "annexes." And so the book was finished at last and, he believed, endowed with the structure of something monumental found in nature or made by man, a great tree with many growth rings, a cathedral, a modern city like his million-footed Manhattan. It was time to render a final account.

Whitman looked back over traveled roads to the emergence, from stirrings to recognition, of the shaping "desire and conviction" of his life:

> After continued personal ambition and effort, as a young fellow, to enter with the rest into competition for the usual rewards, business, political, literary, &c.—to take part in the great *mêlée*, both for victory's prize itself and to do some good—After years of those aims and pursuits, I found myself remaining possess'd, at the age of thirty-one to thirty-three, with a special desire and conviction . . . to articulate and faithfully express in literary or poetic form, and uncompromisingly, my own physical, emotional, moral, intellectual, and aesthetic Personality, in the midst of, and tallying, the momentous spirit and facts of its immediate days, and of current America—and to exploit that Personality, identified with place and date, in a far more candid and comprehensive sense than any hitherto poem or book.

Leaves of Grass was egotistic and "doubtless self-will'd," but it also sprang from the common experiences of all men and women, from the deep-down, universal imperatives of "Sex and Amativeness, and even Animality," and from the particular nature of "America and today." "I know very well," he said, summing up the tumultuous period he and his book had spanned, "that my 'Leaves' could not possibly have emerged or been fashion'd or completed, from any other era than the latter half of the Nineteenth Century, nor any other land than democratic America, and from the absolute triumph of the National Union Arms." To sing the song of himself, his nation, and his century, he had cut himself loose from conventional themes, stock ornamentation, literary allusions, romance, rhyme—anything that existed for the sake of tradition alone and reflected alien times, alien cultures. As his critics liked to point out, he had also become a tireless self-publicist who, without permission or precedent, had made public use of Emerson's private letter of recognition, written newspaper articles about himself, planted stories, collaborated in biographies, polemics and encomia, and even reviewed his own book on many occasions. ("The public is a thick-skinned beast," he said when he was old, "and you have to keep whacking away on its hide to let it know you're there.") And yet this incessant clamor and posturing possessed a certain purity—it was always and ultimately in the service of the work, *Leaves of Grass*, not the self. He never wanted to live in style or rub feathers with the quality for very long.

In his brave preface to the 1855 edition, Whitman defined poets and readers as peers, joint tenants in reality. "The messages of great poets to each man and woman are, Come to us on equal terms, Only then can you understand us, We are no better than you, What we enclose you enclose, What we enjoy you may enjoy." "The proof of a poet," he had concluded, "is that his country absorbs him as affectionately as he has absorbed it."

In the evening of his life he had to concede a measure of defeat. "I have not gain'd the acceptance of my time, but have fallen back on fond dreams of the future—anticipations." His most fervent readers as a group were not the workingmen, artisans and farmers—the democratic leaven—whom he celebrated and addressed his poems to. They were British writers and intellectuals of the highest degree of cultivation—Wilde; Milnes; Algernon Swinburne; John Addington Symonds; Professor Edward Dowden of Trinity College, Dublin; W. T. Stead, editor of the *Pall Mall Gazette;* Robert Louis Stevenson; Gerard Manley Hopkins; William Michael Rossetti and his circle. "I don't know if you have ever realized what it means to be a horror in the sight of the people about you," Whitman said of his standing in literary America, especially literary New England. But the Poet Laureate Alfred Lord Tennyson wrote him warm letters, offered him the hospitality of his house in Surrey, and at an evening's entertainment in London read aloud from *Leaves of Grass* for half an hour. In 1885, when Whitman had a total income of $1,333, including $67 in American royalties, $686, a little over a half, came in the form of outright gifts from English admirers. The steelmaster-philanthropist Andrew Carnegie called it a disgrace to "triumphant democracy" that financial support for "the great poet of America so far" should have to come from abroad.

Whitman had absorbed a great deal of abuse and ridicule ever since 1855, but so far from being neglected, as he often charged, he had in fact become renowned for the obscurity in which he supposedly languished. The New York stockbroker and man of letters,

Edmund Clarence Stedman, had recently confronted this paradox in a prominent, evenhanded, but (according to Whitman) somewhat "grandmotherly" magazine article. ("You can't put a quart of water into a pint bottle," Whitman remarked. "Stedman holds a good pint, but the pint is his limit.") The article appeared in *Scribner's Monthly*, an ultrarespectable journal heretofore, under its editor Dr. Josiah Gilbert Holland, unwaveringly hostile to *Leaves of Grass*.

Let us be candid : no writer holds, in some respects, a more enviable place than burly Walt Whitman. As for public opinion of the professional kind, no American poet, save Longfellow, has attracted so much notice as he in England, France, Germany, and I know not what other lands. Here and abroad there has been more printed concerning him than concerning any other, living or dead, Poe only excepted. Personal items of his doings, sayings and appearance constantly have found their way to the public. In a collection of sketches, articles, debates, which have appeared during the last ten years, relating to American poets, the Whitman and Poe packages are each much larger than all the rest combined. Curiously enough, three-fourths of the articles upon Mr. Whitman assert that he is totally neglected by the press.

But the fact remained: despite the skillfully managed publicity of martyrdom and neglect, Whitman's great poem of joy and liberation —his gospel for the century of democracy, science, and steam—had come nowhere near being affectionately absorbed. "From a worldly and business point of view" as well, Whitman said in "A Backward Glance," *Leaves of Grass* was "worse than a failure." This outlaw book continued to subject him to "frequent bruises" and public humiliations. He counted among them his dismissal, as the author of an immoral book, from his government clerkship in 1865 and, more recently, the expulsion of that same book from Boston, an event that aroused hardly a word of protest from the paladins of literary culture there. All of this, he said with only an occasional hint of bitterness and "sulky vanity"—surprisingly restrained, given his overriding ambition—was "probably no more than I ought to have expected. I had my choice when I commenc'd. I bid neither for soft eulogies, big money returns, nor the approbation of existing schools and conventions. . . . I have had my say entirely my own way and put it unerringly on record—the value thereof to be decided by time."

Uncompromised, its offending passages still in place contrary to all sorts of advice received over the years, *Leaves of Grass* remained "a candidate for the future" and lived "on its own blood." The essential nature of his book was indicated by a few simple words, he said: "Suggestiveness" ("The reader will always have his or her part to do, just as much as I have had mine"), "Comradeship," "Good Cheer," and "Hope"—"The strongest and sweetest songs yet remain to be sung."

Meanwhile, as he wrote in an autumnal poem called "After the Supper and Talk," he remained a grateful and contented guest, "a far-stretching journey" ahead of him, who at evening's end, "shadows of nightfall deepening," delays in the exit door and on the steps,

> loth, O so loth to depart!
> Garrulous to the very last.

II

Shamed by the English, Whitman's American partisans launched several earnest but imperfect schemes to provide for him in old age. In 1886, one such scheme took the form of a private bill, introduced in the Committee on Invalid Pensions by Congressman Henry B. Lovering, of Lynn, Massachusetts, to award Whitman $25 a month in recognition of his hospital work during the war. The bill immediately aroused the ire of an implacable old Boston enemy, Colonel Thomas Wentworth Higginson, a war hero who commanded the Union's first black regiment. His career in peacetime letters was as remarkable for his recognition of Emily Dickinson's genius as for his hatred of Whitman, whose work he had first encountered during a violent bout of seasickness. (He said that Whitman's chief mistake was not that he wrote *Leaves of Grass*, but that "he did not burn it afterwards.") Having already played a part in running the book out of Boston, Higginson opposed the Lovering bill on the grounds that it rewarded a malingerer who should have fought in the front lines instead of hiding in the wards. Even Whitman, who had some reason to believe that nursing the sick and wounded had permanently undermined his own health, was unhappy with the bill—in seeking to make him a public charge it made him a public target as well. "I do *not* expect the bill to pass," he said, and it did not.

One of the bill's instigators, the Boston journalist Sylvester Baxter, succeeded in raising a subscription fund of eight hundred dollars that was presented to Whitman in the summer of 1887. The understanding among the subscribers was that he would buy himself a second home—a little cottage in the country or by the seashore—as a refuge from the oppressive heat of Camden. Having encouraged this scheme, he accepted the money gratefully, but he resisted all advice about the location and purchase of his cottage. As he told Baxter, "I feel as if I could suit my wants and tastes better probably deciding and directing the practicality of the whole thing *myself.*" In the end he neither bought the place nor was willing to give any accounting of what he had done with the money. "It is a closed book," he said testily, "it is a question not again to be reopened." He apparently commingled the "Summer Cottage Fund" with his savings, interpreted "second home" to mean, in a Scriptural sense, "long home," and used the money to build a tomb for himself in Harleigh Cemetery.

"Hot—hot," "the bad vertigo fits—bad fall," he wrote in his daybook in August 1885, the month a cyclone struck Camden and a fireball was seen passing overhead. Recognizing that Whitman had for some time been in danger of declining into a shut-in, Thomas Donaldson, a Philadelphia lawyer, authority on the American Indians, and future biographer of his friend, organized a therapeutic surprise: the gift of a horse and buggy for daily outings.

Without Whitman's knowledge, Donaldson sent out thirty-six letters describing his project and soliciting individual gifts of ten dollars. One letter went to John Greenleaf Whittier, the aged Quaker poet who, as Whitman liked to believe, had long ago flung his copy of *Leaves of Grass* into the fire. Whether this was true was open to question, but the fact remained that for years Whittier had maintained an aggrieved silence about a book that he found morally offensive. Now he was torn between a fear of associating himself with it and a wish to help a needy fellow author who once served the Union cause. He discussed his dilemma with an old friend, Dr. Oliver Wendell Holmes, whose name also appeared on Donaldson's quixotic mailing list. The Autocrat had never yet had a good word to say for Whitman. (He was soon to tell the readers of the *Atlantic Monthly* that Whitman's "rhapsodies" reminded him of "fugues played upon a big organ which has been struck by lightning.") Holmes wrote a blandly favorable note to Donaldson—"I shall be happy to contribute my ten dollars toward the happy object you mention. Will a check on the Hamilton Bank of Boston answer the purpose?"—and privately he advised Whittier to do the same. "Some of his poems are among the most cynical instances of indecent exposure I recollect, outside what is sold as obscene literature," Holmes explained. "But I said to myself just what you did to yourself—he served well the cause of humanity and I do not begrudge him a ten dollar bill."

In his letter to Donaldson, Whittier pointedly expressed his regret that parts of *Leaves of Grass* had ever been written. He hoped that Whitman's horse would be "more serviceable to him than the untamed, rough-jolting Pegasus he has been accustomed to ride—without check or snaffle." Still he was afraid even this grudging benefaction would be misinterpreted. "My friend, Dr. Holmes, who was also a contributor," he wrote to the Boston *Transcript*, "wishes me to say that his gift, like my own, was solely an act of kindness to a disabled author, implying no approval whatever of his writings."

Donaldson apparently knew better than to solicit James Russell Lowell, who had just returned to private life after serving as minister to Great Britain; years earlier, when he was Professor of Modern Languages at Harvard he had dismissed *Leaves of Grass* as "a solemn humbug" and assured an irate clergyman, "I will take care to keep it out of the way of students."* Among more likely prospects whom Donaldson approached were the actor Edwin Booth, the essayist and travel writer Charles Dudley Warner, and Richard Watson Gilder, editor of *The Century*, who like his brother and sister, was an avowed Whitman partisan. Whitman stood among the great loners of American letters along with Emily Dickinson and Herman Melville. "I never read his Book," she told Higginson, "but was told that he was disgraceful." Melville was so much out of the public eye by 1885 that the English poet Robert Buchanan, who came to America looking for him, could learn only that he was "still living somewhere

---

* Possibly on Lowell's initiative, *Leaves of Grass* was removed from the open shelves of the college library and kept under lock and key with other tabooed books. Among those testifying to this was William Roscoe Thayer, a member of the class of 1881 at Harvard, who on a visit to Camden brashly recommended Lowell's work to Whitman—"Although he isn't a poet of the first rank, he stands well in the second place." Whitman stood firm. "You wouldn't persuade me to eat a second-class egg, would you? I don't care for second-class poetry, either." (William Roscoe Thayer, "Personal Recollections of Walt Whitman," *Scribner's Magazine*, LXV [June 1919], p. 683.)

in New York. No one seemed to know anything," Buchanan reported, "of the one great imaginative writer fit to stand shoulder to
shoulder with Whitman on that continent."

Mark Twain, who only a few months earlier had felt the lash of
Boston and Concord on *Huckleberry Finn*, responded instantly and
positively to Donaldson's appeal. "I have a great veneration for the
old man." But the birthday message—also solicited—that he was to
send when Whitman turned seventy in 1889 was so impersonal, so
full of inappropriate sentiments, that Whitman's friends were reluctant to show it to him for fear of souring the occasion. Nearly twenty
years after Whitman's death, when Mark Twain gave a Senate sub-
committee on copyright a list of American authors whose work he
considered of value and therefore deserving of protection under the
law, he named Cooper, Irving, Harriet Beecher Stowe, Poe, Emerson, William Dean Howells (who said Whitman's work was "not
poetry, but the materials of poetry"), and Thomas Bailey Aldrich
(who called Whitman "a charlatan," the author of a mere curiosity
that would survive only if kept in "a glass case or a quart of spirits in
an anatomical museum"). Although his publishing firm had issued a
selection of Whitman's prose, Mark Twain omitted Whitman from
his list, just as he omitted Melville, Thoreau, Hawthorne and Henry
James. Whitman too dismissed Henry James, as "feathers," and as
for Mark Twain—"He might have been something. He comes near
being something; but he never arrives." Not that Whitman was indifferent to American humor. "It is very grim, loves exaggeration,
& has a certain tartness & even fierceness." But he enjoyed this
humor chiefly in the talk of laborers, drivers, boatmen, unlettered
people. "You get more real fun from half an hour with them than
from all the books of all 'the American humorists.' " What was so
striking about the mutual disregard of Mark Twain and Whitman,
both dedicated to the language of American speech as the vehicle for
literature, was not that ships so large could have passed each other
in the night but that they were able to do it on so small an ocean.
Although brought to a successful outcome in mid-September 1885,
the horse-and-buggy fund symbolized Whitman's isolation as well as
the vagaries of literary fame.

"It belongs to you," Donaldson said, pointing to the trim rig that
stood waiting at the curb in Mickle Street. Whitman wept a little,
then climbed in with some assistance, took the reins in hand, and
trotted his sorrel pony around the outskirts of Camden. Visiting him

two weeks later Burroughs noted that they shared a big oyster dinner ("Walt eats very heartily—too heartily, I think, and tell him so") after which "Walt drives me to the station with his new horse and buggy—the first time I ever saw him drive. He is very proud of his present." Whitman's buggy, a phaeton, named for the young god who drove the chariot of the sun, reunited an old man with the sounds and sights of "the rich running day" he celebrated and restored to him some of the exuberance of his youth on Long Island. Half a century earlier he had been a publisher, editor, and delivery man of his own weekly newspaper in Huntington.

"I bought a good horse," he recalled, "and every week went all around the country serving my papers, devoting one day and night to it. I never had happier jaunts—going over to south side, to Babylon, down the south road, across to Smithtown and Comac, and back home. The experience of those jaunts, the dear old-fashion'd farmers and their wives, the stops by hayfields, the hospitality, nice dinners, occasional evenings, the girls, the rides through the brush, come up in my memory to this day."

Driving out daily when the weather was good and the roads clear, with a young neighbor, Bill Duckett, to help him, Whitman slipped back into the country custom of saluting everyone he met along the way and stopping to talk. Driving was his only exercise, he said. He soon wore out the stiff-kneed little pony and replaced it with a bay horse that had more spirit and less of an inclination to balk and stumble. He went for long drives into the flat Jersey farm country or, with the pass given him by the ferry company, crossed over to Philadelphia, Fairmount Park and Germantown. Every few days he visited the graves of his mother and his nephew Walt at Evergreen Cemetery in Camden. When the shad were running in the Delaware he drove to Gloucester, New Jersey, where Billy Thompson, who kept a public house by the water's edge, honored him with gala dinners of planked fish and champagne. He liked to watch the shad boats, rowed by twenty black men, making slow circuits in the river and paying out their seines. In Thompson's kitchen the cooks split and boned the shad, fastened them to scrubbed oak boards with silver nails, broiled and basted them with butter in front of an open coal fire.

Whitman was even up to reviving an old plan, abandoned for five years because of his poor health and a decline in public interest, to give annual lectures commemorating the death of Abraham Lincoln.

He lectured four times in 1886, once at the Chestnut Street Opera House in Philadelphia, where some journalists and actors had organized a benefit performance, preceded by a brief orchestral concert, which earned him nearly seven hundred dollars. At the end of his Philadelphia performance, seated on the half-darkened stage by a rose-globed study lamp, he gave his customary obligatory reading of his most conventional but—virtually to the exclusion of the rest of his work—most popular poem, "O Captain! My Captain!" Sometimes he regretted ever having written it. ("It's My Captain again; always My Captain," he exclaimed when the Harper publishing house asked his permission to print it in a school reader. "My God! when will they listen to me for whole and good?" If this was his "best," he said, "what can the worst be like?") Still he was pleased with the Philadelphia performance—"I am receiving great and opportune kindnesses in my old days—and this is one of them"—and agreed to give his lecture at Madison Square Theatre in New York City on April 14, 1887, the twenty-second anniversary of the assassination.

Robert Pearsall Smith, a prosperous glass manufacturer and frequent host to Whitman in Philadelphia, accompanied him from Camden the day before and put him up at the staid Westminster Hotel, in a suite of rooms once occupied by Charles Dickens. The following afternoon, wearing a black velvet jacket and a lace-trimmed linen shirt open at the collar, he was helped onto the stage by Stedman, one of the sponsors of the lecture, and installed in a large armchair. The theater was barely a quarter full, but this was a flattering turnout nonetheless. In the audience, along with friends like Burroughs and a scattering of young unknown admirers, was James Russell Lowell, sharing a box with Professor Charles Eliot Norton of Harvard (who in 1855 had taken fastidious notice, but notice just the same, of *Leaves of Grass;* Norton called it "superficial yet profound," "preposterous yet somehow fascinating," "a compound of the New England transcendentalist and New York rowdy"). Also in the audience were John Hay, former private secretary to Lincoln and future secretary of state; the popular fiction writers Frank Stockton, Edward Eggleston, Frances Hodgson Burnett, and Mary Mapes Dodge; the sculptor Augustus Saint-Gaudens; José Marti, the Cuban writer and revolutionist; Daniel Coit Gilman, president of the Johns Hopkins University; Mark Twain; and Andrew Carnegie, who subscribed $350 for his box.

In an unemphatic voice, sometimes almost inaudible, Whitman described the bitter convulsions, "more lurid and terrible than any war," that wracked the nation in the years just before Lincoln took office—it was a time when Whitman too had been inwardly divided and confused, torn between "hot passions," "inertia," "incredulity," and "conscious power." Terrible, cleansing and restorative for the nation, the Civil War became the central imaginative event of Whitman's middle life and Lincoln his personal agent of redemption, a symbolic figure who transcended politics, leadership, and victory. Whitman's lecture was his ritual reenactment of the Passion of Abraham Lincoln, a mass offered both to "sane and sacred death" and, as he had also written in his great poem of mourning, "When Lilacs Last in the Dooryard Bloom'd," to "the sweetest, wisest soul of all my days and lands."

As an event frozen in time and deserving to be commemorated in every retrievable detail Whitman recounted his first glimpse of the "strange and awkward figure" of the President-elect passing through New York in February 1861. "I saw him in Broadway, near the site of the present Post-office. He came down, I think from Canal Street, to stop at the Astor House." The night of the assassination Whitman had been away from Washington, but drawing on the eyewitness testimony of his friend Peter Doyle he evoked the lilacs in early bloom, the spirit of victory in the capital, the trivial parlor comedy, then the muffled pistol shot, a moment's hush, the assassin leaping to the stage, a cry of murder, clatter of hooves, soldiers storming the theater with fixed bayonets, a lynch mob roiling in the streets, and all the while Lincoln slowly dying "a heroic-eminent death" that was to filter "into the nation and the race" and give "a cement to the whole People, subtler, more underlying, than anything in written Constitution, or courts or armies." At the end of Whitman's lecture Stedman's little granddaughter carried a basket of lilacs to him, and then he recited "O Captain!" It was as though Lincoln had died "the day before," recalled one listener, the twenty-three-year-old poet Stuart Merrill. "I was there, the very thing happened to me. And this recital was as gripping as the messengers' reports in Aeschylus."

Merrill was among the several hundred who came to a reception that evening in Whitman's suite. Awed and stammering Merrill held out to him a recent issue of a Paris journal containing the symbolist Jules Laforgue's translations of "Children of Adam." "I was sure that a Frenchman would hit upon that part," Whitman said with a smile before the next guest was presented to him. In the quiet of Mickle Street he would later reflect that New York, with its fierce literary politics, its clubs and cabals, its "art delirium" and "crowd of scrawlers," was "death to the spirit . . . a good market for the harvest but a bad place for farming." But now he was made happy by the throng of admirers and enjoyed this "jamboree," "the culminating hour" of his life. It was the nearest he had ever come to savoring social eminence on a large scale. Around midnight, when the popular philosopher John Fiske tried to engage him in a discussion of the immortality of the soul, Whitman slipped away and went to bed, feeling a little dazed and in danger of being killed with lionizing. The next day, refreshed after sleep and a bath, he left for Camden looking "brighter and stronger," Burroughs said, "than I had ever expected to see him."

That June, as Whitman noted in his daybook after he turned 68, he was "almost altogether disabled in walking power & bodily movement—writing & composition power fair—handwriting power pretty good—appetite fair—sleep fair to middling not markedly bad & not really good." But all through the months following he continued to feel well enough to go out for daily rides in his buggy; he was busy preparing *November Boughs* for the printer; and he gladly sat for a procession of painters, sculptors and photographers. In April 1888 he drove out again to Billy Thompson's place at Gloucester. Garrulous, tolerant and playful, red-faced with food and excitement, he lifted his mug of champagne and cracked ice in a toast to President Grover Cleveland, former Prime Minister William Ewart Gladstone, and the emperor of Germany, "three eminent good fellows." He enjoyed the protests of his friends around the table who wished him to be always the radical democrat and were often disappointed. "So you see," he wrote the next day, "I get out & have fun yet—but it is a dwindling business." On May 31 he celebrated his sixty-ninth birthday at the house of Thomas Harned, a Camden attorney, and by his own account did most of the toasting and most of the drinking. The first printer's proofs of his new book, *November Boughs*, were delivered to him that evening as a surprise. "It's more precious than gold," he said, putting the roll of proof sheets in his coat pocket. "It's my baby book just born today—don't you see? I am celebrating two birthdays today."

Later that week, on the night of June 3, he had a succession of strokes, fell to the floor in his locked bedroom, and lay there for several hours, unable to move and unwilling to call out for help. The next day he tried to dismiss the episode as mere "shocks, premonitions," but he had become rambling and sluggish in speech and conversed with the absent Peter Doyle. "Where are you, Pete? Oh! I'm feeling rather kinky—not at all peart, Pete—not at all." He said he was slipping down and nothing could be done. "It is my impression that the whole matter is one but of a short time," his neighbor Horace Traubel told Burroughs. Traubel, Burroughs, and a few other close friends started making plans for the funeral but had prolonged disagreements over questions of "display," "respectability," and the role, if any, of a member of the clergy. Eddy Whitman, on his way to the Insane Asylum at Blackwoodtown, was brought to Mickle Street. They exchanged a few monosyllables and then lapsed into silence, with Walt holding his hand all the while. Walt said to Traubel, "Eddy appeals to my heart, to my two arms: I seem to want to reach out and help him." "Goodbye, boy—I will send for you again," Walt said as Eddy left. "You shall come whenever you choose: goodbye! goodbye!" In September he said goodbye to Burroughs. "He presses my hand long and tenderly, we kiss and part, probably for the last time," Burroughs wrote in his journal. "I think he has in his own mind given up the fight and awaits the end." The end was more than three years away, as it turned out, but after this latest collapse Whitman remained "imprison'd" at Mickle Street, did not go outside until the following May, and then it was in a wheelchair pushed by a male nurse. He no longer had much use for his horse and buggy and sold them "for a song."

2

Burial House

I

WITH THE ONSET of Whitman's final illness, the members of his inner circle drew themselves closely about him. Protective, possessive, and a little stifling, believing themselves a saving remnant, they became his chief audience and he their dependent and captive. The poet of finely articulated isolation accepted the role of guru.

"The scent of these armpits is aroma finer than prayer," he had written in 1855. "This head is more than churches or bibles or creeds." Yet in old age he was the head of an apostolic church whose communicants celebrated his birthdays with eucharistic feasts of adulation and vulgar excess. Wheeled to the table, presented with flowers and plied with iced champagne, he submitted with a mixture of pleasure and distress to the outpourings of the faithful. The proceedings at his seventieth-birthday dinner in 1889, published that year in a book called *Camden's Compliment to Walt Whitman*, struck him as "curious and incredible," "rather too single and unanimous and honeyed for my esthetic sense." One celebrant at the dinner two years later predicted that in years to come Whitman's grave in Camden would be another Mecca, and the city itself would only "be known to the world from the fact of one man living and dying here." "It is because we have travelled the Open Road with him here," concluded the speaker, a local journalist named Harry Bonsall, "that when we come to tread the highway of the spheres and step from constellation to constellation we shall know that Walt Whitman will await us on a still higher 'life' and extend, as now, the hand we will grasp in courage and confidence because of the light he shed on his way thither." "I did not know you were such a speechmaker, Harry," the old man said.

The Saint Peter, rock and chosen successor of the Camden church, was Horace Traubel, son of a Jewish father and a Quaker mother. Twenty-nine when Whitman had his latest stroke, Traubel had already known him for about fifteen years and served him as proxy, editorial assistant, messenger and companion. But he had also become an elective son, "the only thing between me and death," Whitman said. He took Horace's hand and then drew him close and kissed him. "I feel somehow as if you had consecrated yourself to me. That entails something on my part: I feel somehow as if I was consecrated to you. Well—we will work out the rest of my life-job together." Richard Maurice Bucke, a physician and eminent alienist, superintendent of the insane asylum in London, Ontario, was Whitman's Luke as well as his Paul, missionary to the gentiles and to far-flung congregations of true believers. A Whitman fellowship in the Lancashire mill town of Bolton, England, cherished among other sacred objects a lock of the poet's hair and the stuffed body of a canary that had once trilled in the parlor at Mickle Street. On the occasion of Bucke's visit in 1891 the members of the Bolton "college" or "church," mostly business and professional people, welcomed Whitman's "defender," "explicator" and "vindicator" in verses composed to be sung to the tune of "Men of Harlech."

"I wonder what *Leaves of Grass* would have been," Whitman remarked to Traubel, "if I had been born of some other mother and had never met William O'Connor," who for a quarter of a century, and even when they became personally estranged after a quarrel, had been his John the Baptist. Crying in the critical wilderness, at the end of the Civil War, O'Connor had prepared the way by writing and publishing at his own expense *The Good Gray Poet*, a pamphlet that argued for Whitman the stature of a world figure, a prophet of humanity as well as of America; Whitman's physical presence alone, "majestic, large, Homeric," O'Connor wrote, set him apart as an epic hero, and in an allegorical story, "The Carpenter," he also portrayed Whitman as miracle worker and Christ. A master of flesh-creeping invective, learned allusion, and polemic overkill, O'Connor, in Whitman's admiring description, was "a born artillerist," "a battle-ship firing both sides fore and after"; from time to time, it should have been added, the battleship suffered frightful explosions in its own powder magazine. When Traubel and Bucke came to see him in Washington in March 1889, O'Connor had only a few months to live. "Horace is the wonder child of our pilgrimage," O'Connor said, kissing Horace's lips, eyes, and forehead, "the pride of the flock." O'Connor was prepared to depart in peace, having seen salvation in the Whitman church. "It has all been beautiful," his wife said at the end of this sacramental parting. "He will carry it with him into the next world." She had been in love with Whitman for years and had vivid dreams about the mingling of their "astral" bodies.

"I think him the equal, and in many respects the superior of the much misunderstood Jesus," declared William Sloane Kennedy, a former Harvard divinity student turned journalist and professional votary. Whitman had at first been delighted by Kennedy's dramatic conversion from an initial Plymouth Rock distress at the "bad taste," "coarse indecencies," and "moral repulsiveness" of *Leaves of Grass*. Eventually he developed reservations about Kennedy, who, although "granitic" as a partisan, seemed nonetheless to lack a center. "Some day he may get himself all together," Whitman remarked. He maintained a dignified silence when Kennedy, in a Christmas letter in 1890, put a question to him: "Do you suppose in a thousand years from now people will be celebrating the birth of Walt Whitman as they are now the birth of Christ?" There were times, Whitman said, when Kennedy out-Bucked even Bucke.

The doctor had arrived in Camden for a visit just in time to respond to what was clearly the mortal emergency of Whitman's collapse in June 1888. "He took off his coat, rolled up his sleeves, buckled to, saved me," Whitman said a week and a half later. "I thought I was having my last little dance." Bucke's devotion was so intense and of such long standing that over the years he came to look like Whitman. Sometimes he even fancied he was Whitman, although in essential respects their personalities were antithetic. "Over-emphasis is his failing—going off half-cocked," said Whitman, who claimed that his own most pronounced trait was "caution." "I must confess he has plastered it on pretty thick," he said once, after Bucke had lectured on *Leaves of Grass* before the Ethical Culture Society of Philadelphia, "plastered it on not only a good deal more than I deserve but a good deal more than I like." "I fear he lacks balance and proportion," said John Burroughs, the most levelheaded member of Whitman's circle; Burroughs had the same criticism to make of O'Connor.

Choleric and peremptory, with a voice that had a "shrieking quality," Bucke was nonetheless, in Whitman's grateful opinion, "a whole man—he has lived down his losses," which included the whole of one foot and the toes of another, amputated long ago when he nearly died of exposure and starvation attempting to cross the Sierra Nevada in winter. As a young man Bucke had been a railroad hand, a wagon-train driver, and a miner in the Utah and Nevada Territories; he once stood off for half a day a Shoshone war party on the banks of the Humboldt River. He knew at first hand the frontier America that Whitman knew chiefly in imagination.

Bucke's discovery of *Leaves of Grass* in 1868, when he was thirty, was the first in a series of events that bound him to Whitman and his work for life and, he believed, perhaps even for eternity. "I am satisfied that I know something of it and of you," he declared. "That is greatness enough for me—yes and greatness enough to carry my name down thro' all the ages." In 1872, after an evening spent reading Whitman, Wordsworth, Shelley, Keats and Browning, Bucke experienced what he described as an unforgettable, never-to-be repeated moment of "illumination," "exultation," "Brahmic Splendor," and "immense joyousness." He felt he was at the center of a "flame-colored cloud." He "knew," in a way in which he had known nothing before, that "the foundation principle of the world is what we call love, and that the happiness of everyone is in the long run absolutely certain." From that ecstatic moment on, Bucke, like the hedgehog, knew one great thing and knew it very well.

He met Whitman face to face for the first time in 1877 and—like others who came to Camden and were exposed to the strangely affective personality in residence there—experienced "a sort of spiritual intoxication."* Until he died, twenty-five years later, he de-

---

* Similarly, J. W. Wallace, a prominent member of the Bolton group, claimed to have had "a strange and unique experience" when he visited Whitman in September 1891. "Quite suddenly there came into my mind what I can only describe as a most vivid consciousness of my mother, who had died six and a half years before. I seemed to see her mentally with perfect clearness . . . and to feel myself enwrapped in and penetrated by her living and palpitating presence. I record it here because it seemed equally indubitable that Walt was somehow the link between us, and as if his presence had made the experience possible." According to Wallace, who could hold his own with Bucke in the obscurantism department, Whitman's own "illu-

voted himself to the study of spiritual evolution, publishing two books on the subject, *Man's Moral Nature* (1879) and *Cosmic Consciousness* (1901), in addition to a biography of Whitman (1883). He had found that ecstatic illuminations were by no means so uncommon as supposed—ordinary people leading ordinary lives testified to them as well as great moral and ethical leaders, a conclusion supported by subsequent researchers (including William James, who cited Bucke at length in *Varieties of Religious Experience*). But Bucke derived some preposterous inferences from his empirical data; and despite Whitman's attempts to moderate them, Bucke's conclusions about personal immortality, cosmic purpose and the perfectibility of the human race became doctrine for many of the poet's followers and were inevitably vulgarized in the transmission.

In Bucke's account—which supported Whitman's canny representations of the 1855 *Leaves of Grass* as a fully matured work without rehearsals or literary antecedents—there was no need to look for a biographically rational line of development that led from the journalist-loafer to the incomparable poet. Everything one needed to know about Walt Whitman was in *Leaves of Grass;* the long foreground that intrigued Emerson was irrelevant except as it provided a contrast. To a degree unprecedented in the annals of mankind, according to Bucke, Whitman was endowed with "cosmic consciousness" and "the highest moral nature." In one moment of supreme illumination, comparable to the conversion of Saint Paul and believed to have taken place when Whitman was about thirty-four years old, a mere "Man" had been transformed into a "Titan." For public consumption, at any rate, this was a view Whitman endorsed. "I have had a thousand books and essays," he said at his birthday dinner in 1891, "and Dr. Bucke's is about the only one that thoroughly radiates and depicts and describes in a way I think thor-

---

mination" "had been accompanied by a liberation and vast expansion of consciousness and vision, and by a readjustment of all the diverse elements of his nature, which related them thenceforth with the universal and eternal. In this was his home, withdrawn and silent, from which he drew his inspiration and power. It was this—together with his long, resolute and uncompromising faithfulness to the promptings of his deepest nature—which invested him with the personal majesty that, with all his simplicity and spontaneity, always characterized him. And this was the main source of the silent influence of his personality and bodily presence." (John Johnston and J. W. Wallace, *Visits to Walt Whitman in 1890–1891* [London, 1917], pp. 99, 220.)

oughly delineates me." He had exercised such total editorial control over Bucke's biography that they were practically collaborators. He deleted as "intrusion and superfluity" long discussions of man's moral nature and other "metaphysical" subjects, but he let stand Bucke's fevered account of how *Leaves of Grass* came into being and subsequently provided "a picture of the world from the standpoint of the highest moral elevation yet reached." Whitman, too, identified himself with Christ—"My spirit to yours dear brother," he had written, "I understand you"—and lived at the center of a flame-colored cloud that prevented him from seeing himself plain.

II

Ever since his early twenties, when a New York daguerreotypist posed him as a man about town, wearing a soft-brimmed, raked hat and a figured necktie and complacently resting the handle of his walking stick on his shoulder, Whitman had been generating a gallery of images. "I've been photographed, photographed and photographed until the cameras themselves are tired of me," he said to Traubel. "I've run the whole gamut of photographic fol-de-rol," from snapshots to portraits by Mathew Brady. Bucke estimated there were several hundred photographs of Whitman and perhaps a dozen oil portraits and half a dozen busts in addition to innumerable drawings, caricatures and printed materials. His face appeared on cigar boxes although he never smoked. Probably no other contemporary writer, with the single exception of Mark Twain, was so systematically recorded or so concerned with the strategic uses of his pictures and their projective meanings for himself and the public. He had once written these lines "To Confront a Portrait":

> Out from behind this bending, rough-cut Mask,
> (All straighter, liker Masks rejected—this preferr'd,)
> This common curtain of the face contain'd in me for you, in you for
>   you, in each for each.

During one brief visit to New York, for his Lincoln lecture in April 1887, Whitman made an appointment with Augustus Saint-Gaudens, sat for a portrait by the painter Dora Wheeler, a friend of the Gilders, and was photographed at the Broadway studio of

George C. Cox. He liked one of Cox's portraits so much that he titled it "The Laughing Philosopher," sent an autographed copy to Tennyson, and put other copies on sale to supplement his income.

In July he sat simultaneously for the Philadelphia artist Thomas Eakins (more than "a painter," Whitman said—"a force"), for Herbert Gilchrist, the son of his English friend Anne Gilchrist, and for the sculptor Sidney Morse. Between sessions, enjoying every minute of the experience, he served them hot mutton stew and cold sangaree at his kitchen table. The results of these sittings were more satisfactory to him than the "Bostonese" portrait painted by John White Alexander in 1886 and acquired by the Metropolitan Museum. Gilchrist's picture, Whitman said, lacked "guts," but Morse's full-length seated figure reflected "poise, equanimity, power." As for Eakins' portrait, finished in 1888 and later hung at the Pennsylvania Academy of the Fine Arts, Whitman was moved by its realism and penetration, its suggestion of Shelley's George III, "an old, mad, blind, despised, and dying king." "It is not perfect but it comes nearest being me," "faces the worst as well as the best," he maintained, even though the disciples said it made him look fat and self-indulgent. It reminded Kennedy of a "somewhat dissipated old Dutch toper." Gilchrist warned that it was "a dangerous picture to make current."

In the self-absorption of old age Whitman became his own iconographer and, in the judgments he passed on pictures, directly or indirectly revealed how he wished to see himself. "Don't like that portrait in the illustrated paper," he said. "It gives me a foxy, professional look, both distasteful." He preferred one that had "a sort of Moses in the burning bush look." He puzzled for weeks over a "mysterious" photograph that David McKay had found in a New York bookstore. He said he had never seen it before, had no recollection of anything about it, not even the vivid, cast-off–looking outfit he wore—loosely knotted necktie, striped trousers and rumpled matching vest, heavy coat, plug hat held in his right hand. Shaggy and negligent, he could have been a miner come back from California. "What bothers me most of all, piques me, tantalizes me," he said, "is the expression of benignity." "Such benignity, such sweetness, such satisfiedness"—he admitted that this may have been a trick of the camera, but still, "of all the pictures I know, that new one most fills and satisfies me—and whatever people may say and think I am content with it just as it stands."

Despite the avowed skepticism of Bucke and Traubel and even of his brother George, Whitman insisted the picture showed him at a time when his poetry was still "in gestation," antedating the 1855 *Leaves of Grass* by at least five or six years, and he inscribed McKay's copy, "Walt Whitman in 1850 or '49." Bucke dated it 1856, but the outfit Whitman was wearing and his apparent age suggest that even this was too early (the picture was printed in line, as a contemporary photograph, in the *New York Illustrated News* for June 2, 1860). Whitman planned to use this "mysterious," chronologically elastic picture as frontispiece in his seventieth-birthday edition of *Leaves of Grass*. Eventually he settled on an even more benign picture that showed him gazing at a butterfly that appears to have just alighted on the forefinger of his outstretched right hand.

"How do you like that for free and easy," he said, pointing to another old picture. "Is that the picture of a tough? Maybe I am sensitive—maybe I am a tough—maybe the people who don't like toughs, don't like me, are right." Once he fished up from the floor a formal portrait, with "a sort of thanatopsis look," of William Cullen Bryant, a friend from the old days, who had turned cold and distant after he read *Leaves of Grass*. He compared the Bryant with a soiled old photograph of himself. "Do you think this could ever be tinkered into that?" he asked Traubel. "That this loafer, this lubber, could ever be transmuted into that gentleman? All I've got to say is, that I wouldn't like to undertake the contract."

He assigned to a minor place in the canon two crucial pictures of the emerging poet, both of them taken in New York in 1854. The first—Bucke called it "the Christ likeness"—shows a strong-featured, handsome full-lipped man in his prime, wearing an open shirt. His head is delicately, dreamily and sensuously inclined to one side. The eyes are brimming and entranced, caressing, searching, and at the same time removed. The second, the "carpenter" picture he used for the famous frontispiece of 1855, Kennedy was now urging him to suppress as "repulsive, loaferish," and Whitman tended to agree, even though Bucke read into the picture chiefly "sadness and good nature." The point was that this picture was "not a likeness," Whitman said. "I look so damned flamboyant, as if I was hurling bolts at somebody—full of mad oaths—saying defiantly, to hell with you!"—which is more or less what he had wanted that picture to say in 1855, when his poetry stemmed in part from "a hot unqualifying temper, an insulting arrogance." The picture had outlived its purpose. Poise, "benignity," "sweetness," amplitude—these, not flamboyance and hot temper, were the qualities of a sage.

III

"I don't worship the ground you tread on or kiss the hem of your garment," Horace Traubel said to Whitman, "but I think I know how you are bound to be regarded in the future." In anticipation he saved every scrap of Whitman's papers he was able to take away with him. He recorded Whitman's conversations, working from shorthand notes he often made in the semidarkness of the bedroom at Mickle Street—the five volumes so far published, under the title *With Walt Whitman in Camden*, run to over a million words for the relatively brief period of eighteen months in 1888 and 1889, and at least a million additional words still remain in manuscript. Traubel's other published writings about Whitman contain serious distortions. He tried to create a patron saint of American radicalism and socialism, even though Whitman as an old man, having written a revolutionary book, was conspicuously impatient with movements and across-the-board solutions of any sort. Traubel contributed his share of what James Gibbons Huneker called the "slush, hash, obscurity, morbid eroticism, vulgarity, and preposterous mouthings [that] well nigh spoil one's taste for what is really great in *Leaves of Grass*." But even John Burroughs acknowledged that Traubel's conversational records were a remarkably devoted and dependable job of reporting. In some places, he said, he could almost hear his old friend breathe. "Be sure to write about me honest," Whitman had instructed Traubel. "Whatever you do, do not prettify me: include all the hells and damns."

For all his intimacy with Whitman, Traubel realized there were stories he would never be allowed to hear and papers he would never be allowed to see. "Some day when you are ready and I am ready," Whitman told him in September 1888, "I will tell you about one period in my life of which my friends know nothing: not now—not tomorrow—but some day before long. I want to tell you the whole story with figures and all the data, so that you will make no mistake about it." He noticed Traubel's puzzlement and added, "Of course you do not understand an allusion so vague—but you ought to know: I have made up my mind to confide in you to the fullest extent." A week later he said, "You'll hear that in due time—not tonight. That cat has too long a tail to start to unravel at the end of an evening." The subject came up time and again, with Whitman hinting solemnly that it involved something "sacred" and "serious" that "would open your eyes." It was "the one big factor, entanglement (I may almost say tragedy) of my life about which I have not so far talked freely with you." It might "even disgust you," he said, a verb he rarely used.

Traubel could only speculate about what this volatile secret might be, for Whitman hated to be questioned—"catechized"—and when pressed he closed down into stubborn silences, just as he locked his bedroom door each night. Peter Doyle too found that Whitman had "a freezing way" about him that showed whenever someone "stepped across what he thought was his private border-line." As hard as he tried for an answer and as patiently as he waited, Traubel had to suspect—or at least so he said, hoping to force Whitman's hand—that the great secret was that there was no secret. But Whitman insisted—"You will sometime see that there is a secret." At Christmastime, after three months of playing cat and mouse, Traubel once again brought up the subject. "That question about the great secret—you've never answered that." "No," the old man said. "I want you to keep on asking till I answer; only not tonight—not tonight." Promising to tell and then not telling was the Penelope's web of Whitman's last years, and perhaps "secret" was only a metaphor he had chosen for his collective mysteries—his transformation into a "Titan," for one, and the price he may have paid for it in denial of impulse and sustained intimacy with women, men, and "the Me myself," "the real Me."

Like other members of the Camden circle Traubel assumed that Whitman was hinting at a particular love affair of some intensity. Certainly he had never lacked for opportunities. "To use the simple and hearty old scripture phrase," Bucke had written in his biography, " 'the love of women' has, of course, been, and is in a legitimate sense one of the man's elementary passions." Bucke quoted what John Burroughs, again with Whitman's approval, had written in 1867: "without entering into particulars, it is enough to say that he sounded all experiences of life, with all their passions, pleasures, and abandonments. He was young, in perfect bodily condition, and had the city of New York and its ample opportunities around him. I trace this period in some of the poems of 'Children of Adam.' "

"Free love?" Whitman remarked. "Is there any other kind of love?" It was rumored that in addition to casual couplings he had had affairs in New York (perhaps with the "old sweetheart of mine" whose portrait now hung over his bedroom mantelpiece), in Washington (perhaps with a married woman), and in New Orleans. The evidence for these affairs was almost totally hearsay, sometimes even at third or fourth remove. Peter Doyle was reported to have said he knew about the woman in Washington; Ellen O'Connor told a story about "a certain lady" there, but this may have been only a screen for Nelly's own feelings about Walt. Doyle, who believed that fornication was a mortal sin and that one served the unmarried dead by denying them any sexuality, also said, "I never knew a case of Walt's being bothered up by a woman . . . His disposition was different. Women in that sense never came into his head. Walt was too clean, he hated anything which was not clean." George Whitman shared the same morality and the same protective responsibility not only to Walt but to himself—his own respectability was vicariously at stake in the issue of Walt's affairs. "As for dissipation and women," he told Horace Traubel, "I know well enough that his skirts were clean. I never heard the least bit about his doings with women." But it was undeniable that a number of women, among them Nelly O'Connor and Anne Gilchrist, but also some complete strangers who knew him only through his book, had offered themselves to him. "I have loved you for years with my whole heart and soul," a Chicago woman wrote in 1882. "No man ever lived whom I have so desired to take by the hand as you. I read *Leaves of Grass*, and got new conceptions of the dignity and beauty of my own body and of the bodies of other people, and life became more valuable in consequence."

A New York *Herald* interviewer in September 1888 quoted Whitman as saying, "I am an old bachelor who never had a love affair." At first, apparently not having read the interview thoroughly, he found it "friendly" on the whole. After a closer reading he denied he had ever made the old bachelor statement, called the interviewer a liar, and ended up volunteering what appeared to be the sort of story Traubel had been unable to extract by frontal methods. Ten days after the interview appeared, Horace found him in a state of panic. "There's that last paragraph—the bad taste of it: I 'never had a love affair,' he says. 'Taint true—'Taint true." Whitman went on to make an unexpected connection, from which it was only natural to recon-

43

struct a tale of illicit love, pregnancy out of wedlock, enforced separation to avoid disgrace, and an unacknowledged heir. "Why, just these last two weeks I've been in a great worry: a young fellow wants to come on here—I don't want him to come. There's a little fortune hanging on it—thirty or forty thousand dollars—I don't want him to sacrifice it for a sentiment." Then he lapsed into silence after promising as usual to tell the whole thing "some other time." "This must be the 'big story' he has intended to confide in me," Traubel noted. It was the first, but not the last, time that he was to hear of Whitman's children.

Men too interpreted *Leaves of Grass*, especially the section called "Calamus," in fervid, preoccupied ways and sought Whitman out as a great sexual liberator. The first poem in this group seemed to promise nothing less than a new dispensation for some of the outcasts of society.

In paths untrodden,
In the growth by margins of pond-waters,
Escaped from the life that exhibits itself,
From all the standards hitherto published—from the pleasures,
      profits, conformities,
Which too long I was offering to feed to my Soul;
Clear to me now, standards not yet published—clear to me that my
      Soul,
That the Soul of the man I speak for, feeds, rejoices only in
      comrades;
Here, by myself, away from the clank of the world,
Tallying and talked to here by tongues aromatic,
No longer abashed—for in this secluded spot I can respond as I
      would not dare elsewhere,
Strong upon me the life that does not exhibit itself, yet contains all
      the rest,
Resolved to sing no songs to-day but those of manly attachment,
Projecting them along that substantial life,
Bequeathing, hence, types of athletic love,
Afternoon, this delicious Ninth Month, in my forty-first year,
I proceed, for all who are, or have been, young men,

To tell the secret of my nights and days,
To celebrate the need of comrades.

Edward Carpenter, a leading exponent of progressive causes and "The New Thought," who now lived openly with his male lover on a farm in Derbyshire, had come over from England to pay tribute to Whitman for permitting "men not to be ashamed of the noblest instinct of their nature. Women are beautiful, but to some there is that which passes the love of women." The critic and scholar Edmund Gosse, who struggled most of his life to hide what he called an "obstinate twist" in his nature, brought messages from "common friends in England," among whom was the Honorable Roden Noel, a relative of Lord Byron; Noel had written to Whitman earlier, "The proclamation of comradeship seems to me the grandest and most tremendous fact in your work and I heartily thank you for it." The future author of *Dracula*, Bram Stoker, and Charles Warren Stoddard, a literary scholar who found in Tahiti the sexual paradise he had been seeking, declared their love in long, emotional letters to Whitman. An English sailor, Charles William Dalmon, finding himself stranded in Jersey City without money for train fare to Camden, also had to settle for a letter. "I cannot write the things I would write to you—I could not speak the words I would wish to speak—but if I could see your face—if I could hear your voice! I hope—you will see me? yes—you are good—may I come to see you when my ship returns in about a month?"

In Whitman's experience his most persistently troublesome reader was John Addington Symonds, author of a classic work of cultural history, *The Renaissance in Italy*. "Horribly literary and suspicious," was the way Whitman described him in 1891, "a great fellow for delving into persons." Symonds had discovered Whitman's poetry at Trinity College, Cambridge, when he was twenty-five. "I might have been a mere English gentleman had I not read *Leaves of Grass*," he was to say. "It revolutionized my previous conceptions, and made another man of me." He wrote a group of poems about "passionate friendship" between men and took to visiting soldiers' barracks and male brothels in the company of Roden Noel; he also married "a woman of noble nature and illustrious connections" who bore him three children.

"I desire to hear from your own lips—or from your pen—some story of athletic friendship from which to learn the truth," he wrote in 1872, addressing Whitman as "My Master." "What the love of man for man has been in the Past I think I know. What it is here now, I know—alas! What you say it can and shall be I dimly discern in your Poems. But this hardly satisfies me—so desirous am I of learning what you teach. Some day, perhaps—in some form I know not what, but in your own chosen form—you will tell me more about the Love of Friends! Till then I wait. Meanwhile you have told me more than anyone beside." ("Perhaps I don't know what it all means—perhaps never did know," Whitman said to Traubel when he reread this letter. "Maybe I do not know all my meanings.")

After nearly twenty years of being chivvied by Symonds to explain the meaning of "Calamus," Whitman felt like Polonius pursued by mad Hamlet—" 'Still harping on my daughter,' " he quoted several times when these letters came up in conversation. In July 1890 Symonds sent his essay, "Democratic Art, with Special Reference to Walt Whitman," and the quarry became downright exasperated. "I doubt whether he has gripped 'democratic art' by the nuts, or L of G either," he said. By this time Symonds was ill with tuberculosis and had begun to entertain a fantasy of meeting Whitman in the next world and asking him there "about things which have perplexed me here—to which I think you alone could have given me an acceptable answer." But the matter was too urgent to be postponed and in August he finally brought himself to ask some relatively forthright questions:

In your conception of Comradeship, do you contemplate the possible intrusion of those semi-sexual emotions and actions which no doubt do occur between men? I do not ask, whether you approve of them, or regard them as a necessary part of this relation? But I should much like to know whether *you are prepared to leave them to the inclinations and the conscience of the individuals concerned?* . . . I agree with the objections I have mentioned that, human nature being what it is, and some men having a strong natural bias toward persons of their own sex, the enthusiasm of 'Calamus' is calculated to encourage ardent and *physical* intimacies. But I do not agree with them in thinking such a result would absolutely be prejudicial to social interests.

At first, as Whitman told Bucke, he had no intention of answering this "singular letter." But consternation and anger prevailed, and they remained in evidence even in the calculatingly casual reply to Symonds that he drafted on August 19.

Y'rs of Aug: 3d just rec'd & glad to hear f'm you as always—Abt the little portraits, I cheerfully endorse the Munich reproduction of any of them you propose or any thing of the sort you choose—(I may soon send you some other preferable portraits of self)—Suppose you have rec'd papers & slips sent of late—Ab't the questions on Calamus pieces &c: they quite daze me. L of G. is only to be rightly construed by and within its own atmosphere and essential character—all of its pages & pieces so coming strictly under *that*—that the calamus part has even allow'd the possibility of such construction as mention'd is terrible—I am fain to hope the pages themselves are not to be even mention'd for such gratuitous and quite at the time entirely un-dream'd & unreck'd possibility of morbid inferences—wh' are disa-vow'd by me & seem damnable. Then one great difference between you and me, temperament & theory, is *restraint*—I know that while I have a horror of ranting & bawling I at certain moments let the spirit impulse, (?demon) rage its utmost, its wildest, damnedest—(I feel to do so in my L of G. & I do so). I end the matter by saying I wholly stand by L of G. as it is, long as all parts & pages are construed as I said by their own ensemble, spirit & atmosphere.

I live here 72 y'rs old & completely paralyzed—brain & right arm ab't same as ever—digestion, sleep, appetite, &c: fair—sight & hear-ing half-and-half—spirits fair—locomotive power (legs) almost ut-terly gone—am propell'd outdoors nearly every day—get down to the river side here, the Delaware, an hour at sunset—The writing and rounding of L of G. has been to me the reason-for-being, & life comfort. My life, young manhood, mid-age, times South, &c: have all been jolly, bodily, and probably open to criticism—

Tho' always unmarried I have had six children—two are dead—One living southern grandchild, fine boy, who writes to me occasion-ally. Circumstances connected with their benefit and fortune have separated me from intimate relations.

I see I have written with haste & too great effusion—but let it stand.

"It is obvious that he has not even taken the phenomena of abnor-mal instinct into account," the exasperated Symonds was to con-clude, and "entertains feelings at least as hostile to sexual inversion as any law-abiding humdrum Anglo-Saxon could desire." The consensus among Whitman's friends was that this newly revealed chapter in a life previously well known to them was moonshine, the children being the fantasy—panicky, defensive, pathetic, senile, melodramatic or megalomaniac—of a sick man who, as Burroughs said, "was not exactly himself at times toward the last." Hostile outsiders like the historian William Roscoe Thayer, accepted the story as further proof that Whitman was "a strangely dissolute man who . . . shamelessly spread the records of his debauches on the printed page." But Bucke, who was professionally familiar with deluded states, at least gave the appearance of accepting the story too. "I know little about Walt's children," he told Kennedy, "do not know how many there were—believe there were several. He and their mother were not married. That is the whole story." ("My belief," added Nelly O'Connor, looking back to Whitman's trip to New Orleans in 1848, "is that some probably light colored woman loved him, and perhaps followed him north and no doubt a child was born.") After Whitman's death, however, and even with "the secret" out, the chronically tireless Bucke seems to have made no effort to track down children or grandchildren, and no plausible claimant has ever come forward. Given the thrust of Symonds' line of questioning, Bucke may have decided it was tactful to endorse a story that showed that Whitman may have been immoral, by the standards of his time, but immoral in a socially acceptable way.

If Whitman's children were only a fantasy, it was one he had entertained intermittently throughout his life and then settled down with in earnest after his first mention of "a young fellow." Hinting further about the scandal, he said "it involves bad feeling, passion, families, even a fortune . . . it would in at least one place create great unhappiness." Once he mentioned a grandson who had just come to see him but exclaimed "God forbid!" when Traubel said he wanted to meet the boy. In May 1891, when his tomb at Harleigh Cemetery in Camden was being constructed, Whitman wrote to Bucke, "I have two deceased children (young man and woman—illegitimate of course) that I much desired to bury here with me, but have ab't abandon'd the plan on acc't of angry litigation and fuss generally and disinterment f'm down south." In December, when he was obviously failing, Bucke called on him and made notes of their conversation:

I asked him if he did not want to say something to me about that Southern matter. He said "my children?" I said "yes." He said "well I guess not." I said Harned thinks someone ought to know the main fact in case of any trouble arising hereafter—he said "in money matters you mean?" I said "yes." "Oh" he said "there will be no trouble of that kind" and went on to say that the people were of good family and would of themselves never come forward and claim connection.

According to Traubel, on one occasion, shortly before he died, Whitman offered to make "a sort of deposition" on the subject of his children. "He wished to set down this affair in an unquestionable record and proposed signing the paper we drew up. But he was taken sick in our presence and was unable to proceed. There the thing rested." By this time Whitman's tomb was finished and waiting.

IV

On a twenty-by-thirty-foot plot, gift of the Harleigh Cemetery Association, the former housebuilder ordered the construction of his tomb, "a plain massive stone temple" of unpolished Quincy granite. He designed it himself, with one of William Blake's symbolic etchings, "Death's Door," in mind. He regularly had himself driven out to Harleigh to oversee the progress of his tomb and took pride in it as a celebration of personality, like his book. He encouraged reporters to write about the tomb, sent photographs to his friends, and gave happy thought to how it would look in the years to come, reclusive and secure in its wooded hillside, half-hidden among vines, shrubs, creepers and mature trees. He enjoyed his reviews—the cemetery superintendent told him that many visitors expressed their admiration of the tomb and that a certain old army captain who had traveled a great deal pronounced it the best he ever saw.

"Whenever he gets a little flutter of hope that he may live longer," Traubel complained, "he seems to start in at once to husband what money he has so he may not get stranded. His economies last a day or two. Then he lets himself go again. This is the only frailty in him which rubs me." Whitman let himself go in the contract he signed in October 1890 with Reinhalter and Company, monumental manufacturers, of Broad Street, Philadelphia. He obligated himself to pay

$4,000 for a mausoleum, more than twice what his house and lot in Mickle Street had cost. "I do not complain," he told Bucke, who, like Traubel and Harned, made no secret of the fact that they considered this expenditure outrageous, the contract a "swindle," and the tomb a "foolishness or freak," a "false step" of Whitman's declining years. (Said an old friend, John Townsend Trowbridge, "That such a man should have cared about his tomb, anyway, or have hoarded money for it, when he was living on the bounty of others, is something heart-sickening.") By October 1891, when Reinhalter delivered the key to the tomb and rendered a final bill, Whitman was convinced he had been a victim of "black mail or extortion" and refused to honor the contract. A worrisome squabble went on for months—eventually he paid out $1,500 and Harned settled with the builders for the balance, apparently paying all or most of it out of his own pocket. "I am greatly rejoiced that the *Tomb* matter is settled," Bucke told Traubel three weeks before Whitman's death. "All seems to be clearing off for the final scene which cannot now be much delayed."

"My foothold is tenoned and mortised in granite," Whitman had written in 1855. "I laugh at what you call dissolution." Built according to his specifications, the granite burial house—"the rudest most undress'd structure . . . since Egypt, perhaps the cave dwellers"— was also tenoned and mortised, and it was guarded by an iron gate with a massive bronze lock (the granite door he originally called for proved to be too heavy to be hung). Some of the blocks weighed eight or ten tons; the roof was a foot and a half thick. The vault, built deep into the hillside, was faced with marble and tile and contained eight burial spaces. He had told his sister Hannah, "It is my design to gather the remains of our dear father and mother and have them buried here in the tomb I have built for myself." After his death his parents were moved there from graves in Brooklyn and Camden, and in time the burial house also held Hannah's coffin and those of Eddy Whitman, George, Louisa, and their infant son. In death Whitman reunited his scattered family under his granite roof and also, in a lasting assertion of self, merged their identities into his; the pediment of his mausoleum bore only one name, "Walt Whitman," carved in high relief. For a while during construction his name had a date below it, "May 31, 1890," the stone masons having inserted it under the grotesque misapprehension that the tomb was a birthday present from Whitman's friends when he turned seventy-one. (The masons might as well have added a cartouche of ribbons and candles.) Whitman ordered the date chipped off—"an improvement." The deletion left his name standing oddly high above visual center.

Something more fundamental than vanity in old age had led Whitman to build this tomb, completed at just about the same time as the final (or "Death-Bed") edition of *Leaves of Grass*. To the last he obeyed the motto he kept by his writing table, "Make the Works." At the end of January 1892, two months before he died, he sent Bucke a copy of an announcement prepared for the New York *Herald*.

Walt Whitman wishes respectfully to notify the public that the book *Leaves of Grass*, which he has been working on at great intervals and partially issued for the past thirty-five or forty years, is now completed, so to call it, and he would like this new 1892 edition to absolutely supersede all previous ones. Faulty as it is, he decides it as by far his special and entire self-chosen poetic utterance.

Whitman's tomb too was a special and self-chosen utterance. As a boy he had been enthralled by a knowledge of death that in time became more compelling even than the knowledge of sex. He grew up near the neglected burial grounds of his forebears on Long Island —"depress'd mounds, crumbled and broken stones, cover'd with moss." In Brooklyn and Manhattan he saw the graves of soldiers of the Revolution, "the Sacred Army," dug up to make way for shops and dwellings. His heroes Thomas Paine and the Quaker preacher Elias Hicks had not remained safe in the earth; Emanuel Swedenborg's skull was stolen from the grave; for twenty-six years after Poe's death his grave remained unmarked; the unburied dead of the Civil War, "the *strayed* dead," strewed the fields and valleys and woods of the South; in 1876, the centennial year of the Republic, Abraham Lincoln's tomb at Springfield was violated—the grave robbers were about to break into the inner lead casket when they were caught; two years later the body of Alexander T. Stewart, the New York merchant prince, was stolen and held for ransom. But even in Whitman's earliest work the violated and neglected grave had become a constitutive metaphor, and this was a decade before the poet of *Leaves of Grass* began to celebrate the earth as a vast compost heap and life as the rich leavings of many deaths:

I bequeath myself to the dirt to grow from the grass I love,
If you want me again look for me under your boot-soles.

But the old Whitman demanded more pharaonic arrangements. He built himself a burial house that was stark, elemental and secure, declaring, without any need for inscriptions or conventional symbolism, that he had seen yesterday and knew tomorrow. An earthquake and an angel of the Lord would have to roll back the stone from his door. Like his book, Whitman in the tomb was "a candidate for the future."

"Day by day he seems to suffer deeper inroads, a bit sapped here, a bit there, by subtle ways which count for so much," Traubel noted in January 1891. As he wrote he could hear Whitman moaning and gasping for breath in the next room. "Walt very frankly expresses his anxiety to die, to shake off this burden, which increases and is heavier with each day." From his boyhood along the Atlantic shore, Whitman remembered the sea whispering to him "the low and delicious word death, and again death, death, death, death." He remembered, from his time in the hospitals during the war, deaths that arrived "like an invisible breeze after a long and sultry day" and brought with them a brief restoration of mental and emotional clarity, a remission of all pain and fear, even "a sort of ecstasy." Yet for a year and more the dark mother and strong deliveress dealt teasingly with him. Once he had celebrated perfect health and perfect bodies —"Of physiology from top to toe I sing . . . of Life immense in passion, pulse, and power." Now he lay on a decrepit bedstead in a shabby bug-ridden room with paper peeling off the walls and the ceiling plaster beginning to fall. He subsisted mainly on milk punch and month after month lingered on, but so tuberculous, wasted, congested, atrophied, abscessed, tumored, collapsed, and obstructed that his body, like that of Poe's M. Valdemar, was a carnival ground of decay, and his survival evidence of the countervailing force of constitution and unconscious will. Recognizing the anomaly, Whitman gave his permission for an autopsy in the interests of medical science.

When he visited Mickle Street for the last time, Burroughs found Whitman pathetically feeble but more beautiful than ever. He lay with his eyes closed but rallied to tell Burroughs about the new

Leaves of Grass and also to comfort him. "It is all right, John," he said.
"I think of you morning noon & night," his sister Hannah wrote in
March 1892, "and would like to write every day but are going to
wait till you get better, well enough *dear brother* to sit up, in your
chair again & that will be such good news to hear. your letters & all
the money you send all arrive safely." He sent her a last letter and
gift on March 17:

> Unable to write much—$4 enc'd—y'r good letter rec'd—God bless
> you—W W

To relieve his pain he was moved onto a sort of water bed on the
floor. "O I feel so good!" he said when he heard the water splashing
like waves against the side of a ship. He died the evening of March
26.

The next day Thomas Eakins and a pupil made a death mask.
Whitman's literary executors, Traubel, Bucke, and Harned, took
possession of his papers and packed them into barrels. George Whitman
refused to allow the autopsy; the doctors waited until he left the
house that afternoon and then went ahead with their work, discovering
in the course of a nearly three-hour exploration that the immediate
cause of death was pulmonary emphysema; the left lung
had collapsed entirely, and the right was only fractionally functional.
The doctors removed his brain and sent it to be measured
and weighed at the American Anthropometric Society, where it was
destroyed when a laboratory worker accidentally dropped it on the
floor.

The day of the funeral, March 30, people swarmed in Mickle
Street waiting to file into the parlor and look at Whitman in his
polished-oak coffin. Peter Doyle came on from Washington and was
nearly turned away from the door. Some of the New York literary
people sent wreaths of ivy and laurel. Around two o'clock, in the
spirit of a spring celebration—this was "a red letter day in the annals
of the town," said a local paper—the crowds followed the coffin to
Harleigh Cemetery, where, under a canopy in front of the tomb, an
unusual service was heard. From the reader came the words, "I am
the resurrection and the life." The celebrated agnostic Colonel Robert
Ingersoll said that "death is less terrible than it was before. Thousands
and millions will walk into the dark valley of the shadow,
holding Walt Whitman by the hand." There were readings from

53

Confucius, Buddha, Plato, the Koran, the Bible, and *Leaves of Grass*. Kennedy felt as if present at "the entombment of Christ." The speakers claimed for Whitman the unshakable certainty of a mighty prophet fulfilled in his mission. But the dead poet had said he did not know all his meanings and was not afraid of contradicting himself. It would have been fitting for someone at his funeral to read from a poem called "Facing West from California's Shores," shores that Whitman never reached but imagined to be the starting point for a journey through time and culture. Here was Walt, "a child, very old," facing home again, "looking over to it, joyous, as after long travel, growth, and sleep," asking,

> But where is what I started for, so long ago?
> And why is it yet unfound?

3

"Mother, Father, Water, Earth, Me..."

WHEN WHITMAN AT SIXTY-TWO came back for the last time to his birthplace, West Hills, near Huntington, Suffolk County, Long Island, he was reminded again of the rootedness in place his family had once known. His forebears on his father's side were English farmers who came over in the mid-seventeenth century, some in the ship *True Love*, and lived in Connecticut before settling in Huntington township. Through grants and purchases they acquired about five hundred acres of fields and timber, a ducal property by Old World standards. The Van Velsors, on his mother's side, were Dutch, with a recent admixture of Welsh blood and Quaker persuasion, and had settled early at Cold Spring in Nassau County, on the border between the opposed Dutch and English colonists. The Van Velsors farmed and bred mettlesome horses; like the Whitmans and other landowners on Long Island, they owned slaves. (Walt was eight years old when New York State abolished slavery.) Both families risked all when they took up the cause of American independence, and they passed on undiminished to their descendants the sacred purpose of 1776. The Revolution was very nearly lost that August, at the Battle of Long Island, when Sir William Howe drove the Americans from Brooklyn Heights. Walt believed a granduncle of his died in that engagement. "I remember when a boy hearing grandmother Whitman tell about the times of the revolutionary war," he wrote. "The British had full swing over Long Island, and

55

foraged everywhere, and committed the most horrible excesses—
enough to make one's blood boil even to hear of it now." The farmers
endured seven harsh years of enemy occupation; eleven thousand
patriots died in the black hulks of British prison ships anchored in
Wallabout Bay, by Whitman's time the site of the Brooklyn Navy
Yard.

"Two or three-score graves quite plain; as many more rubbed
out," the poet noted when he visited the Van Velsor burial ground
in 1881. Aside from the belilaced cellar hole and some heaps of
rubble "green with grass and weeds," there was hardly a trace of his
grandfather's rambling gray house, his stables, pens and barn. "All
had been pull'd down, erased, and the plough and harrow pass'd
over foundations, road-spaces and everything." On a slope above an
apple orchard at West Hills, a few miles from Cold Spring, was the
burial ground of his father's family. "The Whitmans must have been
a race of note," Walt said on an earlier visit. "There are I should say
as many as fifty graves there (on the Hill). . . . Besides this, many
others of them must have been buried at Huntington village, for I
remember seeing numerous old gravestones that were brought from
their graves, at the time of the Revolutionary war—for the British
encamped on Huntington hill, and took away grave stones for ovens
and hearths, &c. The stones I saw were brought away, lest they
might be despoiled, and somehow, when the war passed over, they
were never returned." The burial ground became a rank disorder of
headstones broken, toppled, effaced, and overgrown—only two
stones were intact and still legible. The neglected plot, the house
nearby where he was born and the Whitman farms had long since
passed into other hands; the old rootedness had given way to a
steadily accelerating rhythm of subdivision, foreclosure and dispos-
session. By the time he was twelve years old, an apprentice printer
in Brooklyn, Walt had lived in about a dozen different houses, each
one more cramped than the last. Change and loss went hand in hand
and had genetic counterparts. Of the eight Whitman children who
survived infancy one was a mental defective and three were psychic
disasters; three were normal, and one became the chief American
celebrant of what William James called "the religion of healthymind-
edness."

"A stalwart, massive, heavy, long-lived race," Whitman said of
his father's side. "They appear to have been always of democratic
and heretical tendencies." Walter Whitman Sr. was born on July 14,

1789, the day the Parisians stormed the Bastille, and he believed in resisting much, obeying little. He named three of his six sons after heroes of the Republic, George Washington, Thomas Jefferson, and Andrew Jackson, and he trained them as radical Democrats, on the side of the farmer, the laborer, the small tradesman, and "the people"—the banks and "the interests" were the enemy. He read books and journals of a dissenting cast and numbered among his heroes and acquaintances the patriot, pamphleteer, and antisuperstitionist Thomas Paine. When the elder Whitman met him in New York, Paine was a dying man, a pariah, and, some said, a drunkard. "From whence," Paine had once asked with fine Voltairean edge, "could arise the solitary and strange conceit that the Almighty, who had millions of worlds equally dependent on his protection, should quit the care of all the rest, and come to die in our world, because, they say, one man and one woman had eaten an apple!" Paine looked to the inner light for guidance and was proud of his Quaker antecedents, but, as Walt said, in those times there was "no philosophical middle ground" for freethinking. And so Paine was "double-damnably lied about," mocked even by schoolchildren:

Poor Tom Paine! there he lies;
Nobody laughs and nobody cries;
Where he has gone or how he fares,
Nobody knows and nobody cares!

The Whitmans revered Frances Wright, Scottish-born freethinker, feminist, and reformer, an intimate of the Marquis de Lafayette. With Thomas Jefferson as her authority, she announced that "Washington was not a Christian." "The first and last thing I would say to man," she wrote in her utopian tract, *A Few Days in Athens*, "is, think for *yourself*." The elder Whitman owned a copy and subscribed to her paper, the *Free Enquirer;* Walt read these, heard Frances Wright lecture, and remembered her in feature, soul and thought as "more than beautiful: she was grand. . . . She possessed herself of my body and soul." Walt's father also owned a copy of *The Ruins*, a celebrated attack on Christianity and supernaturalism by the French savant Count Constantin de Volney. Like others who grew up on such literature, Abraham Lincoln among them, Walt believed that a long, dark tyranny over man's mind and body was at last coming to an end; the Children of Adam would be able to walk in their parents' garden. *Leaves of Grass* borrowed the insurgent and questioning spirit of these mentors along with literal quotations from their writings. Democratic and heretical from the cradle up, "quite innocent of repentance and man's fall," Whitman determined that he would some day "bear my testimony to that whole group of slandered men and women. . . . I may perhaps be the only one living today," he said in 1888, "who can throw an authentic sidelight upon the radicalism of those post-Revolutionary decades."

The English reformer William Cobbett, who spent a year of exile farming on Long Island shortly before Whitman was born, also determined to do justice to at least one of these "slandered men and women." He had Paine's bones dug up from an infidel's grave in New Rochelle and took them to England, but the monument he planned to raise there in Paine's memory was never built; Paine's bones and his coffin passed into the hands of a furniture dealer and then vanished. During his stay on Long Island, Cobbett had noted the intellectual vitality of farmers and artisans like Walter Whitman, their ability to converse on almost any subject—every one of them, he said, "is more or less of a reader." But he also noted less attractive traits: carelessness with their land, which they allowed to become overgrazed and cropped-out, and, conspicuously, their practice of taking hard liquor on any pretext and at any hour between sunup of one day and the next—"Even little boys at, or under *twelve* years of age, go into *stores*, and tip off their *drams!*" "It is very hard for the present generation . . . to understand the drinkingness of those years," Whitman was to say. "I am familiar with it: saw, understood, it all as a boy." His mother understood it, too. "When they get into that state then nothing can be done for the moment but give them the drink," she said when she and Walt were accosted by a derelict, "it is but mercy to give it to them." Whitman once told Burroughs his father had been "addicted to alcohol," and he cited a line from *Leaves of Grass*—"I knew of the agents that emptied and broke my brother"—to suggest that was the reason for Eddy's being "a poor stunted boy almost from the first. He had the convulsions . . . practically has never had any mental life at all."

By early middle age Walter Whitman Senior's slow, taciturn, and brooding nature had become dominant; he had spells of moody silence and depression. He was not cut out for success, and he developed an ironic and resigned expectation of failure. "Keep good heart," he sometimes said, *"the worst is to come."* As a young man he had learned carpentry from his cousin Jacob Whitman, completed his apprenticeship in New York, and worked there several years for wages before coming back to West Hills as a builder of houses and barns on contract. He leased some land from a farmer, Gilbert Valentine, and put up on it his own two-story cedar-shingled house. "He was a first rate carpenter," Walt said, "did solid, substantial, conscientious work," and this was evident in the stone masonry foundations he laid, the wide-planked floors, ample fireplaces, and hand-hewn timbers mortised and pegged in place; his house was

. . . plumb in the uprights, well entretied, braced in the beams.

In June 1816, when he was twenty-seven, he married Louisa Van Velsor, vigorous, big-boned and florid, and brought her from her parents' farm at Cold Spring to the new house.

Their first child, Jesse, named for his paternal grandfather, was born in March 1818. Their second, Walter—named for his father but always called "Walt" in the family—was born fourteen months later, on May 31, 1819. He was an exact contemporary of Herman Melville, born about thirty miles away on Pearl Street in New York; of James Russell Lowell, born at "Elmwood" in Cambridge; of the royal princess, Victoria, born an ocean away at Kensington Palace. Napoleon was dying of cancer on St. Helena. In the White House, recently rebuilt after the British burned it in the War of 1812, was James Monroe, a Virginian of the old school—he still wore knee breeches. "If we look to the history of other nations, ancient or modern," Monroe had said in his first inaugural address, "we find no example of a growth so rapid, so gigantic, of a people so prosperous and happy." But the financial panic of 1819, a massive contraction of credit and faith, brought in an era of ominous division over the issue of slavery. "Like a fire-bell in the night," Jefferson said in 1820, the Missouri Compromise "awakened and filled me with terror"; he heard "the knell of the Union." "In the four quarters of the globe," mocked the Englishman Sydney Smith, "who reads an American book? . . . Under which of the tyrannical governments of Europe is every sixth man a Slave, whom his fellow-creatures may buy, and sell, and torture?" "Every one for himself," Emerson wrote of this time of moral and relational chaos, "driven to find all his resources, hopes, rewards, society and deity within himself." In place of "the social existence which all shared" there "was now separation." "Not only does democracy make each man forget his ancestors," Tocqueville warned, "but it hides his descendants and separates his contemporaries from him; it throws him back upon himself alone and threatens in the end to confine him entirely within the solitude of his own heart."

"There was a child went forth every day," Whitman wrote,

> And the first object he looked upon and received with wonder or
>   pity or love or dread, that object he became,
> And that object became part of him . . .

Passive, dependent, merging object with subject, the external world with the unboundaried ego, the infant learned the reality of his mother through his skin, by touching and being touched, and thereafter, even in mature sexuality, never having altogether gone beyond that first traffic, he could say,

> I merely stir, press, feel with my fingers, and am happy,
> To touch my person to some one else's is about as much as I can
>   stand.

He was to concern himself with "the most profound theme that can occupy the mind of man": "the relation between the (radical, democratic) Me, the human identity of understanding, emotions, spirit, &c." and the "Not Me, the whole of the material objective universe."

Crying, the child learned the sound of his voice and its power over others. Growing, he distinguished objects, sensations, rhythms. The sun rose in the morning, his father set out for work, pigs and chickens rooted in the apple orchard across the road from his mother's kitchen garden. In the evening herds of mongrel cattle and rat-tailed sheep were driven homeward from their grazing on the Hempstead plains—years later he was still able to hear in memory the clanking of their tin and copper bells and smell "the sweet and slightly aromatic evening air." He remembered too the choking smell of lampblack and oil on the canvas covering of the stage and market wagon his grandfather Van Velsor drove each week from Cold Spring to Brooklyn ferry. Words, when he acquired language, became life itself, links to the external world and to his unconscious. "I sometimes think the Leaves is only a language experiment," he was to say. "A perfect writer would make words sing, dance, kiss, do the male and female act, bear children, weep, bleed, rage, stab, steal, fire cannon, steer ships, sack cities, charge with cavalry or infantry, or do any thing that man or woman or the natural powers can do." Words were instruments of command and of relationship to a world waiting to be named for the first time. "Not only common speech," he was to read in Thomas Carlyle's *Sartor Resartus*, "but Science, Poetry itself is no other . . . than a right *Naming*." But words had a separate existence too, as "eluding, fluid, beautiful, fleshless, realities, Mother, Father, Water, Earth, Me, This, Soul, Tongue, House, Fire, . . . What a history is folded, folded inward and inward again in the single word I."

In the quiet after storms he heard the roar of the Atlantic surf. Half a mile from the house, from the top of Jayne's Hill, the highest point on the island, he could look out over Great South Bay, Jones' Beach, and the ocean beyond—to the north he saw Long Island Sound and the Connecticut shore. A sturdy boy with black hair, he soon learned to swim, dig for clams, gather sea gulls' eggs, fish through the ice on the bay. He heard tales of danger and adventure at sea—whaling ships that set out for the Horn from Sag Harbor and never returned, wrecks off the Hamptons, Fire Island and Hempstead beach;

> I look where the ship helplessly heads end on, I hear the burst as she
> strikes, I hear the howls of dismay, they grow fainter and
> fainter.

All his life he had a recurrent dream: "A stretch of white-brown sand, hard and smooth and broad, with the ocean perpetually, grandly rolling in upon it, with slow-measured sweep, with rustle and hiss and foam, and many a thump as of low bass drums. . . . Sometimes I wake at night and can hear and see it plainly." The seashore was "an invisible *influence*" on all his poetry, he said, "a pervading gauge and tally for me." From the time the symbolizing imagination developed in him he believed that he lived always at the water's edge, with the land his father and his mother the unplumbed sea of self; one could drown there as easily as in water.

"He was a very good, but very strange boy," Louisa Whitman

said. He said, "The time of my boyhood was a very restless and unhappy one; I did not know what to do." He was closest to her and to his sisters Hannah and Mary, both born right after him, but he stood apart from his father and most of his brothers. "We are not alike," he said much later. "That's the part and the whole of it." He scarcely ever mentioned Jesse, unstable, violent, jealous, the only sibling who had a prior claim on their parents—it was a relief when Jesse went off to sea and Walt had no rival as his mother's indisputable favorite. "Being a blood brother to a man don't make him a real brother in the final sense of that term," he said, and this applied to George and Andrew as well as to Jesse. Eddy was more like a son to him. So was Jeff, his one "real brother," born in 1833 when Walt was fourteen. "He was a very handsome, healthy, affectionate, smart child, and would sit on my lap or hang on my neck for half an hour at a time. . . . O, how we loved each other—how many jovial times we had!"

The child (in Whitman's poem) who went forth every day had a father who was "strong, self-sufficient, manly, mean, angered, unjust," given to "the blow, the quick loud word, the tight bargain, the crafty lure." For the most part this was probably a generalized sex-typed representation rather than a literal character of Walter Whitman Senior. He tended to be the victim rather than the instigator of tight bargains and crafty lures, was fond of children and animals, quiet, and slow to react. But when aroused he was capable of "memorable vehemence," and he had stormy scenes with Walt, who resented "undue parentalism" and appeared to be hopelessly indolent and stubbornly wayward. In a stormy scene that took place when he was about seventeen Walt categorically refused to do farm work; he chose instead to teach school and write stories, one of them about a farmer who falls a victim to alcohol and "wretched sensuality," strikes his eldest son in "a fit of drunken passion" and is directly responsible for the invalidism and early death of his youngest. It was only after Walter Whitman died in 1855, within a few days of the publication of *Leaves of Grass*, that Walt the victor and survivor began to speak at all freely and affectionately about "my dear father" and to acknowledge, in however conflicted and grievance-heavy a way, the ties between them and his desire for reconciliation. "What is yours is mine," he wrote in an 1859 poem of self-questioning, "As I Ebb'd with the Ocean of Life":

I throw myself upon your breast my father,
I cling to you so that you cannot unloose me,
I hold you firm till you answer me something.

Kiss me my father,
Touch me with your lips as I touch those I love,
Breathe to me while I hold you close the secret of the murmuring I
    envy.

"All through young and middle age," Whitman was to say, "I thought my heredity stamp was mainly decidedly from my mother's side; but as I grow older, and latent traits come out, I see my father's also." For a long time he thought of himself as his mother's child only. Louisa Whitman was not a reader like her husband, but she was "strangely knowing," Walt said. "She excelled in narrative— had great mimetic power; she could tell stories, impersonate; she was very eloquent in the utterance of noble moral axioms—was very original in her manner, her style." In ruddy complexion, features, gait, and voice he took after her—"favored her," the people on Long Island said. He idealized her extravagantly, overlooked her chronic peevishness after she became a widow, and came to attribute to her every creative and feeling impulse in himself. "Leaves of Grass is the flower of her temperament active in me," a reflection of her "reality," "simplicity," and "transparency," of her mingled Dutch strain of the "practical and materialistic" and the "transcendental and cloudy." "Mothers precede all"—he believed that the women of his ancestry had richer natures than their men.

He venerated Frances Wright, Margaret Fuller, George Sand, all of them feminists and agents of spiritual liberation. The "I" of *Leaves of Grass* is almost as often a woman as a man, and the book is a supremely passionate argument for the androgynous union of strength and tenderness, sagacity and impulse. But he had grown up so bound to his mother that oneness with her and separation from her were equally as terrifying as death and the ocean. "The child who went forth every day . . . now goes and will always go forth every day"—in his folded recesses that child remained a child.

A man, yet by these tears a little boy again,
Throwing myself on the sand, confronting the waves.

II

During an epidemic of foreclosures in 1821 Walter Whitman bought at a sheriff's sale the rented property his house stood on. This attempt to remain in place, like others that followed it in his lifetime, proved to be at best a delaying action. As a result of the depression, new building in Huntington township had come to a standstill; the population was in decline, having been drawn away to the hinterlands or to New York, already "the great commercial emporium" of the New World. On May 27, 1823, a few days before Walt's fourth birthday—"I was still a little one in frocks"—Whitman moved his family westward on Long Island to Brooklyn, a bustling market town of around seven thousand people. He settled them in a rented house on Front Street and went out expecting to find steady work at good wages.

Brooklyn was growing so fast that by 1855 it was the third-largest city in the United States and had a population of 200,000, which doubled in the fifteen years after. "The child is already born, and is now living, stout and hearty," Walt was to write in the Brooklyn *Standard* in 1862, "who will see Brooklyn number one million inhabitants!" All through its magical translation from farmers' market to metropolis Brooklyn had offered "treasures of speculation" in real estate, "richer than a California gold mine." He figured proudly that within the past forty years certain choice downtown acres had increased in value a thousandfold. As a civic booster and civic historian writing for a Brooklyn newspaper he had no obligation to report that during those same forty years he and his father, trading in houses and house lots, had failed to obtain a modest share of speculative treasure.

Even in this boom city, with new houses and stores being put up every day, the elder Whitman had trouble making a go of it. "A Methodist elder," Walt recalled, "contracted with my father . . . drawing up the contract so cutely from his own side—so shrewdly worded—as to make it possible for him, when the time for settlement came, to evade here a sum, there a sum, until my poor straightforward father was nearly swindled out of his boots." (Walt's autobiographical notes for those years mention other Brooklynites who figured in the family fortunes in the roles of "villain," "miserable scoundrel," or "old devil.") His father had little better luck with the houses he bought or built for his own use. "We occupied them one after the other, but they were mortgaged, and we lost them"— the mournful and diminishing cadences of that sentence from *Specimen Days* speak for themselves. On an average the Whitmans moved once each year, and in later life he wrestled with the chronology of dislocation:

> We moved to Brooklyn (Front st.) in May 1823
> Moved to Cranberry st. (opposite the church) in '24
>   ″   ″   Johnson st. May 1st 1825 . . .

On Independence Day, a month after the move to Johnson Street, Walt saw and stood near the Marquis de Lafayette, chief living hero of the Sacred Army, and he remembered the event to the end of his days. Accompanied by his son, George Washington Lafayette, the Marquis had returned to the United States as the nation's guest. He had made a pilgrimage to Mount Vernon, pressed his lips to Washington's lead coffin, and stood before it in silence; nearly half a century earlier, as a young major general, he had stood and fought at the Commander's right hand. As he traveled the length and breadth of the country for sixteen months he was greeted everywhere with a fervor that went beyond patriotism and gratitude to an acknowledgment of the miraculous. The newspapers hailed him as "a venerated father, returned from the grave" to bless a grateful child.

Lafayette crossed over to Brooklyn on the ferry early in the forenoon of July 4. In a simple ceremony, staid, antique, and even austere, without brass bands, policemen, or military display, he was welcomed at the ferry landing by a few withered and bent veterans and then rode hatless in an old-fashioned open yellow coach up Fulton Street, the narrow commercial thoroughfare of Brooklyn usually congested with market wagons carrying Long Island meat, fish and produce to New York. The schoolchildren of the town followed the General's carriage to Cranberry and Henry streets, where he laid the cornerstone of the Apprentices Library Building. Some of the smaller children had to be handed down into the cellar excavation. Recalling the occasion for the Brooklyn *Daily Times* in 1857, Whitman described "the childish pride [I] experienced in being one of those who were taken in the arms of Lafayette and reached down by him to a standing place." Eventually he came to believe and repeat in a much practiced reminiscence that "as a little boy I have been press'd tightly and lovingly to the breast of Lafayette," who kissed him before putting him down. Whether the kiss was history or, more likely, pseudo history, an early incident glorified and embroidered, Whitman remembered Lafayette's visit that July for tacitly conferring on him grace and mission.

In October the boom of cannon in the harbor signaled the completion of the Erie Canal; along five hundred miles of inland waterway a ton of grain could travel from Buffalo to Sandy Hook in ten days instead of six weeks and for six dollars instead of a hundred. "Let us conquer space," John Calhoun had said. Now canal, roads, coastal seaway, and the fast sailing packets of the Atlantic shuttle had made New York entrepot for the New World and the Old. " 'Our city,' " Whitman was to write in 1842, was "the heart, the brain, the focus, the main spring, the pinnacle, the extremity, the no more beyond."

Moved across the way, (Van Dyke's) were there 4th July 1826.

Americans who were alive on that day recalled it with awe and grief. As cannon boomed again in the harbor and across the land, marking the fiftieth anniversary of the Declaration of Independence, two former Presidents, both signers of the Declaration, died within a few hours of each other—Thomas Jefferson, eighty-three, at Monticello, and John Adams, ninety, at Quincy. Their dying on that jubilee day, it seemed, had been a last heroic act intended to sanctify their republic and inspire their countrymen. The time of Whitman's growing up was a long farewell salute to the receding world of the founders, a series of remarkable deaths, days of national mourning, acts of patriotic commemoration. In 1831, five years after Jefferson and Adams but, like them, on a July 4, died James Monroe, the last President to have served in combat in the Revolution, and over the next few years other emblematic Americans departed: Charles Carroll of Maryland, ninety-five, sole surviving signer of the Declaration of Independence; John Marshall, architect of constitutional law, in the thirty-fifth year of his chief justiceship ("His death at this time," said the diarist Philip Hone, "is a greater national calamity than Washington's was when it occurred"); James Madison, less happily remembered as fourth President than as father of the Constitution. Each year the circles left by British tents on the grass in Boston

Common grew fainter, the band of veterans of Bunker Hill and Lexington, Valley Forge and Brandywine, smaller. When the last soldier of the Sacred Army was gone, and then in turn the post-Revolutionary generation, what father-heroes would take their place, Whitman was soon to ask; how would the faith of the founders be transmitted? The founders led a revolution, but they left a tradition. How could he reconcile tradition with the revolutionary imperative to be his single self alone?

Moved to Adams st. lived there spring of '27
    "   "   Tillary co[rner] of Washington, (Miller's), 1st May 1827
    "   "   own house in Nov. . . .

By then there were five children (a sixth, born in 1825, died in infancy); Walter Whitman had achieved a temporary measure of economic stability; and Walt was a pupil in District School Number 1 at Concord and Adams streets, the beneficiary of a thrifty and rational scheme of education devised by an English Quaker, Joseph Lancaster. Assisted by hierarchies of student monitors, one teacher was able to distribute rote learning, together with fundamental social values and strict notions of the good and the useful, to two hundred and more pupils. Sometimes he invoked muscular Christianity and resorted to the birch rod, the cowhide strap, and, in Whitman's words, "other ingenious methods of child torture," mental as well as physical. He demanded unison, unquestioning obedience to regulations, undivided attention, and a physical discipline that dictated the precise way to hold and close a book during recitations and the position of hands when the pupils stood at parade rest. The Lancastrian method was designed to separate children from their ignorance as cleanly and impersonally as Eli Whitney's cotton gin separated fibers from seeds. It proved to be stupefying even for pupils less jealous of their emotional freedom than Walt. In later years one of his teachers remembered him as a good-natured boy, clumsy and slovenly in appearance and too big for his age, but otherwise unremarkable; he expressed surprise that Walt had amounted to anything, but added, "We need never be discouraged over anyone."

Walt's most vivid recollection from his five or six years in the common school was a dull shock, something like an earthquake, he imagined, that jarred half the city one day in June 1829, when he was ten years old. The frigate *Fulton*, the first steam vessel to be built by a government, blew up at its mooring in the Brooklyn Navy Yard—a disaffected sailor, it was said, had fired the powder magazine. Forty or fifty of the crew died in the explosion. Their funeral a few days later moved the boy to tears. The procession started for the Fulton Street graveyard from St. Ann's Episcopal Church at Washington and Sands streets:

> It was a full military and naval funeral—the sailors marching two by two, hand in hand, banners tied up and bound in black crepe, the muffled drums beating, the bugles wailing for the mournful peals of a dead march. We remember it all—remember following the procession, boylike, from beginning to end. We remember the soldiers firing the salute over the grave. And then how everything changed with the dashing and merry jig played by the same bugles and drums, as they made their exit from the graveyard and wended rapidly home.

"With music strong I come," he wrote in "Song of Myself,"

> . . . with my cornets and my drums,
> I play not marches for accepted victors only, I play marches for
>   conquer'd and slain persons.
>   .   .   .   .
> I beat and pound for the dead,
> I blow through my embouchures my loudest and gayest for them.

Five months after the *Fulton* explosion, on an evening in November, the ten-year-old boy accompanied his parents to the ballroom of Morrison's Hotel on Brooklyn Heights, and in this opulent and worldly setting, with its sparkling chandeliers and velvet divans, heard a sermon by Elias Hicks. In the audience, along with working-class people like the Whitmans, were the city's dignitaries and social leaders, merchants and judges, men and women of fashion, naval officers in uniform, and elderly Quakers in broad-brimmed hats and black bonnets. Some had come out of mere curiosity, others out of partisanship; Hicks was then at the center of the doctrinal storm that two years earlier had split the Society of Friends into liberal and orthodox communions. "The blood of Christ—the blood of Christ," Hicks had said publicly, according to Whitman, "why, my friends, the actual blood of Christ in itself was no more effectual than the blood of bulls and goats," and his hearers had risen to their feet and thumped their canes on the floor in anger. But that evening on Brooklyn Heights Hicks, a gaunt-faced man of eighty-one—he looked like a cross between an Indian and a black, "without a drop of white blood in his veins," Whitman recalled—did not speak of doctrinal disputes but only of "the light within," the single guiding principle, as it impressed itself on the boy, of man's "religious conscience" and "moral nature." As Hicks rose to the theme his "passionate unstudied oratory," neither argumentative nor intellectual, turned into a naturally cadenced prose that at times seemed to strive to achieve the condition of poetry.

> If there is, as doubtless there is [Whitman was to write], an unnameable something behind oratory, a fund within or atmosphere without, deeper than art, deeper even than proof, that unnameable constitutional something Elias Hicks emanated from his very heart to the hearts of his audience, or carried with him or probed into, and shook and arous'd in them—a sympathetic germ, probably rapport, lurking in every human eligibility, which no book, no rule, no statement has given or can give inherent knowledge, intuition—not even the best speech, or best put forth, but launch'd out only by powerful human magnetism.

Hicks's presence persisted in Whitman's passion for oratory and "natural eloquence," in the loosely cadenced verse of *Leaves of Grass*, in his wooing of ecstasy and in his fundamental creed, that "the fountain of all naked theology, all religion, all worship, all the truth to which you are possibly eligible" was the single self and its inherent relations. In the making of a poet's vision of reality and identity Hicks preceded Emerson and outlasted him—he was "a greater man than Carlyle," Whitman said. As he himself neared seventy, his Quaker traits and mannerisms became more pronounced; and he labored against feebleness, ill health, and a wandering mind to set down on paper, in "Elias Hicks," a fervent account of the "most *democratic* of the religionists," "the democrat in religion as Jefferson was the democrat in politics."

Hicks died in February 1830, when the entire country seemed to be in the grip of a great religious awakening. The following year a farmer in upstate New York, William Miller, predicted the imminent return of Christ followed by the end of the world, and many people prepared themselves for the final outcome.

That was the time of "Revivals" [wrote Whitman]. A third of the young men in Brooklyn, particularly the mechanics and apprentices, and young women of the same class in life, (and O, what pretty girls some of them were!) "experienced religion," as it is still called. In many cases it was no doubt a reality; but in many, alas! it was but an ebullition of the moment; and as such soon became "backsliders."

But the Whitmans remained immune to all this, even in Brooklyn, already known as a city of churches. They tended toward Quakerism but belonged to no meeting. Louisa Whitman attended church sometimes—"She pretended to be a Baptist," George said, but "went almost anywhere"—and her husband never; religious exercises or observances did not figure in their home life; and when Walt was sent to Sunday school at St. Ann's Episcopal Church it was because St. Ann's offered a free supplement to the free education he was getting at the district school the other days of the week, and in any case the lasting effect on him was of a nondoctrinal nature. At St. Ann's (and later, when he was an apprentice, at the Dutch Reformed Church on Joralemon Street), he was duly instructed in Scripture and catechism, but what remained with him was the Bible's rhythms and imagery, and he grew up unscathed by the conviction of sin and damnation that oppressed so many of his contemporaries and made the Sabbath a day of gloom and horror for them.

When he was about twenty he debated with himself whether he should become a Hicksite Quaker, but he put this aside as impossible. "I was never made to live inside a fence"—he was certain *Leaves of Grass* could never have been written on the inside of anything. Judging from this outcome, the orthodox Quakers may have been right, after all, when they denounced Elias Hicks as being little better than a deist and a heretic, and for Whitman himself even this exemplary preacher—a "brook of clear and cool and every healthy, ever-living water"—could go only so far.

Logic and sermons never convince,
The damp of the night drives deeper into my soul.

At eleven, all the formal schooling he was to have behind him, Walt worked as an office boy for a firm of lawyers, James B. Clarke

and his son Edward, on lower Fulton Street. They gave him a desk
and a window nook to himself, and he remembered gratefully that

> Edward C. help'd me at my handwriting and composition, and, (the
> signal event of my life up to that time,) subscribed for me to a big
> circulating library. For a time I now revel'd in romance-reading of all
> kinds—first, the "Arabian Nights," all the volumes, an amazing treat.
> Then, sorties in very many other directions, took in Walter Scott's
> novels, one after the other, and his poetry.

"If you could reduce the Leaves to their elements," he was to tell
Traubel, "you would see Scott unmistakeably active at the roots."
He read Cooper's *The Spy, The Last of the Mohicans* and *The Red Rover*,
a tale of insurgency and ocean adventure that stirred him up "clar-
ionlike: I read it many times." He became and remained "a most
omniverous novel-reader."

Running errands for the Clarkes (and later for a doctor) he explored the two cities along the East River. Downtown and water-
front Brooklyn had become a hive of shipyards and ship chandlers,
distilleries and glass works, casting furnaces, white-lead factories,
professional offices and mercantile establishments. But it remained
fundamentally rural, its character more accurately suggested, in
Whitman's recollection, by homely village fixtures—venerable drug-
stores and grocery stores, a wooden church, the scene of many tear-
ful revival meetings. Rows of elms shaded the grassy walks along
Fulton Street. Boys baited bent pins for killifish in stagnant ponds
and creeks and on hot days climbed up to Fort Greene, the site of
the American defeat in August 1776 and of an American garrison in
the War of 1812. They played on the grassy hill and looked out over
the shingled roofs of the village, a sweep of river, bay and shipping,
and six counties. Except for the area around the Navy Yard, Brooklyn had a reputation for stability and "a character for morals," one
of its leading editors said. On street after street below the Heights,
mechanics, tradesmen and clerks, many of them employed across
the river, built rows of trim boxlike houses on standard lots 25 by
100 feet and for the most part lived quiet lives. In Brooklyn, Whitman was to write, "men of moderate means" could find homes "at a
moderate cost." Writing for a city newspaper and loyal to his city,
he added, "The most valuable class in any community . . . is the

middle class." Brooklyn, somewhat like Camden when Whitman came to live there, lacked those extremes of grandeur and squalor, high challenge and defeat, for which New York was already known the world over.

When he first crossed Brooklyn ferry to Manhattan as a child some of the boats were still powered by horses yoked to a capstan in the deckhouse. The gatekeepers and deckhands made a pet of him, and allowed him to deadhead back and forth and feed what was to become a lifelong passion for river crossings. Now, running errands for the Clarkes, he rode the steam ferry to New York. A few times he delivered legal papers to Aaron Burr, fallen archangel, at seventy-five practicing law again. Stately and courteous, Burr greeted him with "amused interest, alertness, smiling old eyes, and hearty laugh" and with small acts of generosity and favor not to be forgotten. "He had a way of giving me a bit of fruit on these occasions—an apple or a pear." One January day the boy stopped in the street to take in the spectacle of the richest man in America, John Jacob Astor, bundled in furs and wearing an ermine hat, being helped by servants into his gorgeous sleigh; it was drawn by as fine a pair as Walt had ever seen, horses, like his grandfather's, bred for speed and mettle.

> Moved to Henry St. (Nr. Cranberry) the winter [1831–1832] before the first cholera summer.

> It must have been in 1832 *the bad cholera year*, we (the family) were domiciled in Liberty street—all hands except me moved for several weeks out in the country leaving me alone in the house.

Cholera, the characteristic epidemic disease of the century, entered the cities of the eastern seaboard that June, and churchgoers in Brooklyn and New York awaited the scourge with days of fasting, prayer and humiliation. The Masque of the Red Death soon played out its familiar drama. Some victims lived only a few hours after the first warning symptoms; others dragged on through days of diarrhea and retching, dehydration and pain, their skin turning bluish-gray toward the end. At the height of the epidemic over a hundred people died each day, and nearly a third of the population had fled. They carried contagion to the country districts and left behind them a hushed Pompeiian metropolis where grass had begun to grow in deserted thoroughfares. "For various reasons," Whitman wrote in an early story, "large numbers still remained. While fear drove away so many, poverty, quite as strong a force, also compelled many to stay where they were." Walt, printer's apprentice on a daily newspaper, was one of those who stayed where they were, "alone in the house."

> Moved from Liberty st. to Front st. (eastern part), and lived there in spring and early summer of 1833. Mother very sick.

President Andrew Jackson, waving a white beaver hat, his white hair brushed stiffly up from his forehead, rode up Fulton Street in an open barouche that June; the fourteen-year-old boy stood in the crowd that welcomed the Hero and Sage, Man of the People. Sometime around July, when Louisa Whitman gave birth to her eighth child, Jeff, her husband, having failed in Brooklyn, moved his family back out on Long Island. There he farmed and continued to pursue the building trade "with varying fortune," Walt said. The Whitmans may have lived with Cornelius Van Velsor at Cold Spring and moved on after a short while because of domestic frictions—Van Velsor had recently remarried and, according to Walt, his new wife "was not a good investment." Walt's terse note on the family hegira signals the nominal end of his dependent boyhood—

> I remained in Brooklyn.

4

"The Shadow and
the Light of a
Young Man's Soul"

I

The Long Island *Patriot*, the newspaper for which Walt had begun working in 1831, when he was twelve, occupied an old brick building on Fulton Street. It had once served as General Israel Putnam's headquarters. In the basement, along with a stationery shop, was the composing room of William Hartshorne, who had grown up in Philadelphia during the Revolution and rubbed shoulders with some of its heroes; he entertained his apprentices with personal anecdotes about Washington, Jefferson and Franklin. The hand press he used for printing the *Patriot*'s single sheet of four pages was scarcely more sophisticated than the one Franklin worked a century earlier, and in other ways, too, Hartshorne was a link to a principled past that seemed to be receding with alarming speed during the presidency of Andrew Jackson. "He had the old-school manner," Walt said, "rather sedate, not fast, never too familiar, always restraining his temper, always cheerful, benevolent, friendly, observing all the decorums of language and action."

Standing at the type case, the apprentice was instructed by his master in "the pleasing mystery of the different letters and their divisions—the great 'e' box—the box for spaces . . . the 'a' box, 'l' box, 'o' box, and all the rest—the box for quads away off in the right hand corner—the slow and laborious formation, type by type, of the first line." Words formed this way were tangible, vital, the incarnation of thought; when the boy's thumb pressed the composing stick too hard and pied the line he set, words seemed to show a resistant purpose of their own. More than twenty years later, in another print shop in Brooklyn, Whitman was to stand at the case again; as he set type for the first edition of *Leaves of Grass* he remembered a kind and patient master:

> The jour printer with gray head and gaunt jaws works at his case,
> He turns his quid of tobacco, and his eyes get blurred with the
> manuscript.

The *Patriot*, a weekly founded and conducted as the organ of the Democratic Party in Kings County, reflected none of Hartshorne's antique constancy. During Whitman's employment it was the creature of a flamboyant editor, Samuel E. Clement, a tall, hawk-nosed Quaker of Southern antecedents who walked the village lanes in a long-tailed blue coat with gilt buttons and a leghorn hat. As a reward for services rendered the Democratic Party, Clement also held the Brooklyn postmastership (his predecessor was now customs inspector for the port of New York). During his tenure of office at the *Patriot* the Fulton Street premises were a clearinghouse for the United States mails as well as for political and newspaper business.

In this easygoing atmosphere the young Whitman played pranks on such visitors as Henry Murphy, future Democratic boss of Brooklyn. He felt that Clement was "a 'good fellow'" and went along for the ride and for company when the editor drove his buggy out to Bushwick and New Lots delivering papers to country subscribers. Despite his verve and other attractive qualities, Clement managed at one stroke to turn the public and his political patrons against him. He was a grave robber. Loud demands were heard for his banishment, and after a period of simmering down and then oblivion he resurfaced on an opposition newspaper in Camden, New Jersey. What had come to light, in the course of a lawsuit in May 1831, was Clement's participation in a Poe-like adventure that touched on his apprentice's deepest springs of terror—

> A shroud I see and I am the shroud, I wrap a body and lie in the
> coffin,

It is dark here under ground, it is not evil or pain here, it is blank
      here, for reasons.

(It seems to me that every thing in the light and air ought to be
      happy,
Whoever is not in his coffin and the dark grave let him know he has
      enough.)

More than twenty-five years afterward Whitman wrote a remarkably detailed account of the Clement affair. "Several gentlemen," he
wrote in the Brooklyn *Daily Times* in 1857, "were very anxious to
have the sculptured counterfeit presentment of Elias Hicks, the renowned preacher of 'inner light,' who had then lately [February 27,
1830] died at Jericho, Long Island." One of the gentlemen was John
Henri Browere, of New York, a noted maker of life masks who
numbered among his subjects Lafayette, Jefferson, Hamilton, and
Dolly Madison; another of the gentlemen was Browere's son, who
inherited his father's trade secrets and went into the business of
casting heads for phrenological examination. Clement and the Brow-
eres stole into the graveyard at night, dug up Hicks's body, and took
a plaster cast of the head and face.

> From this mould a permanent one was made and several busts of Elias
> were formed, quite perfect, it is said. But soon a quarrel arose, in
> reference to the division of the anticipated profits from the sale of the
> bust—for the whole thing was as much intended for a speculation as
> to rescue the likeness of Elias, and transmit it to posterity. The quar-
> rel became at length so exasperated that, either from sullen agree-
> ment, or in some crisis of excitement, the moulds and the few busts
> made from them were all smashed to pieces! Thus ended this singular
> and in some of its particulars revolting affair.

He must have thought of this affair again at the end of his life, when
he was writing his sketch of Hicks. He had a large plaster bust of
him, "one of my treasures," in the parlor at Mickle Street, and he
included a copperplate "portrait of E. H. from life" in *November
Boughs*. "There's one reason in particular I want this picture to appear," he explained, perhaps with a trace of sympathy for what
Clement had attempted. "With the damnable unreason of a sect the
Quakers—too many of them—are fiercely opposed to pictures,

music, in their houses. I want this head, therefore, to flaunt itself in the faces of the Quakers who see this book."

By the summer of 1832 young Whitman had also left the *Patriot*, to work in the printing office of the opposition Whig weekly in Brooklyn, the Long Island *Star*. Unlike Clement, the *Star*'s owner and editor, Alden Spooner, was rooted in the community and a power behind its remarkable growth; he led the fight for the city charter granted in 1834. At a time when stage plays as well as the doctrines of Frances Wright were anathematized in the city of churches, Spooner's paper was sympathetic to both, gave enlightened attention to science and ideas, lyceum lectures and demonstrations, art and literature, and offered houseroom in its pages to poetry and prose by local authors, some of them quite accomplished. "America has hitherto produced very few writers of distinction; it possesses no great historians and not a single eminent poet," Alexis de Tocqueville noted in the course of his travels through the United States in 1831 and 1832. "The inhabitants of that country look upon literature properly so called with a kind of disapprobation." Whitman heard reflections of this sort all through his early years, and eventually he set himself the goal of being not just an eminent poet but his nation's chosen bard. Meanwhile, the *Star* did its best to answer the literary challenge, and though serving the Whigs just as the *Patriot* served the Jacksonian party, it made a serious effort to do more than merely advance political schemes that, according to Tocqueville, were often "very ill-digested" and whipped readers up into partisan frenzies. "As men become more equal and individualism more to be feared," he said, newspapers would have to become instruments of "intellectual and moral association . . . To suppose that they only serve to protect freedom would be to diminish their importance. They maintain civilization."

Ventilated by the winds of civilization, change, and the great world, the *Star* was Walt's college and trade school, and he graduated a journeyman printer in May 1835, when he was sixteen and practically full-grown; "grew too fast," he said, but he was proud when others admired his strong, well-shaped body naked in the public swimming bath. He was a peaceful child no longer—he had awakened to manhood, the prospect of death, and

77

. . . the fire, the sweet hell within,
The unknown want, the destiny of me.

He took as a sign and portent the dazzling Leonid meteor shower he watched in the night sky in November 1833, "year 58 of the States." "Myriads in all directions," he wrote in a pre-*Leaves of Grass* manuscript fragment, "some with long shining white trains, some falling over each other like falling water—leaping, silent, white apparitions around up there in the sky over my head." His imagination fed on novels, romances, and poetry and on the plays he saw across the river in the theaters along Park Row, Chatham Square, and the Bowery. At first, "a fat-cheeked boy, in round jacket and broad shirt-collar," he went to the theater in the company of other apprentices. "How well I remember my first visit," he wrote in 1850. "The play was the School for Scandal. I had a dim idea of the walls of some adjoining houses silently and suddenly sinking away, to let folks see what was going on within. Then the band; O, never before did such heavenly melodies make me drunk with pleasure so utterly sweet and spiritual!" After a while, stage-struck, he preferred to go alone—"I was so absorbed in the performance, and disliked anyone to distract my attention." From his seat in the pit he saw plays by Shakespeare along with melodramas like *Jonathan Bradford, or the Murder at the Roadside Inn; The Last Days of Pompeii; Napoleon's Old Guard;* and the indestructible *Mazeppa*, featuring an athletic actor and a well-trained horse. At the Bowery Theatre on June 8, 1835, he saw the tragedian Junius Brutus Booth as Shakespeare's *Richard III:*

> I can, from my good seat in the pit, pretty well front, see again Booth's quiet entrance from the side, as, with head bent, he slowly and in silence, (amid the tempest of boisterous hand-clapping,) walks down the stage to the footlights with that peculiar and abstracted gesture, musingly kicking his sword, which he holds off from him by its sash. Though fifty years have pass'd since then, I can hear the clank, and feel the perfect following hush of perhaps three thousand people waiting. (I never saw an actor who could make more of the said hush or wait, and hold the audience in an indescribable, half-delicious, half-irritating suspense.) And so throughout the entire play, all parts, voice, atmosphere, magnetism, from

"Now is the winter of our discontent,"
to the closing death fight with Richmond, were of the finest and
grandest.

Richmond held the crown aloft, and cried, "The day is ours; the
bloody dog is dead." Like a green waterfall, the Bowery's crepe
curtain came down to a tempest of hand clapping—"no dainty kid-
glove business, but electric force and muscle from . . . full-sinew'd
men." It had been an unforgettable evening of "fire, energy, *abandon*"
that stirred the young Whitman to the keel of his being. He felt a
dilation of plenitude and possibility, he was intoxicated with the
human voice:

O what is it in me that makes me tremble so at voices?
Surely whoever speaks to me in the right voice, him or her I shall
     follow,
As the water follows the moon, silently, with fluid steps, anywhere
     around the globe.

Booth's genius "was to me one of the grandest revelations of my
life," a lesson in "artistic expression" and "electric personal idiosyn-
crasy"—"As in all art-utterance it was the subtle and powerful *something special in the individual* that really conquer'd."*

He said that the first time he ever wanted to write anything enduring was "when I saw a ship under full sail, and had the desire to
describe it exactly as it seemed to me." As an apprentice he wrote
"sentimental bits," then "a piece or two," not now identifiable, in
the *New-York Mirror*, a "celebrated and fashionable" weekly of literature and the fine arts edited by George Pope Morris, the popular
author of "Woodman, Spare that Tree" and "By the Lake Where

---

* During the Civil War, Whitman saw one of Booth's sons, John Wilkes, in the
role of *Richard III*. The performance, he wrote in May 1862, "is about as much like
his father's, as the wax bust of Henry Clay, in the window down near Howard
street, a few blocks below the theatre, is like the genuine orator in the Capitol,
when his best electricity was flashing alive in him and out of him." This was three
years before the younger Booth's unscheduled appearance at Ford's Theatre in
Washington at a performance of *Our American Cousin*. ("The Bowery," *New York
Leader*, May 3, 1962—reprinted in *Walt Whitman and the Civil War*, ed. Charles I.
Glicksberg [Philadelphia, 1933], p. 56.)

Droops the Willow." Walt waited impatiently for the fat, red-faced carrier who delivered the *Mirror* in Brooklyn, and he opened and cut the pages with trembling fingers. "How it made my heart double-beat to see *my piece* on the pretty white paper, in nice type." By the time he reached twenty-two he had published, in addition to his routine journalism work, ten didactic essays written "From the Desk of a Schoolmaster." The series title of these pieces, *Sun-Down Papers*, anticipates the great "Sun-Down Poem" of 1856, in later editions titled "Crossing Brooklyn Ferry." He had also published about a dozen poems, most of them dealing with ambition, pride, and the vanity of human wishes; their titles are explicit enough—"The Love That Is Hereafter"; "The End of All"; "We Shall All Rest at Last"; "Our Future Lot"; "My Departure"; "The Punishment of Pride." "O, many a panting, noble heart," he wrote in the opening stanzas of "Fame's Vanity" (1839),

> Cherishes in its deep recess
> Th'hope to win renown o'er earth
> From Glory's priz'd caress.
>
> And some will reach that envied goal,
> And have their fame known far and wide;
> And some will sink unnoted down
> In dark Oblivion's tide.
>
> But I, who many a pleasant scheme
> Do sometime cull from Fancy's store,
> With dreams, such as the youthful dream,
> Of grandeur, love, and power—
>
> Shall I build up a lofty name,
> And seek to have the nations know
> What conscious might dwells in the brain
> That throbs aneath this brow?

Ego confusion intermittently surfaces in these poems along with a terror of drift, lawless imperatives, and the obliteration of identity. Even the best of them are wooden and imitative and show a consistent, perhaps uncompromising lack of promise that could be redeemed only by a radical transformation—a quantum surge—in language, vision, and the self, and by a faith that new beginnings are always possible. ("There are such things as fountains in the world," Coleridge said, even in the desert.) Walt appeared to be unworried. "Nobody, I hope, will accuse me of conceit in these opinions of mine own capacity for doing great things," he wrote in a "Sun-Down Paper."

> Who should be a better judge of a man's talents than the man himself? I see no reason why we should let our lights shine under bushels. Yes: I would write a book! And who shall say that it might not be a very pretty book? Who knows but that I might do something very respectable?

As a description of *Leaves of Grass*, "very pretty" and "very respectable" may serve as one measure of the extent of Whitman's eventual self-transformation.

His apprenticeship over, in the spring of 1835 he found work as a typesetter in New York. When, as an old man, he looked back over his traveled roads he did not say, and probably no longer remembered, whom he had worked for or where he lived; a year of his life went up in the smoke and flames of the city's history. A terrible fire that summer was to devastate the printing and publishing district alongside City Hall Park. The new brick buildings put up in a recent period of expansion and prosperity were too high to be reached by fire brigade ladders and hoses; walls buckled and collapsed into the streets. Several thousand workers, suddenly thrown out of work, found themselves in worse straits after a second fire in December, a calamity that Philip Hone, in the consternation of the moment, called "the greatest loss by fire that has ever been known with the exception perhaps of the conflagration of Moscow." Seven hundred buildings around Wall Street were destroyed, among them the Customs House and the domed Merchants' Exchange with its oval trading hall and heroic statue of Alexander Hamilton; United States Marines and armed militia patrolled nineteen burned-out blocks against looters; property owners, businessmen, investors and insurance companies were ruined; the value of the property and goods destroyed was estimated to be $20,000,000.

Without tenure in the printing trades, unable to find satisfactory work in any other trade, Walt soon became an economic casualty of this disastrous year—it was a foretaste for New Yorkers of the long economic depression that lay ahead. He left the city at the beginning of May 1836 and spent the month with his family. "Long ago we lived on a farm," George Whitman said, and he recalled an instance of the stubborn finality that he associated with his brother. "Walt would not do farm work. He had things he liked better—school-teaching, for instance." Between farming and teaching the choice was clear; still, as Walt suggested in a story called "The Shadow and the Light of a Young Man's Soul," it may have been with dread and a sense of defeat that he took up the first in a series of irregular and poorly paid appointments as a country schoolmaster on Long Island. In the aftermath of the fires of 1835 the story's hero—"unstable as water"—ransacks "every part of the city for employment," gives up and becomes a schoolmaster. "When the young Archibald Dean went from the city—(living out of which he had so often said was no living at all)—went down into the country to take charge of a little district school, he felt as though the last float plank which buoyed him up on hope and happiness was sinking, and he with it."

II

Seventeen when he first stood behind the teacher's desk, Whitman was younger than some of the seventy or eighty farmers' sons who were his pupils. He had been hired to wield a paternal authority in leading or driving them through a "bare and superficial" curriculum of reading, writing, grammar, arithmetic and geography. Education in the country districts was as poverty-struck and grudgingly maintained as the schoolhouse itself, a cheerless, drafty one-room structure without a bell, a clock or a stove—like a farm outbuilding, it had a crude batten door with a padlock. "To teach a good school," he later said, "it is not at all necessary for a man to be inflexible in rules and severe in discipline. Order and obedience we would always have; and yet two of the best schools we ever knew appeared always to the casual spectator to be complete uproar, confusion and chaos." He did not go so far as Emerson's friend Bronson Alcott, who, when physical chastisement was called for at his school in Boston, had the child strike the teacher, but he retired the birch and rule he had experienced as a boy, played twenty questions with his scholars, engaged them in general discussions, told them stories, had them do exercises in description and mental arithmetic and memorize poetry. Charles Roe, a pupil in the school at Little Bay Side, near Jamaica, was to remember him with "respect and affection . . . We were all deeply attached to him, and were sorry when he went away."

George Whitman too, his pupil for about a year, said it was generally agreed that "Walt made a very good schoolmaster." But it was also said he was too easygoing, appeared not to have his heart in his work, and spent much of his time musing and writing. The same school examiners who had been casual about his qualifications when they hired him were probably unimpressed by what they saw on visits to the schoolroom; only a few of the eight or nine quarter-year teaching appointments Walt held between 1836 and 1841 were renewed.

The customary rewards of country schoolteaching, he said, were "poor pay," "coarse fare"—sometimes a pickled hog's head with an olla-podrida of fried turnips, potatoes and cabbage—and a straw mattress with little privacy in the homes of his pupils' parents; he was once invited to bed down with a sick cow. He recalled long winter nights of loneliness and boredom when he would escape the family circle and go back to his teacher's desk to drink solitary hot toddies and play doublehanded checkers. Once, he said, "I had a literary fit, and wrote a story." The title of his story, "Death in the School-Room (a Fact)," speaks for itself. It was only years later that he decided that the common practice of "boarding round"—"moving from house to house and farm to farm, among high and low, living a few days alternately at each"—had been "one of my best experiences and deepest lessons in human nature behind the scenes, and in the masses."

Country schoolteachers were "apt to be eccentric specimens of the masculine race." The Island farmers and tradesmen and their families—"hospitable, upright, commonsensical"—regarded him as more of a puzzle than most of their itinerant boarders. He was big and muscular, but he moved slowly and with a curious indolence. Others bustled; he waited. "Of all human beings, none equals your genuine, inbred, unvarying loafer," Walt wrote in 1840. "What was Adam, I should like to know, but a loafer?" Boarding round, Walt led an interim existence and drew on what he claimed was a family trait, "the ability to tide over, to lay back on reserves, to wait, to take time." (It was because of this same "lethargic waitingness," he said after the Civil War, that George was able to come out alive after five months in Confederate military prisons.) He described his own patient and moratory character in some early notes for a story:

> This singular young man was unnoted for any strange qualities; and he certainly had no bad qualities. Possessed very little of what is called education. He remained much by himself, although he had many brothers, sisters, relations, and acquaintance. He did not work like the rest. By far the most of the time he remained silent.

"One of the greatest things about Walt," George recalled, "was his wonderful calmness in trying times when everybody else would get excited. He was always cool, never flurried." But Walt's composure was more willed than organic, and George had witnessed vivid exceptions. Once, when Walt was out in a boat fishing in a pond near the family farm at Babylon, a neighborhood boy, Benjamin Carman, provoked him by throwing stones in the water and rowing across his lines. Walt met him ashore and thrashed him with his pole. The boy's father brought charges of assault, but they were dismissed, on the grounds the boy deserved worse, and, according to George, "Walt even gave the fellow a devil of a licking after the trial . . . He was a muscular young man at that time—very strong." In later years Walt was to be seen kicking a politician down the stairs, manhandling a verger in a church, and grappling with a carpet-bag senator who insulted him; these demonstrations of explosive temper were memorable because they were infrequent and because he had been trying so hard to cultivate Quaker peaceableness.

For the most part, the Islanders found him mild enough in demeanor, correct in his language and conversation, simple in his living habits and the way he dressed. In his plain black suit he could have passed for an impoverished divinity student if he had not been "rather atheistic" in his views, as Roe said, and openly contemptuous of churchmen, churches, and doctrinal matters in general. He did not care much about public opinion—"Never mind what they think," he told his mother—and the villagers left him alone. At recess he played baseball with his pupils, and when school was out he was politely friendly with the young men of the village and played cards with them once in a while. He never danced or flirted with girls even though, boarding round with large families in districts where young men without barnyard muck on their shoes were in short supply, he had plenty of opportunities; some teachers he knew of had made good marriages that way and were set for life. "The girls did not seem to attract him. He did not specially go anywhere with them or show any extra fondness for their society," Roe once told Horace Traubel, "seemed, indeed, to shun it." Until he left Long Island for good and was free to explore the beckoning island of Manhattan, women remained "a class of beings of whose nature, habits, notions, and ways," Walt wrote in 1840, he had "not been able to gather any knowledge, either by experience or observation."

Between teaching jobs he lived at home and accepted "stormy scenes" and recriminations as the price he had to pay for refusing to do farm work. Otherwise, he and his father managed to coexist on even, although guarded, terms. "I don't think his father ever had an idea what Walt was up to, what he meant," George said. With his sisters and younger brothers, on the other hand, Walt assumed— perhaps, in unacknowledgable striving, even usurped—his father's role. It was "as if he had us in his charge," George said, and he added, "Now and then his guardianship seemed excessive. . . . He was like us—yet he was different from us, too." He was their companion, playmate, and counselor, but as an early sketch, "My Boys and Girls," suggests, he entertained explicit fantasies about being their parent as well.* The claim he made to John Addington Symonds in 1890, "Tho' always unmarried I have had six children," was anticipated in the first sentence of this sketch: "Though a bachelor, I have several boys and girls that I consider my own."

Whitman published "My Boys and Girls" in 1844 but probably wrote it long before then, during his family's stay in Babylon. Four of his brothers and sisters—George, Jeff, Andrew and Hannah

---

* In psychoanalytic terms Whitman at this stage may be described as "subject-homoerotic." "There is, in a sense, no true external love-object—at least initially. Such men love boys as a way of loving the boy in themselves and themselves in the boy. They need have no antipathy for women and may have warm friends among them, but are likely to be too self-centered to pay much attention to them. The situation may be pictured very crudely by thinking of the subject-homoerotic man as virtually encapsulated—more or less intact—within the personality of, usually, his mother . . . he behaves as if he were caught in the predicament of earliest adolescence and tries to escape from it through his love for the young men he might have become. His intense identification with them may lead to an almost uncanny empathy." (Edgar Z. Friedenberg, *The Vanishing Adolescent* [Boston, 1973], pp. 121–22.)

Louisa—figure in it by name and by their relative ages in 1835–1836. Walt's other sister, Mary Elizabeth, born in 1821, appears unnamed as "a very beautiful girl, in her fourteenth year"; with an implicit dread of sexuality, the sketch looks with foreboding to a time when this "child of light and loveliness" will lose her "purity" and "the freshness of youthful innocence." ("Who, at twenty-five or thirty years of age," asks the narrator, "is without many memories of wrongs done, and mean or wicked deeds performed?" Whitman was twenty-five when he published "My Boys and Girls.") The sketch mentions another child who, like Louisa's fifth-born, died in infancy and, in a period when infant deaths were common, was hardly mourned: "It was not a sad thing—we wept not, nor were our hearts heavy." As always, Jesse is excluded from Walt's family picture; also excluded, but for other reasons, is Eddy, an infant at the time of writing and intellectually an infant ever after. Another of Whitman's imaginary "children" invokes a familiar homoerotic theme, the deaths of young men:

> Very beautiful was he—and the promise of an honorable manhood shone brightly in him—and sad was the gloom of his passing away. We buried him in the early summer. The scent of the apple-blossoms was thick in the air—and all animated nature seemed overflowing with delight and motion.

Walt's exercise of a pseudo-parental role already extends beyond the members of his family. He has begun to acknowledge "the need of comrades," the central theme of his "Calamus" poems. Strangely naïve as well as strangely knowing, covert as well as unconsciously revealing, he yearns to become all things to younger men—father, brother, lover, friend; he becomes restive under the restraints society imposed on the expression of his yearnings.

> Then there is J. H., a sober, good-natured youth, whom I hope I shall always number among my friends. Another H. has lately come among us—too large, perhaps, and too near manhood to be called one of my *children*. I know I shall love him well when we become better acquainted—as I hope we are destined to be.

Looking back to this period, Whitman once told Nelly O'Connor that "the grown-up son of the farmer with whom he was boarding while he was teaching school became very fond of him, and Walt of the boy, and he said the father quite reproved him for making such a pet of the boy." Even in this summary version the phrase "quite reproved" suggests a residue of anguish on Whitman's part. Nelly deleted the episode from her published memoir, but it is at least compatible with a story originating in Southold, where Whitman taught for a while, that he got into trouble there and was forced to leave.* And the same farmer's-son episode appears to figure in two short stories Whitman published in 1841, just after he gave up teaching for good. In "Bervance," a father becomes jealous of his son's intimacy with a resident tutor and plots to have the boy put away in a lunatic asylum. The second story, "The Child's Champion," has a happier ending. The hero, John Lankton, becomes the protector of a twelve-year-old farm apprentice. He rescues the boy from the attentions of drunken sailors in a saloon, and takes him to his room, where they spend the night in each other's arms. An angel, "a spirit from the Pure Country," blesses their union with a kiss. Lankton is reborn. His love for the boy "grew not slack with time."

Like Lankton before his regeneration, Whitman nearing twenty "lived without any steady purpose." Like Archibald Dean, the country schoolmaster of "The Shadow and the Light of a Young Man's Soul," he lacked "energy and resolution" but was "not indisposed to work, and work faithfully, could he do so in a sphere equal to his ambitions." He explored this "sphere" at Smithtown, where he taught school for two terms in 1837–1838 and was one of the organizers of a debating society. Its members were the town's achievers, present or future doctors, lawyers, businessmen, holders of public office; they elected him secretary. Such societies, from Benjamin

---

* The general situation will be familiar to readers of Sherwood Anderson's "Hands" (in *Winesburg, Ohio*): "A half-witted boy of the school became enamored of the young master. In his bed at night he imagined unspeakable things and in the morning went forth to tell his dreams as facts. Strange hideous accusations fell from his loose-hung lips." In one version of the Southold episode, Whitman is supposed to have been denounced from the pulpit as a "Sodomite" and then tarred and feathered. This hardly jibes with the fact that during the 1840s and 1850s Whitman regularly spent his vacations around Southold. (Horace Gregory, ed., *The Portable Sherwood Anderson* [New York, 1949], p. 48; Katherine Molinoff, *Walt Whitman at Southold* [Privately printed, 1966].)

Franklin's Junto Club on, had served Americans as gymnasia for mental exercise and substitutes for theatrical entertainment. The habit of public argument acquired in these societies left a peculiar impress on the native character, Tocqueville said. "An American cannot converse, but he can discuss. He speaks to you as if he was addressing a meeting; and if he should chance to become warm in the discussion, he will say 'Gentlemen' to the person with whom he is conversing."

Wednesday evenings in the schoolhouse on the green, the Smithtown debaters addressed themselves to the role of nature and nurture in the formation of character, the rights and wrongs of capital punishment and unrestricted immigration, the injustices done the Indians by the European settlers of the continent, the relative merits of Queen Elizabeth and Mary Queen of Scots, and the achievements for good or evil of the late Emperor of the French, Napoleon Bonaparte. Like their counterparts elsewhere, the Smithtowners also debated issues that were to have a more electrifying importance for Walt Whitman, chrysalid poet of self and nation. At a meeting of the Transcendental Club in Boston in October 1836, Emerson, Alcott, Orestes Brownson, and George Ripley had discussed a familiar topic, "American Genius—the Causes which Hinder Its Growth Giving Us No First-Rate Productions." The following August, Emerson, then a thirty-four-year-old clergyman, addressed the members of the Harvard chapter of Phi Beta Kappa, gathered in the wooden meetinghouse of the First Parish, Cambridge, and announced a new age. "Our day of dependence, our long apprenticeship to the learning of other lands, draws to a close," he said.

> We will walk on our own feet; we will work with our own hands; we will speak our own minds. The study of letters shall no longer be a name for pity, for doubt, and for sensual indulgence. The dread of man and the love of man shall be a wall of defense and a wreath of joy around all. A nation of men will for the first time exist, because each believes himself inspired by the Divine Soul which also inspires all men.

Emerson's "American Scholar" address, said Oliver Wendell Holmes, who was present that day in the meetinghouse, was "our intellectual Declaration of Independence." Later that year, at a public meeting in Boston's Faneuil Hall, another orator touched with heavenly fire, Wendell Phillips, paid tribute to a courageous editor, Elijah Lovejoy, murdered by a pro-slavery mob in Alton, Illinois; the abolitionist cause had found its martyr and its champion.

"Have the arts and sciences flourished more under a Republican form of government than any other?" Whitman argued and carried the affirmative with the Smithtown debaters. "Is the system of slavery, as it exists in the South, right?" He was an emancipationist then and later, not an abolitionist, but he argued and carried the negative. Intoxicated with oratory, the human voice, and for a while with party politics, Whitman was to envision a career for himself as "wander speaker," a public teacher—"The greatest champion America ever could know"—discoursing on public issues to the President, the Congress, and the people. In *Leaves of Grass* a lonely poet often seems to be "addressing a meeting" and tasting "the orator's joys":

> To inflate the chest, to roll the thunder of the voice out from the ribs
> and throat,
> To make the people rage, weep, hate, desire, with yourself,
> To lead America—to quell America with a great tongue.

When Whitman's teaching appointment at Smithtown ran out, he returned from dreams of oratory to newspapering. He bought a used press and a case of types, rented space above a stable, and in June 1838 went into business as founder, publisher and editor of a Huntington weekly, the *Long Islander*. His father, who had some cash in hand after recently mortgaging the farm, may have been a backer, with George, Walt's assistant but also a "part proprietor," holding his proxy. When the first number came out on June 5, 1838, a week after Walt turned nineteen, the Long Island *Star* wished its former apprentice well, warning him, however, that he may have taken on a dubious business enterprise—"Few country places feel a proper pride in sustaining a newspaper." As Whitman later acknowledged, there was not a great deal for any country place to sustain in the usual "dingy" compilation of advertisements (often, like subscriptions to the paper, paid for in potatoes and cordwood), columns scissored out from metropolitan journals, and local stories that chronicled "the details of a big pumpkin or a three-legged cow." No file of the *Long Islander* under Whitman's editorship survives, but two items—his earliest known published writing—were reprinted in the August 8, 1838, issue of the Long Island *Democrat*, a Jamaica newspaper for which he was soon to work:

> Our neighbor of the L. I. Star intimated some time ago, in his peculiarly pleasant style, that though in Suffolk county, the harvest had not been very good, in the Whig counties generally it had never been quite abundant. Whatever the condition of the summer produce may be, we believe the fall crops in this county have hitherto been semi-annually of so abundant and peculiar a nature as quite to excite the ire of the Brooklyn editor.

The second item, titled "Effects of Lightning," was in the pumpkin and cow tradition:

> At Northport, on Saturday, 28th ultimo [July], an unfortunate and somewhat singular accident occurred from the lightning. Mr. Abraham Miller of that place, had been in the fields, engaged in some farm work, and was returning home, as a storm commenced in the afternoon, carrying in his hands a pitchfork. A friend of his who was with him advised him not to carry it, as he considered it dangerous. Mr. Miller, however, did not put down the fork, but continued walking with it; he had gone some distance on his way home, and had just put up the bars of a fence he passed through when a violent clap of thunder, occurred, followed by a sharp flash. The acquaintance of Mr. Miller was slightly stunned by the shock and turning around to look at his companion he saw him lying on his face motionless. He went to him and found him dead; the lightning having been attracted by the steel tines of the fork, had torn his hand slightly, and killed him on the instant.

"Everything seem'd turning out well," Walt said about his Huntington newspaper. "Only my own restlessness prevented me gradually establishing a permanent property there." His own master for the first time in his life, he was careless of schedules, money and toil, the villagers said, devoted instead to books and other pastimes, like the game of ring toss he and George played in their office for stakes of a mince pie or twenty-five cents. Along with the press and types Walt had bought a white mare named Nina. Once a week when he first published the paper, later less regularly when his interest waned, he rode her along the inland and shore roads from Huntington to Babylon, Smithtown and Commack, and delivered his copies to the farmers. He stopped to visit with them in the hayfields; sometimes they asked him to stay for supper and the night —"I never had happier jaunts." There were other jaunts then, day-long excursions to the Atlantic shore, that were to remain in his memory and shape his imagination. "It is a universal summer custom on Long Island," he wrote in 1845, "to have what are called 'beach-parties.' " The young men ran dancing and laughing along the sand, bathed in the surf, fished, dug clams, speared messes of fat, sweet-meated eel. He loved swimming, of a passive sort—"I was a first rate aquatic loafer," he recalled. "I possessed almost unlimited capacity for floating on my back." Cradled, rocked and drowsing, his body rolling "silently to and fro in the heave of the water," he lay suspended between the depths and the light, between the unconscious and the world of necessity. Poets and painters of Whitman's century took up the subject of young men bathing—Gerard Manley Hopkins in "Epithalamion," for example; Seurat in "Une Baignade"; and Eakins in "The Swimming Hole"—and it became familiar in English poetry around the time of the first World War. But Whitman, in Section 11 of "Song of Myself," was to create its most loving and lyrical evocation:*

Twenty-eight young men bathe by the shore,
Twenty-eight young men and all so friendly;
Twenty-eight years of womanly life and all so lonesome.

She owns the fine house by the rise of the bank,
She hides handsome and richly drest aft the blinds of the window.

* Robert K. Martin describes this poem as "a clear defense of the anonymity of sexual encounter. In the dream-vision of Whitman there are no persons, but rather a general feeling of the delight of sexual experience regardless of the partner. They are totally tactile, since they take place in the dreamworld of closed eyes. The experience could well be repeated in almost any steam bath of a modern large city. But the important point to see is that not asking, not knowing and not thinking are integral parts of Whitman's *democratic* vision, and anonymous sexuality is an important way station on the path to the destruction of distinctions of age, class, beauty *and* sex. Whitman loves all being, and will love, and be loved by, all being. It is perhaps at this juncture that the implications of Whitman's perspective become most revolutionary." (*The Homosexual Tradition in American Poetry* [Austin, Texas, 1979], pp. 19–20.)

Which of the young men does she like the best?
Ah the homeliest of them is beautiful to her.

Where are you off to, lady? for I see you,
You splash in the water there, yet stay stock still in your room.

Dancing and laughing along the beach came the twenty-ninth
        bather,
The rest did not see her, but she saw them and loved them.

The beards of the young men glisten'd with wet, it ran from their
        long hair,
Little streams pass'd all over their bodies.

An unseen hand also pass'd over their bodies.
It descended tremblingly from their temples and ribs.

The young men float on their backs, their white bellies bulge to the
        sun, they do not ask who seizes fast to them,
They do not know who puffs and declines with pendant and
        bending arch,
They do not think whom they souse with spray.

The "beautiful gigantic swimmer" of *Leaves of Grass*, "swimming naked through the eddies of the sea" and viewed through the water's green lens or in blood-stained turbulence, makes a first appearance in the literary prose of Whitman's Long Island period.

> I felt myself carried along, as it were, like some expert swimmer, who has tired himself, and to rest his limbs, allows them to float drowsily and unresistingly on the bosom of the sunny river. Real things lost their reality.—A dusky mist spread itself before my eyes.

A current of associations carries him along to "a regular and most sentimental fit of . . . Low Spirits."

> Shall I become old without tasting the sweet draughts of which the young may partake?—Silently and surely are the months stealing along.—a few more revolutions of the old earth will find me treading the paths of advanced manhood.—This is what I dread: for I have not enjoyed my young time. I have been cheated of the bloom and nectar of life.—Lonesome and unthought of as I am, I have no one to care for, or to care for me.

Some of his companions at beach parties were dreaming of girls who had captured their hearts, but he fell into the reveries of William Cullen Bryant's "Thanatopsis" and wondered, How shall I face death? With Bryant's lines and phrases echoing in his mind, he composed a poem, "Our Future Lot," and set it in type at his Huntington newspaper office.

This breast which now alternate burns
    with flashing hope, and gloomy fear,
Where beats a heart that knows the hue
    Which aching bosoms wear;

This curious frame of human mould,
    Where craving wants unceasing play—
The troubled heart and wondrous form
    Must both alike decay,

Then cold wet earth will close around
    Dull, senseless limbs, and ashy face,
But where, O Nature! will be
    My mind's abiding place?

After a year of vagrant management, increasingly subject to such reveries, Whitman's backers sold the *Long Islander* out from under him. The new proprietor made a point of explaining that under his predecessor the paper had been virtually "discontinued." "Came down to New York (after selling Nina) in the summer of 39," Whitman noted, job-hunted, again found nothing there, and retreated to Jamaica, thriving gateway town along the route of the Long Island Rail Road. He worked for the *Democrat* and lived in the house of its editor, James Brenton, who liked him and believed that Walt had promise as a writer of stories and poems but no notion of what it meant to work regular hours—unless summoned after the midday meal, he might spend entire afternoons looking at the sky, a study in indolence and irresolution. Brenton's wife complained that Walt was always "under foot" in the house, always "sitting around" in his shirtsleeves and that he ignored her two small children, even seemed to resent them as intrusions upon his solitude. Brenton was sorry, nonetheless, when Walt left the *Democrat* and went back to teaching school, at Little Bay Side near Jamaica, at Trimming Square and Woodbury, both near West Hills, and during the winter and spring of 1840–1841 at Whitestone, within sight of the farms at the northern extremity of his eventual goal, New York. Whitman's two terms at Whitestone, the last teaching he was to do, survive in his records in the form of a notebook entry, "Winter of 1840, went to White stone, and was there till next spring," and a letter of reference, written in his plain and conventional hand, on behalf of someone otherwise unknown:

> Miss Clarissa Lyvere has been assistant teacher in this school for several months past, and I would cheerfully testify to her competence and her general capability as a teacher. Her knowledge of the ordinary branches of a common school education is complete, and I unhesitatingly recommend her to any and all who may desire a good teacher for their children.
>
> WALTER WHITMAN
>
> Whitestone School
> March 30 [1841]

Like Herman Melville, a schoolteacher before he shipped out for the Pacific whaling grounds that year, "with nothing particular to interest me on shore," Whitman had waited in the schoolhouse for better opportunities to come. In May he went to New York again, but this time, as he wrote in another early poem, there was to be "No Turning Back."

5

"This is the city
and I am
one of the citizens..."

IN THE SWIRL AND BOIL of Jacksonian democracy, half of New York's population, 325,000 in 1841, lived in boardinghouses, families with children as well as single people. Those with money boarded in converted mansions along Broadway; navvies, seamen on the beach, and bankrupts lived in grub cellars near the North River docks or off the Bowery. Whitman made his home with the clerk and trades-man class and explored the great metropolis from "Mrs. Chipman's" at 12 Centre Street, "Mrs. R. in Spring st.," "Mrs. Bonnard's in John st.," "Mrs. Edgarton's in Vesey," "Mary's" and "Brown's in Duane st." Soon after his arrival in the city he described one of these establishments, the landlady presiding over tea and coffee urns at the head of her breakfast table.

> Mr. K. the gentleman at the corner, is a good humored New Eng-lander, and Mr. D., next to him, is from the same section of our country. W. is a dry goods keeper in Greenwich street, and H. an elderly bachelor who has a clothing store down town. A. is a Jewish gentleman of Chatham street, S. one of a well known publishing firm in this city, and the next two young fellows are clerks in Broadway. Mr. B., at the lower head of the table, is a jeweller and a gentleman;

95

Y. is from Saratoga Springs; W., a salesman in a shop near by; Dr. H., a dentist and physician; Mrs. H., his wife; an elderly woman, the mother of our landlady; and several others, ladies, &c., whom we feel delicate about mentioning.

Despite the need that boardinghouses filled in a pre-apartment era, critics considered them a deterrent to ambition, stability, and the homemaking impulse. "I can hardly imagine a contrivance more effectual for ensuring the insignificance of a woman, than marrying her at seventeen, and placing her in a boarding-house," said Frances Trollope, the novelist's mother; she noted a "cold heartless atmosphere . . . where hospitality can never enter, and where interest takes the management instead of affection." One of Whitman's boardinghouse acquaintances, a seventeen-year-old junior clerk named Henry Saunders, forged thirty thousand dollars in checks before he was transferred from the lodgings they shared at 68 Duane Street to the Tombs, a few blocks away in Centre Street. "Boarding houses are no more patronized by me," says the repentant hero of Whitman's 1842 novel, *Franklin Evans*. "I have often thought that the cheerless method of their accommodations drives many a young man to the bar-room, or to some other place of public resort." Whitman figured that nineteen out of twenty young men living in the cities visited prostitutes "as an ordinary thing." There is no reason to believe he was the lone holdout. Instead of denouncing "the social evil," as newspaper moralists invariably did, he denounced police harassment and "kidnapping" of prostitutes; he advocated the progressive policy of combating venereal disease in the brothels through regulation and inspection. He wrote warmly about the "handsome" and "good-hearted" girls who thronged the Broadway pavements after dark, and at times he liked to think not of the city's pageants, the ships at the wharves and the bright store windows,

> Not those, but as I pass O Manhattan, your frequent and swift flash
>   of eyes offering me love,
> Offering response to my own . . .

Passionate about oratory and, for a while, party politics, Whitman surfaced briefly from obscurity two months after his return to the island city and addressed a Democratic rally in City Hall Park (the Tammany paper *New Era* claimed a crowd of fifteen thousand). He

Walt Whitman's parents, Walter Whitman and Louisa Van Velsor Whitman, were living in this house at West Hills, near Huntington, Long Island, when he was born in 1819.

4

5

The poet's favorite brother, Thomas Jefferson Whitman (Jeff), married Martha Mitchell (Mattie) in 1859.

6

Walt Whitman in the 1840s at about twenty-five.

7

The Whitmans occupied this house on Cumberland Street in Brooklyn in 1852. The Fulton Ferry (below) joined the cities of Brooklyn and New York.

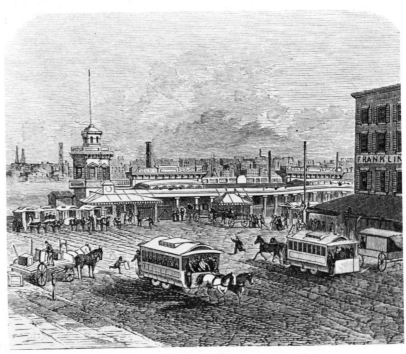

8

9

Broadway at City Hall Park. The view above shows Barnum's American Museum (with flag) and the Astor House, New York's most elegant hotel. In the view below, Broadway stages rumble past St. Paul's Church.

10

The first (and only surviving) number of Whitman's Free Soil newspaper and the title-page cover of his temperance novel. The cover of the *American Phrenological Journal*, published by Fowler & Wells, pictures the organs and activities of the mind.

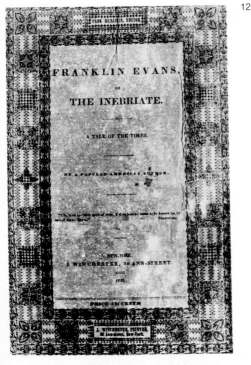

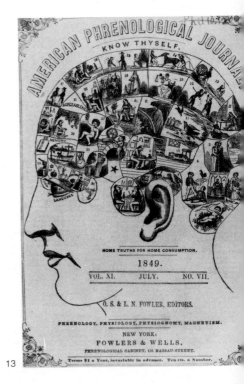

14

"What bothers me most of all, piques me, tantalizes me, is the expression of benignity. Such benignity, such sweetness, such satisfiedness . . ." Whitman dated this "mysterious" picture "1850 or '49," but it was probably taken ten years after that.

15

Above, New York from the north, 1853. In the foreground are the Murray Hill distributing reservoir and the Crystal Palace—on the present sites, respectively, of the New York Public Library and Bryant Park. The view from the south shows (at left) Castle Garden, where Jenny Lind sang.

16

17

Walt Whitman in 1854, a year before he published *Leaves of Grass*. His friend and disciple, Dr. Bucke, called this "the Christ likeness."

18

19

Star performers: the actresses Fanny Kemble (18) and Charlotte Cushman (19), the singers Marietta Alboni (20) and Jenny Lind (21), the actors Edwin Booth (22) and Edwin Forrest (23).

20

21

Ralph Waldo Emerson acknowledged the receipt of *Leaves of Grass* with this letter of recognition. Whitman regarded it as the charter of "an emperor"—"I supposed the letter was meant to be blazoned."

Concord 21 July
Mass'ts } 1855

Dear Sir,

I am not blind to the worth of the wonderful gift of "Leaves of Grass." I find it the most extraordinary piece of wit & wisdom that America has yet contributed. I am very

the book advertised in a newspaper, that I could trust the name as real & available for a Post-office. I wish to see my benefactor, & have felt much like striking my tasks, & visiting New York to pay you my respects.

R. W. Emerson.

Mr Walter Whitman.

The first edition of *Leaves of Grass*. The frontispiece was engraved from a daguerreotype made by Gabriel Harrison in July 1854. Only this page of the 1855 manuscript survives, presumably because Whitman used the verso as memo paper.

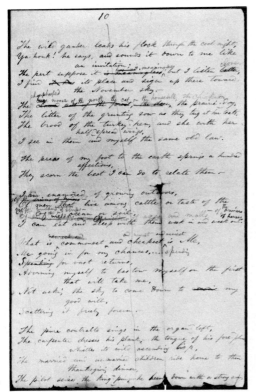

28

Fanny Fern.

29

Thomas Carlyle.

30

Tennyson, the poet laureate.

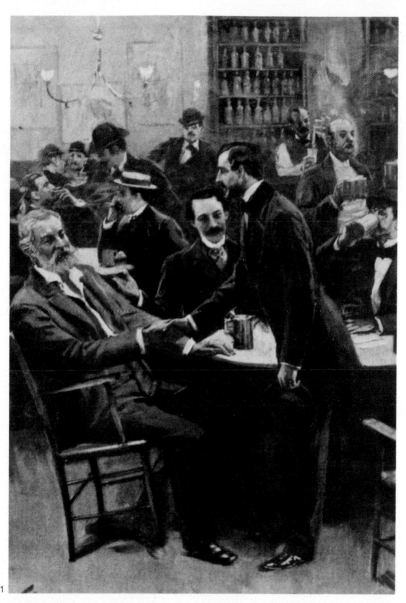

31

William Dean Howells meets Whitman at Pfaff's beer cellar.
The illustrator for Howells' *Literary Friends and Acquaintances*
used turn of the century fashions in this 1860 scene. The
presiding genius of Pfaff's (not shown) was Henry Clapp,
editor of the *Saturday Press* and a Whitman partisan.

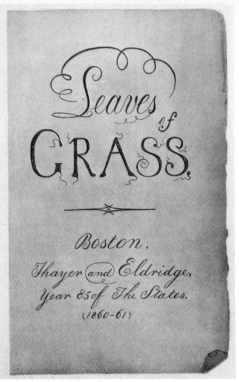

32

Frontispiece and title page of Whitman's third edition of *Leaves of Grass*. Calamus, or sweet-flag, his symbol for "the love of comrades." The photograph shows Whitman in 1860, aged forty-one.

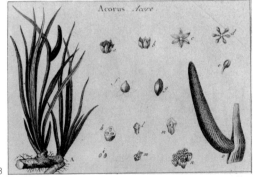

33

34

had a good record in the party, having campaigned the year before for Martin Van Buren; according to his own account he also had a good voice and no stage fright, although he later admitted that "forensically" he was like a drowning man. He had a place of honor in the program, following Major Auguste D'Avezac, a former personal aide to Andrew Jackson and now a power at Tammany Hall. "My fellow citizens," Whitman said in a spread-eagle peroration,

> I beseech you to entertain a noble and more elevated idea of our aim and struggles as a party than to suppose that we are striving to elevate this man or that man to power. We are battling for great principles —for mighty and glorious truths. I would scorn to exert even my humble efforts for the best Democratic candidate that ever was nominated, in himself alone. It is our creed—our doctrine; not a man or set of men, that we seek to build up . . . The guardian spirit, the good genius who has attended us ever since the days of Jefferson, has not now forsaken us. I can almost fancy myself able to pierce the darkness of the future and behold her looking down upon us with those benignant smiles she wore in 1828, '32, and '36. Again will she hover over us, encouraging us amid the smoke and din of the battle, and leading us to our wonted victory, through "the sober second thoughts of the people."

"Heaven save the mark," gibed the *Star*, the Whig paper on which he had served part of his apprenticeship. "Teaching very small children may be an easy life, but teaching those big children of Tammany Hall . . . seems very farcical." ("Only come-day go-day palaver," Whitman himself was to say of his speechifying many years later; "what I really had to give out was something more serious, more off from politics and towards the general life.") The *New Era* printed his speech the next day, and soon after he was made to feel at home at Tammany Hall, then a hotel as well as party headquarters. In the dining room, or at the Pewter Mug, a politicians' saloon around the corner in Spruce Street, he passed the time with a local celebrity, Colonel John Fellows. Fellows had fought at Bunker Hill in the Continental Line, corresponded with Jefferson and Madison, and enjoyed the friendship of Thomas Paine; in an adverse time he remained loyal to Paine's name and memory. Fellows' history and bearing, his silver-white hair, formal manners, and antique, brass-buttoned blue tailcoat gave him an eminence disproportionate to the minor sinecure he now held as tipstaff in the city courts. To the spoilsmen of Tammany and City Hall he was a reminder of "manly rectitude and the instincts of absolute justice," Whitman said, and he was also a symbolic personage. He suggests the Revolutionary warrior, "white-haired remnant of a past age," in "The Last of the Sacred Army," one of the eight stories that during 1841 and 1842 the young Whitman, making a vigorous bid for fame as a fiction writer, published in the *Democratic Review*.

"A monthly magazine of a profounder quality of talent than any since," Whitman said; the *Democratic Review* was the voice of cultural nationalism and the messianic movement that called itself "Young America." Andrew Jackson had been the *Democratic Review*'s first subscriber in 1837; stories and poetry by Hawthorne, Whittier, and Bryant appeared in its pages along with articles of substance on fiscal policy, transcendentalism, capital punishment, the Catiline conspiracy, animal magnetism, and the like. Trading on his renown as a frequent contributor—and on a literary precocity that was not part of his later, "official" character—Whitman reached out, unavailingly, in the direction of Boston. "My stories, I believe, have been pretty popular, and extracted liberally. Several of them in the *Democratic Review* have received public favor," he wrote in June 1842 to the Boston literary editor Nathan Hale, Jr. "The undersigned takes the liberty of offering you the accompanying MS ["The Angel of Tears"] for your 'Miscellany.' The price is $8." Hale declined the offer.

Meanwhile, Whitman labored obscurely as a printer in the thunderous Ann Street pressroom of the *New World*, a popular weekly paper. Its founding editors, Park Benjamin and Dr. Rufus Griswold, powerful figures in the literary politics of the day, had parted company after a few issues, leaving Benjamin in command of a paper whose title and some of its contents—including Whitman's fiction and poetry—still reflected Griswold's championship of "Americanism" and native authors. But for the most part the *New World* could have been an English paper that happened to be printed in New York. Without earning a penny in fees or royalties for their authors, the latest novels of Dickens, Marryat, Bulwer, G. P. R. James, and other popular writers appeared serially in Benjamin's mammoth pages—sometimes more than four feet long and eleven columns wide—or complete, in "extras" set in type by night-and-day pressroom gangs and rushed out in competition with other pirated editions of the same books. ("Dickens' *American Notes* were received by us at eight o'clock on Sunday evening," the *New World* boasted. "They make two octavo volumes in the English edition of six hundred pages. We printed them complete in a double extra number . . . and issued them at one o'clock on Monday—being precisely seventeen hours from the time 'the copy was put in hand.' ") When Benjamin's newsboys howled and bellowed their wares in the streets, said the diarist George Templeton Strong, these "extras" made as great a sensation as the arrival of the *Great Western* from Liverpool with news of a break in the price of cotton. Dickens, the unchallenged favorite of two hemispheres, was the chief victim of the pirate publishers, and when he came to America in 1842 he made his grievances known right away. "There must be an international copyright agreement," he said in the first of several speeches that enraged printing and publishing interests. "It becomes the character of a great country; firstly because it is justice; secondly, because without it you can never have, and keep, a literature of your own."

The press in general claimed that such remarks were churlish and confirmed Dickens' fundamentally antidemocratic bias. On the last point Whitman was willing to take issue even with the *Democratic Review*. "I consider Mr. Dickens to be a democratic writer," he argued in February 1842:

> Mr. Dickens never maligns the poor. He puts the searing iron to wickedness, whether among poor or rich; and yet when he describes the guilty, poor and oppressed man, we are always in some way reminded how much need there is that certain systems of law and habit which lead to this poverty and consequent crime should be remedied . . . I cannot lose the opportunity of saying how much I love and esteem him for what he has taught me through his writings —and for the genial influence that these writings spread around them wherever they go.

But, Dickens' work aside, the pages of the *New World* and similar black-flag publications were, as Whitman saw them, little better than cheap boardinghouse tables that provided a gobbling public with imported works of "tinsel sentimentality," "vulgar coarseness," and "dish-water senility." These "cataracts" of aristocratic and feudal fancy eroded "the ideas of republican freedom and virtue" and, just as Dickens had warned, drowned the American writer. "Shall Hawthorne get a paltry *seventy-five dollars* for a two-volume work—shall real American genius shiver with neglect—while the public run after this foreign trash?" "We have not enough confidence in our own judgment," Whitman said; "we forget that God has given the American mind powers of analysis and acuteness superior to those possessed by any other nation on earth." But that mind remained in bondage to the Old World "as much as Gulliver was bound by the Lilliputians." To the end of his days he remembered Margaret Fuller's challenge. "It does not follow because many books are written by persons born in America that there exists an American literature. Books which imitate the thought and life of Europe do not constitute an American literature. Before such can exist, an original idea must animate this nation and fresh currents of life must call into life fresh thoughts along its shores."

For more than a decade Whitman lived at the center of a great debate over democracy, nationalism and culture. Old John Quincy Adams, invited to contribute to the *Democratic Review*, flatly declined and registered his conviction "that literature was, and in its nature must always be, aristocratic; that democracy of numbers and literature were self-contradictory." In the first number of the magazine in October 1837 its chief editor, John L. O'Sullivan, had announced an altogether opposite creed. "The vital principle of our literature must be democracy . . . All history is to be rewritten; political science and the whole scope of moral truth have to be reconsidered in the light of the democratic principle." Eight years later, arguing in support of the annexation of Texas and of America's messianic imperative—to lead the world to salvation by the road of republicanism—O'Sullivan announced a corollary imperative. It was the nation's "manifest destiny"—a phrase he put into circulation—"to overspread the continent allotted by Providence for the free development of our yearly multiplying millions." ("The footsteps of Providential Intelligence," as the historian George Bancroft said, were visible in America's future as well as her brief past.) Democratic space, practically limitless, shaped the democratic vision—America offered fewer subjects for poetry than the Old World, but, according to Tocqueville, these subjects were "more vast." "Oregon and Texas are yet unsung," said Emerson. He awaited the arrival of a native genius possessing "nerve and dagger" and a "tyrannous" command of "our incomparable materials"—"America is a poem in our eyes; its ample geography dazzles the imagination, and it will not wait long for metres." Eventually it was Whitman who had the last word in the debate. "The United States themselves," he announced in 1855, "are essentially the greatest poem."

During the first two weeks of March 1842, at the New-York Society Library at Broadway and Leonard Street, Whitman joined the fashionable audience that came to hear Emerson, "this great gun of transcendentalism," lecture for six evenings on "The Times" and proclaim an era of individual self-fulfillment—"All Souls' Day." ("I have taught one doctrine," Emerson said in his journals, "the infinitude of the private man.") Emerson's lecture on March 5, "The Poet," Whitman described at the time as "one of the richest and most beautiful compositions, both for its matter and style, we have heard anywhere, at any time." In answer to the familiar conundrum, "whether Poetry is possible in the present time," Emerson, infidel among public philosophers, said, "Why not?" In other countries and other centuries the Poet—"the fortunate, the adapted, the timely man"—had celebrated the symbolism of naked facts, the wonders of the human heart and of gods walking in flesh. "The genius of poetry is here," Emerson said:

> He worships in this land also, not by immigration but he is Yankee born. He is in the forest walks, in paths carpeted with leaves of the chestnut, oak, and pine; he sits on the mosses of the mountain, he listens by the echoes of the wood; he paddles his canoe in the rivers and ponds. He visits without fear the factory, the railroad, and the wharf. When he lifts his great voice, men gather to him and forget all that is past, and then his words are to the hearers, pictures of all history; and immediately the tools of their bench, and the riches of their useful arts, and the laws they live under, seem to them weapons of romance. As he proceeds, I see their eyes sparkle, and they are filled with cheer and new faith.

To doubt that America's poet would yet appear, Emerson concluded, "is to doubt of day and night." He might have been speaking to Whitman alone, fixing him with a tyrannous eye. "Ralph Waldo Emerson, of New England," tall and slender, "at the lecturer's desk lecturing," is commemorated in "Pictures," a preliminary study—a montage or inventory of images—for *Leaves of Grass*. "Afoot with my vision," the poet arrived was to be a sharer in all the places and occupations of democratic man and to make an Emersonian pledge:

You will hardly know who I am or what I mean,
But I shall be good health to you nevertheless,
And filter and fibre your blood.

II

Early in 1842 Whitman moved up and out of the pressroom of the *New World* to become a free-lance writer for the *Aurora*, one of fifteen or twenty newspapers that in the era of Horace Greeley, James Gordon Bennett, and the fiery James Watson Webb scrambled daily for their share of New York's readers and advertisers by means fair and foul.* The *Aurora*'s proprietors, Anson Herrick and John F. Ropes, had built its circulation to about five thousand, half that of Greeley's *Tribune*, when in March, after a period of trial, they appointed Whitman at twenty-two their chief editor. They hailed him as "a bold, energetic and original writer," gave him the services of a police reporter and a battery of printers, and put him in charge of filling their four-page metropolitan daily with news, editorials, and penny-a-line material by outside writers. The *Aurora* "is bound to no party," he announced, but is "fearless, open, and frank in its tone"; he was determined, he said, to make the *Aurora* "*the* paper of the city" and "the most readable journal in the republic." From across the river the Brooklyn *Daily Eagle* soon noted "a marked change for the better [that] has come over this spirited little daily since the accession of Mr. Whitman" but warned, "There is, nevertheless, a dash of egotism occasionally."

For weeks, rewarded by a substantial gain in circulation, he assailed Bishop John Hughes, "a hypocritical scoundrel," who, along

---

* After his first visit to New York Dickens characterized the press there as

"dealing in round abuse and blackguard names . . . pimping and pandering for all degrees of vicious taste, and gorging with coined lies the most voracious maw; imputing to every man in public life the coarsest and the vilest motives; scaring away from the stabbed and prostrate body-politic, every Samaritan of clear conscience and good deeds; and setting on, with yell and whistle and the clapping of foul hands, the vilest vermin and worst birds of prey." (*American Notes* [Penguin, 1972], pp. 135–36.)

with "bands of filthy wretches," "Catholics and ignorant Irish," had insulted and trampled upon "American citizenship." (Whitman's version of the "Young America" gospel was practically indistinguishable from the anti-Catholic, antiforeigner creed of the Native American Party.) At issue was a bill in the state legislature allowing public moneys to be diverted to the parochial schools. "We have taken high American ground," Whitman wrote, shifting from coarse abuse to a statement of principle:

> There are a thousand dangerous influences operating among us—influences whose tendency is to assimilate this land in thought, in social customs, and, to a degree, in government, with the moth eaten systems of the old world. Aurora is imbued with a deadly hatred to all these influences; she wages open, heavy, and incessant war against them.

But even from high American ground he had helped whip up "the indignation of large numbers of our citizens . . . to a pitch altogether ungovernable." On Election Day, April 12, Catholics and Protestants battled in the streets "in open combat," as Whitman had urged earlier, and not by "the Indian method." A No-Popery mob attacked St. Patrick's Cathedral and stoned the bishop's residence. ("Had it been the reverend hypocrite's head, instead of his windows, we could hardly find it in our soul to be sorrowful.") After midnight, as he put the morning edition to bed, Whitman heard sounds of martial array in City Hall Park. From his office window he watched two companies of mounted troops file into Chatham Street headed for the Bowery.

Probably on orders from Herrick, Whitman turned conciliatory. "We go for the widest liberty—the widest extension of immunities of the people, as well as the blessings of government. Let us receive these foreigners to our shores, and to our good offices." According to William Cauldwell, an *Aurora* compositor, Whitman bridled at Herrick's interference and his attempts to "tone" the paper's editorials. They quarreled, Herrick by this time having become disenchanted with Whitman's "egotism," his elusive and apparently indolent disposition. "For the next two or three hours," Whitman wrote in the *Aurora*, describing what might have been a typical day of dining, reading, and strolling on Herrick's time, "we possess no recollection of having done anything in particular. And at half past

8 P.M. (fifteen minutes before this present writing) the chilling consciousness came over us that we hadn't written anything for a leader."

"There is a man about our office so lazy that it takes two men to open his jaws when he speaks," said a management squib in the May 3 *Aurora*. "If you kick him he's too idle to cry, for then he'd have to wipe his eyes. *What* can be done with him?" The solution was obvious. On May 16 Whitman announced that he had been "for three or four weeks past, and now is, entirely disconnected with the editorial department of the Aurora." Soon, mustering the conventional invective of the day in his trade, he looked back on "a trashy, scurrilous, and obscene daily" run by two "dirty fellows . . . ill bred vagabonds," who, before they disgusted him into resigning, had engaged him, a "literary person," to "take the editorial charge of their sheet" and " 'do' their paper for them." Herrick and Ropes abused him as "a 'pretty pup,' " whose "indolence, incompetence, loaferism and blackguard habits forced us to kick him out of the office." When the *Aurora* gave up the ghost three years later, the New York *Herald* put the blame on Whitman's "outrageous system of blackguarding the Catholics and the Irish"—he belonged to "a set of men in New York perpetually revolving about in the current of political events, like chips in an eddy of the Mississippi."

In his notoriously unstable profession Whitman knew more instability than most editors. By September 1845, when he moved back to Brooklyn, he had worked for about ten different papers; their names—*Tattler, Sunday Times, Statesman, Plebeian, Sun, Democrat, New Mirror*—merged and blurred in his memory. Meanwhile, he had been eking out his wages, often part time or suddenly terminated after a few weeks, by selling fiction to the magazines. A few months after leaving the *Aurora*, for seventy-five dollars cash down he supplied Park Benjamin with a 60,000-word novel, *Franklin Evans;* in the bravado or embarrassment of retrospect he claimed that he had dashed it off in three days at Tammany Hall and the Pewter Mug while under the influence of port, gin and whiskey. Its shabby melodrama, false sentiment and Gothic dodges suggest that Whitman may also have been in the grip of guilt and self-loathing bound up with perturbations over leaving home, the breakdown of the family and the traditional order, postadolescent sexuality, and living alone in the great city.

Franklin Evans; or The Inebriate, A Tale of the Times is the story of a farmer's apprentice from Long Island—"a mere boy, friendless, unprotected, innocent of the ways of the world—without wealth, favor, or wisdom"—who comes to New York, rents an attic room in a boardinghouse, falls in with bad company, and succumbs to the temptations of the "wicked" and "deceitful" city, in particular the gin mills and whorehouses; the critic Leslie Fiedler has said that *Franklin Evans* is "quite what one would expect from the perpetual mama's boy . . . and the refugee from a small town." Later, Franklin visits "one of the southern counties of Virginia" and in the course of a drinking spree marries a slave woman who becomes "an object of hate." Just as it seems that he is about to lurch into a drunkard's grave he pledges himself first to "temperance" and finally to "total abstinence" from alcohol, and presumably "vice" and the passional life in any form. "It was damned rot—rot of the worst sort—not insincere, perhaps, but rot, nevertheless," Whitman said to Traubel. "It was not the business for me to be up to. I stopped right there; I never cut a chip off that kind of timber again." George Whitman recalled that Walt never took any pride in his book. "Quite the contrary. He rather disliked or laughed at the mention of it."

The *New World* announced on November 5, 1842, the forthcoming publication of *Franklin Evans*, written "by a popular American Author . . . one of the best Novelists of this country," and dedicated by him to "the Temperance Societies and the friends of the Temperance Cause throughout the Union." Promising that the book would "create a sensation, both for the ability with which it is written [and] the interest of the subject," Benjamin brought it out as a *New World* "extra" and sold about twenty thousand copies. Whitman himself, in one of the first of his many self-reviews, recommended *Franklin Evans* to the readers of the New York *Sun*, and four years later, when he was editor of the Brooklyn *Daily Eagle*, serialized the novel in his own paper. Meanwhile, contrary to his recollection, he had begun writing another novel, *The Madman*, cut from exactly the same kind of timber as *Franklin Evans*.

In his preface to *Leaves of Grass* in 1855, Whitman described the poet of America as "the equable man" who indicates to others the path between reality and the soul and who "judges not as the judge judges, but as the sun falling around a helpless thing." But before the great poet stirred, the long foreground of *Leaves of Grass* had been

dominated by an inconstant newspaper editor, a sometime dema-
gogue, and a writer of imitative fiction. During the 1840s the casually assured workingman of the 1855 frontispiece presented himself
as a *boulevardier*, *flaneur* and man of fashion. ("He was rather stylish,"
George said. "He started in with his new notions somewhere around
1850–1855," which was when he began thinking of himself as Walt
Whitman instead of Mr. Walter Whitman.) Now he sported a high
hat worn at a careful angle and a frock coat with a flower in his lapel.
Swinging a cane of dark polished wood he sauntered with an air of
leisure, self-contentment, and amused curiosity. In Battery Park,
where society people enjoyed the sea air and harbor sights, children
interrupted their sidewalk games to let him pass—"There comes a
gentleman." At the swimming barge moored near Castle Garden he
floated on his back in the green water. Afterward, leaning on the
stout wooden railing that edged the park's flagstone walk, he looked
out over the press of shipping in the bay.

> On one hand lay the majestic three-decker North Carolina, the beau-
> tiful Sicilian frigate, a revenue cutter, with a host of smaller craft; and
> on the other side were the stately Columbus, the corvette Vincennes,
> and a crowd of East river sloops, intermingled with a Liverpool packet
> and a dozen small steamers; the large Sound-boats, Narragansett,
> Rhode-Island, and Worcester, came plunging their vast white bodies
> with a multitude of human beings on their upper decks, and setting
> everything afloat in commotion by the waves raised by their huge
> paddles. A tow-boat from Philadelphia with a long string of barges in
> her wake, and another from Albany, looking like a floating village,
> came along at the same moment, and filled up the picture, when
> suddenly there darted out from the apparently inextricable mass of
> floating worlds, a little fairy looking yacht, with "Osprey" embla-
> zoned on her stern, and with sails that sat like a new coat on a dandy.
> The wind was brisk and for a moment appearances threatened a
> general crash, but there proved to be sea room enough, and each bark
> went on its way rejoicing, throwing the spray like snow-drifts all over
> the broad Bay.

On such a day Whitman too could go on his way rejoicing.
"Wasn't it brave!" he wrote about the exhilaration of being alive in a
city so brilliant and bustling. "And didn't we laugh (not outwardly
—that would have been vulgar; but in the inward soul's bedcham-
ber) with very excess of delight and gladness? O, it is a beautiful

world we live in, after all!" His prose was mannered and sprinkled with locutions like "*nous verrons*" and "*en militaire,*" and it reflected a benign condescension. "What jovial dogs they are!" he said about the butchers in the Grand Street market.

> With sleeves rolled up, and one corner of their white apron tucked under the waist string—to whoever casts an enquiring glance at their stand, they gesticulate with the grace, the affected bendings and twistings of a French dancing master. Neither does rebuff discourage them. With amusing perseverance, they play off on every new passenger the same lures and the same artifice that have been tried and failed in so many previous cases. And when they have nothing else to do, they amuse themselves with a jig, or a break-down. The capacities of the "market roarers" in all the mystery of a double shuffle, it needs not our word to endorse.

In 1855 one of these well-remembered jovial dogs repeated his minstrel-show turn in "Song of Myself":

> The butcher-boy puts off his killing-clothes, or sharpens his knife at
> the stall in the market,
> I loiter enjoying his repartee and his shuffle and break-down.

The gentleman-saunterer Walter Whitman absorbed what the great poet was to celebrate:

> The glories strung like beads on my smallest sights and hearings, on
> the walk in the street and the passage over the river.

"Mannahatta!" the old Whitman was to exclaim. "How fit a name for America's great democratic island city! The word itself, how beautiful! how aboriginal! how it seems to rise with tall spires, glistening in sunshine, with such New World atmosphere, vista and action!" He preferred the name to "New York," which commemorated a mean and feeble tyranny. America's first urban poet began as a student of the city's rhythms and sounds. Soon after daybreak a trickle of pedestrians along Broadway—laborers with lunch pails, cleaning women, news vendors with bundles of morning papers still damp from the press, sleepy underclerks who swept shop floors and kindled fires before opening time—became a tidal surge of youth, vigor and gaiety. "We have often wondered, of a bright morning, how everybody could dress so well"—foreigners remarked on the fact that even journeymen mechanics wore sleek coats, glossy hats, bright watch fobs, and doeskin gloves—"and where on earth they could find business enough to employ them, and make it necessary for them to hurry along at that helter-skelter pace." The avenue became clogged with carts, lumbering freight wagons, white-and-gold omnibuses, liveried carriages; they generated a din of shouts and curses, warning bells, whips cracking, iron wheels and iron shoes striking the cobblestones. At noon "the patricians of our great metropolis" arrived from their mansions and took possession of Broadway. They flocked to the fashionable stores and galleries, hairdressers, oyster cellars, ice-cream palaces, and bar-rooms, the lobbies of the City Hotel and the lordly, granite-fronted Astor House, the most opulent caravansary in the New World. At day's end the tidal flow of humanity, nabobs and clerks alike, surged and then trickled away, and the city once again was briefly surrendered to the spirits of silence.

Broadway, America's "great thoroughfare and fashionable playground," vindicated democratic society and culture. ("We were taught every day and in every way," said Thomas Low Nichols, Whitman's predecessor at the *Aurora*, "that ours was the freest, the happiest, and soon to be the greatest and most powerful country in the world.") Yet pigs scavenged in the Broadway gutters and were set upon by packs of homeless dogs; troops of ragged child prostitutes, twelve and younger, haunted the crossings; thieves and pickpockets darted like fish through the crowds. White light from the city's gas lamps flooded the thoroughfare, but a few blocks to the east dark streets, vacant squares, and unfenced lots frightened away even the police.

The lowest houses of prostitution, nests of disease, drunkenness, and violence, were located around the Five Points and in Cherry, Water and Walnut streets. "Poverty, wretchedness, and vice," Dickens noted, "hideous tenements which take their name from robbery and murder: all that is loathsome, drooping, and decayed is here." Two thousand European immigrants might arrive on a single day and pour into the rookeries of Pitt, Ridge and Attorney streets, "some of the dirtiest looking places in New York," Whitman said. These newcomers were not "paupers and criminals" but the Republic's most needed asset, *the wealth of stout poor men who will work.*

But he wished they could be speeded "to the cheap lands of the West" instead of encouraged to settle in a city hostile to foreigners and notorious for its extremes of luxury and squalor, conspicuous waste and hopeless destitution.

"Between seven and eight o'clock last evening we visited the scene of the fire in Broome and Delancey streets," Whitman wrote in 1842; five years later, changing only a detail or two, he was able to turn in the same news story to the Brooklyn *Daily Eagle*.

> Women carrying small bundles—men with heated and sweaty faces —little children, many of them weeping and sobbing—met us every rod or two. Then there were stacks of furniture upon the sidewalks and even in the street . . . the hubub, the trumpets of the engine foremen, the crackling of the flames, and the lamentations of those who were made homeless by the conflagration—all sounded louder and louder as we approached, and at last grew to one continued and deafening din. It was a horrible yet magnificent sight! . . . a sight to make a man's heart sick, and keep him awake at night, when lying in his bed.

("Agonies are one of my changes of garments," he wrote in "Song of Myself"—"I am the mash'd fireman with breastbone broken, / Tumbling walls buried me in their debris.") Fire destroyed the entire printing, binding and storage establishment of Harper and Brothers in June 1842; fire destroyed the New York *Tribune* in February 1845, and in July, ten years almost to the day since the great fire of 1835, an explosion like an earthquake turned Broad Street into a heap of ruins and leveled nearly three hundred buildings. Whitman and other practiced observers acquired after a while a sort of firebug discrimination. ("The fire last night was a small affair, as fires burn nowadays, only about $200,000," a diarist wrote. "On the whole this was a very fair fire.") They noted the red glow of iron shutters heated by the blaze within, streams of molten lead flowing across the pavement from the linings of tea chests, hailstorms of sparks and cinders, blistered paint and cracked window glass in houses a street away, the click of picks and shovels in the smoldering ruins the next morning.

New buildings went up on the hot rubble of the old, stores replaced residences, the character of streets and entire neighborhoods changed overnight. But fire was only one of the agents of the city's will to exploit and expand at any cost, its "pull-down-and-build-all-over again spirit," Whitman called it, asserting a deep-down although intermittent conservatism that equated "rabid, feverish itching for change" with "that father of restlessness, the Devil." It seemed to him that everywhere he looked—in the individual, the family, the social aggregate—stability, tradition and piety were being eroded, and the uprooting and scattering of the Whitmans reenacted. Trinity Church, "sombre, sulky, and proud," still towered over Wall Street and over the graves of Alexander Hamilton and Commander James Lawrence, naval hero of the War of 1812, but in the Baptist burial ground at Delancey Street a woman with a loaded pistol guarded the graves of her husband and children against the real-estate developers. A mob rioted in sympathy, Whitman reported in March 1842, but "the divinity of trade" prevailed. The burial ground was dug up and sold for house lots by the Hudson Fire Insurance Company. The company directors

> actually set people to work with spades and pick axes to dig down and pitch out the decayed relics of bodies buried there. Fleshless bones, and ghastly skeletons, and skulls with the hair still attached to them, and the brittle relics of young infants and the shrouded ashes of age, and forms of once beautiful maidens, now putrid in corruption—all these, fearful and sickening, and making the very heart of the looker-on to thrill with horror—were struck in by the cold steel, and pitched to and fro, as loafers pitch pennies upon the dock.

Whitman said that savages would not have tolerated such desecrations and removals, claiming churchyards, potter's fields, and even battle sites "made sacred by the blood of freedom's martyrs." The sepulchral literary tradition of Thomas Gray and Edward Young, Philip Freneau and William Cullen Bryant, now had to accommodate a distinctive fact of nineteenth-century life. In cities along the Eastern seaboard the ancient dead were dug up and the new dead banished from the habitations of the living to suburban "parks of repose" like Mount Auburn in Cambridge (1831) and Greenwood in Brooklyn (1837).

"We like to walk aside from the beaten path," Whitman wrote about one of his visits to Greenwood, "to creep up the knolls, and into the more retired groves, where affection seems to have selected the prettiest burial spots." The terms "burial ground" and "graveyard" gave way to the more consoling "cemetery," a sleeping place; the dead were no longer dead and gone but sweetly "Asleep in Jesus." The horses of finality had been gentled, broken to the prevailing mode of euphemism. Tourists with guidebooks and excursion tickets came to Mount Auburn and Greenwood to enjoy the landscaping and the statuary. Pensive female figures, winged cherubs, draped urns, broken lutes, weeping willows, and other creations of the stonecutter's chisel replaced the simple headstone with its symbolic skull and stark recital of the facts of mortality.

Even Brooklyn Ferry sometimes suggested to Whitman the anomie and affectlessness that were among the aspects of city life. It moved to and from its slip "like iron-willed destiny."

> Passionless and fixed, at the six-stroke the boats come in; and at the three-stroke, succeeded by a single tap, they depart again, with the steadiness of nature herself. Perhaps a man, prompted by the hell-like delirium tremens, has jumped overboard and been drowned: still the trips go on as before. Perhaps some one has been crushed between the landing and the prow—(ah! that most horrible thing of all!) still, no matter, for the great business of the mass must be helped forward as before. A moment's pause—the quick gathering of a curious crowd, (how strange that they can look so unshudderingly on the scene!)— the paleness of the more chicken-hearted—and all subsides, and the current sweeps as it did the moment previously. How it deadens one's sympathies, this living in a city!

Not the city alone but life itself, as Whitman read in *Sartor Resartus*, could seem an "immeasurable steam-engine, rolling on, in its indifference, to grind me limb from limb." If the celebrated American traits of "rushing and raging," " 'indomitable energy' and 'chainless enterprise' " are "remembered down to posterity, and put in the annals," Whitman reflected, "it will be bad for us. Posterity surely cannot attach anything of the dignified or august to a people who run after steam-boats, with hats flying off, and skirts streaming behind!" The future moralist of *Democratic Vistas* also had little respect for "*showy*," new Grace Church at Broadway and Tenth Street, fashionable place of Sabbath assembly for ladies in *mousseline-de-laine* dresses, dandies in high-heeled boots, and other preferred stockholders in divine favor. "It is a place where the world, and the world's traits, and the little petty passions and weaknesses of human nature, seems to be broad blown and flush as upon the Exchange in Wall Street, Broadway, or any mart of trade, of a week day."

And yet "chainless enterprise" produced its monuments and delights. With cannon, church bells, a banner proclaiming the victory of Neptune over the Demon of Fire, and a great procession, on October 14, 1842, New York marked the completion of a water system that had been five years building. An aqueduct thirty-eight miles long, one of the century's engineering triumphs ("a performance which all Europe cannot parallel" Whitman declared), replaced wells long polluted by seepage from graveyards and privies with the sweet waters of the Croton basin in Westchester County. The Croton system contributed two new monuments: at Fifth Avenue between Fortieth and Forty-second streets the Murray Hill distributing reservoir, its tawny Egyptian-style walls topped with a broad promenade from which one could view the bay, both rivers, and the village of Harlem; and in City Hall Park a broad marble basin with a fountain that jetted Croton water to the height of a five-story building. Facing the fountain and, Whitman said, looking out over "one mighty rush of men, business, carts, carriages, and clang," was P. T. Barnum's flag-decked American Museum, the world's most celebrated assembly of freaks, monsters, relics, and curiosities, genuine and bogus; the star attraction of these "dusty halls of humbug," as Henry James remembered them, was the twenty-five-inch-high General Tom Thumb, whose marriage to another midget, Lavinia Warren, would be celebrated at Grace Church. Plumbe's daguerreotype gallery stood a few blocks north of the American Museum:

> In whatever direction you turn your peering gaze, you see naught but human faces! There they stretch, from floor to ceiling—hundreds of them . . . Even as you go by in the door you see the withered features of a man who has occupied the proudest place on earth: you see the bald head of John Quincy Adams, and those eyes of undimmed but still quenchless fire. There too, is the youngest of the Presidents, Mr. Polk. From the same case looks out the massive face of Senator Benton . . . Indeed, it is little else on all sides of you, than a great legion of human faces—human eyes gazing silently but fixedly upon you, and creating the impression of an immense Phantom concourse— speechless and motionless, but yet *realities*. You are indeed in a new world—a peopled world, although mute as the grave.

In 1846 yet another attraction declared the city's growing awareness of itself as a historic human invention, the yoking of nature and artifice under a benign democratic dispensation. In the Minerva Room on Broadway, E. Porter Belden exhibited his model of the city of New York. The work of one hundred and fifty artists and artisans, surmounted by a gorgeous canopy adorned with nearly one hundred paintings of business establishments and places of note, Belden's creation occupied 480 square feet of floor space. "It is a perfect fac-simile of New York," he declared, "representing every street, lane, building, shed, park, fence, tree, and every other object in the city." Over 200,000 houses, stores, and public buildings were depicted in carved wooden miniature along with five thousand boats and ships in the harbor. Belden's model replicated New York, he said, "almost as accurately as if the latter had been by some Immense Mechanical Power compressed into narrower limits!"

Uncompressed by mechanical power, bustling and self-contradictory, New York, as Whitman knew it then, was itself a "model," of the nation reduced, of personality and the mental life enlarged, and of the sunshine places and dark patches, the lawless energies and contrarieties in each. In the city he explored democracy, and in democracy he explored himself and the raw experience that went into *Leaves of Grass*. "Remember," he was to say, "the book arose out of my life in Brooklyn and New York . . . absorbing a million people . . . with an intimacy, an eagerness, an abandon, probably never equalled." In the end he compared his book with "a great city," epitome of "modern civilization."

6

"The word final, superior to all… what is it?"

WHITMAN CAUGHT SIGHT of a number of literary celebrities going about their business or pleasure in New York—Dickens; William Cullen Bryant, bound for his office at the *Evening Post;* the country squire James Fenimore Cooper, bound for the courts to teach yet another newspaper editor lessons in civility; the dandy and international favorite Nathaniel Parker Willis; Washington Irving, the first American author to make a living from his work. At the office of the *Plebeian*, he had a glimpse of an up-and-coming celebrity, the patrician poet and scholar James Russell Lowell, fat and handsome; wearing his auburn hair to his shoulders he looked like a Yankee Keats. They exchanged a few words and parted, not to meet again for fifteen years and more. "Whitman, I remember him of old," Lowell was to say. "He used to write stories for the *Democratic Review* under O'Sullivan. He used to do stories then, *à la* Hawthorne."

Whitman stood shoulder to shoulder with the *Democratic Review* writers—Bryant, Whittier, Major D'Avezac, and other believers in "a good time coming"—in advocating progressive measures, in particular the abolition of capital punishment, the subject of a "Dialogue" he published in the November 1845 number. But for the most part Whitman's contacts with the literary community, even with the *Democratic Review* group, were random and transient. In addition to O'Sullivan he had dealings of an irregular sort with his former employer Park Benjamin and with a relative newcomer, Thomas Dunn English, author of the popular lines,

Oh! don't you remember sweet Alice, Ben Bolt?
Sweet Alice, whose hair was so brown,
Who wept with delight when you gave her a smile,
And trembled with fear at your frown?

English was also the founder of the *Aristidean*, a magazine of "Reviews, Politics and Light Literature" that died under him after only six issues. According to Poe, with whom he carried on a losing feud, this debacle proved English had talent enough as a man of letters "to succeed in his father's profession—that of a ferryman on the Schuylkill." Unequal antagonists, grotesquely antithetic talents, Poe and English had one taste, at least, in common: they published Whitman in 1845, English a novelette, two tales, and a cluster of five "Fact-Romances," and Poe two articles in his *Broadway Journal*.

"Poe was very cordial in a quiet way," Whitman recalled, "appear'd well in person, dress, &c. I have a distinct and pleasing remembrance of his looks, voice, manner, and matter: very kindly and human, but subdued, perhaps a little jaded." Poe had begun to tire of being known as the author of "The Raven." His dusky phantom vied with the eagle for the title of America's national bird, and he had become identified with it virtually to the exclusion of everything else he had written. In Lowell's couplet,

Here comes Poe, with his raven, like Barnaby Rudge,
Three fifths of him genius and two fifths sheer fudge.

"Somehow," Whitman said, the poem "did not enthuse me. . . . Poe was morbid, shadowy, lugubrious—he seemed to suggest dark nights, horrors, spectralities." Thirty years after they met in the *Broadway Journal* offices at the corner of Beekman and Nassau streets Whitman developed that impression in a series of images that linked the daylight splendor of New York harbor with the nightmare ending of Poe's "MS Found in a Bottle": "the ship is quivering, oh God! —and going down."

In a dream I once had, I saw a vessel on the sea, at midnight, in a storm. It was no great full-rigg'd ship, nor majestic steamer, steering firmly through the gale, but seem'd one of those superb little schooner yachts I had often seen lying anchor'd, rocking so jauntily, in the waters around New York, or up Long Island sound—now flying uncontroll'd with torn sails and broken spars through the wild sleet and winds and waves of the night. On the deck was a slender, slight, beautiful figure, a dim man, apparently enjoying all the terror, the murk, and the dislocation of which he was the centre and the victim. That figure of my lurid dream might stand for Edgar Poe, his spirit, his fortunes, and his poems—themselves all lurid dreams.

If Emerson spoke for the brave and sunny oversoul of *Leaves of Grass*, its vital principle of strength, health and hope, then Poe spoke for its id, even though Whitman claimed that at the outset he had rejected Poe's "dark nights, horrors, spectralities." "I could not originally stomach him at all," he said to Traubel. But the nearly two dozen pieces of fiction he published between 1841 and 1845 were as much "*à la* Poe" as "*à la* Hawthorne."* Their ambience of symbol,

---

* Whitman's "The Last of the Sacred Army" (1842) is virtually a rewriting of Hawthorne's "The Gray Champion" (1835); symbolic of his other borrowings are the names "Reuben" (in "Reuben's Last Wish," 1842) and "Bourne" (in *Franklin Evans*, 1842), which, taken together, recall "Reuben Bourne" in Hawthorne's "Roger Malvin's Burial" (1832). Whitman's "The Angel of Tears" (1842) shows that he had been "a good pupil" of Poe, according to Professor Roger Asselineau. "Bervance: or, Father and Son" (1841) is a Poe-like tale of "a deep revenge—a fearful redress," just as "Revenge and Requital" (1845) joins the same major theme of Poe with the cholera epidemic rendered in symbolic terms in "The Masque of the Red Death" (1842). Whitman's obsession with sepulture suggests several stories by Poe (in particular "Berenice," 1835) and by Hawthorne as well as the opening chapter of Sir Walter Scott's *Old Mortality* (1816).

Two items from the Brooklyn *Daily Eagle* when Whitman was editor dramatize his ambivalence toward Poe. On December 17, 1846, Whitman quoted the following from another publication as a laudable example of "humor and drive-away-careism":

A NICE JOB.—We understand that Mr. E. A. Poe has been employed to furnish the railing for the new railroad over Broadway. He was seen going up street a few days ago, apparently laying out the road.

The second item, written by Whitman, followed this cruel joke by a day:

It is stated that Mr. Poe, the poet and author, now lies dangerously ill with brain fever, and that his wife is in the last stages of consumption.—They are

nightmare, and dramas of the inner soul was only slightly relieved by Whitman's borrowings in theme and manner from Cooper and Scott as well as from lesser writers. His fiction was derivative and imitative, preachy and didactic; it dripped with false sentiment, cliché, and melodramatic contrivance. Nonetheless the stories are freer and more distinctively articulated than his early poetry; they have a peculiarly intense, dreamlike absurdity, which may have derived from a collision of borrowed materials with imperatives he was not able to acknowledge in frontal ways. In bulk alone the stories represent a creative surge that Whitman was not to experience again until he wrote *Leaves of Grass;* they earned him his first literary reputation and proved to him that he had been right when he decided to strike off on his own.

Many years later he said that the tales had come "from the surface of the mind, and had no connection with what lay below—a great deal of which indeed was below consciousness. At last came the time when the concealed growth had come to light, and the first edition of *Leaves of Grass* was written and published." But despite Whitman's claims to the contrary the tales share with *Leaves of Grass* a source "below consciousness." More than any other biographical testimony, they illuminate his inner life from the age of about twenty-one to twenty-six, and taken as a cycle, they represent the working-out of a temporary resolution of forces. He had published the first of these stories in 1841, when he went off to New York alone. With one exception—possibly a reprinting of a story whose earlier appearance is unrecorded—he published the last of them in 1845, when he moved to Brooklyn and lived with his parents again.

Whitman's stories are basically fantasies about the erosion of relationship and about the terrors of growing up, separation from par-

---

said to be "without money and without friends, actually suffering from disease and destitution in New York."

In the end Whitman judged him "a victim of history—like Paine. The disposition to parade, to magnify, his defects has grown into a habit: every literary, every moralistic jackanapes who comes along has to give him an additional kick." Whitman was apparently the only writer of any standing present at Poe's reburial in Baltimore in 1875. (Roger Asselineau, *The Evolution of Walt Whitman* [Cambridge, Mass., 1960], I, 46; Cleveland Rogers and John Black, eds., *The Gathering of the Forces* [1920], II, 272–3; Horace Traubel, *With Walt Whitman in Camden* [Philadelphia, 1953], 23; Floyd Stovall, ed., *Prose Works, 1892* [1963], 231–32.)

ents, death (in particular the death of the young), and the obliteration of identity. Typically the hero-victim of these fantasies —call him "Walt"—is a young man prevented from fulfilling himself and even literally destroyed by a father (or symbolic father) who is harsh and arbitrary, given to "cruelty and punishment and whippings and starvation"; sometimes the father is drunk, and then his "intemperance" becomes synonymous with rage, unreasoning hatred, and sexual aggression. The father in "Bervance" plots to have his younger son put away in a lunatic asylum; the teacher in "Death in the School-Room" bullies a pupil to death and flogs the corpse. The father in these stories favors "Walt's" older brother just as the mother favors "Walt" and finds his "kiss ever . . . sweetest to her lips." "Walt's" relationship to his mother is infantile, narcissistic —his life is so intertwined with hers that, from his point of view, their identities and even deaths are indistinguishable. Often the parental background in these stories has been foreshortened: at the start the father is a widower, or "Walt" is alone with his widowed mother. In the latter instance their undivided and unchallenged possession of each other threatens to be as destructive to "Walt" as his father's enmity and his own terrifying passional self. On all sides "Walt" sees a world of loss, menace and isolation. "Wherefore is there no response?" he asks in "Eris: A Spirit Record," a symbolic tale of "unreturned and unhallowed passion" ("Eris," it may be worth noting, is "sire" spelled backwards).

"Wild Frank's Return," the second of Whitman's stories in the *Democratic Review*, was introduced by an editorial note. "The main incidents in this and another story, 'Death in the School-Room,' . . . were of actual occurrence; and in the native town of the author, the relation of them often beguiles the farmer's winter-fireside." Whitman's main source, merely a springboard, was an anecdote Louisa Whitman told about her childhood on the Van Velsor farm near Cold Spring. One morning her father rode off on his favorite horse, "Dandy," to do business in the countryside. By nightfall, when he failed to return as expected, his wife and daughter became uneasy; later, in the midst of a storm, Dandy returned, saddled, bridled, but riderless. Ghostly footsteps are heard in the house.

> The dark hours crept slowly on, and at last a little tinge of day-light was seen through the eastern windows. Almost simultaneously with it, a bluff voice was heard some distance off, and the quick dull beat

of a horse galloping along a soft wet road. . . . My grandmother opened the door this time to behold the red laughing face of her husband, and to hear him tell how, when the storm was over and he went to look for Dandy, whom he had fastened under a shed, he discovered the skittish creature had broken his fastening and run away from home—and how he could not get another horse for love or money, at that hour—and how he was fain forced to stop until nearly daylight.

The ghostly footsteps were peaches dropping to the floor from a branch hung over the parlor fireplace. As Whitman retold it in 1846, this "Incident on Long Island Forty Years Ago" ends in laughter.

"Wild Frank's Return" ends, as it begins, in anger. Frank, about twenty years old and his mother's favorite, has a "hot dispute" with an older brother over the ownership of Black Nell. The horse is described in terms appropriate to its traditional cryptosexual symbolism: "a fine young blood mare—a beautiful creature, large and graceful, with eyes like dark-hued jewels, and her color that of the deep night." The father, a Long Island farmer, takes the brother's side in the dispute, even though it is plain that Frank is the rightful owner.

Wild Frank's face paled with rage and mortification. That furious temper which he had never been taught to curb, now swell'd like an overflowing torrent. With difficulty restraining the exhibition of his passions, as soon as he had got by himself he swore that not another sun should roll by and find him under that roof. Late at night he silently arose, and turning his back on what he thought an inhospitable home, in [a] mood in which the child should never leave the parental roof, bent his steps toward the city.

Frank runs off to sea. "His poor mother's heart grew wearier and wearier. She spoke not much, but was evidently sick in spirit." After two years Frank comes back, has a cool reunion with his brother in a village tavern, and accepts the loan of Black Nell for the journey to his parents' farm. On the way he stops to rest under an oak tree and becomes drowsy; time passes unnoted, a mist veils the landscape; Frank sleeps through a thunderstorm. Frank's sleep is a sort of negative conversion, the opposite of the summer loaf in the grass and the ecstatic illumination Whitman was to write about in Section 5 of "Song of Myself." "Thus in the world you may see men steeped in lethargy," the narrator comments, "while a mightier tempest gathers over them." Frank sleeps on "like a babe in its cradle," but Black Nell, whom he had tethered to his wrist with "a piece of strong cord," starts up in fright,

> an image of beautiful terror, with her fore feet thrust out, her neck arch'd, and her eyes glaring balls of fear. At length, after a dazzling and lurid glare, there came a peal—a deafening crash—as if the great axle was rent; it seemed to shiver the very central foundations, and every object appeared reeling like a drunken man. God of Spirits! the startled mare sprang off like a ship in an ocean-storm! Her eyes were blinded with light; she dashed madly down the hill, and plunge after plunge—far, far away—swift as an arrow—dragging the hapless body of the sleeper behind her!

Wild Frank's "return" is an act of revenge against the family, his mother in particular.

> The clattering of a horse's hoofs came to the ears of those who were gather'd there. It was on the other side of the house that the wagon road led; and they open'd the door and rush'd in a tumult of glad anticipations, through the adjoining room to the porch. What a sight it was that met them there! Black Nell stood a few feet from the door, with her neck crouch'd down; she drew her breath long and deep, and vapor rose from every part of her reeking body. And with eyes starting from their sockets, and mouths agape with stupefying terror, they beheld on the ground near her a mangled, hideous mass—the rough semblance of a human form—all batter'd and cut, and bloody. Attach'd to it was the fatal cord, dabbled over with gore. And as the mother gazed—for she could not withdraw her eyes—and the appalling truth came upon her mind, she sank down without shriek or utterance, into a deep, deathly swoon.

The "fatal cord," like its umbilical counterpart "dabbled over with gore," is the real or symbolic instrument of "Walt's" death in other stories. It becomes the hangman's rope in "Richard Parker's Widow" (1845), much of which Whitman lifted verbatim from a published account of a mutiny in the British Navy in 1797: the same episode and its central character were to inspire Herman Melville's *Billy Budd*. Somewhat like Wild Frank, Parker, "in a fit of despondency," left his family and became a common seaman. "Gentlemanly in his manners," "the bravest of the brave," when the crews of several warships mutiny for just cause Parker is chosen their leader and spokesman, a rebellious son confronting a stern father. Parker is tried before a naval court-martial and sentenced to be hanged. "He said nothing to his mates on the forecastle but 'Good-bye to you!' and expressed a hope that his death would be considered a sufficient atonement, and would save the lives of others. He was then strung up at the yard arm, and in a few moments dangled lifeless there." Melville's *Billy Budd* is a redemptive drama of love, justice, and an innocence like that of "young Adam before the Fall," "a child-man." Whitman, typically, concerns himself with the rights of sepulture and recounts in disproportionate detail the widow's efforts to rescue the body of the hanged man from the anatomist's knife. (In Whitman's treatment it scarcely matters whether she is Parker's wife or his mother). With her own hands she digs up the corpse from its shallow grave in the churchyard, takes it with her to London, and keeps it in her room until the Lord Mayor prevails upon her to give it burial at Whitechapel.

One of Whitman's manuscript fragments introduces a boy who has quarreled with his mother and fallen asleep "with the tears of foolish passion yet undried upon his cheeks." He dreams he has become rich and powerful, with the world at his feet, and is summoned to her deathbed but arrives too late. "He bent down his ear to the cold blue lips and listened—but the cold blue lips were hushed forever." He remembers the times he tormented her by allowing her to believe he had drowned or disappeared. "Now for two little words, *I pardon*, that proud rich man would amost have been willing to live in poverty forever." In another fragment "Walt" has powers of clairvoyance. "He very often knew days beforehand of a death that should happen, and who it was and how it came to be. This terrible consciousness came to him irrespective of place or occasion." In the grip of this consciousness he sees his sister in her linen shroud. He also sees himself in a shroud and is a spectator at his own funeral, an irresistible adolescent fantasy, as Tom Sawyer knew, that allows him to savor injustice and exercise retributive power over adults; it also allows him a way of mastering his fear of death.*

---

* "It is indeed impossible to imagine our own death, and whenever we attempt to do so we can perceive that we are in fact still present as spectators. Hence . . . at bottom no one believes in his own death, or, to put the same thing in another way

"Whitman is a very great poet, of the end of life," D. H. Lawrence said. "A very great post-mortem poet, of the transformations of the soul as it loses its integrity. The poet of the soul's last shout and shriek, on the confines of death." *Leaves of Grass* was the accommodation with death Whitman tried but failed to reach in his fiction. Even in the wastelands of these narratives there are passages of the most vivid and emotionally charged writing he had as yet been capable of, a complex texture of reference, symbol, and confessional parallel that looks ahead to the poetry. The title of one of the stories, "The Tomb Blossoms," is in itself a central Whitman trope, one of the constitutive metaphors of *Leaves of Grass*. ("Walt's great poems," said Lawrence, "are really huge fat tomb-plants, great rank graveyard growths.") In the village burial ground described in "The Tomb Blossoms," "Walt" meets a "withered female," the widow Delaree, "a very old inmate of the poor-house," "a native of one of the West India Islands."

> With the careless indifference which is shown to the corpses of outcasts, poor Delaree had been thrown into a hastily dug hole; without any one noting it, or remembering which it was. Subsequently, several other paupers were buried in the same spot; and the sexton could only show two graves to the disconsolate woman, and tell her that her husband's was positively one of the twain. . . . The miserable widow even attempted to obtain the consent of the proper functionaries that the graves might be opened, and her anxieties put at rest! When told that this could not be done, she determined in her soul that at least the remnant of her hopes and intentions should not be given up. Every Sunday morning, in the mild seasons, she went forth early, and gathered fresh flowers, and dressed *both* the graves. So she knew that the right one was cared for, even if another shared that care.

Widow Delaree's flowers were

> fresh, and wet, and very fragrant—those delicate soul-offerings. And this, then, was her employment. Strange! Flowers frail and passing, grasped by the hand of age, and scattered upon a tomb! White hairs and pale blossoms, and stone tablets of Death!

. . . in the unconscious every one of us is convinced of his own immortality." (Sigmund Freud, "Thoughts for the Times on War and Death," *Standard Edition of the Complete Psychological Works of Sigmund Freud* [London, 1963–74], XIV, p. 289.)

"Blossoms and branches green to coffins all I bring," the great poet was to write. "This grass is very dark to be from the white heads of old mothers"; death was "an old crone rocking the cradle," a "dark mother." But the widow with her basket of leaves and buds was not the only one "who panted for the long repose, as a tired child for the night," "Walt" concludes, anticipating the invocation to "lovely and soothing death" in his elegy for Abraham Lincoln. "The grave—the grave. What foolish man calls it a dreadful place? It is a kind friend. . . . I do not dread the grave. There is many a time I could lay down, and pass my immortal part through the valley of the shadow, as composedly as I quaff water after a tiresome walk. For what is there of terror in taking our rest?"

But it was only through poetry that Whitman learned to walk with his terror as a friend. The "low and delicious word death," "word final, superior to all," became his mantra, like Lear's

Never, never, never, never, never

and he repeated it until he achieved stillness of mind. A mother endlessly rocking the cradle, the sea

> Lisped to me constantly the low and delicious word DEATH,
> And again Death—ever Death, Death, Death,
> Hissing melodious, neither like the bird, nor like my aroused child's
> heart,
> But edging near, as privately for me, rustling at my feet,
> And creeping thence steadily up to my ears,
> Death, Death, Death, Death, Death.
>
> Which I do not forget,
> But fuse the song of two together,
> That was sung to me in the moonlight on Paumanok's gray beach,
> With the thousand responsive songs, at random,
> My own songs, awaked from that hour,
> And with them the key, the word up from the waves,
> The word of the sweetest song, and all songs,
> That strong and delicious word which, creeping to my feet,
> The sea whispered me.

So he was to write in 1859. Meanwhile he whistled in the graveyard.

7

Manifest Destiny

I

DURING THE SUMMER OF 1845 Walter Whitman Senior gave up farming at Dix Hills, rented a house on Gold Street in Brooklyn, near the Navy Yard, and listed his occupation in the city directory as "carpenter." During the ten years of life remaining to him he was to continue his struggle for security with diminishing vigor, which after 1850 trailed off into invalidism. Walt came back to Brooklyn at about the same time as his father, to work again for the *Star*. Four years earlier the paper had mocked Whitman for presuming to teach politics to "those big children of Tammany Hall" and recommended that he come back and finish up his apprenticeship. Edwin Spooner, the founder's son, was willing to put aside past and present differences in order to acquire the services of a seasoned editor who had the beginnings of a literary reputation.

Whitman wrote about fifty pieces for the *Star*, mainly on music, theater, books and education, and he stayed on for five months before he left in circumstances that were superficially similar to those of his parting of the ways with his *Aurora* employers. The *Star*, "incarnation of nervelessness," he wrote, was in so terminal a stage of "inanimation" that it needed help just to "lean against the wall and die." Spooner saluted him from a distance as a disreputable "country schoolmaster" and "hectoring scrivener" whose political convictions and utterances invariably "throw his Democratic friends into convulsions." But this latest blowup inaugurated a period of stability in his profession and in his personal life. William B. Marsh, editor of the *Daily Eagle*, Brooklyn's leading paper, died suddenly at the end of February 1845; by early March Whitman had been hired to succeed him; and he was to remain with the *Eagle* for nearly two years, his longest tenure as a daily journalist.

Even while the Whitmans as a family were still living out on Long Island Walt assumed the role of guardian of his brothers and sisters. Now he became his father's surrogate or regent. In October 1844 the elder Whitman made a down payment of twenty-five dollars on a mortgaged lot on Prince Street in Brooklyn; the following May he paid an additional one hundred dollars on the property; and by the beginning of 1846 the family had moved from Gold Street to the new house, Number 71, that he built at Prince Street. Yet from the start Walt was at least a part owner; the original document of indenture and various receipts for down payments and mortgage interest bear his endorsement. In June 1847 he took title in his own name to the Prince Street property and assumed responsibility for the $900 mortgage held by the Long Island Insurance Company, the semi-annual interest payments of $31.50, and the city taxes. He asserted his new primacy in other ways, buying a silver watch for ten dollars, a gold ring, a gold pencil, and a proper suit with a frock coat (the outfit cost him thirty-two dollars, a sizable sum). Probably for his mother or sisters he bought a carnelian pin, some fancy thimbles, a purse. He bought new boots for his brothers and paid to have the old ones repaired. He paid for domestic odds and ends at Prince Street—$56 worth of masonry work, eighteen gilt picture frames, some furniture, an engraved front-door nameplate, emblem of someone who had come to stay; he set out trees and shrubs.

Whatever transformations were ahead, in 1846 "The Poet of America" eagerly awaited by Emerson was a dutiful son, newspaper editor, and citizen of Brooklyn. He was active in the councils and affairs of the Democratic Party of Kings County, was secretary of its General Committee, officiated at an open-air rally. At parades he marched in the vanguard with other dignitaries and occupied a place in the reviewing stand. On July 4 veterans of the War of 1812 fired off an artillery salute from Fort Greene, and church bells rang; just before the benediction closed the patriotic exercises at the fort an "Ode" by Whitman was wrenchingly accommodated to the tune of "The Star-Spangled Banner."

O, God of Columbia! O, shield of the Free!
   More grateful to you than the fanes of old story,
Must the blood-bedewed soil, the red battle-ground, be
   Where our fore-fathers championed America's glory!

Then how priceless the worth of the sanctified earth,
We are standing on now. Lo! the slopes of its girth
Where the Martyrs were buried: Nor prayers, tears, or stones,
Mark their crumbled-in coffins, their white, holy bones!

These halting verses, dealing as usual with the neglect of graves, were part of a successful campaign Whitman waged in the *Eagle* to save Fort Greene from the developers. Patriotic emotions came easily to him. In one of his *Eagle* columns he concelebrated Washington's farewell to his army.

When the last of the officers had embraced him, Washington left the room followed by his comrades, and passed through the lines of light infantry. His step was slow and measured—his head uncovered, his large breast heaving, and tears flowing thick and fast as he looked from side to side at the veterans to whom he then bade adieu forever. Shortly an event occurred more touching than all the rest. A gigantic soldier, who had stood at his side at Trenton, stepped forth from the ranks, and extended his hand, crying, "Farewell, my beloved General, farewell." Washington grasped his hand in convulsive emotion, in both his. All discipline was now at an end! the officers could not restrain the men, as they rushed forward to take the Beloved One by the hand, and the convulsive sobs and tears of the soldiers told how deeply engraven upon their affections was the love of their commander. Reaching the barge at Whitehall, through this most sad avenue, the retiring Leader entered it; and, at the first stroke of the oar, he rose, and turning to the companions of his glory, by waving his hat, bade them a sad adieu; their answer was only in tears; officers and men, with glistening eyes, watched the receding boat till the form of Washington was lost in the distance.

The same charged episode, much compressed in the retelling, was to appear in one of Whitman's major poems of 1855, "The Sleepers."

He stands in the room of the old tavern, the well-belov'd soldiers all
         pass through,
The officers speechless and slow draw near in their turns,

The chief encircles their necks with his arm and kisses them on the
    cheek,
He kisses lightly the wet cheeks one after another, he shakes hands
    and bids good-by to the army.

"I had one of the pleasantest sits of my life" on the *Eagle*, Whitman
said, "a good owner, good pay, and easy work and hours." Daylong
outings sponsored by grateful holders of public franchises and con-
tracts took him to Coney Island for a tumble in the surf and a
clambake with champagne. In the gleaming new omnibus "Excel-
sior" drawn by six white horses he rode out to Greenwood Cemetery
with children from the orphan asylum, played and loafed on the
grass with them, enjoyed strawberries, cake and lemonade. He was
a guest of the Long Island Rail Road on "a flying pic-nic" to Greenport, whaling and resort village a hundred miles away. "The company was excellent—no small portion being ladies. A car was
attached, filled with first-rate refreshments; and the obliging waiters
served the passengers just as the latter might have been served in an
ordinary public dining or ice-cream room." At Greenport he visited
his sister Mary, who lived there with her shipwright husband Ansel
Van Nostrand and their children. He was treated to a dinner, "not
to be beat," at the Peconic House and was back home in Brooklyn
later the same day, happy and tired, carrying flowers.

Soon after Whitman was appointed editor, the *Eagle* acquired new
readers, larger quarters, new type, and a Napier cylinder press,
"about as pretty and clean-working a piece of machinery as a man
might wish to look on," Whitman wrote. His desk vibrated to the
thump and roar of papers printing fast and steady on the floor below.
News traveled " 'in the twinkling of an eye' "—"The Governor's
message, which we publish today, was transmitted, (5000 words)
from Albany to New York yesterday . . . by magnetic telegraph,
after 12 o'clock, and was in type, printed, and for sale in Brooklyn
and New York, by 4 o'clock!" Papers of the Whig opposition, Horace Greeley's New York *Tribune* and even Spooner's *Evening Star*
conceded that the *Eagle* was "exceedingly well got up" and contained
"a brilliant lot of editorials and original articles." On the *Eagle*'s front
page, previously given over to six unrelieved columns of advertisements, Whitman introduced a literary miscellany—among work by
various European and American authors he reprinted eleven of his
own stories.

"The people of the United States are a newspaper-ruled people," he wrote in the *Eagle*. They had cut their ties to "kingcraft," "priest-craft," and "the old and moth-eaten systems of Europe." But they depended on their editors to lead them, sometimes against their wills, to "light and knowledge" about such orthodox Democratic principles as free trade and annexation, and to "noble reforms" concerning the oppression of women and wage laborers, capital punishment, education of the young by rote and rod, the iniquities of the English in Ireland. The editor was also an agent of culture. As the *Eagle*'s book reviewer, Whitman introduced readers to Carlyle, Coleridge, Goethe, George Sand and Schlegel, as well as a hundred native authors of practical, historical, scientific and literary works. In the course of his reading and reviewing he acquired a formidable literary and intellectual culture, ancient and modern, and a close knowledge of the English tradition in poetry, from Chaucer to Tennyson. In the end, of course, he was to strip his writing of "stock poetical touches," disavow the old culture, proclaim a new one, and represent *Leaves of Grass* as antiliterary. Some of his comments as *Eagle* reviewer point the way to this metamorphosis. "We think this man stands above all poets," he said about Coleridge. "He was passionate without being morbid—he was like Adam in Paradise, and almost as free from artificiality." His review of Goethe's *Auto-Biography* (Parke Godwin's translation of *Dichtung und Wahrheit*) was virtually a prospectus for the generic autobiography he was to attempt in his own book.

> What a gain it would be, if we could forego some of the heavy tomes, the fruit of an age of toil and scientific study, for the simple easy truthful narrative of the existence and experience of a man of genius, —how his mind unfolded in his earliest years—the impressions things made upon him—how and where and when the religious sentiment dawned in him—what he thought of God before he was inoculated with books' ideas—the development of his soul—when he first loved—the way circumstances imbued his nature, and did him good, or worked him ill—with all the long train of occurrences, adventures, mental processes, exercises within and trials without, which go to make up the man—for *character* is the man, after all.

On May 11, 1846, citing enemy incursions in Texas, recently annexed from Mexico, and the consequent shedding of American blood on American soil, President James K. Polk asked Congress for a declaration of war—"The cup of forbearance has been exhausted." General Zachary Taylor's troops crossed the Rio Grande and inaugurated the unequal contest that ended when Winfield Scott took Vera Cruz and Mexico City. Santa Fe fell to Colonel Stephen Kearny's Army of the West; Commodore John Sloat's Pacific Squadron raised the American flag over Monterey and claimed all of California for the United States. "*Annexation* is now the greatest word in the American vocabulary," Philip Hone said in his diary. " 'Veni-vidi-vici!' is inscribed on the banners of every Caesar who leads a straggling band of American adventurers across the prairies, over the mountains, up the rivers, and into the chaparral of a territory which an unprovoked war has given them the right to invade." Greeting with a sick heart the day of the snake and the lizard, Emerson asked.

> . . . who is he that prates
> Of the culture of mankind,
> Of better arts and life?
> Go, blindworm, go,
> Behold the famous States
> Harrying Mexico
> With rifle and with knife.

James Russell Lowell saw the Mexican adventure as "essentially a war of false pretenses . . . it would result in widening the boundaries and so prolonging the life of slavery." "I call it murder," said his cracker-barrel Yankee, Hosea Biglow—

> They jest want this Californy
>   So's to lug new slave-States in
> To abuse ye, an' to scorn ye,
>   An' to plunder ye like sin . . .
> Chaps that make black slaves o' niggers
>   Want to make wite slave o' you.

On occasion Whitman had taken issue with saber-rattling articles that came out in O'Sullivan's *Democratic Review*. "If our fame and honor could come in no other path except the path of the cannon-balls," he said about the long-festering Oregon boundary dispute with Great Britain, "and if our advance is to be signalized by the smoke of cannon and the groans of dying men—we could turn our faces aside and almost say, let us never be a great nation!" But when Polk's war message came over the telegraph from Washington, Whitman, a Democratic regular writing for a Democratic paper in support of a Democratic President, took up the rant of the war party. "Yes: Mexico must be thoroughly chastised!" He demanded "prompt and *effectual* hostilities. . . . Let our arms now be carried with a spirit which shall teach the world that, while we are not forward for a quarrel, America knows how to crush, as well as how to expand." In October he attended an open-air meeting of the Democratic party of Kings County and, as secretary, recorded a resolution that had been enthusiastically proposed and enthusiastically adopted:

> Resolved, that while we deplore the existence of war at any time, we acknowledge its necessity when our territory is invaded or hostilities are threatened by an enemy—and that the invasion of Texas, peaceably and lawfully annexed to this country by consent of its people who had achieved and then professed their independence, and the declarations of Mexico that it considered such annexation a war measure, required from our national administration the prompt and energetic measures which they have pursued against the latter country.

His army outnumbered by three to one on the sun-baked plains of Buena Vista, Zachary Taylor, agent of manifest destiny, flung back the enemy general's demand for surrender—"Tell him to go to hell!"—and won a victory that stood "Bright Among the Brightest Emanations of American Glory," said Whitman, comparing Taylor with Caesar and with George Washington. Continentalism and Union were to shape Whitman's poetic vision. ("I am large, I contain multitudes.") "California's shores" were not only the Western boundaries of the Union—they were the boundaries of the found and the "yet unfound," the measure of his psychic growth. ("Eastward I go only by force," Thoreau said, "but westward I go free.") "The daring, burrowing energies of the Nation will never rest till the whole of this northern section of the great West World is circled in the mighty Republic—there's no use denying that fact!" Whitman wrote this after a visit to Governors Island to watch a regiment of volunteers training for the invasion of California. These raggle-taggle conquistadors, scarecrow youths and toothless old bachelors in military castoffs, were right out of *The Pickwick Papers*, but even as he laughed at their tanglefoot drills he could not help musing on the emergence of American empire and the beauties of New York harbor, "one of the most magnificent views God ever spread out for mortal eyes to admire!" Whitman's day at the "California camp" ended in the mood of a fete:

> The band of the station, (and a fine band it was), brought out their music, and practiced some choice German and Italian marches. The drummer boys, and juvenile fifers, collected together. A large body of the regulars were paraded on the green, and went through their evolutions like clock-work; *that* was indeed discipline. Then the drums beat for roll call—after which the men were dismissed. After which we saw a famous game at foot ball, incident to the same being any quantity of mishaps and tumblings down—all, however adding to the glee of the time.

On a hot Saturday evening, August 8, 1846, the House of Representatives prepared to approve an administration bill appropriating, as a step in the direction of a negotiated peace, two million dollars for the purchase of disputed territory from Mexico. Routinely recognized by the chair, a hitherto inconspicuous Democratic member from Pennsylvania, David Wilmot, introduced a proviso: "as an express and fundamental condition to the acquisition of any territory from the Republic of Mexico . . . neither slavery nor involuntary servitude shall ever exist in any part of said country." (Wilmot later explained that he had "no morbid sympathy for the slave," only the desire to protect white men from "the disgrace which association with negro slavery brings upon free labor.") President Polk puzzled over Wilmot's "mischievous and foolish amendment. . . . What connection slavery had with making peace with Mexico it is difficult to conceive." But a week later opposition papers in the North had no such difficulty understanding what the Proviso had achieved. "As if by magic," said the Boston *Whig*, "it brought to a head the great question which is about to divide the American people."

Whitmans and Van Velsors had been slaveowners for a century and more. Sarah White, one of Walt's great-grandmothers, chewed tobacco, swore like a squire, and rode out daily to oversee her field hands; when she became an invalid and was confined to her chair and bed she kept order by shying chunks of wood at her house-slaves, "a whole troop of 'em," he said. Hannah Brush Whitman, his paternal grandmother, told him she used to see a dozen or more slave children at supper in the kitchen of the main house. Some of these children were the half-breed offspring of Long Island's other subject race, the dispossessed Indians, "degraded, shiftless, and intemperate, very much after the lowest class of blacks."

Many of the free blacks he saw in Brooklyn when he was growing up were unemployed and did odd jobs or begged in the streets. When he was twenty-two he began hearing rumors, based on statistics in the sixth United States Census, that the incidence of insanity and idiocy among free blacks was some ten times higher than it was among slaves. These statistics were later discredited, but not before they had been found to be useful in supporting the a priori conclusion that blacks could never be assimilated into American life ("Nature has set an impassable seal against it," Whitman wrote in the 1850s) and were unfitted for freedom ("No race can ever remain slaves if they have it in them to become free. Why do the slave ships go to Africa only?"). "The African race here is a foreign and feeble element," said William H. Seward a few months before he became Lincoln's Secretary of State, "like the Indians incapable of assimilation. . . . A pitiful exotic unnecessarily transplanted into our fields." In Whitman's day-to-day social policy and conduct he was no different from most Northerners, including abolitionists, who deplored slavery in principle and in practice denied free blacks the most rudimentary civil rights. "You loathe them as you would a snake or a toad, yet you are indignant at their wrongs," St. Clare says to his New England cousin in *Uncle Tom's Cabin*. "You would not have them abused; but you don't want to have anything to do with them yourselves."

Whitman's stereotypical black person was a muddle of ascriptive traits. The slave Margaret, whom Franklin Evans marries in his drunken passion, is sexual, magnetic, calculating, vindictive, murderous—"the fire of her race burnt with all its brightness in her bosom." One *Leaves of Grass* fragment speaks for the anger and despair of slaves:

I am a curse: a negro thinks me;
You cannot speak for yourself, negro;

I lend him my own tongue;
I dart like a snake from your mouth.

My eyes are bloodshot, they look down the river,
A steamboat paddles away my woman and children.

Another fragment suggests a benign helplessness:

Poem of the black person.—Infuse the sentiment of a sweeping, shielding protection of the blacks—their passiveness—their character of sudden fits—the abstracted fit . . .

In one of his *Aurora* editorials Whitman commented on a popular lithograph of the period that contrasted "Slavery as It Exists in America" with "Slavery as It Exists in England." As pictured, life in the slave quarters of the Cotton Kingdom was cheerful, contented and secure, while the English laborer either starved in his hovel or was driven into the parish workhouse. "The British," Whitman wrote, "have within the borders of their own country miseries compared to which those of the southern slaves are as a wart to Ossa." Nevertheless, banded together under the powerful slogan "Am I Not a Man and a Brother?" English reformers were sending over money for abolitionist lectures and propaganda. While neglecting their own enslaved masses, these reformers had the temerity to export benevolence and teach Americans "what is our duty to 'our colored brethren.' " In Whitman's eyes the villains were the abolitionists. Their "ranting" and "abominable fanaticism" defied "all discretion, the settled law of the land, the guaranteed power of citizens," "free thought," and "liberal sentiments." The chief issue for Whitman was not black slavery in itself but the oppression of spirit that black slavery, and all other forms of servitude, fostered in what Emerson called "the republic of Man." Whitman remembered hearing Emerson say at the end of a lecture, "What right have I to speak of slavery? Are we not *all* slaves?"

The New York lawyer and civic leader George Templeton Strong, a practical man above all, also denounced abolitionism as "false, foolish, wicked and unchristian," and he was even willing to argue that "slave-holding is no sin." Still, when the time came, he made a crucial distinction. "N. B. The question of the expediency of slave-holding, and of the policy of upholding the institution, is a very different affair." Whitman's attitudes crystallized early in the long debate over the extension of slavery into the territories. "Set Down Your Feet, Democrats!" he wrote in the *Eagle* on December 21, 1846.

> If there are to be States to be formed out of territory lately annexed, or to be annexed, by any means to the United States, let the Democratic members of Congress, (and Whigs too, if they like,) plant themselves quietly, without bluster, but fixedly and without compromise, on the requirement that *Slavery be prohibited in them forever*.

The *Eagle* had been "the very first Democratic paper" to take a decisive stand on the issue of Free Soil, Whitman claimed; he claimed also that the party in the North had become "*one solid unbroken phalanx.*" What appeared, briefly, to be a coalition of conscience had been joined even by Daniel Webster, "a cynical, bad, corrupt man," as Whitman had described him a year earlier, "indebted to the brandy bottle for his indignant eloquence and to the ill-got funds of the Whigs for the supplies of his pocket book." Webster, the arch-Whig, was now a supporter of the Wilmot Proviso in the Senate. Abraham Lincoln, a one-term Whig member of the House, figured he voted for it "as good as forty times" before it was killed. In one form or another the Proviso was debated for a decade and a half before the bombardment of Fort Sumter. Instead of setting down their feet in unity, the Democrats of New York State first declined to take any stand at all—according to Whitman they lost the November 1847 local election as a result—and then, in 1848, nominated for President Michigan Senator Lewis Cass, largely on the strength of his assertion that only the people living in the territories, not the Congress, had the power to decide the slave issue there.

Meanwhile the Free Soil Democrats bolted, leaving the party in control of "Old Hunkers" like Isaac Van Anden, who was treasurer of the General Committee in Kings County as well as publisher of the *Eagle*. The party regulars compared the dissidents to the farmer who set fire to his barn in order to get rid of the rats. The Barnburners merged with abolitionists and anti-slavery Whigs at a national convention in August 1848 and nominated Martin Van Buren for President under the slogan "Free soil, free speech, free labor, and free men." (The victor in November was the Whig candidate, Zachary Taylor.)

On January 3, 1848, in the last Barnburner editorial he was to write for the *Eagle*, Whitman assailed Cass's popular-sovereignty doctrine and demanded from him "a better show of sense." On the eighteenth the Brooklyn *Advertiser* reported that a "great disturbance" had recently taken place at the *Eagle* office; this was possibly a cryptic reference to an episode that the *Advertiser* subsequently detailed: "When personally insulted by a certain prominent politician, Mr. Whitman kicked the individual down the editorial stairs," as if the prominent politician had been just another Benjamin Carman interfering with the editor's freedom to fish in troubled waters. Several Brooklyn and New York papers reported Whitman's dismissal along with the news that the *Eagle* had turned a political somersault back into the Old Hunker camp. On the twenty-first, brazening it out, Van Anden denied any change in the *Eagle*'s political coloration, conceding only that in the course of "business arrangements" he "has found it necessary to dispense with one of its editors." And "business," meaning party business, was as fair an explanation as any of a change that involved little personal rancor on either side—during the spring Van Anden published at least seventeen pieces by Whitman and went out of his way to compliment him.

It was only after Whitman had been gone for a year and a half that Van Anden, responding to the mounting bitterness of the party schism and to renewed gossip about Whitman's firing, felt that he had to take a familiar rhetorical tack. "Slow, indolent, heavy, discourteous, and without steady principles," he wrote in the *Eagle*, "he was a clog upon our success, and reluctant as we were to make changes, we still found it absolutely necessary to do so. . . . Mr. W. has no political principles, nor, for that matter, principles of any sort. . . . Whoever knows him will laugh at the idea of his *kicking any body*, much less a prominent politician. He is too indolent to kick a musketo." Whitman's account in *Specimen Days* is closer to the level truth. "The troubles in the Democratic party broke forth . . . and I split off with the radicals, which led to rows with the boss and 'the party,' and I lost my place."

According to Bryant's *Evening Post* and Greeley's *Tribune* on the twenty-first, the Brooklyn "radicals" were planning to start their own paper and put Whitman in charge of it. But that scheme hung fire until summer, and in any case he had had his fill of local politics for a while. In the lobby of the Broadway Theatre he ran into a man from New Orleans, J. E. McClure, who was starting up a new daily there, the *Crescent*, and needed a chief editor. Over drinks during the intermission McClure made him an offer, and less than forty-eight hours after the final curtain went down Whitman was on his way south with a two hundred dollar cash advance in his pocket to bind the agreement and pay for travel. His fourteen-year-old brother Jeff, an apprentice printer, accompanied him.

"Left Brooklyn for New Orleans, Feb. 11th '48," Walt noted. Until then he had never been much west of the Hudson or south of Sandy Hook; with the exception of trips to Virginia during the Civil War, it was not until he was in his early sixties, when he visited Colorado and Canada, that he again ventured far from home; like Thoreau, he never went to Europe. But now, because of a casual meeting and a decision made quickly in a theater lobby, the future poet of continentalism looked beyond familiar scenes. By the time he returned to Brooklyn from New Orleans he had traveled five thousand miles and seen democratic vistas of city and wilderness, river and lake, mountain and plain. In 1855 he was to celebrate the American "space and ruggedness and nonchalance" that had been awaiting "the gigantic and generous treatment worthy of it."

II

At Cumberland, eastern terminus of the National Road, trade artery to the Ohio and upper Mississippi valleys, Walt saw Tartar encampments of white-canvased juggernaut-wheeled Conestoga wagons by the hundreds loaded with freight; wagon men and drovers, a race of giants and heroes, warmed themselves by stupendous fires of soft coal. The nine-passenger coach of the National Road and Good Intent Stage Company toiled and clattered across the Alleghenies to Wheeling, 131 miles between sunset and dawn, stopping every ten miles for fresh teams of horses. A mountain relay station visited an hour after midnight was a challenge to native Michelangelos and Caravaggios. "There were some ten or twelve great strapping drovers," Whitman wrote in his notebook, reclining about the room on benches, and as many more before the huge fire. The beams overhead were low and smoke-dried. I stepped to the farther end of the long porch; the view from the door was grand, though vague, even in the moonlight. We had just descended a large and very steep hill, and just off on one side of us was a precipice of apparently hundreds of feet. The silence of the grave spread over this solemn scene; the mountains were covered in their white shrouds of snow—and the towering trees looked black and threatening; only the largest stars were visible.

Two and a half days out of New York, at Wheeling on the Ohio River he boarded the steam packet *St. Cloud*, bound for New Orleans from Pittsburgh and calling at Cincinnati, Louisville, Cairo (no " 'great shakes' except in the way of ague"), Natchez and innumerable dismal landings and woodyards populated by loafers, children, and an occasional group of "tall, strapping, comely young men." For the most part the river voyage was twelve days of yellow-brown muddy water, barren winter-blasted landscapes, and social monotony relieved to some extent by the *St. Cloud*'s handsome accommodations and first-rate food.

> Mother you have no idea of the splendor and comfort of these western river steam boats [Jeff wrote]. The cabin is on the deck, and staterooms on each side of it, their are two beds in each room. The greatest of all these splendors is the eating (you know I always did love eating) department. Every thing you would find in the Astor house in New York, You find on these boats. I will give you a little description of the way we live on board. For breakfast we have: coffee, tea, ham and eggs, beef steak, sausages, hot cakes, with plenty of good bread, sugar &c &c. For dinner: roast beef, d[itt]o mutton, d[itt]o veal, boiled ham, roast turkey, d[itt]o goose, with pie and puddings, and for supper every thing that is good to eat.

Passengers gobbled up these feasts as if they were in a railroad station buffet with five minutes between trains.

Below Louisville, where the Ohio dropped twenty feet in three miles, the *St. Cloud*'s pilot by-passed the canal on the Kentucky side and caromed the ship down the river's boiling chute. "The *fright* we all had," Jeff wrote, "some of the passengers went to bed, others walked the cabin floor, looking as gloomy as if they were going to be hung. Altho I was frightened a good deal, it was not so much as some of the *men* were. If the boat had sunk we were within a few feet of the shore, but I dont think we could have got there, the current was so swift." It had been an "ugly part of the river," Walt wrote—he voiced his own apprehensiveness about the voyage, and perhaps about the new life ahead of him, in a poem he published in the *Crescent*.

> River fiends, with malignant faces!
>   Wild and wide their arms are thrown,
> . . . the river a trailing pall,
> Which takes but never again gives back.

Late Friday, February 25, after two weeks and 2,400 miles of almost continuous travel by train, stage and steamer, Whitman arrived in New Orleans, spent the night on board the *St. Cloud*, and the next day took a room for himself and Jeff at a boardinghouse in Poydras Street. "You could not only see the dirt, but you could taste it, and you had to too if you ate anything at all," Jeff complained to his mother—he already missed her compulsively tidy housekeeping. "And the rooms too, were covered with dirt an inch thick." They moved out of the Poydras Street establishment on March 4, after Walt found that nine dollars a week could buy them decent food and good beds at the Tremont House. It was around the corner from the handsome park in Lafayette Square and directly across St. Charles Street, the Broadway of New Orleans, from the *Crescent* offices at Number 93. "Walter will get the first number of his out on Sunday next," Jeff wrote home on February 28. On Monday March 6 the *Crescent* began publishing on a regular weekday schedule. Whitman was in charge of a staff that included an editorial writer, a city news reporter who was "amiable-hearted . . . but excessively intemperate" and died young, and a general hand who translated foreign items and was the grandson of Mozart's librettist, Lorenzo Da Ponte. Jeff, hired as office boy and printer's devil at five dollars a week, earned an additional dollar or two bundling and selling for newsprint the exchanges the *Crescent* received from other papers.

Across the street the octangular barroom of the St. Charles Hotel, New Orleans' showiest and most expensive example of Greek Revival architecture, served snow-topped cobblers, champagnes, and French brandies. Planters and cotton traders at tables in the recesses did steady business with each other—auctions, conferences, deals of one sort or another—while the bar was two or three deep with officers returned victorious from the war in Mexico and in a mood to celebrate and be entertained. Gaming houses, fancy brothels, and a year-long spirit of Mardi Gras had already made New Orleans famous as the wickedest city in Christendom.

Among the tamer attractions during Whitman's stay were Dr. Collyer's Model Artists, fresh from "the Royal Academies of London and Paris" by way of a successful run in New York. They presented, at the St. Charles Theatre, breathtaking tableaux of Adam's first sight of Eve, the Temptation, the Medici Venus, and similar subjects. When the house lights went up on Collyer's flesh show one night they revealed, seated in the dress circle and flanked by uniformed aides, a plain-looking man, in civilian clothing, with a wrinkled, dark-yellow face and an easy laugh, Major General Zachary Taylor. The orchestra struck up "Hail Columbia," and the audience stood in ovation to the hero of Buena Vista and, many predicted, the next President of the United States. (Writing in the *Crescent*, Whitman doubted the wisdom of raising a man to the presidency "merely because he has shown courage and skill in maneuvering men, horses, and cannon.")

Victorious war with Mexico had added Texas, Arizona, New Mexico and California to the national domain, an acquisition of over 500,000 square miles, second in size only to the Louisiana Purchase. During nearly two years of war New Orleans had served as "our channel and *entrepot* for everything going and returning," troops, ships, supplies, booty and news, Whitman said, and had taken on "a strange vivacity and *rattle*." The city's jubilant mood was a response not only to American victory but to what promised to be victories for democratic nationalism all over Europe in 1848.

"For a few weeks after I commenced my duties at New Orleans, matters went on very pleasantly," he noted in a diary. "People seemed to treat me kindly." McClure and his partner needed him to get their paper launched and were willing, at least for a while, to put up with his Free Soil politics. The *Crescent* solicited advertising from slave traders, reported their arrivals and their auctions, and in other ways was committed to serving the interests of a city in which every sixth person was a slave. Visionaries like James De Bow, professor of political economy at the new University of Louisiana, believed that the Crescent City, already a sort of second Athens (even the saloons looked like Greek temples), was proof that a great civilization could again be raised on a foundation of human bondage. Working for the *Daily Crescent* and savoring New Orleans life for its existential delights Whitman felt no more compromised in principle than another visitor from the North, Henry Adams, trained from the cradle in Boston and Quincy to abhor slavery as "the sum of all wickedness" and slave states as "dirty, unkempt, poverty-stricken, ignorant, vicious!" Like Emerson and Bronson Alcott, both of whom lived for a while in the South, young Adams discovered that "the picture had another side," frankness, courtesy, grace and ease. His indignation yielded before a brooding, indolent sensuality that hung in the air heavier than wistaria and the scent of catalpas. "Quick mettle, rich blood, impulse and love!"—these were some of the memories Whitman was to invoke in a poem of 1860, "O Magnet-South."

In the steamy imaginings of *Franklin Evans*, Whitman had prepared himself for a place of sexual license, and after his downriver passage he moralized his safe arrival in New Orleans.

> But when there comes a voluptuous languor,
>   Soft the sunshine, silent the air,
> Bewitching your craft with safety and sweetness,
>   Then, young pilot of life, beware.

Suspending conclusions, Whitman gave himself over to the city.

Went into St. Mary's Market, saw a man, a good old man in a blue jacket and cottonade pantaloons, with a long stick of sugar cane in his hand. Wondered who he was, and much surprised to find that he was a lawyer of some repute. At the lower end of the market there was a woman with a basket of live crabs at her feet. . . . Came down town —shops all open—and heard the news boys calling out the names of the different papers that they had for sale. . . . Went down town further—all was business and activity—the clerks placing boxes upon the pavements—the persons employed in fancy stores were bedecking their windows with their gaudiest goods, and the savory smell of fried ham, broiled beef-steaks, with onions, etc., stole forth from the half unshut doors of every restaurant. . . . Passed down Conti street and looked at the steamboat wharf. It was almost lined with steamboats; some were puffing off steam and throwing up to the sky huge columns of blackened smoke—some were lying idle, and others discharging sugar, molasses, cotton, and everything else that is produced in the great Valley of the Mississippi. Came to the conclusion that New Orleans was a great place and *no* mistake.

Allegiance and the senses were wooed at every turn. His parents huddled by the stove and heard the windows rattling in their house at Prince Street, but in New Orleans the peach trees blossomed in spring sunlight. Sailors and stevedores worked bare-legged and shirtless by the wharves. "Dark Creole beauties" at Holy Thursday Mass in the Cathedral of St. Louis approached the communion rail "with an air that seemed to say that beauty was part of their religion." When they strolled along St. Charles Street their gowns brushed against baskets of roses and violets offered for sale by other beauties. Standing in the gaslight of theater and hotel entrances, the flower girl plied her timeless trade.

She sells her flowers, and barters off sweet looks for sweeter money [Whitman wrote in the *Crescent*]. She has a smile and a wink for every one of the passers-by who have a wink and a smile for her. . . . What becomes of the flower-girl in the day time would be hard to tell: perhaps it would be in bad taste to attempt to find out.

When the talk one evening in September 1888 turned to the subject of mixed blood in the South, Whitman described the flower-girl class of New Orleans with unusual explicitness.

The Octoroon was not a whore [he told Traubel] and yet *was*, too: a hard class to comprehend: women with splendid bodies—no bustles, no corsets, no enormities of any sort: large, luminous, rich eyes: face a rich olive: habits indolent, yet not lazy as we define laziness North: fascinating, magnetic, sexual, ignorant, illiterate: always more than pretty—"pretty" is too weak a word to apply to them.*

His letter to John Addington Symonds about his "times South" and

---

* Whitman was unconsciously echoing a passage from his *Franklin Evans*, written six years before his trip to New Orleans. "Among the slaves on Bourne's estate lived a young woman, named Margaret, a creole. . . . She was of that luscious and fascinating appearance often seen in the south, where a slight tinge of the deep color, large, soft, voluptuous eyes, and beautifully cut lips, set off a form of faultless proportions—and all is combined with a complexion just sufficiently removed from clear white, to make the spectator doubtful whether he is gazing on a brunette, or

his six illegitimate children introduced a mystery he promised to unravel but never did. Thirteen years after Whitman's death an English biographer, Henry Bryan Binns, supplied the omission: he came up with a class-bound but—as demonstrated in several subsequent biographies—irresistible surmise about the New Orleans period.

> It seems that about this time Walt formed an intimate relationship with some woman of a higher social rank than his own—a lady of the South where social rank is of the first consideration—and that she became the mother of his child, perhaps, in after years, of his children; and that he was prevented by some obstacle, presumably of family prejudice, from marriage or the acknowledgement of his paternity.

In support of this conjecture Binns cited a poem by Whitman.

> Once I pass'd through a populous city imprinting my brain for
>   future use with its shows, architecture, customs, traditions,
> Yet now of all that city I remember only a woman I casually met
>   there who detain'd me for love of me,
> Day by day and night by night we were together—all else has long
>   been forgotten by me,
> I remember I say only that woman who passionately clung to me,
> Again she holds me by the hand, I must not go,
> I see her close beside me with silent lips sad and tremulous.

---

one who has indeed some hue of African blood in her veins. Margaret belonged to the latter class."

This meaning of the word "creole," a notorious semantic gumbo, was one of several current in the 1840s. "Understand, good reader," noted the journalist, lawyer, and politician, A. Oakley Hall, who lived in New Orleans from 1846 to 1851, "that Creole is a word signifying 'native,' and applies to all kinds of things and men indigenous to New Orleans," a definition also acceptable to Benjamin Moore Norman, author of a reliable guide to the city published in 1845. When applied to blacks, "creole" distinguished the native-born from those brought over from Africa. In writing about Whitman's New Orleans "romance," the English biographer Henry Bryan Binns, as will be seen, chose to understand "creole" to mean an upper-class white person descended from French or Spanish settlers. (A. Oakley Hall, *The Manhattaner in New Orleans; or, Phases of "Crescent City" Life* [New York, 1851; repr. Baton Rouge, 1976], p. 17; *Norman's New Orleans and Environs* [New Orleans, 1845; repr. Baton Rouge, 1976], pp. 73–74.)

According to Binns this encounter was responsible for the "quickening of emotional self-consciousness" that, along with other changes, led Whitman to write *Leaves of Grass*. Binns's method was to accept as literal, truth-bound testimony lines by a poet who represents himself elsewhere in *Leaves of Grass* as growing up in Virginia and Texas and hunting polar bears in Alaska. In justice to his method Binns's hypothesis should have suffered a terminal setback in 1920, when another biographer, Emory Holloway, discovered the manuscript of "Once I Pass'd through a Populous City." It appears that Whitman intended originally to celebrate "adhesiveness" or manly love, for the second line read,

> But now of all that city I remember only the man who wandered
> with me, there, for love of me.

The "woman who passionately clung to me" was a

> . . . rude and ignorant man who, when I departed, long and long
> held me by the hand, with silent lip, sad and tremulous.—

Even in the face of this discovery, the New Orleans mistress survived in the biographies, and as late as 1960 Holloway himself, like the bereft whaling ship *Rachel* at the end of *Moby Dick*, was still deviously cruising in search of Whitman's children.

"The actual journey has no interest for education," Adams said about his trip south. "The memory was all that mattered," and it is the memory that matters for Whitman, too. Regardless of whatever romances he did or did not have there, New Orleans stood for a heightened recognition of the self and its needs.

> I saw in Louisiana a live oak growing,
> All alone stood it and the moss hung down from the branches,
> Without any companion it grew there uttering joyous leaves of dark
> green,
> And its look, rude, unbending, lusty, made me think of myself,
> But I wonder'd how it could utter joyous leaves standing alone there
> without its friend near, for I knew I could not,
> And I broke off a twig with a certain number of leaves upon it, and
> twined around it a little moss,

143

And brought it away, and I have placed it in sight in my room,
It is not needed to remind me of my own dear friends,
(For I believe lately I think of little else than of them,)
Yet it remains to me a curious token, it makes me think of manly
      love;
For all that, and though the live oak glistens there in Louisiana
      solitary in a wide flat space,
Uttering joyous leaves all its life without a friend a lover near,
I know very well I could not.

"If you only keep well till I get home again, I think I shall be satisfied," Walt wrote to his mother on March 28. "I began to feel very uneasy, not hearing from you for so long." Since leaving early in February he had received only one letter from home and relied on a friend at the *Eagle* for family news. "O how I long to see you," he said a month later, but he was also thinking of the mortgage payment about to fall due on the Prince Street property—"Hannah must get $31 ½ from the Bank to pay the interest." Sometimes he worried about whether his trees and shrubs had survived the winter, but in general he considered himself "quite happily fix'd" where he was and with bright prospects "in the money line." "He thinks this place agrees with him very much," Jeff reported, "and says he feels better than ever he did in New York." But Jeff had lingering attacks of "the disintery" and summer complaint and was desperately homesick from the start—his family's strange silence probably attributable to a break in postal service from the North, made the distance from home intolerable. "This will be the eighth or ninth letter we have sent you, and we have not received a single one from you," he scolded. "Do write to us, Father, even half a sheet would be better than nothing." He continued to sound the same tearful note. "Mother, Just think what you would think of us if we had writtin you only one letter since we came away. . . . If you do not write to us pretty soon we will do something but I don't know what."

After two months, the *Crescent* owners decided that their founding editor had outlasted his short-term function and was likely to be an embarrassment to the paper in the coming presidential elections. (The major political parties either supported or tolerated the extension of slavery.) McClure and his partner now treated him with "a singular sort of coldness" and began to bully Jeff, as if holding him hostage against his brother's departure. On May 27, three days after a final squabble with McClure over a cash advance, the Whitmans were on their way home.

Walt celebrated his twenty-ninth birthday aboard the steamer *Pride of the West* near Memphis. He was bound for St. Louis, Chicago, and then New York by way of the Great Lakes and the Hudson River. When he returned in mid-June he was "more radical than ever," the *Advertiser* said, and once again embroiled in antislavery politics. In August he addressed a meeting of Brooklyn Barnburners and was chosen a delegate to the national convention of the recently formed Free Soil Party. On September 9, after two months of recruiting backers and subscribers, he began to publish the Brooklyn *Freeman*, a weekly dedicated to the election of Martin Van Buren and Charles Francis Adams and to opposing, "under all circumstances the addition to the Union, in future, of a single inch of *slave land*, whether in the form of state or territory." "How he hated slavery!" Whitman wrote about Thomas Jefferson in his first editorial. "He hated it in all its forms—over the mind as well as the body of man." *Leaves of Grass* was to grow in "Free Soil."

8

Wonderland

I

"HYDROPATHY," or water cure, was supposedly discovered by a peasant, Vincent Priessnitz, when he immersed his aching bones in the rills and streams of Austrian Silesia. During the 1840s it became big business in New York, already a world market center for all sorts of schemes promising social and individual happiness. James Russell Lowell, President Eliphalet Nott of Union College, James Fenimore Cooper, Professor Calvin E. Stowe of Cincinnati, and his wife, Harriet Beecher Stowe, were among the sufferers who came from far and near to have their body poisons flushed away by enemas, wet packs, long soaks, cascades, and other means of "exomosis" or "transudation" employing pure Croton water. Whatever its long-range effectiveness, the water cure was bracing to the spirits and a sovereign treatment for drunkenness, hangovers, and colonic stasis. Some of its practices leaked into general acceptance and encouraged people to drink water, bathe regularly and eat moderately. This was no small gain in a time of intemperance, low standards of personal cleanliness, and huge meals of greasy batter-coated meats and underbaked breads stoked away when their already dyspeptic victims were at the gallop or comatose with exhaustion and surfeit.

Sylvester Graham, temperance reformer, physiological guru, and eponym of the delicious cracker, joined in the battle against dyspepsia, or indigestion, a malady of epidemic proportions for Americans. The "Peristaltic Persuader," as he was called, favored internal and external applications of cold water and repasts of boiled vegetables and bread made from unsifted whole-wheat flour. Alcohol, tea, coffee and red meat were proscribed, on the grounds that they stimulated the lower nature. In a celebrated lecture on chastity Graham argued that there had to be something amiss with any organ that sent priority messages to the brain—an erect penis was no more wholesome than a bloated stomach or an infected finger. According to him and other popular theorists of the day, the seminal loss for a man in one act of sexual intercourse was the equivalent of forty ounces of blood, a fifth of the body's supply. This appalling figure was a warning that sexual overindulgence—meaning more than once a month—could cause tuberculosis, convulsions, indigestion, and even imbecilism; sex—especially masturbation—withered the thinking organs of men, just as thinking withered the reproductive organs of women. Sex was a major disorder, even a catastrophe; it was a wonder the species had lasted as long as it had. In the name of health and public order the body was banished from polite society, and its external shape and structure were denied. By 1855, when Whitman presented himself coatless and bare-necked, his pelvis thrust forward, in his *Leaves of Grass* frontispiece, men of fashion were dressed from head to toe like black tubes. Women of fashion looked like tea cozies, jam pots, and other gently rounded objects of manufacture. Their breasts, buttocks and legs were hidden by nearly one hundred yards of gown, petticoat and underclothing.

"I see through the broadcloth and the gingham," Whitman was to write.

> As Adam early in the morning,
> Walking forth from the bower refresh'd with sleep,
> Behold me where I pass, hear my voice, approach,
> Touch me, touch the palm of your hand to my body as I pass,
> Be not afraid of my body.

No other poet of his century wrote about the body with such explicitness and joy, anatomizing it at rest and cataloguing its parts, celebrating it as an instrument of love.

> Without shame the man I like knows and avows the deliciousness of
>   his sex,
> Without shame the woman I like knows and avows hers.

No other poet of his century paid such a continuing high price for his boldness: ostracism, ostentatious neglect, ridicule, censorship, suppression. In his *Education*, Henry Adams asked himself

> whether he knew of any American artist who had ever insisted on the power of sex, as every classic has always done; but he could think only of Walt Whitman. . . . All the rest had used sex for sentiment, never force; to them, Eve was a tender flower, and Herodias an unfeminine horror. American art, like the American language and American education, was as far as possible sexless. Society regarded this victory over sex as its greatest triumph.

In his typically Victorian pursuit of health as the supreme good, Whitman was drawn to more humane schemes than Graham's, in particular to phrenology, or the science of mind. One of its founders, Johann Kaspar Spurzheim, had been hailed as a messiah when he arrived on American shores in 1832. He said that the intellectual faculties had specific localities in the folds and fissures of the brain, the *size* of these localities varying with the strength or weakness of these faculties in each person. Since the skull, as described, was a bony fabric that fitted the brain like the skin of a pumpkin and conformed to its contours, it was possible to measure faculties from the outside. The examination and classification of living skulls— "bump reading"—was a form of palpation, the classic diagnostic procedure applied this time not to livers, uteruses and prostates, but to personality, temperament and ability.

The corollary of Spurzheim's elegant propositions was electrifying: if you found out what you were, you could then become what you wanted to be by "depressing" faculties that were too prominent and "elevating" those that were too small. The chart of bumps appeared to be a scientific tool for harnessing the present in the service of the future; perhaps the beleaguered human race had found a way to purge itself of crime, insanity and bafflement. For Americans, who were already fired up with the gospel of self-reliance and democratic mission, Spurzheim's teachings were like drinks on the house. "Self Made or Never Made" was one of the mottoes of the new science when it became naturalized; another was, "*Phrenologize our nation, for thereby it will reform the world.*"

Spurzheim planned to spend two years lecturing in the principal American cities and visiting the Indians. He was giving a course in brain anatomy at the Harvard Medical School when he collapsed from exhaustion and fever. His death on November 10, 1832, at the age of fifty-six, was memorialized by the Massachusetts Medical Association as "a calamity to mankind." Escorted by a committee of distinguished citizens, Spurzheim's body went to Mount Auburn Cemetery, and his brain went to Harvard, but his happy spirit marched the length and breadth of the American continent for more than thirty years, trailing behind it more believers than there were in all the world beside.

Phrenology "assumed the majesty of a science," Poe said in 1836, "and as a science ranks among the most important which can engage the attention of thinking beings." The educator Horace Mann pronounced it "the guide of philosophy, and the handmaid of Christianity." Henry Ward Beecher, Ralph Waldo Emerson, and Daniel Webster had their bumps read; Webster's skull, which measured 25 inches around, was said to be to common skulls "what the great dome of St. Peter's is to the small cupolas at its side." At the age of sixteen George Templeton Strong consulted a phrenologist who "gave me a true account of what I believe to be my real character— and without any previous knowledge of me and without any information gained by 'pumping.' " Dr. Oliver Wendell Holmes was told that his bumps indicated a capacity for success "in some literary pursuit; in teaching some branch or branches of natural science, or as a navigator or explorer." Shabby quacks plying their trade along the frontier were just as accommodating and furnished their clients "character-charts that would compare favorably with George Washington's," said Mark Twain, who also recalled one steamboat captain who "had more selfish organs than any seven men in the world . . . They weighed down the back of his head so that it made his nose tilt up in the air."

"One of the choice places of New York to me then," Whitman wrote about the period after his return from the south, "was the 'Phrenological Cabinet' of Fowler & Wells, Nassau street near Beekman. Here were all the busts, examples, curios, and books of that study obtainable. I went there often, and once for myself had a very elaborate and leisurely examination and 'chart of bumps' written out (I have it yet)." Orson Squire Fowler, the founding partner of the establishment, had been introduced to phrenology by Henry Ward Beecher when they were students together at Amherst College. He went on to become its chief American promoter and popularizer, the author, publisher and retailer of manuals that gave phrenology philosophic underpinnings and also converted it to a precise applied science claiming to measure more than forty separate faculties. Assisted by his brother Lorenzo, Lorenzo's wife Lydia, their sister Charlotte (billed as the Mother of Phrenology), and her husband Samuel R. Wells, Fowler built up a conglomerate of cures and pseudosciences. His firm conducted a "Hydropathic and Physiological School," dispensed information about roughage, high colonics, and the like, published several mass-circulation periodicals in their field, and also promoted yet another European import, animal magnetism.

"I openly avow my belief in Animal Magnetism," Orson announced, "because I have seen so many facts and experiments that I know it to be true." The universe was represented as a vast battery of "irradiating power" or "nervous force" that worked on principles conveniently confused with those of the magnetic telegraph. Men and women, horses, cows, and chickens, maples, cornstalks, and raspberry canes, even rocks and puddles, were all part of a network of sending and receiving stations relaying an invisible electric fluid. Human beings transmitted this fluid by means of hypnosis, arcane passes, handholding, and more forthright forms of expression. "The sexual organs are electric; no part of the body is richer in nerves," said one authority whose work Whitman was familiar with. "The male in health is positive; the female negative. All substances living or dead are either in a positive or negative condition of electricity." Like phrenology, animal magnetism bridged mind and matter, the individual and the mass, and was supposed to cure disease and extend life. It also accounted for spiritualistic phenomena such as telepathy, clairvoyance and communication with the dead.

As he entered the decade of his thirties, a decisive time of passage and redefinition of the self, Whitman was a sort of storage battery or accumulator for charged particles of the contemporary. Animal magnetism, among other ephemeral orthodoxies, became part of his vocabulary of concept and metaphor. He was to sing "the body electric" and announce,

Mine is no callous shell,
I have instant conductors all over me whether I pass or stop,
They seize every object and lead it harmlessly through me.

The sexual force was magnetic:

> Does the earth gravitate? does not all matter, aching, attract all
>   matter?
> So the body of me to all I meet or know.

Both hypnotist and clairvoyant, the poet bent "with open eyes over
the shut eyes of sleepers" and imagined all mankind to be bound
together by mesmeric flow and electric touch:

> The sleepers are very beautiful as they lie unclothed.
> They flow hand in hand over the whole earth from east to west as
>   they lie unclothed.
> The Asiatic and the African are hand in hand, the European and
>   American are hand in hand,
> Learn'd and unlearn'd are hand in hand, and male and female are
>   hand in hand.

Phrenologists and spiritualists "are not poets, but they are the
lawgivers of poets," Whitman was to say. He bathed and swam
daily, studied texts on water cure, diet, physique, exercise, longev-
ity, personal magnetism, eugenics, sexology, heredity. "Morality
and talent," he noted, citing Orson Fowler as his authority, "are
affected more by food, drink, physical habits, cheerfulness, exercise,
regulated or irregulated amativeness than is supposed." The poet-
hero of *Leaves of Grass*, "well-begotten, and rais'd by a perfect
mother," endowed with perfect health, beautiful blood and a beautiful brain, made outrageous boasts.

> I do not press my fingers across my mouth,
> I keep as delicate around the bowels as around the head and
>   heart . . .
> Divine am I inside and out, and I make holy whatever I touch or am
>   touch'd from,
> The scent of these arm-pits aroma finer than prayer.

Phrenology, Whitman wrote in the *Eagle*, had "gained the victory"
over skeptics and detractors and stood firmly established "among the
sciences." The hero of one of Whitman's short stories made himself

over into a new and better person: he had learned "that he *could* expand his nature by means of that very nature itself." This is what Whitman hoped for himself when he came to the Clinton Hall cabinet of Fowler and Wells on July 16, 1849, and paid three dollars to have his bumps read. Red-faced and vigorous, a shade under six feet tall and weighing about 180 pounds, he could vault a six-barred fence and swing aboard a Broadway stage moving at a trot.

"This man has a grand physical constitution, and power to live to a good old age," Lorenzo Fowler reported in his phrenological notes. "He is undoubtedly descended from the soundest and hardiest stock. Size of head large." (According to Orson Fowler's *Practical Phrenology*, a copy of which Whitman kept to the end of his life, great men had large heads and large chests—these were features that he was to emphasize in his official portraits.) "Leading traits of character appear to be Friendship, Sympathy, Sublimity and Self-Esteem, and markedly among his combinations the dangerous faults of Indolence, a tendency to the pleasure of Voluptuousness and Alimentiveness, and a certain reckless swing of animal will, too unmindful, probably, of the conviction of others." Even "dangerous faults" were to serve Whitman's purposes—the poet of *Leaves of Grass*, a work of "hot, unqualifying temper" and "insulting arrogance," was also a loafer who was in love with eating and the pleasures of his body.

On Fowler's scale of measurement, "1" was "very small"; "4" average; and "7," the highest reading possible, was "very large." Whitman scored "6" on "Amativeness" ("Sexual love"); "Philoprogenitiveness" ("Parental love; fondness for children and pets"); "Adhesiveness" ("Friendship; attachment; fraternal love," symbolized by "two women embracing each other"); and "Cautiousness" ("Watchfulness, fear, restraint, solicitude, prudence, sense of danger"). Several faculties measured between 6 and 7: "Self-Esteem"; "Firmness"; "Benevolence"; and "Sublimity." Potentially morbid faculties such as "Acquisitiveness" and "Veneration" were safely in the middle range. Perhaps Whitman's "5" and "5–6" for the poetic faculties of Language and Ideality were a bit disappointing, but he was proud of this inventory all the same, and on three separate occasions between 1855 and 1860 published it as a credential for *Leaves of Grass*.

Altogether wrongheaded, as "scientific" as Dante's cosmography and as chimerical as perpetual motion, phrenology nevertheless served Whitman well: it supplied him with a structure of belief, the underpinnings of a personal mythology. He found a way of reasoning from a limited present to the poet he was to become. It scarcely matters that he drew the right conclusions from the wrong data. Spurzheim's rosy pseudoscience served Whitman like the scaffoldings around the speculative houses he was putting up in Brooklyn. In time he dismantled his phrenological staging and uprights and the new self stood unaided, but he never disavowed its origins. "I know what Holmes said about phrenology," he told Traubel, "—that you might as easily tell how much money is in a safe feeling the knob on the door as tell how much brain a man has by feeling the bumps on his head: and I guess most of my friends distrust it—but then you see I am very old fashioned—I probably have not got by the phrenology stage yet." He assured his friends that the phrenologists had rated his caution at six, practically cowardice, and when he told Edward Carpenter, "There is something *furtive* in my nature like an old hen," he may have been thinking of Orson Fowler's emblem for caution, "A hen surprised by a hawk; her chickens having been warned, are fleeing for safety," and of how *Leaves of Grass* had needed shelter.

"Pictures," a decisive preliminary study that he wrote around 1853–1854, began with a riddle:

> In a little house pictures I keep, many pictures hanging suspended—
>   It is not a fixed house,
> It is round—it is but a few inches from one side of it to the other
>   side.

The interior of the human head resembled Plumbe's daguerreotype gallery on Broadway and also the symbolic gallery that regularly appeared as the cover illustration of Orson Fowler's *American Phrenological Journal*. Thirty-nine multitiered vignettes of people, animals, birds, and familiar objects were displayed within a profiled human head; they represented the organs and activities of mind. In the rough and fragmentary lines of "Pictures," Whitman rendered in comparable vignettes his inventory of the imagination, memory and aspirations of the poet to be.

> Who is this, with rapid feet, curious, gay—going up and down
>   Manahatta, through the streets, along the shores, working
>   his way through the crowds, observant and singing?

"Whatever I have heard has given me perfect pictures," he said:

> And every hour of the day and night has given me copious pictures,
> And every rod of land or sea affords me, as long as I live, inimitable
> pictures.

Among them were pictures of the Stoic and Epicurean philosophers who had set him "free in a flood of light" when he was a very young man—"It was like being born again." From Epictetus he had learned a liberating doctrine, that the basis of happiness was in behaving conformably to nature:

> . . . the master appears advancing—his form shows above the
> crowd, a head taller than they.
> His gait is erect, calm and dignified—his features are colossal—he is
> old, yet his forehead has no wrinkles,
> Wisdom undisturbed, self-respect, fortitude unshaken, are in his
> expression, his personality.*

Epicurus is represented in a "Pictures" fragment as

> the old philosoph in a porch teaching
> His physique is full—his voice clear and sonorous—his phrenology
> perfect.

These philosophers, phrenological models of physique and personality, had helped release him from his terror of death. Phrenology, in turn, offered him a way of controlling life: only the completely healthy, integrated and functioning man, exercising all faculties and embracing all experience, was able to collaborate, as a peer, with nature.

Wonderful in physique and temperament, as Lorenzo Fowler told him in writing, Whitman knew for a certainty he had escaped the

---

* Whitman was thinking of a passage from his early and enduring idol Frances Wright's *A Few Days in Athens:* "Zeno advanced into the midst; he stood by the head and shoulders above the crowd . . . his gait, erect, calm, and dignified; his features . . . seemed sculptured by the chisel for a colossal divinity; the forehead . . . was marked with the even lines of wisdom and age; but no harsh wrinkles . . . Wisdom undisturbable, fortitude unshakeable, self-respect . . . were in his face, his carriage, and his tread." (David Goodale. "Some of Walt Whitman's Borrowings." *American Literature* X, No. 2 [May 1938], pp. 205–6.)

family pattern of psychological and genetic decline. In life he would redeem and subsume his parents, brothers, and sisters, just as in death they would all lie together in a tomb marked with his name only. According to Fowler's reading, it had been perfectly natural for him to be father-guardian-companion to George, Jeff, Eddy, the Long Island farmer's son, and other young men. "Philoprogenitiveness" and "adhesiveness" were joys as well as faculties:

In winter I take my eel-basket and eel-spear and travel out on foot on
    the ice—I have a small axe to cut holes in the ice,
Behold me well-clothed going gayly or returning in the afternoon,
    my brood of tough boys accompanying me,
My brood of grown and part-grown boys, who love to be with no
    one else so well as they love to be with me,
By day to work with me, and by night to sleep with me.

Sexuality, for the time being, ceased to be a riddle and a torment. Powerfully endowed in "amativeness" and "adhesiveness," he could now rationalize confused emotions and celebrate, while at the same time naïvely distinguishing, "sexual love" and "the love of comrades." He was to be a perfected man and also a new type of the poet, robust, sensual, joyous, a universal sharer, lover, companion and teacher. Poe's Roderick Usher, presiding over the fall of a doomed house, represented in all its self-destructive and brief brilliance the "Mental Temperament," or "Nervous Temperament," that phrenologists associated with poets and artists. Usher was cadaverous in complexion, like Poe himself. His skin had "a ghostly pallor"; his hair was "silken," "of a more than web-like softness and tenuity"; his eyes were "large, liquid, and luminous beyond comparison"; and his expression was remote from "any idea of simple humanity."

The thirty-year-old editor of the Brooklyn *Freeman* was soon to describe himself as a "tall, large, rough-looking man, in a journeyman carpenter's uniform. Coarse, sanguine complexion; strong, bristly, grizzled beard; singular eyes, of a semitransparent, indistinct light blue, and with that sleepy look that comes when the lid rests half way down over the pupil; careless, lounging gait." His companions—drivers, mechanics, ferryboat hands—epitomized "simple humanity." In the cabinet of Fowler and Wells he had entered a wonderland of funhouse mirrors. But he saw reflected in them the lineaments of "Walt Whitman, an American, one of the roughs, a kosmos," "a man cohered out of tumult and chaos."

II

Shortly before midnight on September 9, 1848, fire broke out along Fulton Street in Brooklyn. Augmented fire brigades and Marines from the Navy Yard brought it under control, but twenty acres of residences and commercial properties were destroyed, including the basement office at 110 Orange Street, where earlier in the day Whitman published the first number of his Brooklyn *Freeman*. "We had not much to lose," he said, "but of what we had not a shred was saved—no insurance." On November 1 he managed to get the paper started up again in a shop two blocks away, at the corner of Middagh and Fulton, where he also conducted a hand-to-mouth business as job printer.

The *Freeman* did well enough by spring for him to convert it from a weekly to a daily, and in anticipation of ultimate victory for the Free Soilers with Missouri Senator Thomas Hart Benton as their candidate, he entertained himself with the prospect of fat publishing profits that would enable him to retire "when we get too much vexed with our official duties." But a year after he launched his paper the Barnburners of New York, maneuvering and compromising in the name of party unity, trooped back to the Hunker fold and left him high and dry. "I withdraw entirely from the Brooklyn *Freeman*," he announced. "To those who have been my friends, I take occasion to proffer the warmest thanks of a grateful heart. My enemies . . . I disdain and defy just the same as ever." Aside from quotations in other papers, the *Freeman*, high-water mark of Whitman's commitment to political journalism, survives only in the single known copy of the first number printed on Orange Street the day of the fire.

He managed to get a commission to write travel letters for the New York *Sunday Dispatch* and went to Greenport to stay with his sister Mary. Her white frame house looked out over a splendid harbor busy with sloops and sailing skiffs by the hundreds. They worked the waters off Plum Island and Montauk Point, where great schools of bluefish were taken on hooks baited only with rags and bones. The Greenport fishing fleet in action was a more exhilarating sight "than any New York yacht race," he said. In the stiff breeze the boats darted about like swallows and made impossibly sharp turns across one another's bow. Their daredevil crews—"great unshaved, gigantic-chested beings, with eyes as clear as coals," "eyes of hawks, piercing and sharp"—took poses like Greek statues as they cast out their trolling lines and hauled them in again with a flourish; they stripped the fish off and piled them into the boats as fast as a lightning compositor setting type. These heroes lived on fish, salt pork, potatoes and rum, worked for days half naked and up to their waists in water, and at night slept soundly on beds of furled sails and marsh hay. In imagination he became one with them:

> . . . trailing for blue-fish off Paumanok, I stand with braced body,
> My left foot is on the gunwhale, my right arm throws far out the
>   coils of slender rope,
> In sight round me the quick veering and darting of fifty skiffs, my
>   companions.

He declined to sentimentalize life in the country districts—"In *proportion*, there is as much wickedness in country as in towns," and probably more misery. Isolation and a hard struggle for existence nurtured avarice, "barbarous" ignorance, alcoholism, drug addiction, and a strange sort of egotism. Old people lived like hermits, and when they died their cottages stood deserted, except for a cat gone wild that prowled under the floor boards. "The country child is put to hard work at an early age," he wrote, recalling his own aversion to farming:

> he soon loses the elasticity of youth, and becomes round-shouldered and clumsy. He learns to smoke, chew, and drink, about as soon as his town prototype. The diet of country people is generally abominable: pork and grease, doughy bread, and other equally indigestible dishes, form a large portion of their food. They work very much too hard, and put too heavy labors upon the youthful ones. The excessive fatigue of a hurried harvest, in the hottest season of the year, thoroughly breaks the constitution of many a boy and young man. . . . no matter what moralists and metaphysicians may teach, *out of cities the human race does not expand and improvise so well morally, intellectually, or physically.*

Seeking "perfect pictures," pictures "copious and inimitable," he found them more readily in libraries and art galleries and when he rode the Fulton Ferry. He admired the forests of shipping topped by the spire of Trinity Church, walked the broad battlements of the Murray Hill Reservoir, and envisioned New York a hundred years into the future. "You and I, reader, and quite all the people who are now alive, won't be much thought of then," he said in November 1849, "but the world will be just as jolly, and the sun will shine as bright, and the rivers off there—the Hudson on one side and the East on the other—will slap along their green waves, precisely as now; and other eyes will look upon them about the same as we do now." Unconsciously and infallibly, he had begun to rehearse "Crossing Brooklyn Ferry," his great "Sun-Down Poem" of 1856. The ferry plying between Brooklyn and Manhattan also plied between now and forever, the one and the many:

> It avails not, time nor place—distance avails not,
> I am with you, men and women of a generation, or ever so many
>   generations hence,
> Just as you feel when you look on the river and sky, so I felt,
> Just as any of you is one of a living crowd, I was one of a crowd,
> Just as you are refresh'd by the gladness of the river and the bright
>   flow, I was refresh'd,
> Just as you stand and lean on the rail, yet hurry with the swift
>   current, I stood yet was hurried,
> Just as you look on the numberless masts of ships and the thick-
>   stemm'd pipes of steamboats, I look'd.

III

After Walt came back from New Orleans "we all lived together," George recalled. Walt "made a living now—wrote a little, worked a little, loafed a little," spent a lot of time in the libraries and "wrote what mother called 'barrels' of lectures"—on politics, language, slavery, diet, exercise, physique, and the like. Early in 1849 he rented a store-front forum in Granada Hall, apparently planning to set himself up as the Fowler of Fulton Street and move on to a career as national teacher or "wander speaker," a "Professor of Things in General" like Diogenes Teufelsdröckh in *Sartor Resartus*. This scheme came to nothing, although some of the lecture material, along with the lecture manner itself, passed into *Leaves of Grass*. In December he took a job as principal editor of a new paper, the *Daily*

News, on Nassau Street in New York; two months later the paper went out of business. During the late spring of 1850 he wrote potboiling journalism for the *Daily Advertiser*—weekly "Sketches of Brooklynites" and "Church Sketches"—and he tried, without success, to sell Moses and Alfred Beach, owners of the New York *Sun,* his twenty-two-part serial adaptation of *The Childhood of King Erik Menved* by B. S. Ingemann, a virtually impenetrable (and by his own admission, "voluminous" and "prolix") novel about regicide in fourteenth-century Denmark.

In June he visited Greenport again, and in September, traveling by train to Woodbury and then on foot along the Jericho turnpike and across the fields, he went back to West Hills with his father. The elder Whitman's sister Sarah and her daughter Hannah, both widows, now lived in a house he had put up when he was a vigorous young man of thirty. "I plumped in at the kitchen door," Walt wrote.

> Aunt S. (father's sister) was standing there—I knew her at once, although it is very many years since I saw her, and she looked very old and bent. . . . Hannah her daughter, came in, after a moment. Their appearance was peculiar; but both H. and Aunt S. made us heartily welcome—after the latter recovered from a momentary shock and surprise; for she didn't at first know what to think of it.
>
> Richard Colyer died about five years ago. Hannah, the widow, is certaintly a clever hearted creature; she made us very welcome, and was evidently sincere about it. Hard work, losing her husband, and some troubles among her children, have made her a little vaporish, and she complains of bad health. . . .
>
> Aunt S. is indeed an original. She has very little regard for dress; but is craving for money and property. She has always shown a masculine, determined mind. Soon after her marriage, (to one Walters) her husband took to drink; she separated from him, and would never live with him afterward.

Father and son visited the family burial hill and the homestead of the Whitmans during the eighteenth century. The old house, long since passed out of the family, was now "a carriage house and granary. The largest trees near it, that I remember, appear to have been cut down." Walter Whitman, Sr., with five years of failing health ahead of him, was seeing the old places for the last time. Some of the dominant mood of that return—defeat, scatter, sadness, decline

—infected the unavailing letter his son wrote a month later to Carlos Stuart, a New York editor and a West Hillsian by marriage. Stuart, Walt heard, was about to start his own newspaper.

> I take the liberty of writing, to ask whether you have any sort of "opening" in your new enterprise, for services that I could render? I am out of regular employment, and fond of the press—and, if you would be disposed to "try it on," I should like to have an interview with you, for the purpose of seeing whether we could agree to something. My ideas of salary are *very* moderate.

Despite the pattern of bafflement in some of his affairs, Walt responded energetically and with measurable results to the boom in Brooklyn real estate that lasted until the spring of 1854. His credit was good with contractors, and he had little trouble financing and building a series of houses, which he and his family occupied rent free until he was able to sell at a profit. George and Andrew, who still lived at home, worked as carpenters like their father. Walt was primarily a businessman. During 1849 he moved to a new house at 106 Myrtle Avenue and cleared $600 on the sale of the Prince Street house. By 1853, in addition to miscellaneous properties, he owned three houses in Cumberland Street that had been financed by a loan of $2,000 at 1 percent monthly interest, and $3,500 from the profitable sale of the Myrtle Avenue property. After advertising in New York papers, he sold two of the houses on Cumberland Street and occupied the third, a two-story building with a shop signed "Carpenter & Builder." It was Walt who patiently docketed the payment receipts for surveying and interest, lumber and paint, doors and window glass, brackets and moldings, sashes and blinds, tin and tinning, and it was Walt who drew up specifications for floorings, partitions, casings, shed roofs, stair rails, and masonry work, including "Stone wall for cellar, chimneys and fireplaces, Plastering, Cistern, Privy, Cess Pool, Flagging in front," and so on.

On June 14, 1852, as Walter Whitman, Jr., he wrote out an agreement with Minard S. Scofield, carpenter, for work on the Cumberland Street houses—"framing, and setting partitions, enclosing with weather-boards, furnish windows and outside door frames"—for a total of $635 to be paid in installments during the summer. A related notebook entry has been used as evidence that in addition to being owner-builder Walt himself hired out as a journeyman carpenter:

July 31st 1852—Mr. Scofield owes W. W. for eleven days work
Aug 14—Inclusive of to-day—(half a day for the week ending Aug.
    7th)—six days and a half—altogether 17 ½ days
Aug 21—Made full week the past week (Scofield owes for 23 ½ days)
    $26.42

Yet the precise accounting that Walt kept on the back of the Scofield agreement clearly indicates that the $26.42 due was for 23 ½ days of work put in by "W. Whitman, Sr." Walt was to claim that in 1854, the year before he published *Leaves of Grass,* he did construction work and brought his lunch pail to the job like any common laborer. But he had soft hands, and John Burroughs doubted that Walt ever had enough skill with hammer and saw to make him "an acceptable carpenter."

Built according to Walt's specifications, the Myrtle Avenue house, which he kept from 1849 to 1852, was nothing if not practical. Like other tradesmen's families, the Whitmans lived over the store. On June 4, 1851, from the shop and job-printing office he installed at street level, Walt issued the *Salesman and Traveller's Directory for Long Island,* a weekly advertising sheet that offered practical information about routes, schedules and accommodations; homeliest of all his ventures with the printed word, it died within the month. He had somewhat better luck at Myrtle Street selling toys, playing cards, stationery, books and phrenological items. On what must have been an unusually good day at the store in 1850 one customer, S. Knae-bel, a musician, spent $12.31 for thirty varied items. Among them were a history of the American Revolution, an etiquette book, two volumes of the Reverend Jacob Abbott's Lucy stories for children, a phrenological head, and two Fowler and Wells publications, *Love and Parentage* and *The Phrenological Guide.*

Looking beyond his own situation to the world of event, Whitman saw few encouraging signs in 1850. Democratic hope was at ebbtide. Two years earlier, the overthrow of Louis Philippe in France had touched off a wave of revolutions all over Europe. Americans rejoiced in the expectation that soon no throne would be left standing anywhere. "God, 'twas delicious!" Whitman wrote,

That brief, tight, glorious grip
Upon the throats of kings.

But the forces of liberal nationalism—Emerson's "party of the Future," "the Movement"—were crushed with appalling ferocity. The revolutionaries of 1848 died on the battlefields, at the barricades and before firing squads, or they fled into exile. Karl Marx spent the rest of his life in London writing *Das Kapital* in the reading room of the British Museum; Giuseppe Mazzini and Carl Schurz also took shelter in London; Giuseppe Garibaldi dipped candles on Staten Island; Whitman was to see the Hungarian patriot Louis Kossuth riding up Broadway. Reaction, repression and militarism prevailed once again.

Four years after the first debates on the Wilmot Proviso, the word "secession" hung over the Senate floor. On March 7, speaking "not as a Massachusetts man, nor as a Northern man, but as an American," Daniel Webster threw his support to the Kentuckian Henry Clay's compromise resolutions. Disunion was an even greater evil than slavery, Webster argued. "I would rather hear of natural blasts and mildews, war, pestilence and famine, than to hear gentlemen talk of secession. To break up this great government! to dismember this glorious country! to astonish Europe with an act of folly such as Europe for two centuries has never beheld in any government or any people!!" New Englanders who until then had looked up to him as a champion of humanitarian causes now believed, as the Boston clergyman Theodore Parker said, that Webster must have been "begotten in sin, and conceived in iniquity," for the Compromise he endorsed upheld the constitutional rights of slaveholders and even called for stricter laws governing the return of fugitive slaves. "It seems to me," Parker said, "that there is no such life of crime long enough to prepare a man for such a pitch of depravity." "When faith is lost, when honor dies," Whittier wrote, "the man is dead!" "The word *liberty* in the mouth of Mr. Webster sounds like the word *love* in the mouth of a courtezan," said Emerson, who thereafter commemorated March 7 as a day of humiliation.

Whitman's poem "Blood-Money," published in the New York *Tribune* two weeks after Webster's speech, invoked inevitable parallels with Judas Iscariot. But it also addressed itself to Whitman's fellow Democrats—"Doughfaces," Northern men with Southern principles—who rallied behind the Compromise of 1850. They figured as well in his "Song for Certain Congressman" (New York

Evening Post, March 2) and "The House of Friends" (New York *Tribune,* June 14). The latter opened with an allusion to the Old Testament prophet Zechariah—

> If thou art balked, O Freedom,
> The victory is not to thy manlier foes;
> From the house of thy friends comes the death stab.

—and went on to a passage of invective:

> Doughfaces, Crawlers, Lice of Humanity—
> Terrific screamers of Freedom,
> Who roar and bawl, and got hot i' the face,
> But, were they not incapable of august crime,
> Would quench the hopes of ages for a drink—
> Muck-worms, creeping flat to the ground,
> A dollar dearer to them than Christ's blessing;
> All loves, all hopes, less than the thought of gain;
> In life walking in that as in a shroud.

Quoting from this "queer little poem" a week later, the editor of a Whig paper in Brooklyn mocked both the poet and his former Democratic cohort. "Here, now, is a specimen of the way one of the young democracy, Master Walter Whitman, lays it on the members of 'the party' whom he has had the pleasure of knowing:—Master Walter has evidently a very poor opinion of his old cronies. . . . See now how he talks to 'em."

In the bafflement and despair of defeated principle, Whitman had turned to poetry again after publishing scarcely a line since 1846: he wrote and published four politically inspired poems between March and June 1850, and this brief surfacing was to be followed by five years of silence until the first edition of *Leaves of Grass.* Despite their awkwardness, the 1850 poems have a peculiar prominence in the long foreground of the book. Three of the four poems provoked by the Compromise debate and by events in Europe are unrhymed and irregular in form; they are "Biblical" both in allusion and in their loosely cadenced verse. "Resurgemus," the last of the group, appeared in the New York *Tribune* on June 21. A bridge to the future, it was Whitman's only poem published in 1850 or in any year previous to 1855 that he included in *Leaves of Grass.* His tribute to the

European martyrs of 1848–1849 moved beyond its topic toward his matured style and concerns. Invoking one of his shaping metaphors, the benign and ever-renewing cycle of sour corpses and sweet grass, it links insurgency with eternal life:

> Not a grave of those slaughtered ones,
> But is growing its seed of freedom,
> In its turn to bear seed,
> Which the winds shall carry afar and resow,
> And the rain nourish.

> Not a disembodied spirit
> Can the weapon of tyrants let loose,
> But it shall stalk invisibly over the earth,
> Whispering, counseling, cautioning.

> Liberty, let others despair of thee,
> But I will never despair of thee:
> Is the house shut? Is the master away?
> Nevertheless, be ready, be not weary of watching,
> He will surely return; his messengers come anon.

In July one of the goddesses in Whitman's pantheon, Margaret Fuller, intellectual, transcendentalist, author of the first major American feminist treatise, *Woman in the Nineteenth Century*, drowned off Fire Island at the end of a two-month voyage home from Leghorn. A fugitive from tyranny and reaction in Europe, she had seen Garibaldi, Mazzini, and the infant Roman Republic broken by the French. Her body was never recovered, a "great and noble lady gone down into the sea," said Bronson Alcott. Looking for a resurrection of lost hopes, and the life of the age to come, Whitman turned to the gospel of the self redeemed through art.

9

Phalanxes

I

"THEY WERE big strong days—our young days," Whitman recalled, looking back on the early 1850s, "days of preparation: the gathering of the forces." Many of his friends then were artists beginning to define themselves as insurgents in the service of the people. In William Cullen Bryant's New York *Evening Post* Whitman called for American painters and sculptors to band together in "a close phalanx, ardent, radical, and progressive" and create a "grand and true" art worthy of their country and the times they lived in. He went on to pay tribute to "the young artist race" of his acquaintance: they were warm, impulsive, and independent, "instinctively generous and genial, boon companions, wild and thoughtless often, but mean and sneaking never."

One exception, as he acknowledged to his dying day, was his French-born brother-in-law, Charles L. Heyde, a landscape painter. In the first stages of their acquaintance Walt was admiring enough to bring the great Bryant, "High Priest of Nature," to Heyde's Brooklyn studio to see his work. With more fateful results Walt brought Charley home with him. "I wish to God he had been in hell before we ever saw him," Jeff was to say. In March 1852 the painter married their sister Hannah and took her to Vermont, where they shared four childless decades of domestic warfare. According to Hannah, Charley was tyrannical, abusive and unfaithful; he attacked her physically and called her "crazy," "a mean stinking selfish wretch" who had no more intellect than her half-wit brother Eddy. According to Charley, Hannah was sluttish, violent and hypochondriacal. "She makes a half barbarous life for herself," he complained to Walt, "and almost baffles all my efforts at times to humanize her." In all likelihood both Heydes were psychotic—after Charley had to be put away in a condition diagnosed as chronic dementia, Hannah spent her days in a darkened room and hallucinated about the Whitman family fortune. Charley was a whelp, cur, skunk, leech and snake, Walt said of him at various times, "the bed-buggiest man on earth," "almost the only man alive who can make me mad; a mere thought of him, an allusion, the least word, riles me." Still, it was Charley Heyde, painter, occasional poet, amateur musician and flower lover, who, alone of all the Whitmans by blood or marriage (with the exception of Jeff), took an informed interest in *Leaves of Grass* although he finally decided it was only a literary version of his wife.

Whitman had more level dealings with Gabriel Harrison, painter, photographer and playwright, a friend of Poe and the great actor Edwin Forrest. He admired Harrison's daguerreotype portraits— they were "perfect works of truth and art" that went beyond mechanical likeness to capture the "spirit," the psychological aura, of his sitters. On a hot July day in 1854, Harrison was to pose the "carpenter" portrait that, in Whitman's judgment, captured the spirit of *Leaves of Grass* and should face the title page of the first edition. Another Brooklyn artist, Walter Libbey, painted a portrait of him in oils. Libbey appeared to have a promising career ahead of him, but he died young, "with nothing practically accomplished— not even a name won." Yet for Whitman, then undergoing a concentrated education of the eye, Libbey had served as a tutor, an exemplar of apparently simple and spontaneous artistry that mediated between the material and the spiritual. Commenting on a picture by Libbey of a boy playing the flute Whitman articulated his own developing aesthetic:

> I don't know where to look for a picture more *naïve*, or with more spirit or grace. The young musician has stopped, by the way-side, and putting down his basket, seats himself on a bank. He has a brown wool hat, ornamented with a feather; rolled-up shirt sleeves, a flowing red cravat on his neck, and a narrow leather belt buckled round his waist—a handsome, healthy country boy. . . . There is richness of

coloring, tamed to that hue of purplish gray, which we see in the summer in the open air. There is no hardness, and the eye is not pained by the sharpness of outline which mars many otherwise fine pictures. In the scene of the background, and in all the accessories, there is a delicious melting in, so to speak, of object with object; an effect that is frequent enough in nature, though painters seem to disdain following it, even where it is demanded.*

Libbey's work was democratic as well as accessible and transcendent.

Abroad, a similar subject would show the boy as handsome, perhaps, but he would be a young boor, and nothing more. The stamp of class is, in this way, upon all the fine scenes of the European painters, where the subjects are of a proper kind; while in this boy of Walter Libbey's, there is nothing to prevent his becoming a President, or even an editor of a leading newspaper.

Among other Brooklyn artists whom Whitman knew and visited were Frederick A. Chapman, who worked in stained glass as well as in oils, and the more eminent Jesse Talbot, whose elegiac portraits and landscapes hung in the National Gallery of Design in New York. Whitman wrote glowingly about Talbot's work in at least four articles published between 1850 and 1853 and owned one of Talbot's

---

* This applies to Whitman's *plein-air* "Farm Picture"—

Through the ample open door of the peaceful country barn,
A sunlit pasture field with cattle and horses feeding,
And haze and vista, and the far horizon fading away.

This in turn recalls the luminous realism of the Long Island genre painter William Sidney Mount, whose work Whitman knew. Genre painting—an "art for the people," in Oliver Larkin's definition, that interprets "man to himself by showing how he behaves on simple and present occasions"—was integral to the democratic vision of *Leaves of Grass*. Section 9 of "Song of Myself" also recalls Mount:

The big doors of the country barn stand open and ready,
The dried grass of the harvest-time loads the slow-drawn wagon,
The clear light plays on the brown gray and green intertinged,
The armfuls are pack'd to the sagging mow.

Whitman and painting are sensitively discussed in F. O. Matthiessen, *American Renaissance* [New York, 1941], pp. 595–613. For genre painting, Oliver W. Larkin, *Art and Life in America* [New York, 1960], pp. 214–23.

oils, "an original of marked beauty and value . . . illustrating a scene from Pilgrim's Progress." (He also owned the Libbey portrait and a large print of Osceola the Seminole chief given him by the artist George Catlin.) He often came to the studio where Henry Kirke Brown, National Academician and sculptor of the equestrian statue of Washington in Union Square, worked with his young assistant, the vigorous and brilliant Ohioan, John Quincy Adams Ward.

With the habitués of Brown's studio, young artists who had recently returned from their studies in Paris, Rome and Florence, Whitman felt more at home than with any comparable literary group. He shared their commitment to native subjects and to the gospel of John Ruskin, whose *Modern Painters* he had praised in the *Eagle* for its "intellectual chivalry, enthusiasm, and . . . high-toned sincerity." At Brown's, Whitman recalled fancying in particular "one sparkling fellow" who talked to him at length, apparently from personal acquaintance, about Pierre Béranger, the French Robert Burns. In the Brown circle, Whitman recalled proudly, "I was myself called Béranger." The younger men looked up to him as a prematurely graying sage of progressivism in art, literature and politics, and a faithful promoter of their work. In gratitude they invited him to speak at the first awards ceremony of the Brooklyn Art Union.

"To the artist," he said in his talk on March 31, 1851, "has been given the command to go forth into all the world and preach the gospel of beauty. The perfect man is the perfect artist." But one did not have to be an artist to recognize that "in the life we live upon this beautiful earth there may, after all, be something vaster and better than dress and the table, and business and politics." By recognizing "the truly great, the beautiful and the simple," ordinary Americans of the age of steam and cast iron could adorn their nation and their lives as with a halo and recapture the freshness of Eden. Looking ahead to Harrison's open-shirted portrait, Whitman mocked "the orthodox specimen of a man of the present time," a mere tailor's dummy confined in high-heeled boots, a swallow-tailed coat, many swathings at the neck, and a ridiculous hat. Citing "great rebels and innovators," he argued that the highest art was the art most totally engaged.

> I think of few heroic actions which cannot be traced to the artistical impulse. He who does great deeds, does them from his sensitiveness to moral beauty. Such men are not merely artists, they are artistic

material. Washington in some great crisis, Lawrence in the bloody deck of the *Chesapeake*, Mary [Stuart] at the block, Kossuth in captivity and Mazzini in exile,—all great rebels and innovators, especially if their intellectual majesty bears itself out with calmness amid popular odium or circumstances of cruelty and an infliction of suffering, exhibit the highest phases of the artistic spirit. A sublime moral beauty is present to them, and they realize them. It may be almost said to emanate from them. The painter, the sculptor, the poet express heroic beauty better in description; for description is their trade, and they have learned it. But the others *are* heroic beauty, the best beloved of art.

Talk not so much, then, young artist, of the great old masters, who but painted and chiselled. Study not only their productions. There is a still better, higher school for him who would kindle his fire with coal from the altar of the loftiest and purest art. It is the school of all grand actions and grand virtues, of heroism, of the death of captives and martyrs—of all the mighty deeds written in the pages of history —deeds of daring, and enthusiasm, and devotion, and fortitude. Read well the death of Socrates, and of a greater than Socrates. Read how slaves have battled against their oppressors—how the bullets of tyrants have, since the first king ruled, never been able to put down the unquenchable thirst of man for his rights.

In tribute to the "hot and baffled struggle" for these rights that had been raging in Europe for years, Whitman concluded his address with eighteen lines from his own "Resurgemus."

"Make no quotations and no references to other writers," Whitman instructed himself when he was composing *Leaves of Grass*. "Take no illustrations whatsoever from the ancients or classics . . . nor from the royal and aristocratic institutions and forms of Europe. Make no mention or allusion to them whatever, except as they relate to the new, present things—to our country—to American character or interests." Culture and tradition appeared to him as repressive, barriers to self-transcendence and the construction of "a poem on the open principles of nature." Whitman's call for the shucking-off of old symbols had a counterpart in German romantic philosophy, and he had also heard it from the apostles of high European culture. Himself cautious and hot-blooded, furtive and brash, hen as well as eagle, Whitman subscribed to both culture and anarchy, tradition and revolution, and he sailed toward a new dispensation under the opposed slogans, "Let us now praise famous men," and, word of the modern, "make it new." He issued his own letters of marque and obliterated from his booty the evidences of its origin. His transactions with culture were as complex as those of Captain Nemo, the Byronic hero who exiled himself from man and his works and lived under the sea's surface in an electric palace of literature, music, and art.

On Broadway, in the heart of the striving capital of the New World, Whitman discovered such a palace, the private museum where Dr. Henry Abbott displayed his celebrated collection of Egyptian antiquities. Whitman's serious interest in Egyptology went back to books he read and lectures he heard in the 1840s—now it fed on Abbott's treasure of papyrus scrolls, mummies, and funerary relics, incised tablets, ornaments of beaten gold, figures of gods with the bodies of men and the heads of hawks. "I went to the Egyptian Museum many, many times; sometimes had it all to myself—delved at the formidable catalogue—and on several occasions had the invaluable talk, correction, illustration and guidance of Dr. A. himself. He was very kind and helpful to me in those studies."

Absorbed in those studies Whitman shut out the clatter of traffic and commerce from the street and became a tiny creature standing alone in an enormous vista of time and space. "Three thousand years ago—five thousand—ten thousand years ago—and probably far back beyond that—those huge African cities, peopled by the race we call Egyptians, existed in just as much vigor and reality as the United States exists today," he was to write in 1855. "They had cities equal or superior in architectural grandeur to any now upon the earth. . . . They not only had books, but these books were plentiful. Epics were common. They had novels, poems, histories, essays, and all those varieties of narrative forever dear to the people."

On his deathbed the Frenchman Jean François Champollion, who unlocked ancient Nilotic culture by deciphering the Rosetta stone, pointed to the manuscript of his *Grammar of Egyptian Hieroglyphics* and said, "Be careful of this—it is my *carte de visite* to posterity." This was the way Whitman was to describe his own book, "my definitive *carte visite* to posterity." *Leaves of Grass* was a modern Book of the Dead, in Whitman's day also titled "the book of going forth in the day" (possibly echoed in his line, "There was a child went forth every day"). The grass was

. . . a uniform hieroglyphic,
And it means, Sprouting alike in broad zones and narrow zones . . .
All goes onward and outward, nothing collapses,
And to die is different from what any one supposed, and luckier.

He was to model his poet-hero on the god Osiris, a wise and bene-
ficent ruler who reclaimed his people from slavery and before whom
"all human beings were equal." In some of the texts Whitman studied, Osiris, the god of eternal renewal, was depicted with stalks
growing from his corpse.

Scented herbage of my breast,
Leaves from you I glean, I write, to be perused best afterwards,
Tomb-leaves, body-leaves growing up above me above death . . .

Whitman's Art Union talk, a polymorph perverse stage in his
development toward the sourcelessness of *Leaves of Grass*, was a mo-
saic of "quotations" and "references to other writers," among them
Rousseau, Longfellow, Bryant, Shakespeare, Pope, Horace, and a
Persian poet of "hundreds of years ago." It cited Jesus, the Bible,
Mary Queen of Scots, Columbus, and the ancient Greeks, specifi-
cally Socrates, Plato, and Alcibiades. Framing ideas came from
Ruskin, George Sand, Frances Wright, Coleridge, Emerson, and
Thomas Carlyle, Emerson's own master and conduit to German
philosophy.

For the generation that came to maturity in the 1830s and 1840s
Carlyle was so towering a spiritual guide and social critic that his
influence became like the air bathing the globe and was consequently
taken for granted, as Margaret Fuller suggested in the *Dial* in 1841.
"Where shall we find another who appeals so forcibly, so variously
to the common heart of his contemporaries?" No living writer "exercises a greater influence than he in these United States," she said.
She summarized the timeless creed, "as old and as new as truth
itself," that Carlyle had "reenforced" with unexampled power and
brilliance:

To *be* and not to seem; to know that nothing can become a man which
is not manlike; that no silken trappings can dignify measures of mere
expediency; and no hootings of a mob, albeit of critics and courtiers,

can shame the truth, or keep Heaven's dews from falling in the right place; that all conventions not founded on eternal law are valueless, and that the life of man, will he or not, must tally with the life of nature.

In Carlyle's idiom, it was the duty of "two-legged animals without feathers" to look the universe in the eye and ask it for the time, to be as clear-eyed and uncoerced as if "dropped from the moon," to assert their membership in "a living, literal *Communion of Saints*, wide as the World itself, and as the History of the World."

Carlyle's heroic affirmations, "Natural Supernaturalism," and radical critique of capitalist-industrial society had a long induction period in Whitman's intellectual system. Carlyle's essays introduced him to Goethe, Schiller, Jean Paul (Richter) and the *Nibelungenlied*. During 1846 and 1847 he reviewed six of Carlyle's books. *On Heroes, Hero Worship and the Heroic in History* proved to be as incantatory in content as in title. It celebrated founders of religions, prophets, leaders and universal poets, an apostolic succession that for Whitman pointed the way for a modern Poet Prophet, a man of the people, simple, unschooled, coarsely garbed, who in passionate, spontaneous and unrhymed verse would speak for his century—

I am your voice—It was tied in you—In me it began to talk

—and create for it a "New Bible," *Leaves of Grass. Sartor Resartus*, Whitman wrote in the *Eagle*, "has all of Mr. Carlyle's strange wild way;—and all his fiery breadth and profundity of meaning—when you delve them out," fair warning to readers that this was a queer and enigmatic as well as a brilliant book. Purportedly it was the biography of "a quite new human Individuality, an almost unexampled personal character": Diogenes Teufelsdröckh, *Professor der Aller-ley-Wissenschaft* ("Professor of Things in General") and author of *Die Kleider, ihr Werden und Wirken* ("Clothes, Their Origin and Influence"). Teufelsdröckh's biography was a mélange of social criticism, fantasy, pedantry, obscurantism and colossal egotism, St. Augustine's *Confessions* and Sterne's *Tristram Shandy*, strange words and ridiculous phrases, apostrophes, perorations, catalogues and asides, pledges of allegiance and disbelief, passages of self-quotation and self-parody, the ravings of a maniac and the pure intellection of an angel whose vision penetrates costumes and the smoky counterpanes of cities. Like Whitman in "The Sleepers," wandering all night in his vision and exploring the collective dream life, Teufelsdröckh, "alone with the stars" in his attic apartment over the town of Weissnichtwo, peers through the "vast, void Night" and shares life with the dying and the newborn, the lover, plotter, gambler, condemned man, grieving mother.

In this "rapt," "weird" and "grotesque" book, as Whitman described *Sartor Resartus*, Carlyle had written his spiritual autobiography and a secular gospel on the pattern of Rousseau, Goethe and Nietzsche, but it was impossible to tell where the skylarking left off and the seriousness began—the romantic irony of the Europeans had been carried over wholesale into English. Like "Song of Myself," *Sartor Resartus* was a reflexive work that told the story of how it came to exist. The resemblance did not end here. "Song of Myself"—described (by Richard Chase) as an "extraordinary collection of small imagist poems, versified short stories, realistic urban and rural genre paintings, inventories, homilies, philosophizings, farcical episodes, confessions and lyric musings"—was a comparable mélange or what-not. The astonished or perplexed reader discovered in it, along with ecstasy, pain and surreal journeyings, a strange admixture of wit, humor, clowning, comic boasting, Western brag, Yankee laconism, conscious absurdity and colossal egotism:

> Unscrew the locks from the doors!
> Unscrew the doors themselves from their jambs!
> I dote on myself, there is that lot of me and all so luscious . . .
> I think I could turn and live with animals . . .
> I discover myself on the verge of a usual mistake.
> I do not say these things for a dollar or to fill up the time while I
>   wait for a boat . . .
> I sound my barbaric yawp over the roofs of the world.

Still, for all such parallels, resemblances, echoes, borrowings, or influences, whether direct or reflections of the spirit of the age, it is useless to look outside Whitman himself for the matrix or occasion for *Leaves of Grass*. Eventually he rejected Carlyle, the most obstreperous Victorian critic of democracy, for his sheer "*cussedness*," for his "ever-lurking pessimism and world-decadence," and for lacking "a soul-sight of that divine clue and unseen thread which holds the whole congeries of things, all history and time, and all events, however trivial, however momentous, like a leash'd dog in the hand of the hunter." In the long run neither Emerson nor Carlyle was the "master" of Whitman, any more than George Sand or Sir Walter Scott. Brought toward a pitch of aroused readiness by art and history, radical politics and magical pseudo sciences, Whitman was soon to acknowledge an emerging purpose to be "a master after my own kind."

II

At antislavery meetings in the New York Tabernacle on Broadway near Pearl Street, Whitman drank in the hot eloquence of Cassius Marcellus Clay of Kentucky and Senator John Parker Hale of New Hampshire, both of them natural orators, as he recalled, and also "tough, tough"—they had to hold their ground against bands of hecklers and thugs sent in by Isaiah Rynders, Sixth Ward Tammany boss and an instigator of the bloody Astor Place riot. On August 14, 1852, writing out of the blue as "a stranger, a young man, and a true Democrat, I hope," Whitman called on Hale, the unanimous but reluctant presidential nominee of the Free Soilers, to lay his candidacy before the people "in the old heroic Roman fashion." He offered Hale a creed rather than a platform, a litany of hopes rather than a reasoned assessment of the forthcoming campaign. He believed that his "close phalanx" of artists, "young," "ardent," and "generous," had a mighty counterpart in "the young men of our land," as he told Hale, in their "ardent and generous hearts."

"You are at Washington, and have for years moved among the great men," Whitman wrote from his house on Cumberland Street in Brooklyn.

I have never been at Washington, and know none of the great men. But I know the people. I know well, (for I am practically in New York,) the real heart of this mighty city—the tens of thousands of young men, the mechanics, the writers, &c &c. In all these, and behind the bosh of the regular politicians, there burns, almost with fierceness, the divine fire which more or less, during all ages, has only awaited a chance to leap forth and confound the calculations of tyrants, hunkers, and all their tribe. At this moment New York is the most radical city in America. It would be the most anti-slavery city, if that cause hadn't been made ridiculous by the freaks of the local leaders here.

Despite his displays of Roman heroism at public meetings and in the Senate—a colleague once promised that Hale would not go ten miles into Mississippi before gracing "one of the tallest trees of the forest, with a rope around his neck"—Hale was no Coriolanus or Caesar. He was the justifiably despairing candidate of a third party that had been bleeding to death since the Compromise of 1850. In a dull November election even the Whig runner-up, General Winfield Scott, managed to win less than a tenth the electoral votes of the colorless and inoffensive Democratic victor, Franklin Pierce, plain evidence that in 1852 "the great mass of the common people"—including the people of New York, for all the radicalism that Whitman credited them with—valued sectional tranquillity and the middle road. But the future poet-prophet of *Leaves of Grass* continued to hold it as a certainty that "the souls of the people ever leap and swell to any thing like a great liberal thought or principle" and that the world would again see, as in the age of Jefferson half a century back, "an American Democracy with thews and sinews worthy this sublime age." "Look to the young men," he told Hale.

Whitman's "musical passion," he recalled in *Specimen Days*, "follow'd my theatrical one" by several years. During the middle 1840s he listened appreciatively enough to Mendelssohn's oratorio *St. Paul* and to the pyrotechnics of foreign virtuosos like the Frenchman Henri Vieuxtemps and the Norwegian Ole Bull, who could play on all four strings of his violin at the same time. But his passion fixed itself for a while at the homelier level of simple music sung by family trios and quartettes: the Hutchinsons from New Hampshire, who often appeared at antislavery rallies; the Cheneys, children of a Vermont preacher; the Alleghanians, the Amphions, the Harmoneons, and Father Kemp's Old Folks. These popular touring ensembles exemplified "heart-singing" as opposed to "art-singing"—so Whitman wrote in an article for Poe's *Broadway Journal* in November 1845. He was moved by their sentimental and topical ballads—"The Soldier's Farewell," "My Mother's Bible," "Lament of the Irish Emigrant," "The Mariner Loves O'er the Water to Roam," "The Old Granite State." The unadorned style, easy unison, and simple harmonies of the Cheneys, the fresh faces of the girls, the stout shoulders of their brothers, all reminded him of "health and fresh air in the country, at sunrise," and took him back to his childhood on the Hempstead plains.

"Our gratification was inexpressible," he wrote after hearing the Cheneys at Niblo's Garden in November 1845. "This, said we in our heart, is the true method which must become popular in the United States—which must supplant the stale, second-hand, foreign method, with its flourishes, its ridiculous sentimentality, its anti-republican spirit, and its sycophantic influences, tainting the young taste of the Republic." He was still a narrow cultural nativist—he ignored the fact that the vogue of family singing troupes had begun in 1839 with the Rainers, yodelers from the Austrian Tirol, and the Alpine flavor had persisted. He spontaneously favored "the true method" of the Cheneys over "the agonized squalls, the lackadaisical drawlings, the sharp ear-piercing shrieks, the gurgling death-rattles" that had been his first impressions of Rossini, Donizetti, Bellini and Verdi. He was slow, and as a partisan of native and earthy culture, even reluctant to give in to grand opera, the rage of New York from the middle forties on. Opera companies, lead singers, conductors, and orchestras from Paris, Milan, London, Havana, and New Orleans performed at one or more of some eight theaters, including the elegant 1,800-seat Astor Place Opera House.

After a year of operagoing on *Eagle* passes, Whitman conceded that foreign music was exercising an elevating influence on American taste. Soon his reviews moved from tolerance to sophisticated pleasure and finally to "passion." "Art-singing" and "heart-singing" were no longer opposed but one and the same; grand opera began to reshape his sensibility:

Ah this indeed is music—this suits me.

On August 5, 1847, after hearing the English diva Anna Bishop in Donizetti's *Linda di Chamounix*, he wrote with a new degree of assurance:

Her voice is the purest soprano—and of as silvery clearness as ever came from the human throat—rich but not massive—and of such flexibility that one is almost appalled by the way the most difficult passages are not only gone over with ease, but actually dallied with, and their difficulty redoubled. They put one in mind of the gyrations of a bird in the air.*

By 1850 Whitman belonged to the stubborn minority in New York who kept their heads during the visit of the Swedish coloratura Jenny Lind. Barnum had whipped up such a frenzy of expectation and worship that on September 1 twenty thousand people massed in Broadway in front of the entrance to the Irving House to witness her arrival. A week later, George Templeton Strong noted that "Jenny Lind mania continues violent and uncontrolled. Auction of seats for her first concert Saturday; Genin the hatter took seat number 1 at $225."

Whitman attended her last Castle Garden concert on the twenty-fourth. "She was dressed in pink satin, with black lace flounces and cape—great, green cockades in her hair—white kid gloves, fan, handkerchief, and the ordinary fashionable *et ceteras*. Her cheeks were well rouged, and her walk bad. The expression of her face is a sort of moral milk and honey." He found her performance "showy," remote from "true music"—"She simply has a clear, shrill voice, of wonderful fluency, which will perhaps make you think of rich plate glass." The Swedish Nightingale sang like a sweet bird, he acknowledged, "but there is something in song that goes deeper—isn't there?" He left believing that Barnum and a bought press had humbugged the public with this renowned "cantatrice," a word he apparently borrowed from the English translation of George Sand's *Consuelo*. Its emancipated heroine, an operatic contralto of miracu-

---

* "I hear the trained soprano . . . she convulses me like the climax of my love-grip," Whitman wrote in the 1855 *Leaves of Grass* (he softened the line in later editions). But his response to Anna Bishop in 1847 already has sexual overtones of artful prolongation and ecstatic release. "Dallied," suggesting amorous play, and "the gyrations of a bird in the air" together anticipate his 1880 poem about the mating of eagles:

Skyward in air a sudden muffled sound, the dalliance of the eagles,
The rushing amorous contact high in space together,
The clinching interlocking claws, a living, fierce, gyrating wheel . . .

lous gift, was proof, as the novelist wrote, that the secret of "the grand, the true, the beautiful in art" was simplicity. "Be simple and clear," Whitman instructed himself in his notebook. His line in "Song of Myself"—

The pure contralto sings in the organ loft

—recalled Consuelo singing Pergolesi's "Salve Regina" in the organ loft of Saint Mark's in Venice.

Jenny Lind "never touched my heart in the least," but the tenor Alessandro Bettini, who sang in Donizetti's *La Favorita* at Castle Garden the following summer, made him realize, for the first time, he said, "what an indescribable volume of delight the recesses of the soul can bear from the sound of the honied perfection of the human voice. . . . all words are mean before the language of true music." His conversion became complete during the 1852–53 season when the Italian prima donna Marietta Alboni sang the principal roles in ten different operas and also gave a dozen concerts and a performance in Rossini's *Stabat Mater*. "I heard Alboni every time she sang in New York and vicinity," Whitman said. He remembered her as the "greatest of them all"—"I wonder if the lady will ever know that her singing, her method, gave the foundation, the start, thirty years ago, to all my poetic literary efforts since." "But for the opera," he was to say, "I could never have written *Leaves of Grass*." Rich, supple, expressive, overleaping the stars, Alboni and her music liberated him from the metrical, rhymed "ballad-style" of poetry. The arching, cantabile lines, the stabbing arias, sobbing recitatives, and antiphonal design of "Out of the Cradle Endlessly Rocking" followed "the method of the Italian opera," he said in 1860. The boy in that poem, an "outsetting bard," responds to the song of the mocking bird as Whitman at thirty-three responded to Marietta Alboni:

Now in a moment I know what I am for, I awake,
And already a thousand singers, a thousand songs, clearer, louder
        and more sorrowful than yours,
A thousand warbling echoes have started to life within me, never to
        die. . . .
My own songs awaked from that hour.

Music had become the great "combiner, nothing more spiritual, nothing more sensuous, a god, yet completely human," and the human voice was its godlike instrument.

"Talents of gold, and endowments of silver, are possessed by every human being, if he did but know it," Whitman wrote in November 1850, arguing that "music, in the legitimate sense of that term, exists independently of technical music . . . just as poetry exists independently of rhyme." "I advise each and every young person early to commence the study of music, and persevere in its practice and enjoyment all their days." Following his own advice he traded ten daguerreotypes and some artist's supplies from his Myrtle Street store for Charley Heyde's guitar, valued at twelve dollars. During 1852 he traded a lot in Cypress Hills plus $54 for a melodeon and, a gift for Jeff, paid $180 for a seven-octave rosewood-case piano with a two-year warranty. On the Fulton Street ferry late at night, with only a few sleepy passengers aboard, he sang operatic scraps and airs. He sang when he rode the Broadway omnibus, and he sang when he walked on the beach at Coney Island. In love with his own voice—"somehow it's always magnetic"—he sent it out into a relational void where his unrequited single self attempted to merge with the "not Me."

III

One redeeming feature of the brutally hot summer of 1853— Whitman noted "400 deaths in three or four days in N. Y."—was the World's Fair, America's first, that filled the Crystal Palace, a gorgeous octagonal building of glass and iron on the site of present-day Bryant Park. The exterior of this architectural wonder was viewed to best advantage from the Latting Observatory on the north side of 42nd Street, a 280-foot-high tower served by a steam elevator that hoisted visitors from an ice-cream parlor at ground level to banks of telescopes on the upper landings. Sam Clemens, a seventeen-year-old journeyman printer, was entranced by the view from the tower, a great city surrounded by water and farmland, the broad promenades of the reservoir, and adjoining them "a perfect fairy palace—beautiful beyond description." Bold in construction and materials, the Crystal Palace outstripped its counterpart in London's Hyde Park and promised to inaugurate an entire order of architecture in iron, from train sheds to mile-high buildings.* It had the largest dome in the Western world—123 feet high, 100 feet in diameter, and supported by twenty-four columns—and it enclosed nearly five acres of display space for steam and electric engines; bridge elements; printing presses; guns; gold bars from California; lighthouse lenses; lifeboats; grain separators; apple parers; furniture, carved and inlaid; works in precious metals; and paintings and sculptures, including Hiram Powers' celebrated nude, the "Greek Slave" ("so undressed," Henry James said, "yet so refined").

The centerpiece of the Crystal Palace, a colossal equestrian statue of George Washington by Baron Carlo Marochetti, an Italian residing in London, loomed beneath the apex of the great dome. It had earned this place of honor more by its size and subject than by its excellence. The horse belonged in the knacker's yard, while the plaster Father of his Country, sitting braced in his saddle eye to eye with spectators in the gallery, reminded some of them of a raw recruit anxious to please his drillmaster. "In short," said the authors of the exhibition catalogue, "it is not a statue of Washington, but a huge man on a huge horse."

"Undoubtedly the great artistic feature of the Exhibition," the same authors said, was the equally looming but more universally admired sculpture group, *Christ and His Apostles*, by the Dane Bertel Thorwaldsen—"Christian art has reached . . . its noblest expression." Thirteen gigantic figures, intended for the cavernous apse of a church in Copenhagen, were crowded together against a lunette of maroon wall, as if the Last Supper were being served in a railway buffet. Still, one visitor who had dragged through the Crystal Palace's endless courts of edification was to recall that his tiredness and hunger as a boy of eleven had faded before the "sugary or confectionary sweetness" of Thorwaldsen's "shining marble company." "I was somehow in Europe, since everything about me had been 'brought over,' " Henry James wrote. "The Crystal Palace was vast and various and dense, which was what Europe was going to be." (The young Mark Twain thought instead of home. "The visitors to

* This promise died with the Crystal Palace. Although cheap, strong, and technically fireproof, iron had no integrity in high temperatures, a flaw that was demonstrated on October 5, 1858, when, within fifteen minutes after its combustible contents caught fire, the dome, roof and walls of the Crystal Palace collapsed. (Waring Latting's observatory tower had burned to the ground two years earlier.)

the Palace average 6,000 daily," he told his sister, "—double the population of Hannibal.")

"New York, Great Exposition open'd in 1853," Whitman wrote much later. "I went for a long time (nearly a year)—days and nights." He remembered Thorwaldsen's "colossal" figures along with inexhaustible displays of the products of art, commerce, science and industry. With characteristic emphasis he described the Crystal Palace as "an original, esthetic, perfectly proportioned American edifice—one of the few that put modern times not beneath old times, but on an equality with the best of them."

High rising tier on tier with glass and iron facade,
Gladdening the sun and sky, enhued in cheerfulest hues,
Bronze, lilac, robin's egg, marine and crimson . . .

Not very good Whitman, to be sure, but a suggestion at least that the Crystal Palace continued to have vital meaning for him after his own vitality as a poet had waned. In delights of the mind, eye and soul, as well as in material comforts and conveniences, no feudal lord had ever been so abundantly blessed as the American common man of the mid-nineteenth century: this was one lesson of the Crystal Palace, a temple of the useful and uplifting that also suggested that the mission of an American poet was

To exalt the present and the real,
To teach the average man the glory of his daily walk and trade.

He dressed like men who worked on ferryboats, drove stages, fire engines and express wagons, and worked with their hands, and he shared with them a quality of something "rankly common," John Burroughs said, "like freckles and sweat." A tall rough-looking man who weighed 179 pounds on the scale at the Crystal Palace on November 18, 1853, he wore a slouch hat over his grizzled hair and weathered red forehead, clean, cheap knockabout clothes, checked shirt open at the neck, and baggy trousers with the bottoms tucked into his boots. Crossing the river he stood in the wheelhouse with the pilots. He rode the Broadway stages by the hour and sat up on the box with the drivers, "a strange, natural, quick-eyed and wondrous race":

They had immense qualities, largely animal—eating, drinking, women—great personal pride, in their way—perhaps a few slouches here and there, but I should have trusted the general run of them, in their simple good-will and honor, under all circumstances. Not only for comradeship and sometimes affection—great studies I found them also. (I suppose the critics will laugh heartily, but the influence of those Broadway omnibus jaunts and drivers and declamations and escapades undoubtedly entered into the gestation of "Leaves of Grass.")

He enjoyed their yarns, their mimicry, and their virtuoso memories —they could cite passenger tallies for a particular time of day from trips a month back. Most had got their muscles and their skill with horses from years on the farm. They had to be quick, strong and brave to thread their lumbering stages through anarchic thorough-fares, and often they fetched up in the accident ward where Whitman, unconsciously rehearsing his wartime occupation as wound-dresser, came to comfort and minister to them. Sometimes he followed their bodies to the cemetery:

> He was a goodfellow,
> Freemouthed, quicktempered, not badlooking, able to take his own
>   part,
> Witty, sensitive to a slight, ready with life or death for a friend,
> Fond of women . . . played some . . . eat hearty and drank hearty,
> Had known what it was like to be flush . . . grew lowspirited
>   toward the last . . . sickened . . . was helped by a
>   contribution,
> Died aged forty-one years . . . and that was his funeral.

He felt easy and loved with these men, loving and alive. Drivers are archangels in "Song of Myself":

> The young fellow drives the express wagon, (I love him, although I
>   do not know him;) . . .
> The driver thinking of me does not mind the jolt of his wagon . . .

The force he felt was as strong as gravity, and yet for all his sensitiv-ity and candor he did not fully understand it. He believed he was doing neither more nor less than claiming for men the emotional freedom and physical expressiveness—holding hands, touching, hugging, kissing—that society allowed women to enjoy with each other. Why should the sexes be so manacled by custom and decree, by an irrational terror of gender confusion, that aggressiveness was reserved to the male and tenderness to the female? Androgyny, the beautiful integrating principle that had stirred poets and philosophers from Plato to Coleridge, seemed only natural and right to Whitman standing "all alone," "myself," "solitary," a self-contained classless society of one.

On the other side of a sheet of manuscript containing draft lines of "Song of Myself"—

I claim for one of those framers over the way framing a house,
The young man there with rolled-up sleeves and sweat on his superb
   face,
More than your craft three thousand years ago, Kronos, or Zeus his
   son, or Hercules his grandson

—Whitman described some of his companions at the Crystal Palace:

20 March '54.

Bill Guess—aged 22. A thoughtless, strong, generous animal nature, fond of direct pleasures, eating, drinking, women, fun etc. Taken sick with the small-pox, had the bad disorder and was furious with the delirium tremens. Was with me in the Crystal Palace, a large, broad fellow, weighed over 200. Was a thoughtless good fellow.

Peter _____ _____, large, strong-boned young fellow, driver. Should weigh 180. Free and candid to me the very first time he saw me. Man of strong self-will, powerful coarse feelings and appetites. Had a quarrel, borrowed $300, left his father somewhere in the interior of the State, fell in with a couple of gamblers, hadn't been home or written there in seven years . . .

George Fitch—Yankee boy, driver. Fine nature, amiable, sensitive feelings, a natural gentleman, of quite a reflective turn. Left his home because his father was perpetually "down on him." When he told me of his mother his eyes watered . . .

10

Illuminations

I

"WE DID NOT KNOW WHAT HE WAS WRITING," George Whitman said about the period just before *Leaves of Grass* came out. Walt was still a part-time builder, but the bottom had fallen out of the market. In the aftermath of a recession in 1854 houses were selling at thirty percent or more below cost; unemployed carpenters lined up at soup kitchens in the City of Churches.

> Built in Skillman st. and moved there, May 1854. Moved in Ryerson st. May 1855.

Walt bought the Ryerson Street house in his mother's name, for her to hold, in the wording of the deed, "without concurrence of her husband at any time." Walter Whitman, Sr., who forty years earlier had built the plumb and sturdy house at West Hills with his own hands, had suffered a stroke and gradually sank into helplessness through many bad spells and negligible remissions. Even in this darkening time, Walt "did not seem more abstracted than usual," George said. "He would lie abed late, and after getting up would write a few hours if he took the notion." George was unimpressed when early in the summer of 1855 Walt brought home the first copy of *Leaves of Grass*. "I saw the book—didn't read it at all—didn't think it worth reading—fingered it a little."

Sometimes, as in "A Backward Glance," Whitman claimed for his book a long, deliberate history and said that after years of competing for "the usual rewards" he had determined to become a poet. "At the age of thirty-one to thirty-three, a desire that had been flitting through my previous life, or hovering on the flanks, mostly indefinite hitherto, had steadily advanced to the front, defined itself, and finally dominated everything else." But he also said that he had started "elaborating the plan of my poems . . . experimenting much, and writing and abandoning much," when he was twenty-eight, in 1847, and in 1855 he "commenced putting Leaves of Grass to press, for good—after many MS doings and undoings—(I had great trouble in leaving out the stock 'poetical' touches—but succeeded at last.)" On other occasions he suggested instead that patient purpose had yielded to an unfathomable urgency. He spoke of the "perturbations" of *Leaves of Grass* and said that "very much of it" had been written under "great pressure, pressure from within," that had made his book, "launched from the fires of *myself*," inevitable and immediately necessary. He "felt that he must do it."

His conflicting, overlapping, or vague "explanations" of an event that may have been by its nature inexplicable were further confounded by his habitual mystifications and his casualness with chronology and documentary evidence. One of his notebooks contains trial lines and fragments—

The poet is a recruiter
He goes forth beating the drum—O, who will not join his troop?

—along with this memorandum, possibly for the Skillman Street house:

Front windows on first floor—lights 13 x 17—Window five lights high—a sash of two lights across top—the other eight lights made in two door-sides, hung each with hinges.

Ultimately the year of his surge of "MS doings and undoings" became so blurred that some biographers have supposed it to be as early as 1847, before he went to New Orleans. But it is hardly likely that he would have reverted to the relatively conventional verse he was still writing in 1850 or that he would have deferred until 1855 publishing at least some evidences of a great discovery. (Even Whitman's "A Boston Ballad," written around June 1854 in response to the arrest and rendition of the fugitive slave Anthony Burns and included in *Leaves of Grass*, is preliminary in style.) Delay and patient preparation are not in character with Whitman's first edition, assembled in hot and arrogant haste and even in a sort of desperateness. The long prose preface of 1855 was, in part, a series of loosely connected notes—a warehouse of ideas—for poems he was planning even as his book was in press. A year later, his surge still far from peaking, he published a second edition with twenty new poems, among them the great "Crossing Brooklyn Ferry," added to his original twelve. "I wish now to bring out a third edition," he was to say two years later, "I have now *a hundred* poems ready (the last edition had thirty-two)." Like "Song of Myself," the earliest editions of *Leaves of Grass* both celebrated and reenacted the act of becoming.

He was probably nearest the historical truth when he said, only six years after the event described, that he "definitely" began writing out his poems in 1854. This was the year he turned thirty-five, the mid-point of a life decade that he associated with "the perfection and realization of moral life" and that many other writers knew also to be a crossroads, perhaps a last chance. "I have heard that after thirty a man wakes up sad every morning," Emerson said. "Where the top of this arch of life may be, it is difficult to know," Dante said. "I believe that in the perfectly natural man, it is at the thirty-fifth year." At thirty-five, "the middle of the journey of our life," Dante is supposed to have had his vision of awaking in a dark, pathless wood and finding his way to paradise. Whitman noted that "in the 35th year of his age" Shakespeare was "adjudged already to deserve a place among the great masters." At the same age, and after years of conscious and unconscious rehearsal, Whitman awoke to a new purpose.

On and off since about 1847 he had carried with him a 3½-by-5½-inch pocket notebook bound in green boards with a leather backstrip and three leather loops along the side edges to hold a pencil. Below the signature "Walter Whitman" on the inside front cover he wrote and in turn canceled three of his addresses over a period of five years—71 Prince Street, 30 Fulton Street (the *Daily Eagle* office), and 106 Myrtle Avenue, where he conducted his stationery and job-printing business until 1852. For 1847 he notes a transaction with his employer, Isaac Van Anden of the *Eagle*, and some masonry work ordered for the basement at Prince Street and paid for in full.

He removed seven pages possibly containing similar business memoranda. The bulk of the surviving entries are of another sort and vintage. They appear to be contemporaneous with the 1854 addresses for the artists Jesse Talbot and Frederick Chapman scribbled on the inside back cover and with related entries in other notebooks that can be assigned to 1854 on the basis of internal evidence—references to the sinking of the ship *San Francisco* (retold in section 33 of "Song of Myself"), operatic performances by the star couple Giula Grisi and Giuseppe Mario, the bombardment of Sebastopol, and the charge of the Light Brigade.

In his green notebook the printer, schoolmaster, fiction writer, editor, shopkeeper, and housebuilder began—for the first time, as far as anyone knows—to sound his voice over the roofs of the world. In Biblically cadenced, unrhymed verse he celebrated a psychic revolution: the single self happy merely to exist, enjoying "the ecstasy of simple physiological Being" and chanting "the chant of dilation or pride." Other masters singing the wrath of Achilles and man's first disobedience, had created an epic literature out of war, pain, denial, oppression and enforced belief. In Whitman's own country a century and a half earlier Cotton Mather commemorated "the wonders of the Christian religion, flying from the depravations of Europe to the American strand." A four-word phrase in Whitman's notebook—

Observing the summer grass

—is a cue for the stunning introit of "Song of Myself," in spirit and structure a secular Mass.

> I celebrate myself,
> And what I assume you shall assume,
> For every atom belonging to me as good belongs to you.
>
> I loafe and invite my soul,
> I lean and loafe at my ease. . . . observing a spear of summer grass.

"Test of a poem," he noted. "How far it can elevate, enlarge, purify, deepen and make happy the attributes of the body and soul." Another prose note is a study for both Section 46 of "Song of Myself"—

I tramp a perpetual journey,
My signs are a rain-proof coat and good shoes and a staff cut from
      the woods

—and for his famous "Song of the Open Road." The note reads:

I will take each man and woman of you to the window and open the
shutters and the sash, and my left arm shall hook you around the
waist, and my right shall point you to the endless and beginingless
road along whose sides are crowded the rich cities of all living philosophy, and oval gates that pass you in to fields of clover and landscapes
clumped with sassafrass, and orchards of good apples, and every
breath through your mouth shall be of a new perfumed and elastic
air, which is love.—Not I—not God—can travel this road for
you . . .

Other fragments in prose and Whitman's distinctive free verse, each
line a thought, were just as clearly intended for *Leaves of Grass* in its
achieved form and manner. They tell of release, discovery, a radical
new dimension of knowledge.

I cannot understand the mystery, but I am always conscious of myself
as two—as My soul and I: and I reckon it is the same with all men
and women.

I am the poet of the body,
And I am the poet of the soul

Have you supposed it is beautiful to be born?
I tell you I know it is just as beautiful to die;
for I take my death with the dying
And my birth with the new-born babe.

I am the poet of sin,
For I do not believe in sin

No two have exactly the same language, and the great translator and
joiner of the whole is the poet. He has the divine grammar of all
tongues, and says indifferently and alike, How are you friend? to the
President in the midst of his cabinet, and Good day my brother, to

Sambo, among the hoes of the sugar field, and both understand him and know that his speech is right.

Leaves of Grass was to celebrate the conquest of loneliness through the language of common modern speech. It invokes the profoundest pun in the English language, "eye" and "I," and links the seer with the sayer:

> Speech is the twin of my vision. . . . it is unequal to measure itself.
> It provokes me forever,
> It says sarcastically, Walt, you understand enough. . . . why don't
> you let it out then?

This "Walt" speaks for the collective, timeless "I." Shelley called to the west wind to make him its lyre, "even as the forest is." Wordsworth aspired to be

> . . . obedient as a lute
> That waits upon the touches of the wind.

"I conceive of man as always spoken to from behind, and unable to turn his head and see the speaker," said Emerson; the poet's function was to transmit

> Secrets of the solar track,
> Sparks of the supersolar blaze.

Supreme American inheritor of Romanticism, Whitman too believed the poet was the agency of a transcendent power and created "rapt verse" in an "ecstasy of statement,"

> a trance, yet with all the senses alert—oniy a state of high exalted musing—the tangible and material with all its shows, the objective world suspended or surmounted for a while, & the powers in exaltation, freedom, vision—yet the *senses* not lost or counteracted.

He said he had the capacity to "*stop thinking*" at will, to go "negative" and suspend all conscious striving. He underlined Keats's definition

of "Negative Capability"—"when a man is capable of being in un-
certainties, mysteries, doubts, without any irritable reaching after
fact and reason." When writing *Leaves of Grass* Whitman felt like a
"sonnambulist" who, on awakening, is amazed by the giddy heights
and impossible situations he passed over safely while afoot with his
vision." "The Sleepers"—

> I dream in my dream all the dreams of the other dreamers,
> And I become the other dreamers.

—has been called "perhaps the only surrealist American poem of the
nineteenth century"; it is also the equivalent of a prolonged "out-of-
the-body experience." Unlike many of his contemporaries, for
whom the "vision" was a useful literary convention, Whitman was
being quite literal when he spoke of ecstasies and illuminations. He
may have experienced them in adolescence—

> Now in a moment I know what I am for, I awake

—and in all probability he experienced them again during 1853–54.
Gabriel Harrison's "Christ likeness" of Whitman is the portrait of an
illuminate.

Whitman was not a "mystic." Conversion, discipline, renuncia-
tion of the self, the body, and the world are alien to *Leaves of Grass*.
His lifelong hero Elias Hicks, he said, was *"sentimental-religious* like
an old Hebrew mystic," but "though I may have something of that
kind 'way in the rear, it is pretty far back in the rear & I guess I am
mainly sensitive to the wonderfulness & perhaps spirituality of
things in their physical & concrete expressions—& have celebrated
all that."

He had shared the experience of countless people, irreligious by
common standards, who had flashes of illumination or ecstasy—
even Caliban saw the clouds open and "cried to dream again." These
experiences have a remembered correlative or "trigger." With Whitman it was the sea, music, the grass, the green world of summer.
The rhythm of these experiences is sexual and urgent—tumescence,
climax, detumescence—but the "afterglow" may last a lifetime, as it
did with him, and he invoked it and prolonged it through poetry;

the poet was the shaman of modern society, a master of "the techniques of ecstasy."*

Whitman invited these experiences when he lay on the sunbaked grass or on the sands at Coney Island and when, in shattered health, he sought out stillness at Timber Creek. Like Emerson and Thoreau, he had studied the Eastern literature of ecstasy; a poem he published the year before he died, "A Persian Lesson," was his tribute to the Sufi-inspired poets who in erotic lyrics had celebrated the I-Thou relationship, "the central urge in every atom," Whitman wrote, "to return to its divine source and origin." Perhaps an ecstatic experience is only a neurological event, a spiraling mania or "rush" induced by a biogenic amine in a synapse of the brain, but this scarcely matters: Whitman *knew* what he knew to be transcendent.

> Do you see O my brothers and sisters?
> It is not chaos or death—it is form, union, plan—it is eternal life—it
>   is Happiness.

In sunlight on the summer grass the poet awoke from the first half of life and celebrated "Happiness" in a lyric of astonishing delicacy and finality:

> I believe in you my soul. . . . the other I am must not abase itself to
>   you,

---

* Vincent Van Gogh was reading Whitman in 1888, around the time he was painting the apocalyptic *Starry Night*, and he wrote to his sister, "He sees in the future, and even in the present, a world of health, carnal love, strong and frank—of friendship—of work—under the great starlit vault of heaven a something which after all one can only call God—and eternity in its place above the world. At first it makes you smile, it is all so candid and pure." The German poet Rainer Maria Rilke describes this counterpart to the ecstasy that Whitman invoked in Section 5 of "Song of Myself." "He had never been filled with more gentle motions, his body was somehow treated like a soul, and put in a state to receive a degree of influence which, given the normal apparentness of one's physical conditions, really could not have been felt at all. . . . he insistently asked himself what was happening to him then, and almost at once found an expression that satisfied him, saying to himself, that he had got to the other side of Nature." In part a response to this experience, Rilke's *Duino Elegies* are written in a dithyrambic free verse similar to Whitman's. (*The Complete Letters of Vincent Van Gogh* [London, 1958], Vol. III, p. 445; Rilke, *Duino Elegies*, trans. J. B. Leishman and Stephen Spender [New York, 1939], pp. 124–25.)

And you must not be abased to the other.

Loafe with me on the grass. . . . loose the stop from your throat,
Not words, not music or rhyme I want. . . . nor custom or lecture,
      not even the best,
Only the lull I like, the hum of your valved voice.

I mind how we lay in June, such a transparent summer morning;
You settled your head athwart my hips and gently turned over upon
      me,
And parted the shirt from my bosom-bone, and plunged your
      tongue to my barestript heart,
And reached till you felt my beard, and reached till you held my
      feet.

Swiftly arose and spread around me the peace and joy and know-
      ledge that pass all the art and argument of the earth;
And I know that the hand of God is the eldest brother of my own,
And that all the men ever born are also my brothers. . . . and the
      women my sisters and lovers,
And that a kelson of the creation is love;
And limitless are leaves stiff or drooping in the fields,
And brown ants in the little wells beneath them,
And mossy scabs of the wormfence, and heaped stones, and elder
      and mullen and pokeweed.

Whitman often pondered the example of Emanuel Swedenborg who had undergone "a total change—a revolution, probably one of the most curious in human experience. At that time was opened to him, in the twinkling of an eye, the 'spiritual world,' and he saw it (or was it that he fancied he saw it?). The inference is that this spiritual world exists at all times with us and around us, but that few, indeed hardly any, come into rapport with it. But Emanuel Swedenborg was one of the few." The circumstances of Swedenborg's celebrated illumination—a historic event that, according to Whitman, marked the emergence of the individual consciousness in modern religious thought—were "somewhat comical," "most unromantic and vulgar": as Swedenborg was finishing his dinner at a London inn a mist surrounded him, and when it cleared he saw that he had a visitor, a man radiant with light. "I think Swedenborg was right," Whitman remarked another time, "when he said there was a close connection—a very close connection—between the state we call religious ecstasy and the desire to copulate. I find Swedenborg confirmed in all my experience. It is a peculiar discovery." Whitman made that connection in a manuscript fragment:

> I am a look—mystic—in a trance—exaltation.
> Something wild and untamed—half-savage.
> Common things—the trickling sap that flows from the end of the
>   manly maple.

The sex organ itself was a "poem"

> . . . of the privacy of the night, and of men like me,
> This poem drooping shy and unseen that I always carry, and that all
>   men carry,
> (Know once for all, avow'd on purpose, wherever are men like me,
>   are our lusty lurking masculine poems,)

Poets of ecstasy through the ages rendered the consummated marriage of the soul with God in sexual imagery. But sexuality as sexuality—"the desire to copulate"—is a force in *Leaves of Grass*, a work that celebrates the democratization of the whole person, the liberation of impulse and instinct from involuntary servitude.

> Urge and urge and urge,
> Always the procreant urge of the world . . .
> I will go to the bank by the wood and become undisguised and
>   naked . . .
> Echos, ripples, and buzzed whispers . . . loveroots, silk thread,
>   crotch and vine . . .
> A few light kisses . . . a few embraces . . . a reaching around of
>   arms . . .

Orgasm follows the bulging of "firm masculine coulter":

> Something I cannot see puts upward libidinous prongs,
> Seas of bright juice suffuse heaven.

> Dazzling and tremendous how quick the sunrise would kill me,
> If I could not now and always send sunrise out of me.

The genderless Other who turned over upon the passive Walt that transparent June morning and plunged its tongue to the barestript heart reappears in "The Sleepers" as the active partner in an act of fellation. In the androgynous changes of Whitman's dream-logic, the woman

> . . . who adorned herself and folded her hair expectantly,
> My truant lover has come and it is dark.

becomes an erect penis, described—in a passage Whitman removed from later printings—as "hotcheeked and blushing," "thrust forth":

> I feel ashamed to go naked about the world,
> And am curious to know where my feet stand . . . and what is this
>   flooding me, childhood or manhood . . . and the hunger
>   that crosses the bridge between.
>
> The cloth laps a first sweet eating and drinking,
> Laps life-swelling yolks . . . laps ear of rose-corn, milky and just
>   ripened:
> The white teeth stay, and the boss-tooth advances in darkness,
> And liquor is spilled on lips and bosoms by touching glasses, and the
>   best liquor afterward.

In the detumescent "afterward" the "I" experiences a prolonged glow:

> I descend my western course . . . my sinews are flaccid,
> Perfume and youth course through me, and I am their wake.

"Song of Myself" and "The Sleepers"—the one sunlit, conscious in argument and public in voice, the other nocturnal, secret, surreal —celebrate the same wonders: the flowing springs of being, process, simple existence, ongoing perception that becomes the agency as well as the subject of poems. Together "Song of Myself" and "The Sleepers" are the matrix for all of Whitman's work. *Leaves of Grass* was to grow and change and reflect an evolving persona, but it arrived in 1855 not as a "promising" book but as something completely achieved. There is nothing quite like it in literature, Whitman at his best, and when he is at his awful worst—windy, repetitious, self-imitative—one loves him for that too, he is so un-worried, nonchalant, like animals:

> I think I could turn and live awhile with the animals . . . they are so
> placid and self-contained,
> I stand and look at them sometimes half the day long.
>
> They do not sweat and whine about their condition,
> They do not lie awake in the dark and weep for their sins,
> They do not make me sick discussing their duty to God,
> Not one is dissatisfied . . . not one is demented with the mania of
> owning things,
> Not one kneels to another nor to his kind that lived thousands of
> years ago,
> Not one is respectable or industrious over the whole earth.

II

Whitman's traffic with the poets of his day was mainly of a nega-tive sort—he learned from them what not to do. Tennyson was "an imitation of Shakespeare," "a refined, educated, traveled, modern English dandy." His *Maud; A Monodrama*, published the same year as *Leaves of Grass*, was "tedious and affected, with some sweet pas-sages." (It was "Ulysses," Whitman said, that "shows the *great master*.") Another long poem of 1855, *Hiawatha*, Longfellow's enor-mously popular foray into genteel primitivism, also left Whitman cold—it was at best "a pleasing ripply poem." He had drawn away from the "misty," "windy" style of James Macpherson's fabrications from the Gaelic—"Don't fall into the Ossianic, *by any chance*."

"Be simple and clear.—Be not occult," Whitman instructed him-self around 1854, when he was reading the Scotsman Alexander Smith's *A Life-Drama and Other Poems*, a now-forgotten collection that ran through several editions in England and the States. Smith was ridiculed as the founder of a Spasmodic School of poetry and "a phenomenon of a very dubious character." Whitman found him "imbued with the nature of Tennyson. He is full of what are called poetical images—full of conceits and likenesses; in this respect copy-ing after Shakespeare and the majority of the received poets. He seems to be neither better nor worse than the high average." Nevertheless Whitman discovered in *A Life-Drama* "one electric passage," as he noted in 1854, "where the announcement is made of a great forthcoming Poet." The electric passage was addressed to a character named "Walter," who says that these words "set me on fire."

> My Friend! a Poet must ere long arise,
> And with regal song sun-crown this age,
> As a saint's head is with a halo crowned;—
> One, who shall hallow Poetry to God
> And to its own high use . . .
> A mighty Poet whom this age shall choose
> To be its spokesman to all coming times.
> In the ripe full-blown season of his soul,
> He shall go forward in his spirit's strength,
> And grapple with the questions of all time,
> And wring from them their meanings. As King Saul
> Called up the buried prophet from his grave
> To speak his doom, so shall this Poet-king
> Call up the dead Past from its awful grave
> To tell him of our future.

Whitman echoed this passage in his preface to *Leaves of Grass:*

> The great poet forms the consistence of what is to be from what has been and is. He drags the dead out of their coffins and stands them again on their feet. . . . he says to the past, Rise and walk before me that I may realize you. He learns the lesson . . . he places himself where the future becomes present.

The preface was a "Defense" or "Apology" in the tradition of Sir Philip Sidney, Wordsworth and Shelley, but it could never have been written on their side of the Atlantic. "The Americans of all nations at any time upon the earth have probably the fullest poetical nature," said this child of the democratic century. "The United States themselves are essentially the greatest poem." And he concluded:

> An individual is as superb as a nation when he has the qualities which make a superb nation. The soul of the largest and wealthiest and proudest nation may well go halfway to meet that of its poets. The

signs are effectual. There is no fear of mistake. If the one is true the other is true. The proof of a poet is that his country absorbs him as affectionately as he has absorbed it.

In Whitman's 1855 edition, this logic frames ten crowded, double-columned pages of prose argument often more than halfway to poetry. Writing his preface in hot haste while the book was in press, Whitman punctuated it with strings of periods, ellipses that seem intended to indicate simultaneous and continuous acts of perception instead of omitted connections. His first readers may have rubbed their eyes in amazement, consternation or dismay. ("The Preface," the critic Ivan Marki says, "creates the conditions indispensable to the understanding of the volume, but it cannot explain anything, since it is part of what needs to be explained.")

Although sequential and closely reasoned, Whitman's preface gave a first impression of being a balloon of random *pensées* ballasted with American particularities (cottonwood, persimmons, the convening of Congress, labor-saving machinery, the Yankee swap) and unashamed references to the urge and act of love, "venereal sores or discolorations," "the privacy of the onanist," and the "fatherstuff" with which sinewy races of bards were to be conceived. These Americans of the future, a "new breed of poets"—"There will soon be no more priests"—were to take their religion from a new Bible, *Leaves of Grass*, and a new set of commandments that revolutionized and enhanced their consciousness of being alive. (Whitman "was a great changer of the blood in the veins," D. H. Lawrence said.)

This is what you shall do: Love the earth and sun and the animals, despise riches, give alms to every one that asks, stand up for the stupid and crazy, devote your income and labor to others, hate tyrants, argue not concerning God, have patience and indulgence toward the people, take off your hat to nothing known or unknown to any man or number of men, go freely with powerful uneducated persons and with the young and with the mothers of families, read these leaves in the open air each season of every year of your life, reexamine all you have been told at school or church or in any book, dismiss whatever insults your own soul, and your very flesh shall be a great poem and have the richest fluency not only in its words but in the silent lines of its lips and face and between the lashes of your eyes and in every motion and joint of your body.

"At the moment it seemed vital and necessary," Whitman said long after he had discarded his preface in favor of other declarations. "It seemed to give the book some feet to stand on."

III

On May 15, 1855, two weeks and two days before his thirty-sixth birthday, Walter Whitman, author, proprietor, and publisher of a literary work in press, registered the title *Leaves of Grass* with the clerk of the United States District Court, Southern District of New York. The clerk wrote out a copyright notice that Whitman brought to the printing office of James and Thomas Rome, in a little red-brick building on the southwest corner of Fulton and Cranberry streets in Brooklyn. He was spending nearly every day there that spring, writing, revising, reading proof, even working at the type case, just as he had done twenty years earlier as an apprentice printer. Altogether he set in type about ten of the ninety-five pages of a book that he also designed, produced, published, promoted (shamelessly, his critics said), regarded as "the New Bible," and for nearly forty years made the center of his life, the instrument of health and survival itself.

Still, for a book so momentous, there was something casual, *ad hoc*, even accidental, about its first publication. The 795 copies the Romes ran off on their hand press and delivered to the binder were all there were or could be of the first edition. No plates were made; the book was printed from type, and the type distributed. During June a Brooklyn binder, Charles Jenkins, put two hundred copies in green cloth at a unit cost to the author of thirty-two cents; the remaining 595 copies were contracted out to another establishment and given cheaper bindings. The manuscript, a document of extraordinary literary and historical importance, stayed in the shop until 1858, when it was burned, Whitman recalled offhandedly. "Rome kept it several years, but one day, by accident, it got away from us entirely—was used to kindle the fire or to feed the rag man."

Fowler and Wells, proprietors of wonderland, were Whitman's nominal distributors to the trade. During the first weeks of July their Phrenological Cabinet offered for sale, along with other curious wares, an album-sized book that was as arresting in makeup as in contents, the most brilliant and original poetry yet written in the New World, at once the fulfillment of American literary romanticism and the beginnings of American literary modernism. The words "Leaves of Grass" were stamped on the covers in tendriled letters that appeared to be taking root in the green cloth. Inside the 8-by-11-inch quarto the eye was caught first by the uncaptioned frontispiece portrait of a bearded man, a stipple engraving, with alterations supervised by Whitman, of Harrison's "carpenter" photograph. The first known review, in the New York *Tribune* on July 23, took note of this portrait and of what it suggested about its subject:

> . . . we may infer that he belongs to that exemplary class of society sometimes irreverently styled "loafers." He is therein represented in a garb, half sailor's, half workingman's, with no superfluous appendage of coat or waistcoat, a "wideawake" perched jauntily on his head, one hand in his pocket and the other on his hip, with a certain air of mild defiance, and an expression of pensive insolence on his face which seems to betoken a consciousness of his mission as the "coming man." This view of the author is confirmed in the preface.

The page facing this portrait offered no clue to the author's name. It showed only the title, set in a wood type face with capitals about an inch high, a small decorative swelled rule, and "Brooklyn, New York: 1855." The copyright page was more informative, but the Walter Whitman named in the statutory boilerplate was conceivably the author's publisher or assignee or even, as some readers might have concluded, a conservator appointed in cases of mental instability. Ten pages of eccentrically punctuated prose were followed by eighty-three pages of verse, at first glance simply clusters of prose sentences printed like Bible verses; the twelve poems were untitled except for the insistent head caption for each, again "Leaves of Grass." Only in a passage on page 29 did the reader finally come upon a connection between the bearded loafer of the frontispiece, the anonymous author, and the copyright holder:

Walt Whitman, an American, one of the roughs, a kosmos,
Disorderly, fleshy and sensual . . . eating drinking and breeding,
No sentimentalist . . . no stander above men and women or apart
    from them . . . no more modest than immodest.

In an era of triple-barreled literary eminences who uttered their names in Jovian trochees and dactyls—William Cullen Bryant, John Greenleaf Whittier, Ralph Waldo Emerson, Henry Wadsworth Longfellow, James Russell Lowell—Walter Whitman had chosen to follow the populist examples of Andy Jackson, Kit Carson, and Davy Crockett. The change was more than nominal—it was organic, revolutionary. He had found his soul's true name:

> What am I after all but a child, pleas'd with the sound of my own
> name? repeating it over and over;
> I stand apart to hear—it never tires me.*

On Friday July 6, 1855, Horace Greeley's New York *Tribune* published this small advertisement on page 2:

Walt Whitman's Poems, 'Leaves of Grass,' 1 vol. small quarto, $2, for sale by Swayne, No. 210 Fulton-St., Brooklyn, and by Fowler and Wells, No. 308 Broadway, N.Y.

On Wednesday July 11, three days before his sixty-sixth birthday, Walter Whitman, father of the newly published poet, died in the Ryerson Street house attended by his wife, Louisa. Walt and Jeffy "felt very much to blame themselves for not being at home," she wrote to Hannah, "but they had no idea of any change [.] your father had been [ill] so long and so many bad spells." Alone up in Vermont

---

* "Standing apart" is one of the literal meanings of the word *ecstasy*. Tennyson said he experienced the same sort of autohypnosis through the repetition of his name.

> I have never had any revelation through anaesthetics, but a kind of waking trance (this for want of a better term) I have frequently had, quite up from boyhood, when I have been all alone. This has often come upon me through repeating my own name to myself silently till, all at once, as it were, out of the intensity of the consciousness of the individuality, the individuality itself seemed to dissolve and fade away into boundless being; and this is not a composed state, but the clearest of the clearest, the surest of the surest, utterly beyond words, where death was an almost laughable impossibility, the loss of personality (if so it were), seeming no extinction, but the only true life. I am ashamed of my feeble description. Have I not said the state was utterly beyond words? (Quoted in Walter Franklin Prince, *Noted Witnesses for Psychic Occurrences* [Boston, 1928], p. 144.)

with Charley Heyde, Hannah vied with her grieving mother—"I myself feel the need of comfort and sympathy." Mary also "took it very hard" that she had not been with her father at the end. She came in from Greenport in time to follow the body to the Cemetery of the Evergreens in Williamsburg. In accordance with the widow's wishes, a Baptist minister read the burial service over a lifelong freethinker. Mary was "very sick" after the funeral, and Walt took her back to Greenport. He stayed with her for part of the summer, enjoyed his customary vacation around Shelter Island and Peconic Bay, and recalled this time as "the happiest of my life." He was to come back to New York "with the confirmed resolution, from which I never afterwards wavered, to go on with my poetic enterprise in my own way, and finish it as well as I could." During the same season that saw the birth of *Leaves of Grass* he accepted his father's death with equanimity, having prepared for it during the years of his unacknowledged regency. The concluding lines of his book were an antidote for loss:

> Great is death . . . Sure as life holds all parts together death holds
> all parts together;
> Sure as the stars return again after they merge in the light, death is
> as great as life.

The opening paragraph of the preface he composed that spring in the Rome brothers' printing office described the past as a sort of father and the young nation, whose poet he was determined to be, as a stoic, even jubilant presence, Walt himself, unperturbed in the house of mourning. America, he wrote,

> perceives that the corpse is slowly borne from the eating and sleeping rooms of the house . . . perceives that it waits a little while in the door . . . that it was fittest for its days . . . that its action has descended to the stalwart and well-shaped heir who approaches . . . and that he shall be fittest for his days.

11

"The beginning of a great career"

I

Do you take it I would astonish?
Does the daylight astonish? or the early redstart twittering through
  the woods?
Do I astonish more than they?

Reading these lines at his desk in Concord, in a complimentary copy sent him by an anonymous author, Emerson almost believed he had seen salvation and could depart in peace. "In raptures," as a visitor noted, Emerson pointed to a certain "oriental largeness of generalization" as evidence that an American Buddha, the long-awaited national poet, had spoken at last. "So extraordinary," he told a Boston friend, Samuel Gray Ward, "I must send it to you, & pray you to look it over." He wondered whether the author had not been "hurt by hard life & too animal experience," but still praised *Leaves of Grass* as "wonderful," "the American poem," "a nondescript monster," as he wrote to Carlyle, "which yet had terrible eyes and buffalo strength." After some puzzlement over the identity and whereabouts of the new poet, Emerson composed a letter to Walter Whitman, Esq., in care of Fowler and Wells in New York.

Concord Massachusetts 21 July 1855

DEAR SIR,
  I am not blind to the worth of the wonderful gift of "Leaves of Grass." I find it the most extraordinary piece of wit & wisdom that

America has yet contributed. I am very happy in reading it, as great power makes us happy. It meets the demand I am always making of what seemed the sterile & stingy Nature, as if too much handiwork or too much lymph in the temperament were making our western wits fat & mean.

I give you joy of your free & brave thought. I have great joy in it. I find incomparable things said incomparably well, as they must be. I find the courage of *treatment*, which so delights us, & which large perception only can inspire.

I greet you at the beginning of a great career, which yet must have had a long foreground somewhere, for such a start. I rubbed my eyes a little to see if this sunbeam were no illusion; but the solid sense of the book is a sober certainty. It has the best merits, namely, of fortifying & encouraging.

I did not know until I, last night, saw the book advertised in a newspaper, that I could trust the name as real & available for a Post-office. I wish to see my benefactor, & have felt much like striking my tasks, & visiting New York to pay you my respects.

R. W. EMERSON.

MR. WALTER WHITMAN.

This five-page salute, Whitman later said, was the charter of "an emperor"—"I supposed the letter was meant to be blazoned." In the annals of literary partisanship and the laying-on of hands, Emerson's words are unmatched for their generosity and force, their shrewdness and simple justice. Another insurgent scripture, *Walden*, published the summer before, had drawn only qualified praise from Emerson. Now he proclaimed the greatness of *Leaves of Grass* to friends, casual visitors, and far-flung acquaintances. "Toward no other American, toward no contemporary excepting Carlyle, had Emerson used such strong expressions," said Moncure Conway, the young Harvard Divinity School graduate who was to be Emerson's first legate to the new poet. "Emerson had been for many years our literary banker; paper that he had inspected, coin that had been rung on his counter, would pass safely anywhere." Stripped of its marketplace metaphors the same idea was echoed on the other side of the Atlantic by William Howitt, reviewer for the *London Weekly Dispatch*—"What Emerson has pronounced to be good must not be lightly treated." Even the *Criterion*, a high-toned New York weekly that dismissed Whitman's book as "a mass of stupid filth," had to acknowledge, apologetically, the quality of its credentials—"an unconsidered letter of introduction has oftentimes procured the admittance of a scurvy fellow into good society."

Emerson's letter admitted *Leaves of Grass* to a meeting of Philadelphia abolitionists where Lucretia Mott, the Quaker preacher, heard it discussed and praised. "R. W. Emerson calls it 'the book of the age,' " she wrote to her sister. "It is something Emersonian in style —a kind of unmeasured poetry in praise of America & telling what true poetry is." She had no objection to the purchase of a copy for her seventeen-year-old granddaughter. The patrician critic and scholar Charles Eliot Norton told his friend James Russell Lowell that he had been alerted to the existence of this "literary curiosity" by the revered Emerson, who had apparently written a letter to the author "expressing the warmest admiration and encouragement." In his unsigned review in the September *Putnam's Monthly* Norton described *Leaves of Grass* as "preposterous yet somehow fascinating," a surprisingly harmonious fusion of "Yankee transcendentalism and New York rowdyism" that at times exhibited, in the "rough and ragged thicket of its pages," undeniable boldness and originality. Norton confessed that he had had to overcome his distaste for the book's "disgusting" and "intolerable" coarseness. "One cannot leave it about for chance readers," he told Lowell, "and would be sorry to know that any woman had looked into it past the title-page. I have got a copy for you, for there are things in it you will admire." ("No, no," Lowell replied, "the kind of thing you describe won't do.") Another member of Emerson's circle, the clergyman Edward Everett Hale, future author of *The Man Without a Country*, praised Whitman (in the January 1856 *North American Review*) for his "remarkable power," his "freshness, simplicity, and reality," and for living up to the claims made in the preface. Half a century later Hale was still congratulating himself for having written this review, the first that, in Whitman's recollection, had done his book anything close to justice.

In the summer of 1855, when he returned from his vacation on eastern Long Island, he had been greeted by a review of a different sort, prominent but grudging and even mischievous, by Charles A. Dana of the *Tribune*, Horace Greeley's managing editor. A one-time member of the Brook Farm commune who had lived on admiring terms with its founder, George Ripley, and with Margaret Fuller and Nathaniel Hawthorne, Dana had retrieved some remnants of idealism from the ruins of that experiment in plain living and high thinking. In the "nameless bard" of *Leaves of Grass* he recognized an oafish descendant of Emerson, Bronson Alcott, and other "prophets of the soul." He too praised Whitman's "bold, stirring thoughts," "genuine intimacy with nature," and "keen appreciation of beauty." But he argued that "the essential spirit of poetry" had found "an uncouth and grotesque embodiment." "His independence often becomes coarse and defiant. His language is too frequently reckless and indecent," Dana said, sounding the cry that Whitman was to hear to the end of his days, "and will justly prevent his volume from free circulation in scrupulous circles." Because of such objections William Swayne, the Fulton Street bookseller listed in the original announcements in the *Tribune*, had withdrawn *Leaves of Grass* from his stock and his name from Fowler and Wells's advertisements. Even *Life Illustrated*, the firm's own "Family Newspaper," said the book was "perfect nonsense," "a series of *utterances*" that the public was advised to take or leave, "just as they prefer." Soon Samuel Wells, more of a businessman and less of a crusader than his partner Orson Fowler, suggested that Whitman omit "certain objectionable passages" or look for another publisher.

At Mickle Street Whitman made an almost casual thing of it when he explained how Emerson's letter, a private and privileged communication, came to be published in the New York *Tribune* without the writer's permission or foreknowledge. He said that when he was walking down the street in New York he happened to run into Dana, who had heard about the letter along the transcendental grapevine, was eager to print it in his newspaper, and wanted Whitman to release the text to him. Whitman refused, but a week or so later changed his mind, having been won over by Dana, who represented himself, with some justification, as "a friend of Mr. Emerson" and therefore in a responsible position to decide what was legitimate and proper for everyone concerned. He printed the letter in the *Tribune* on October 10 and prefaced it with a brief paragraph that suggested a turning-point in the public fortunes of *Leaves of Grass*:

> We sometime since had occasion to call the attention of our readers to this original and striking collection of poems, by Mr. Whitman of Brooklyn. In so doing we could not avoid noticing certain faults which seemed to us to be prominent in the work. The following opinion, from a distinguished source, views the matter from a more positive and less critical standpoint.

At first cautious and reluctant, just as his phrenological chart had said, Whitman could justifiably claim to have been, up to this point, the unoffending victim of Dana's good intentions and unreliable assurances.* But once the letter was released he fell on it like a hawk —"I too am not a bit tamed." The life of his sacred book was in the balance. He sent the *Tribune* clipping to Longfellow and other celebrities, arranged to have the letter printed in *Life Illustrated*, and eventually distributed it to editors and critics in the form of a small broadside he printed up. It was headed "Copy for the convenience of private reading only" and changed Emerson's formal "Mr. Walter Whitman" to "Walt Whitman."

The letter became part of the fabric of his plans as he prepared the second edition of his book during 1855 and 1856. "Make no puns / funny remarks / Double entendres / 'witty' remarks / ironies / Sarcasms," he instructed himself in his notebook. "Only that which / is simply earnest, / meant,—harmless / to any one's feelings / — unadorned / unvarnished / nothing to / excite a / laugh / silence / silence / silence / silence / laconic / taciturn." He vows to "Avoid all the 'intellectual / subtleties,' and 'withering doubts' and 'blasted hopes' and 'unrequited / loves,' and 'ennui' and 'wretchedness' and the whole of the lurid and *artistical* and *melo-dramatic* / effects.— Preserve perfect calmness and sanity." He lists some of his casual acquaintances in New York—

> Sam (with black eyes & cap)
> Nick (black eyes 40th st—small)
> Joe (Canadian-Montreal)
> Bill Young (milkman & driver)
> George Applegate (tallest)
> English Johnny (49th st Jockey cap)
> Sam (49th st round shoulders light clothes)

—and also sketches out, in the pride of creation and mastery, his "Sun-Down Poem" ("Crossing Brooklyn Ferry") of 1856:

* The official version of the episode, laid out by Bucke in 1883 with Whitman's approval, even denied there had been any evidence "that the letter was meant to be private." Whitman became more circumspect about such matters. In 1871, after he received a flattering letter from Tennyson, he cautioned a newspaper friend, "I rely on your promise not to publish the letter, nor any thing equivalent to it." But he had no objection to printing the news that he had received such a letter. (Richard Maurice Bucke, M. D., *Walt Whitman* [Philadelphia, 1883], p. 139.)

Poem of passage / the scenes on the river / as I cross the / Fulton ferry / Others will see the flow / of the river, also, / Others will see on both / sides the city of / New York and the city / of Brooklyn / a hundred years hence others / will see them . . . The continual and hurried crowd of / men and women crossing / The reflection of the sky / in the water—the blinding / dazzle in a track from / the most declined sun, / The lighters—the sailors / in their picturesque costumes / the nimbus of light / around the shadow of my / head in the sunset

Further on, along with trial passages for another major new poem of 1856, "Song of the Broad-Axe," is an entry of a different sort. Enclosed within a large bracket, it occupies a page to itself:

"I greet you at the
beginning of a great
career"

R. W. Emerson

Whitman made several layouts of these words on binder's paper left over from the first edition before he had them stamped in gold on the spine of the second edition around August 1856. Torn out of context, gaudily displayed, this Ali Baba formula appeared to be an endorsement even of new poems Emerson could not possibly have seen. And further compounding what a Boston paper had called "the grossest violation of literary comity and courtesy that ever passed under our notice," at the end of the book Whitman once again printed the entire letter along with a vaunting essay in the form of a public thank-you:

Brooklyn *August 1856.*
Here are thirty-two poems, which I send you, dear Friend and Master, not having found how I could satisfy myself with sending any usual acknowledgement of your letter. The first edition, on which you mailed me that till now unanswered letter, was twelve poems—I printed a thousand copies, and they readily sold; these thirty-two Poems I stereotype, to print several thousand copies of. I much enjoy making poems. Other work I have set for myself to do, to meet people and The States face to face, to confront them with an American rude tongue; but the work of my life is making poems. I keep on till I make a hundred, and then several hundred—perhaps a thousand. A few

years, and the average annual call for my Poems is ten or twenty thousand—more, quite likely. Why should I hurry or compromise? . . . Master, I am a man of perfect faith.

Even the loyal and resourceful Bucke, utterly flummoxed for once, had to admit that Whitman's "they readily sold" was "a plain lie." According to Bucke's information, the first edition had "no sale" and the second "little or no sale." "If the reader goes to a bookstore," Hale had pointed out in his review, "he may expect to be told, at first, as we were, that there is no such book, and has not been." Whitman himself said he doubted "if even ten were sold" and that he ended up giving away almost all of his first edition to "friends and relatives"—"Oh, as a money matter, the book was a dreadful failure." It was a "failure" despite the vigorous deployment of his talents as an impresario with one lifelong act to manage. The lessons of P. T. Barnum's American Museum, General Tom Thumb and the Swedish Nightingale had not been wasted on him.

Whitman supplied friendly journals with the information that *Leaves of Grass* created "an extraordinary sensation in the literary world on both sides of the Atlantic"—"the emphatic commendation of America's greatest critic has been ratified by the public." And it was Whitman who wrote three anonymous reviews of *Leaves of Grass* that appeared around the end of 1855. "An American bard at last!" he announced in the *United States Review*. "Politeness this man has none, and regulation he has none. A rude child of the people!—No imitation—No foreigner—but a growth and idiom of America," he wrote in the Brooklyn *Daily Times,* and in support of these and similar claims he subjoined Lorenzo Fowler's reading of the bard's skull and personality. In the *American Phrenological Journal*, a Fowler and Wells enterprise, he cited Tennyson's poetry with admiring tolerance but predicted his own, riding the wave of the future, might yet prove "the most glorious of triumphs, in the known history of literature."

Skillfully managed, Whitman's homemade appreciations made news in their own right. A friendly journalist, William Swinton, praised him in the New York *Times* for the "manly vigor" and "brawny health" of *Leaves of Grass*. "This man has brave stuff in him. He is truly astonishing." In the course of several thousand words of careful and sensitive discussion, Swinton reported that "proof slips of certain articles written about *Leaves of Grass*" had been delivered to the *Times* office together with a copy of the first edition bound in green and gold and the printed text of a letter in which Ralph Waldo Emerson complimented the author "on the benefaction conferred on society":

> On subsequently comparing the critiques from the *United States Review* and the *Phrenological Journal* with the Preface of *Leaves of Grass* we discovered unmistakable evidence that Mr. Walt Whitman, true to the character of a Kosmos, was not content with writing a book, but was also determined to review it, so Mr. Walt Whitman has concocted both those criticisms of his own work, treating it we need not say how favorably.

Sensation generated sensation, Whitman had learned. So did neglect, if it was conspicuous enough. Later he tended to favor a history in which *Leaves of Grass*, far from "an extraordinary sensation," had been greeted in total silence or with howls of derision.

The same appreciations, along with Swinton's "exposé," were to see further service in 1860 in *Leaves of Grass Imprints*, a 64-page promotional pamphlet got up for his third edition. Their authorship was not officially acknowledged until 1893, when they appeared in a memorial volume, *In Re Walt Whitman*, edited by his literary executors. By this time Traubel and the others had almost learned to live with their mortification. "Walt, some people think you blew your own horn a lot," Traubel said to him, "—wrote puffs on yourself—sort of attitudinized and called attention to yourself quite a bit." "Do they say so? Do they? Who are 'some people?' What are 'puffs?' " the old man countered before falling back on the principle he usually invoked on such occasions, that he spoke for his work with better authority than any party of the second part. "I have merely looked myself over and repeated candidly what I saw," he said. "If you did it for the sake of aggrandizing yourself that would be another thing; but doing it simply for the purpose of getting your own weight and measure is as right done for you by yourself as done for you by another." He became testier when Traubel quizzed him about his promotions involving Emerson. What made the whole history so distressing was that Whitman had long since repudiated fealty to his "master" and had done so with such gracelessness that the sincerity of his original declaration became suspect. Perhaps having in mind only the senile relic, much given to intervals of mental removal from reality, who was worshiped by the church of

Emerson after about 1870, Whitman wrote him off as lacking in "red blood, heat, brawn, animality," as another literary gentleman in whose work America "not only plays no important figure . . . but hardly appears." Even more shocking was a statement he made in 1880:

> The reminiscence that years ago I began like most youngsters to have a touch (though it came late, and was only on the surface) of Emerson-on-the-brain—that I read his writings reverently, and ad-dress'd him in print as "Master," and for a month or so thought of him as such—I retain not only with composure, but positive satisfac-tion. I have noticed that most young people of eager minds pass through this stage of exercise. The best part of Emersonianism is, it breeds the giant that destroys itself. Who wants to be any man's mere follower? lurks behind every page.

"It is of no importance whether I had read Emerson before starting L. of G. or not," he told the faithful Kennedy in 1887, and he was barely able to control his exasperation. "The fact happens to be positively I had *not* . . . If I were to unbosom to you in the matter I should say that I never cared so very much for E.'s writings."*

Traubel was the most persistent of the disciples. "According to your letter to Emerson, you sold all the first edition," he said and

* The contrary is suggested by a manuscript note about Emerson that Whitman made (according to Bucke's dating) in the "early fifties," before *Leaves of Grass*.

He has what none else has; he does what none else does. He pierces the crusts that envelope the secrets of life. He joins on equal terms the few great sages and original seers. He represents the freeman, America, the individual. He represents the gentleman. No teacher or poet of old times or modern times has made a better report of manly and womanly qualities, heroism, chastity, temperance, friendship, fortitude. None has given more beautiful accounts of truth and justice. His words shed light to the best souls; they do not admit of argument. As a sprig from the pine tree or a glimpse anywhere into the daylight belittles all artificial flower work and all the painted scenery of theatres, so are live words in a book compared to cunningly composed words. A few among men (soon perhaps to become many) will enter easily into Emerson's meanings; by those he will be well-beloved. The flippant writer, the orthodox critic, the numbers of good or indifferent imitators, will not comprehend him; to them he will indeed be a transcendentalist, a writer of sunbeams and moonbeams, a strange and unapproachable person. (Richard Maurice Bucke, ed., *Notes and Fragments* [London, Ont., 1899], pp. 128–29.)

put the problem to Whitman squarely. "I was wondering whether you were not bluffing Emerson." "You mean bragging? Well—maybe there was something of that sort in it." Traubel held firm. "I can't forget, either, that in that same letter you call Emerson 'master.' Now you repudiate the word. What did you mean by it then? . . . You didn't need to play Emerson: he was on your side without it." "Who the hell talked about playing anybody?" Whitman fired back. "Do you mean to say I'm a liar?" "No," Traubel said. "I only mean to say that I'd like to know the real reason for 'readily sold' and 'master.' " Whitman retreated. "Maybe if you look long enough in the right place you'll find what you're looking for," another cat with a long, long tail.

But Whitman's public dealings with Emerson were imperious from the start. He blazoned the letter like a rescript from a royal cousin who—having already discerned the poet's "free & brave thought," "courage," "great power," and unshakable sense of mission as bard, prophet and oversoul—should not have been altogether surprised to find in him also the naked egotism, "the disdain and calmness," of saints and tyrants. "I am so non-polite," Whitman said in 1857, "so habitually wanting in my responses and ceremonies." His correspondent replied, "I think your judgment of yourself is rather severe"—if Emerson and his aggrieved friends had "expected *common* etiquette from you, after having read *Leaves of Grass*, they were sadly mistaken in your character."

"That was very wrong, very wrong indeed," Emerson said after his letter appeared in the *Tribune*. "Had I intended it for publication I should have enlarged the *but* very much—enlarged the but." It was "a strange, rude thing" Whitman had done, he told Samuel Longfellow, the Cambridge poet's younger brother. The distinguished geologist J. P. Lesley believed Emerson had been victimized. Lesley had found *Leaves of Grass* "trashy, profane & obscene" and "the author a pretentious ass, without decency. I was not a little vexed therefore," he wrote to Emerson, "when a few days afterward my cousin came in with a newspaper slip containing what purported to be a letter of respect and gratitude to the author over the name which of all others among American good men and thinkers I revere and love as a master and leader of the people. . . . I pronounced it at once ungenuine, a malicious jest." Friends who visited Emerson when the blazoned second edition arrived in the mail claimed that until that moment they had never seen him truly angry. His later comments on *Leaves of Grass* were to have an edge of mockery and disparagement, a clear note of "but": "an auctioneer's inventory of a warehouse," for example, "a singular blend of the Bhagvat Ghita and the New York *Herald*," "half song-thrush, half alligator." Yet even in his first dismay over the abuse of a privileged communication Emerson held true to his announced purpose, to strike his tasks and visit New York "to see my benefactor . . . to pay you my respects."

A one-word entry in Emerson's day book for December 11, 1855 —"Brooklyn"—may be the only record he kept at the time of their first meeting. Emerson called at the little wooden house on Ryerson Street. They talked for an hour or so and went off to eat dinner in New York and after, on Whitman's urging, to drink beer at Fireman's Hall, a noisy social club on Mercer Street. "Emerson's face always seemed to me so clean—as if God had just washed it off," Whitman said. He understood why Carlyle, on first meeting Emerson, had called him an "angel," "a beautiful transparent soul." When he was next in Brooklyn, probably in February 1856, Emerson called again, and they had dinner at the Astor House. But before these encounters, Emerson sought out information from others about "the strange Whitman," "our wild Whitman," "a wayward, fanciful man."

II

"As you seemed much interested in him and his work," Conway wrote to Emerson in September 1855, "I have taken the earliest moment which I can command . . . to give you some account of my visit." After a talk with Emerson, Conway had bought a copy of *Leaves of Grass* at Fowler and Wells's Boston branch on Washington Street and read it on the night steamer to New York. The next morning he looked Whitman up in the Brooklyn city directory and called at Ryerson Street; Mrs. Whitman directed Conway to the Romes' printing office. "I found him revising some proof. A man you would not have marked in a thousand; blue striped shirt, opening from a red throat; and sitting on a chair without a back, which, being the only one, he offered me, and sat down on a round of the printer's desk himself. His manner was blunt enough also, without being disagreeably so. . . . He seemed very eager to hear from you, and what you thought of his book." He was amused to hear from

Conway—his first official literary visitor, he said—about the Reverend Mr. Cyrus Bartol, a prominent Boston Unitarian, who had started to read aloud from *Leaves of Grass* in polite company but was so embarrassed that he abandoned the experiment. Apparently a man of leisure, Walt accompanied Conway to the ferry and crossed over with him. He swaggered when he walked, kept his hands in his outside pockets, and greeted as friends and equals fruit peddlers, ticket-takers, and roustabouts that he met along the way—"laboring class," Conway noted. "He says he is one of that class by choice, that he is personally dear to some thousands of such . . . who 'love him but cannot make head or tail of his book,' " a paradox that often bothered Walt. The next day Walt and Conway dined in genteel circumstances at the Metropolitan Hotel with Conway's sister and a friend of hers. Both young ladies had been exposed to passages from his book and were eager to meet him; they found his manners good and his talk entertaining. "I went off impressed with the sense of a new city on my map," Conway concluded, "just as if it had suddenly risen through the boiling sea."

Also put up to it by Emerson, Samuel Longfellow, then pastor of the Second Unitarian Church in Brooklyn, made overtures to Whitman through a mutual friend. To his surprise Whitman paid him an unannounced visit. Wearing his usual knockabout clothes the poet turned out to be "not in the least boisterous in manner," although he persisted in keeping his hat on while he sat in the minister's parlor on Pierrepont Street—

I cock my hat as I please indoors or out.

He talked freely about growing up on Long Island, his experiences as printer, newspaper editor, and now publisher of his own book. He was preparing a second edition, which Fowler and Wells were still willing to distribute for him, and meanwhile writing a series of articles—about the opera and Dr. Abbott's Egyptian Museum—for the firm's *Life Illustrated*. Longfellow was charmed, yet found him "not so handsome a person as his verses are handsome." "Isn't it a quite wonderful book?" he wrote to Hale, whose review he had just read. "Such quick and live senses, such love of men, boys, women, babies, trees—all things that are. So keen to see, so vigorous to touch with right words. Such marvellous little pictures in two or five words. Such human tenderness at times."

Unlike many poets, Longfellow might have noted, Walt dedicated his tenderness to no single lover but to a collectivity of about thirty million souls, the American church, for whom he was writing a Bible. In the course of the great illumination at the heart of *Leaves of Grass* it seemed that Walt had leaped directly from his discovery of identity and vocation to a conspicuously ample stage of generativity, and he had done this, as far as one could tell, without having experienced sustained intimacy with any one person.

O I could sing such grandeurs and glories about you!

he told his readers in one of the new poems of 1856:

Whoever you are, now I place my hand upon you, that you will be
     my poem,
I whisper with my lips close to your ear,
I have loved many women and men but I love none better than
     you. . . .
The hopples fall from your ankles.*

---

* William James quotes this "fine and moving poem," titled "To You," in the concluding chapter of *Pragmatism* (1907). Of two ways of interpreting it, "both useful," he favors the second:

> One is the monistic way, the mystical way of pure cosmic emotion. The glories and grandeurs, they are yours absolutely, even in the midst of your defacements. Whatever may happen to you, whatever you may appear to be, inwardly you are safe. Look back, *lie* back, on your true principle of being! This is the famous way of quietism, of indifferentism. Its enemies compare it to a spiritual opium. Yet pragmatism must respect this way, for it has massive historic vindication.
>
> But pragmatism sees another way to be respected also, the pluralistic way of interpreting the poem. The you so glorified, to which the hymn is sung, may mean your better possibilities phenomenally taken, or the specific redemptive effects even of your failures, upon yourself or others. It may mean your loyalty to the possibilities of others whom you admire and love so, that you are willing to accept your own poor life, for it is that glory's partner. You can at least appreciate, applaud, furnish the audience, of so brave a total world. Forget the low in yourself, then, think only of the high. Identify your life therewith; then, through angers, losses, ignorance, ennui, whatever you thus make yourself, whatever you thus most deeply are, picks its way.
>
> In either way of taking the poem, it encourages fidelity to ourselves. Both ways satisfy; both sanctify the human flux. [Cambridge, Mass., 1975, p. 133.]

But the tender lover, teacher and liberator also had a savage side. When he looked at the turmoil of American politics in 1856 and observed the slaveholding interests apparently coercing an entire free people into the "hopple, the iron wristlet, and the neck-spike," whispers and caresses gave way to a rhetoric of tumors, abscesses and running sores. In the White House Franklin Pierce "eats dirt and excrement for his daily meals, likes it, and tries to force it on The States," Whitman wrote in "The Eighteenth Presidency!" a pamphlet that he wrote, set in type, and offered in proof sheets to "editors of the independent press, and to rich persons":

> Circulate and reprint this Voice of mine for the workingmen's sake. I hereby permit and invite any rich person, anywhere, to stereotype it, or re-produce it in any form, to deluge the cities of The States with it, North, South, East and West. It is those millions of mechanics you want; the writers, thinkers, learned and benevolent persons, merchants, are already secured about to a man. But the great masses of the mechanics, and a large portion of the farmers, are unsettled, hardly know whom to vote for, or whom to believe. I am not afraid to say that among them I seek to initiate my name, Walt Whitman, and that I shall in future have much to say to them. I perceive that the best thoughts they have wait unspoken, impatient to be put in shape; also that the character, pride, friendship, conscience of America have yet to be proved to the remainder of the world.

The American Party, a haven for proslavery politicians, had chosen ex-President Millard Fillmore as its candidate in 1856, and the Democratic Party the chicken-hearted James Buchanan, both of them "disunionists," Whitman raged, political corpses that had been padded, painted and lifted out of putrid graves by "spies, blowers, electioneers, body snatchers, bawlers, bribers, compromisers, runaways, lobbyers, sponges, ruined sports, expelled gamblers, policy backers, monte dealers, duelists, carriers of concealed weapons, blind men, deaf men, pimpled men, scarred inside with the vile disorder, gaudy outside with gold chains made from the people's money and harlot's money twisted together; crawling, serpentine men, the lousy combings and born freedom sellers of the earth." In 1856 the former Democratic regular and Tammany stump speaker was to give his vote to the first presidential candidate of the Republican party, the soldier-explorer John C. Fremont. "The Eighteenth Presidency!"—*Leaves of Grass* restated as campaign literature—declared a faith that was to be put to the test all too soon. "What political denouements are these we are approaching? On all sides tyrants tremble, crowns are unsteady, the human race restive, on the watch for some better era, some divine war," he said, five years before the first cannonade in Charleston Harbor. "No man knows what will happen next, but all know that some such things are to happen as mark the greatest moral convulsions of the earth. Who shall play the hand for America in these tremendous games?"

The most successful literary couple in the United States in 1856 were the biographer James Parton, an acquaintance of Whitman's, and his wife Sara, known to a doting public as Fanny Fern. Hawthorne admired her moralizing sketches; the tendriled cover design of *Leaves of Grass*, and the germ of Whitman's title as well, may have been borrowed from her *Fern Leaves from Fanny's Portfolio*. Parton's first book, *The Life of Horace Greeley* (1855), sold about 30,000 copies within six months of publication and sent him on his way to become the preeminent biographer of his time. And so when Samuel Wells began to consider divesting himself of *Leaves of Grass* he suggested, quite sensibly, that Whitman apply to the Partons, "who are *rich & enterprizing*," and to their publishers, Mason Brothers of New York.

As a pupil at Catharine Beecher's school in Hartford Sara earned the nickname "Sal-Volatile." Her impetuousness, mercurial changes of mood, and hypersensitivity to criticism, along with her coquettish pride in her auburn ringlets and regal manners, had become more pronounced with age. She was forty-four in January 1856, when she married Parton, her third husband and eleven years her junior, and the early years of their marriage were tempestuous and quarrelsome. From the start Sara cast her eye on Walt in a cherishing way. She had not yet read his book, she wrote in her column in the *Ledger* on April 19, 1856 ("Peeps from Under a Parasol"), but she admired his "muscular throat," his broad shoulders, "that fine, ample chest of his," and his voice, "rich, deep, and clear as a clarion note. In the most crowded thoroughfare, one would turn instinctively on hearing it, to seek out its owner." Two days later she sent a clipping of this item to Walt along with a hand-delivered note.

"Leaves of Grass"

You are *delicious!* May my right hand wither if I don't tell the whole world before another week, what *one* woman thinks of you.

"Walt"? "what I assume you shall assume!" Some one evening this week you are to spend with Jemmy [Parton] & me—Wednesday?—say.

She addressed herself to *Leaves of Grass* in her column on May 10. Where Emerson has spoken, "my woman's voice of praise may not avail," she said, archly, considering that each week half a million readers of her column in the New York *Ledger* were in the habit of hanging on her words. She spoke of her "unmingled delight" in the book and extended to the author "the cordial grasp of a woman's hand." She found nothing "limp, tame, spiritless" about *these* leaves, created by a "glorious Native American" who had put aside his labors with chisel, plane, and hammer to write them and set them in type with "toil-hardened fingers." What made her review even more remarkable for 1856 was that, as a woman, she declared her unmingled delight even in poems in *Leaves of Grass* already notorious for "coarseness and sensuality." She admired them because they painted nature nude, celebrated the healthy, living human body and paid tribute to woman as "the bearer of the great fruit, which is immortality." "My moral constitution may be hopelessly tainted or—too sound to be tainted, as the critic wills, but I confess that I extract no poison from these 'Leaves'—to me they have brought only healing. Let him who can do so shroud the eyes of the nursing babe lest it see its mother's breast."

With such publicity Walt inevitably became a Topic—like William Lloyd Garrison, Fanny Kemble, and Henry Ward Beecher—at Brooklyn soirées in 1856. "I was not their kind," he said about Samuel Longfellow's circle, "so preferred not to push myself in, or, if in, to stay in." But Longfellow managed to recruit him from time to time, and although Walt had little to say at these gatherings he was nonetheless the center of attention, according to Bronson Alcott, father of Louisa May, then a fledgling author of thrillers. Survivor of high-principled experiments in living, of Pythagorean diets of squash, turnips, and cold water, Alcott had responded to *Leaves of Grass* when he first read it as if twenty years were suddenly subtracted from his age and he had broken his lifelong vows about alcohol—his empyreal prose took on a Whitman bluster.

Meeting Walt face to face for the first time in October Alcott recognized in him "the very God Pan," "an extraordinary person, full of brute power, certainly of genius and audacity," who, to Alcott's delight, came right out with it and boasted that he spoke for America and its institutions, that he had never been sick a day in his life or taken medicine and was "quite innocent of repentance and man's fall." When they had dinner together at Taylor's Saloon on Broadway early in December Walt said he was planning to go to Washington soon to report on the activities of "the pigmies assembled there at the Capitol." As for full-sized men and women he appeared to believe, if Alcott understood him correctly, that although America was pregnant with them she could presently show only two, Emerson and himself.

Walt was a guest at Longfellow's house a few days after Christmas, when Alcott, itinerant transcendentalist sage, conducted one of his celebrated "Conversations," Orphic and metaphysical rites of sometimes stupefyingly elevated discourse, chiefly monologue. Alcott noted that Walt, who was wearing his trouser bottoms tucked inside his cowhide boots, endured the evening "very becomingly," although he was "not at home, very plainly, in parlours, and as hard to tame as Thoreau."

Henry Thoreau, temporarily employed as a land surveyor at Eagleswood, a nearby Fourierist community, had joined Alcott in New York a few days after Buchanan's election victory. They shared a room at Dr. Russell Traill's Water Cure and Hydropathic Medical College, spent a day with Horace Greeley on his Chappaqua farm, and on Sunday crossed over to Brooklyn to attend services at Henry Ward Beecher's Plymouth Church. Thoreau was fidgety during the sermon on universal justice, delivered with Beecher's accustomed unction, uplift, and eye on the box office (as Whitman said, "We may well doubt whether he is not making people Beecherites instead of Christians").

After midday Sabbath dinner with the merchant Richard Manning, a friend of the eminent Unitarian divine William H. Channing, Thoreau and Alcott walked to Classon Avenue, where the Whitmans had recently moved, and in Walt's absence visited with his mother. Walt had his flaws, she admitted, but he had always been wise and good, much looked up to by his brothers and sisters as well as by any number of "common folks." He had retired from house-building and now "had no business but going out and coming in to eat, drink, write, and sleep." She believed in him "absolutely," Alcott noted. While they were talking in the kitchen Thoreau helped himself to some of her biscuits from the oven. ("He was always doing things of the plain sort—without fuss," said Walt.) They left with the assurance that her son would be at home the next morning and happy to see them. That evening at Manning's house Alcott organized a Conversation on the subject of divine, human, and sav-age attributes. Mrs. Sarah Tyndale, a Germantown abolitionist whom they had met at dinner—Alcott described her as "a solid walrus of a woman"—spoke for the human, citing in particular the candor and compassionateness of women. In any case she preferred Thoreau's savages to Alcott's blessed Jesus, in her view a "fancy man" short on gumption.

She went along with Alcott and Thoreau the next day. Walt showed them up the narrow stairs at Classon Avenue to the attic room he shared with Eddy. Their common bed was still unmade; the chamber pot beneath sat practically in full sight. Walt, it was clear, exhibited the insouciance and rectitude he cherished in ani-mals. A rough worktable and chair stood by the single window; there was a small pile of books on the mantelpiece. Pasted on the bare wall were prints of Hercules, Bacchus, and a satyr. "Which, now, of the three, particularly, is the new poet here?" Alcott asked. Walt declined to be questioned about the pictures, hinting, as Alcott understood, that perhaps he saw himself as Hercules, Bacchus and satyr combined, a sort of pantheon.

Pictures aside, he seemed not only eager to talk about himself but reluctant to have the conversation stray from the subject for long. While his visitors tried to accommodate themselves in this cheerless coop, Walt told them a great deal about himself, his daily baths (even in the coldest weather), his passion for the opera, Broadway omnibuses, their drivers and, above all, his writing. He lived for nothing else but to "make poems," he told them, pronouncing the word "pomes," and had recently brought out a new edition of *Leaves of Grass*, a copy of which he presented to Thoreau before the morning was over. These days he was in the grip of another creative surge and at the rate that he was going would soon need a third edition with about eight times as many "pieces" as the first. All in all, in place of this account of himself, he might just as well have recited a passage from "Song of the Broad-Axe":

Arrogant, masculine, näive, rowdyish,
Laugher, weeper, worker, idler, citizen, countryman,
Saunterer of woods, stander upon hills, summer swimmer in rivers
       or by the sea,
Of pure American breed, of reckless health, his body perfect, free
       from taint from top to toe, free forever from headache and
       dyspepsia, clean-breathed,
Ample-limbed, a good feeder, weight a hundred and eighty pounds,
       full-blooded, six feet high, forty inches round the breast
       and back,
Countenance sun-burnt, bearded, calm, unrefined,
Reminder of animals, meeter of savage and gentleman on equal
       terms, . . .

Thoreau had so far been mainly silent, but he could not have been put off by Whitman's egotism alone. ("I should not talk so much about myself," he had said in *Walden*, "if there were anybody else whom I knew as well.") But neither was he willing to try his strength against the other's. Observing the edgy traffic between them, Alcott was reminded of "two beasts, each wondering what the other would do, whether to snap or run." He decided that either Henry was afraid Walt would steal his woods and wild creatures or Walt had recognized that for once he had met his match in Henry, "a sagacity potent, penetrating, and peerless as his own," an ego as unbiddable, an eye as hawklike. (Emerson surmised that perhaps Henry's "fancy for Walt Whitman grew out of his taste for wild nature, for an otter, a woodchuck, or a loon.") Later in the course of what turned out to be a two-hour visit they went downstairs to the parlor, where they could be reasonably comfortable. Alcott tried to engage Walt and Henry in conversation with each other. After one relatively prolonged exchange—Walt remembered it as "a hot discussion"—they lapsed into formal compliments. Henry departed with Alcott, leaving behind with Walt a new friend and admirer, Sarah Tyndale.

Describing the encounter twelve days later, Thoreau confessed that Whitman "is essentially strange to me," a strangeness compounded by Whitman's claim during their talk that "I misapprehended him. I am not quite sure that I do." "Among the few things which I chanced to say," Thoreau reported, "I remember that one was, in answer to him as representing America, that I did not think much of America or of politics, and so on, which may have been somewhat of a damper to him." Thoreau took a much more radical view of the issues involved in "The Eighteenth Presidency!" ("It is hard to have a Southern overseer; it is worse to have a Northern one," he had said in *Walden*, "but worst of all when you are the slave-driver of yourself.") Each had his own vector of self-willed resistance to a trade- and conformity-minded society.

A great city is that which has the greatest men and women,
  If it be a few ragged huts it is still the greatest city in the world,

Walt proclaimed, and Henry, who knew about huts and life reduced to simplest terms, could approve the sentiment, if not the precise words in which it was put. "Great" was one of Walt's cherished words, while "true" was one of Henry's, and correspondingly Henry's style of dissent was often cool, mocking and precise, nervous and spare. Politics of the sort Walt concerned himself with seemed to Henry "something so superficial and inhuman that practically I have never fairly recognized that it concerns me at all." And as for obligations to the democratic mass—"I feel that my connections with and obligations to society are still very slight and transient." His gibe about America, politics "and so on," intended partly as a corrective to demagogic rant and naïve optimism, seemed to Walt only to reflect a disagreeable trait that Thoreau, in most respects an admirable person in word and deed, an ally, shared with the mighty Carlyle: "disdain" for ordinary people, "inability to appreciate the average life," altogether "a very aggravated case of superciliousness." Walt came to believe that literary New Englanders in general were snobbish, reserved and antidemocratic—"Emerson is the only sweet one among them and he has been spoilt by them" —although Thoreau, like Emerson and Alcott, had come considerably more than half way to meet him.

Thoreau had his asperities and his cold side, there was no doubt of it. "As for taking Thoreau's arm," a Concord woman remarked, "I should as soon take the arm of an elm tree." It was the elm-tree Thoreau whom Whitman saw, not the hot convert who later carried his copy of *Leaves of Grass* like a red flag through the streets of Concord. A month after their meeting, Thoreau was still discovering in "Song of Myself" and "Crossing Brooklyn Ferry" not only "more good" than he had known for a long time but the force of revelation. Whitman's "alarum or trumpet-note ringing through the American camp" Henry was to hear again when Captain John Brown rode on Harper's Ferry.

A prude when it came to sexual matters, Thoreau found "two or three pieces" in *Leaves of Grass* "which are disagreeable, to say the least; simply sensual. It is as if the beasts spoke. I think that men have not been ashamed of themselves without reason. No doubt there have always been dens where such deeds were unblushingly recited, and it is no merit to compete with the inhabitants. But even on this side he has spoken more truth than any American or modern that I know. . . . He occasionally suggests something a little more than human. You can't confound him with the other inhabitants of Brooklyn or New York. How they must shudder when they read him!" Thoreau had neither snapped nor run. "Since I have seen him I find that I am not disturbed by any brag or egotism in his book. He may turn out to be the least of a braggart of all, having a better right to be confident. He is a great fellow."

12

"The Ocean
of Life"

I

WHITMAN'S PLAN to observe "the pigmies" at Washington merged with a grander ambition during the early months of 1857. He was going to be a public teacher who addressed the President, the Congress, the Supreme Court, or the nation at large, "as some great emergency might demand," but always with a single purpose—"to keep up living interest in public questions," *"to hold the ear of the people."* "I see in my country many great qualities," he said in manuscript notes for a speech. "I see in America not merely the home of Americans, but the home of the needy and down-kept races of the whole earth . . . I say the land that has a place for slaves and the owners of slaves has no place for freemen." The public voice he had already raised in "The Eighteenth Presidency!" now had a cycle of poems to recite, "Chants Democratic and Native American," composed during a recent and ongoing surge. The "Chants" were the high-water mark of Whitman's faith in the politics of democracy; they were also a sort of handbook for oratory, a thesaurus of themes and issues. "Now we start hence," he announced in "Wander-Teachers":

We confer on equal terms with each of The States,
We make trial of ourselves, and invite men and women to hear,
We say to ourselves, Remember, fear not, be candid, promulge the
      body and the Soul,

> Promulge real things—Never forget the equality of humankind, and
>   never forget immortality;
> Dwell a while and pass on . . .

Like this one, many of the other "chants" were all too nakedly in the manner of the orator. Still, Whitman believed that with these poems in hand, along with other new "clusters," he was well on his way to achieving the final intention of *Leaves of Grass*. "In the forthcoming Vol.," he told Sarah Tyndale,

> I shall have . . . a hundred poems, and no other matter but poems—
> (no letters to or from Emerson—no notices or anything of that sort.)
> I know well enough that *that* must be the *true* Leaves of Grass—I
> think it (the new Vol.) has an aspect of completeness, and makes its
> case clearer. The old poems are all retained. The difference is in the
> new character given to the mass, by the additions.

This new volume, combining the 32 poems of 1856 with 68 new ones, was to be triple the length of its predecessor. The only difficulty was in finding a publisher. He told her he had finally decided that "Fowler and Wells are bad persons for me. They retard my book very much. It is worse than ever . . . they want the thing off their hands." She promised him that if he came to visit her in Germantown she would give him a concurring version of Fowler and Wells's "malpractice." Meanwhile she sent him fifty dollars toward buying up the plates from them.

For the same purpose, or perhaps just to help a fellow author get through the winter, James Parton, "without the least request or hint from me," offered a loan of two hundred dollars. Early in 1857 Whitman took the money and gave Parton a short-term note. It is not altogether clear what happened between then and late spring when the note fell due. Talking to Traubel about the Parton loan (or scandal, as it became), he referred darkly to "venom, jealousies, opacities: they played a big part; and, if I may say it, women: a woman certainly . . . ." When William Sloane Kennedy investigated the same loan after Walt's death he concluded that Sara Parton had been "sweet" on Walt but had suddenly developed a case of "unquenchable spite." One of Kennedy's sources was Ellen O'Connor, to whom Walt had once confided his side of the story—Ellen's unrequited passion for Walt may have made her especially attentive to the situation. The cause of Sara's about-face was "of too private a nature to be discussed," Kennedy said, but, adopting Ellen's version of events, he supplied a ponderous clue—"see Potiphar story of Bible"—that was beyond mistaking: Potiphar was the Egyptian official whose wife, failing to seduce their slave Joseph, falsely accused him to her husband, who thereupon had Joseph put in prison.

When payment time came and passed, Parton, who needed cash for a trip to New Orleans to research his biography of Andrew Jackson, put Walt's note for collection in the hands of Sara's confidant, Oliver Dyer, one of her publishers and her sole marriage witness. On June 17, acting as attorney for James Parton, plaintiff, Dyer appeared at Walt's door and seized several items of personal property, including books and the oil painting by Jesse Talbot. According to Walt, Dyer later assured him that Parton had accepted these goods in full settlement and that the debt was discharged, but despite reminders when they met again on the street and ferry Dyer never produced Parton's receipt or the canceled note; he may have kept the picture for himself. Walt considered the debt "*paid*," but Parton did not, and neither did a number of detractors who in time confounded the debt with the fact that Walt, apparently flouting the sacred code of commercial honor, had had to be sued for it at all. The legend of the Bad Gray Poet, now bill-jumper as well as immoralist and barbarian, surfaced after the war, during Walt's time in Washington. A quarter of a century later Kennedy was doing battle with Thomas Wentworth Higginson, who charged that the late poet had built a Taj Mahal mausoleum while bilking his benefactors.

When Walt saw his belongings being carted away he also saw a repetition of the Whitman and Van Velsor history of default and foreclosure. But what anger he felt he directed not at Parton, whose work he was to review favorably, but at Sara. "The majority of people do not want their daughters trained to become authoresses and poets," he commented in the Brooklyn *Daily Times* on July 9. "We want a race of women turned out from our schools, not of pedants and bluestockings. One genuine woman is worth a dozen Fanny Ferns."

Two months or so before this gibe, Walt's money troubles forced him to go back to full-time journalism; the surge of poetry that had occupied him for close to a year came to a halt. Around May 1857 he joined the staff of the *Daily Times*, a politically independent paper whose proprietor, George C. Bennett, he was to recall as "a good, generous, honorable man." The paper had endorsed the Republican presidential candidate in 1856—under Whitman it was to welcome the senatorial victory (over Abraham Lincoln) of the Illinois Democrat, Stephen Douglas, as perhaps the beginning of "a great middle conservative party" that alone could avert what the fire-eating Senator William Seward of New York was calling an "irrepressible conflict." Sometime in 1858, midway through his two years with the *Daily Times*, Whitman printed up a circular announcing his intention to travel the United States and Canada lecturing, "henceforth my employment, my means of earning my living . . ." But for the most part he seemed resigned to at least the temporary scaling-down of the bard and wander-speaker to a writer of editorials and leading articles for the citizens of Brooklyn. Years later he cited as his proudest achievement on the *Daily Times* his campaign for the construction of an integrated municipal water system. "With the consent of the proprietor, I bent the whole weight of the paper steadily . . . against a flimsy, cheap and temporary series of works that would have long since broken down, and disgraced the city."

Walt's misadventure with Parton had given him a preview of the financial panic of August 1857 and its trail of constricted credit, business failures and unemployment. He figured in October that at least 25,000 people in the cities of New York and Brooklyn would be out of work by winter and an additional 100,000, their dependents, would suffer with them. The diarist George Templeton Strong worried about preserving peace and order during the coming months. "We are a very sick people," Strong said. "The outward and visible signs of disease, the cutaneous symptoms, are many." Walt's prescription came from personal experience. "We must now return to first principles and acknowledge . . . that the money we have received is not our own until we have satisfied all just demands accruing upon it." Turning to the world of polite letters he took note of the marriage of James Russell Lowell, "one of the truest of our poets," and of the first issue (November 1857) of the new magazine edited by Lowell, the *Atlantic Monthly*, a disappointment, "inferior to the average *Harper's Monthly*. (Subsequent issues proved to be a "credit to American intellect and enterprise.") He came to the defense of Ralph Waldo Emerson, whose little poem in the *Atlantic*, "Brahma"—a "pantheistic thought" expressed "with remarkable grace and melody"—was being ridiculed for "unintelligibility." He

defended the memory of Edgar Allan Poe against the slanders of his
literary executor, Rufus Wilmot Griswold.

As an occasional sports writer he condemned prize fighting for
encouraging "rowdy turbulence instead of calm courage," celebrated
the hygienic virtues of swimming, and covered a New York-
Brooklyn baseball game in the course of which three of the local
players were disabled by injuries. He had opinions on the need for
an American national anthem as stirring as the "Marseillaise," the
vogue of chess, home aquariums, and crossword puzzles, and the
apparent completion—it failed after three weeks in service—of
Cyrus Field's Atlantic Cable, "an electric chain from the New World
to the Old." "Utterly unmoved either by covert sneers, or chilly
neglect," Field, the Hero as Promoter, had "won for himself imper-
ishable fame as the foremost man of the Nineteenth Century." ("The
cities confer with each other from across two thousand miles," Whitman had written in his 1855–56 *Leaves of Grass* notebook, "the continents talk under the waves of seas.")

Walt once said that he never had the makings of "a good journalist"—"My opinions are all, always, so hazy—so slow to come. I am
no use in any situation which calls for instant decision." As artist
and universal lover he obeyed a different rhythm:

> A noiseless patient spider,
> I mark'd where on a little promontory it stood isolated,
> Mark'd how to explore the vacant vast surrounding . . .

Gossamer cables, spun from the self and more "electric" than Cyrus
Field's, linked the single soul to distant spheres of the Not-Me. But
so far from webbing all reality Whitman and his book were still only
"a promise, a preface, an overture," he wrote in what may have been
the draft of yet another review of his own work. "Will he justify the
great prophecy of Emerson? or will he too, like thousands of others,
flaunt out one bright announcement, the result of gathered powers,
only to sink back exhausted." He had announced a brave purpose:

> I, now thirty-six years old, in perfect health, begin,
> Hoping to cease not till death.

But he also doubted his purpose:

Shall I make the idiomatic book of my land?
Shall I yet finish the divine volume [?]
I know not whether I am to finish the divine volume . . .

He lived simultaneously in different stages of the future. Antici-pating the enthusiasm his work would eventually arouse in Ger-many, he gave a copy of *Leaves of Grass* to Frederick Huene, an émigré poet employed in the *Daily Times* pressroom and got him started on a translation—Huene said that he had to give it up be-cause "I could not do justice to his ideas and thoughts." The month of the Parton foreclosure Whitman was laying plans both for the one-hundred-poem *Leaves of Grass* that he told Sarah Tyndale about and for a monumental edition that was to contain one poem for each day of the year:

> The Great Construction of the New Bible. Not to be diverted from the principal object—the main life work—the three hundred and sixty five.—It ought to be ready in 1859.

"The world is young," Emerson said. "We too must write Bibles, to unite again the heavens and the earthly worlds." He himself had set out to write a modern, secular gospel—so had Goethe and Carlyle, Thoreau in *Walden* and Melville in *Moby-Dick*. Whitman intended *Leaves of Grass* to be the trinitarian gospel of natural religion, democ-racy and science, "a modern Image-Making creation" supplying the vision without which, the Scriptural Proverbialist said, "the people perish." The author of this gospel spoke for "the people," but he was a messiah as well:

> I am not content now with a mere majority. . . . I must have the
>   love of all men and all women.
> If there is one left in any country who has no faith in me, I will
>   travel to that country and go to that one.

"Great is language," Whitman had declared in 1855, "it is the mightiest of the sciences." Now he applied himself to the study of historical linguistics with William Swinton, a professor of ancient and modern languages before he joined the *Times*. "Question for Swinton," Walt noted, "To tell me of Etruria." Another question for Swinton: "*What are the Turanian languages?*" A number of passages in the popular text on language that Swinton published in 1859, *Rambles Among Words*, bear the unmistakable imprint of Walt Whitman, an unacknowledged collaborator:

> New thoughts, new things, all unnamed! Where is the theory of literary expression that stands for the new politics and sociology? that puts itself abreast the vast divine tendencies of Science? that absorbs the superb suggestions of the Grand Opera?

Words were "metaphysical beings," evolving, vital, organic realities, Walt argued in *An American Primer*, a collection of notes for a public lecture on language. "A perfect writer would make words sing, dance, kiss, do the male and female act, bear children . . . or do any thing, that man or woman or the natural powers can do." Certain words he favored because they were the correlatives of his own preferred identity: "robust, brawny, athletic, muscular . . . resistance, bracing, rude, rugged, rough, shaggy, bearded, arrogant, haughty. These words are alive and sinewy—they walk, look, step with an air of command." While writing his *Primer* and working with Swinton Walt also collected hundreds of entries for a combined dictionary and phrase book of American English. He had in mind a sequel to Noah Webster's *American Dictionary of the English Language* (1828), in its time a revolutionary instrument in extending the boundaries of approved usage to take in "new thoughts, new things"; for Whitman these included imports from foreign tongues as well as slang—"shin-dig," "spree," "bender," "bummer," "So long" ("a delicious American—New York—idiomatic phrase at parting"). In the end, after compiling a great mass of notes under the working title *Words*, Whitman put the project aside. It threatened to divert his energies from the construction of *Leaves of Grass*, which he once described as "only a language experiment . . . an attempt to give the spirit, the body, the man, new words, new potentialities of speech."

Adamic, *Leaves of Grass* disavows sources, traditions, antecedents, and, in general, what Whitman thought of as "pictures of things" as opposed to "real things themselves." But his book continued to derive blood and fiber, even if only abreactively, from his readings in Rousseau and Voltaire, Plato, Dante, Shakespeare, Cervantes and Goethe, ancient cycles, epics, and sagas, including the Hindu. In his notebook he reminds himself to read Blackstone's *Commentaries* and Montesquieu's *The Spirit of Laws*, books on physiology, the ancient Hebrews, life and manners in Persia. He rejects as much as he accepts. *Paradise Lost* is "offensive to modern science and intelligence. . . . Think of a writer going into the creative action of the deity." "Of life in the nineteenth century it has none, any more than statues have," he says about Keats's poetry. "It does not come home at all to the direct wants of the bodies and souls of the century." He is determined, it seems, to take all knowledge for his province and bend it to his purposes. He reads *Blackwood's Magazine, Edinburgh Review, Westminster Review,* conduits for the culture and learning of Victorian England. He writes newspaper reviews of biographies of Michelangelo and Frederick the Great, a history of France and a sociological study of prostitution, Dr. David Livingstone's *Missionary Travels and Researches in Africa,* Motley's *The Rise of the Dutch Republic.* He collects and annotates chronologies and tables, articles on history, law, geography, exploration, astronomy, archaeology, the fine and applied arts, geology, life in foreign countries, oratory, religion, science. "Go study the human figure—study anatomy—study it along the wharfs and levees, the 'long shoremen, hoisting and lowering cargoes. Study the pose of the drivers of horses." He reads the proceedings of the American Association for the Advancement of Science. Absorbing the spirit of the times, he is already an evolutionist when Darwin publishes *Origin of Species.* His wonder at unimaginable vistas of existence is matched by his interest in the weekly reports of the United States Patent Office and the light they throw on "America and American character."

He dines with Sarah Tyndale's son Hector, a cultivated man who has made many trips to Europe, and he quizzes him about "where he thought I needed particular attention to be directed for my improvement—where I could especially be bettered in my poems." Tyndale tells him to emulate the massiveness and sweeping effects of York Cathedral, and Walt dutifully notes this advice together with a comment solicited from another acquaintance, that *Leaves of Grass* lacked "*euphony*—your poems seem to me to be full of the raw materials of poems, but crude, and wanting finish and rhythm." Walt records a conversation with a traveler recently returned from China who gives him an account of religion, slavery, polygamy, military service, capital punishment, tea production, and other features of life during the T'ai P'ing Rebellion.

Walt often spends hours at a stretch in the house of Mrs. Abby Price, a friend of his mother's, and virtually becomes a family member. Abby's husband runs a pickle works near the Navy Yard. She and her daughter Helen supplement his income by making the rounds of Brooklyn households, including the Beechers', with their Singer sewing machine, a recent improvement. ("What a revolution this little piece of furniture is producing," Walt exclaims—Abby and Helen, booked for a fortnight ahead, could accomplish in a day with their foot-treadle machine what would have taken a seamstress six months with a needle.) Even in this setting the work of self-improvement continues. Walt discourses on books, music, the opera, Marietta Alboni and his other favorite singers, "the spiritual nature of man," "the reforms of the age," and kindred topics. He has friendly debates about politics, patriotism, democracy, and the news of the day with a lodger in the Price house, John Arnold, whom he suspects of harboring a bias against the common people. According to Helen Price, Arnold, a retired preacher, was a Swedenborgian in allegiance although not a church member and "a man of wide knowledge and the most analytical mind of any one I ever knew." "Conversation with Mr. Arnold 7 March '57," Walt notes—the topic is the life of Dr. Joseph Priestley, the British scientist who isolated oxygen, left England because of his allegedly atheistic and Jacobin sympathies, and became one of the vexed figures in American Unitarianism. He "must have been a *real man*," Walt decides. "He was not followed by the American Unitarians. (How these Unitarians and Universalists want to be respectable and orthodox, just as much as any of the old line people!)"

One of these old-line people, the Reverend Dr. Elbert Porter, pastor of the Williamsburg Church (Dutch Reformed) and editor of the *Christian Intelligencer*, surprises Walt when they meet by assuring him that he has not only read *Leaves of Grass* but wants "*more*." He hopes that Walt has retained the Dutch Reformed faith that he must have inherited from the Van Velsor side of the family. "I not only assured him of my retaining faith in that sect," Walt reports to Sarah Tyndale, "but that I had perfect faith in all sects, and was not inclined to reject one single one—but believed each to be as far advanced as it could be, considering what had preceeded it." Porter —"the head man of the head congregation of Dutch Presbyterians in Brooklyn, Eastern District!"—is not put off by this answer and invites Walt to dinner.

"He is a born *exalté*," Helen Price says of Walt—"his *religious sentiment* . . . pervades and dominates his life." Encouraged by Arnold, Walt attends Swedenborgian meetings in New York and studies Swedenborg's life and writings. In the *Daily Times* he calls him a "precursor of the great religious difference between past centuries and future centuries," yet he is puzzled and unsatisfied by the seer's gospel—"There is something in it that eludes being stated." He had his own millennial religion, with the priest surrendering his place at the altar to the poet, "the divine literatus." Religion was too important to be the property of churches, of "Saint this, or Saint that"—it belonged to "Democracy *en masse*, and to Literature."

Dinner at the Reverend Dr. Porter's house was, if not the first, probably the last of Whitman's love feasts with the Brooklyn clergy. His editorials dealt forthrightly with the sexual needs of unmarried men and women, the benefits to be derived from licensing the brothels, and the doctrinal debate over slavery then raging in the Baptist Ecclesiastical Council. After two years on the *Daily Times*, during the summer of 1859 Whitman "resigned his place," Huene said, "in consequence of articles which were very unfavorably criticized by ministers and church people, about which he had quite a philosophic debate with Mr. Bennett." Whitman remembered Bennett warmly, but ministers and church people in general—"institutional, official, teleological goodness"—he came to "thoroughly disapprove of—hate—yes, even fear."

II

A few days after his thirty-eighth birthday in 1857 Walt noted as his "principal object—the main life work . . . the Great Construction of the New Bible." The following year he marked his birthday with an appeal, largely addressed to himself, for "a revolution in American oratory" and the emergence of "a great leading representative man, with perfect power, perfect confidence in his power . . . who will make free the American soul." In later years he commemorated the season of his birthday with other declarations of purpose. But in 1859, when he became forty and rounded the potently symbolic turn into his fifth decade, he entered a dark period. "It is now time to *stir*," he wrote in a notebook entry for June 26, "*To Stir* . . . and get out of this *Slough*." He was either out of work or about to be. For the next three years he was to squeeze out a living—perhaps six or seven dollars a week supplemented by occasional windfalls from his poems—selling articles to the papers. "The New Bible" that was to have been ready in 1859 was still an intention only. The brave persona announced in 1855—hero-poet, "the equable man . . . the equalizer of his age and land"—had not stood up under the test of change and experience, had become more tragic in vision, less "insolent" in certainty.

The poet who walks the Long Island seashore in "As I Ebb'd with the Ocean of Life"—published as "Bardic Symbols" when Whitman managed to sell it to James Russell Lowell at the *Atlantic* in April 1860—hears not a song of celebration but a dirge sung by "the voices of men and women wrecked." His "bardic symbols" are drift, debris, rotting leaves, windrows, tufts of straw, froth, bubbles, the wrack and waste left by the restless intercourse of his father, the land, and his mother, the sea. The poet imagines himself a corpse:

(See! from my dead lips the ooze exuding at last!
See—the prismatic colors, glistening and rolling!)

His work has come to no more than "a trail of drift and debris":

. . . I have not once had the least idea who or what I am,
But that before all my insolent poems, the real Me still stands
    untouched, untold, altogether unreached,
Withdrawn far, mocking me with mock-congratulatory signs and
    bows,
With peals of distant ironical laughter at every work I have written
    or shall write.
Striking me with insults till I fall helpless upon the sand.

He had failed to understand his own meanings. In his language primer he said that American young men were capable of "a wonderful tenacity of friendship, and passionate fondness for their friends" but possessed "remarkably few words [or] names for their friendly sentiments . . . they never give words to their most ardent friendships." The phrenologists had a word for these friendships, "adhesiveness," as distinguished from "amativeness" or "sexual love." The cluster of forty-five poems that became "Calamus" in the third (1860) edition of *Leaves of Grass* was Whitman's attempt to find a language for "manly love" and "the love of comrades," the ultimate democracy of the heart. Poems celebrating "the most copious and

close companionship of men" were themselves "Chants Democratic." On the eve of the Civil War he was still able to imagine a
"continent indissoluble" and raised above sectional strife:

> Affection shall solve every one of the problems of freedom,
> Those who love each other shall be invincible,
> They shall finally make America completely victorious, in my name.

In Fowler's diagram of the human brain "adhesiveness" had been
symbolized by two women embracing, but from now on men too
were to embrace, greet one another with a kiss, walk hand in hand.
More splendid than a warship under full sail or the great city itself
was the sight

> . . . of two simple men I saw to-day, on the pier, in the midst of the
> crowd, parting the parting of dear friends,
> The one to remain hung on the other's neck, and passionately kissed
> him,
> While the one to depart, tightly prest the one to remain in his arms.

Among the hundred poems Whitman had in hand by June 1857
were a dozen or so that were the "embryon" of "Calamus." *Leaves of
Grass* arose in part from an accommodation with death that had now
begun to fail. Love itself became bound up with his own death—

> Scented herbage of my breast,
> Leaves from you I yield, to be perused best afterwards,
> Tomb-leaves, body-leaves, growing up above me, above death,
> Perennial roots, tall leaves . . .

—and with the death of others. He seems almost to foresee the war
years he spent ministering to the torn bodies of soldiers:

> Of him I love day and night, I dreamed I heard he was dead,
> And I dreamed I went where they had buried him I love—but he
> was not in that place,
> And I dreamed I wandered, searching among burial-places, to find
> him,
> And I found that every place was a burial-place,
> The houses full of life were equally full of death . . .

One day he told Helen Price about a young man he knew on the *Daily Times* who had destroyed their "delightful silent friendship" by expressing his affection "in heated language." Psyche must not look on Cupid, Walt said to Helen, citing Apuleius' legend of baffled love. The secret of his own nights and days, as he wrote in "Calamus," could be got at only by "faint indirections."

> Among the men and women, the multitude, I perceive one picking
>   me out by secret and divine signs,
> Acknowledging none else—not parent, wife, husband, brother,
>   child, any nearer than I am;
> Some are baffled—But that one is not—that one knows me.

> Lover and perfect equal!
> I meant that you should discover me so, by my faint indirections,
> And I, when I meet you, mean to discover you by the like in you.

From his schoolteaching years on, Walt had assumed an anomalous sort of role—tender, protective and nurturing—with his pupils, his brothers, even casual acquaintances who are now only names in his notebooks. "You grew up with me," he tells the "passing stranger" in one of the "Calamus" poems.

> We two boys together clinging,
> One the other never leaving . . .

In his soul he wished adolescence could have been frozen in time and adulthood deferred. Yet as pseudo father, as guardian, husband, brother, lover, and comrade to young men, he invested himself in their growth away from him into independence and heterosexual maturity.

For years the chief support of his homoerotic fantasy of "two boys together clinging" had been Jeff, his one "real brother" and only "understander." After their trip to New Orleans Jeff followed Walt's example and worked in the printing trades in Brooklyn and New York. When he began to be interested instead in land surveying and civil engineering he went to work for the municipal water system that Walt was lobbying for so vigorously in *Daily Times* editorials. Jeff was proud of *Leaves of Grass* and passionate about opera and music. "Flocks of ideas," Walt wrote in an early notebook, "beat their countless wings and clutch their feet upon me, as I sit near by where my brother is practising at the piano," which Walt had bought for him. "God's blessing on your name and memory, dear brother Jeff!" Walt wrote in 1890, remembering "how we loved each other —how many jovial good times we had!" Jeff "was very much with me in his childhood & as big boy greatly attached to each other till he got married" (in 1859, the year of Walt's "slough"), moved to his own place with his wife, Mattie, and had his own family; he was Walt's ward and companion no longer. Walt loved Mattie as if she were a sister—she and Louisa Whitman were "the two best and sweetest women I have ever seen or known or ever expect to see." Still, his cherished and exclusive relationship with Jeff had been fractured along with his understanding of "adhesiveness," now divested of its sanctions in brotherly love.

While Walt was in his slough, it seemed to him, as Carlyle had written about his own sickness unto death, that "all things in the heavens above and the earth beneath were but the boundless jaws of a devouring monster." Confronting his bare-stripped heart, the brave and joyous poet yielded to the profoundest melancholy.

The record of that confrontation is, in part, the cycle of twelve lyrics that Whitman composed during the spring and summer of 1859 and preserved in fair copies in his notebook, perhaps with no thought, at first, of ever printing them. They were "fit to be perused," he noted privately, "during the days of the approach of Death." He called them "sonnets," not because of their form, which is typically irregular, but perhaps because they make up a narrative sequence, like Shakespeare's, that dramatizes—not necessarily *recounts*—a passionate attachment to a younger man; the roots in literal happening of Whitman's attachment are just as obscure as those of Shakespeare's, but the *pattern* of this attachment prefigures Whitman's baffled love affairs over the next two decades. "Live Oak with Moss," as Whitman originally titled this cluster, is an act of self-exploration and in the end a recognition of his homosexuality at least as desire if not fulfillment. It is Whitman's poetry, and not any overt act that one can point to, that defines his nature. "Live Oak with Moss" records a perception of possibilities—and a crisis of "intimacy," in Erik Erikson's terms, auguring "a deep sense of isolation and consequent self-absorption"—with which Whitman must come to terms.

"Burning for his love whom I love," as he writes in the opening poem, he compares himself in the second to the Louisiana live oak, emblem of his trip South with Jeff,

> Uttering joyous leaves all its life, without a friend, a lover, near,
> I know very well I could not.

He goes on to make a series of contrasts between success, as he had first thought of it, and a newly discovered kind of happiness:

> For the one I love most lay sleeping by me under the same cover in
>   the cool night,
> In the stillness, in the autumn moonbeams, his face was inclined
>   toward me,
> And his arms lay lightly around my breast—And that night I was
>   happy.

Yet these exquisitely tender and simple commemorations are also fearful. The poet who had once declared it was enough for him "to strike up the songs of the New World" and spend his life singing them now says his lover is jealous of these songs "and withdraws me from all but love":

> I am indifferent to my own songs—I will go with him I love,
> It is to be enough for us that we are together—We never separate
>   again.

He strikes through his "impassive exterior." He wishes to be re-membered "ages hence" as one

> Who was not proud of his songs, but of the measureless ocean of
>   love within him—and freely poured it forth,
> Who often walked lonesome walks, thinking of his dear friends, his
>   lovers,
> Who pensive, away from one he loved, often lay sleepless and
>   dissatisfied at night,
> Who knew too well the sick, sick dread lest the one he loved might
>   secretly be indifferent to him.

He tells of "sullen and suffering hours . . . hours of my torment" when he fears that his lover is lost to him. His lover may little know

. . . the subtle electric fire that for your sake is playing within me

and that threatens the poet himself:

> For an athlete is enamoured of me—and I of him,
> But toward him there is something fierce and terrible in me, eligible
> to burst forth,
> I dare not tell it in words—not even in these songs.

About the time that he finished this sequence Whitman planned another "string of Poems (short, etc.)," this one "embodying the amative love of woman—the same as Live Oak Leaves do the passion of friendship for man." The new cluster—"Enfans d'Adam" in the 1860 *Leaves of Grass* and later, fortunately, "Children of Adam"—is often lacking in felt emotion. In an athletic, impersonal, even ideological way, these poems celebrate "stalwart loins" and the act of procreation.

> A woman waits for me—she contains all, nothing is lacking,
> Yet all were lacking, if sex were lacking, or if the moisture of the
> right man were lacking . . .

Even when his cadences are at their most passionate he seems to be addressing a lover who is not so much a woman as she is a prospect of history.

> Through you I drain the pent-up rivers of myself,
> In you I wrap a thousand onward years,
> On you I graft the grafts of the best-beloved of me and of
> America . . .

Walt the "wander-speaker" and "wander-teacher" has set out to bestow on the people of the New World the freedom Adam and Eve knew in the Garden of Eden before they knew shame; their children were to be readmitted to Paradise by embracing the flesh and nakedness. There is an implicit sexual politics in "Children of Adam": before homosexual men can freely enjoy even a little happiness with one another, heterosexual men and women together must be able to enjoy a great deal more. But perhaps he had put his own balance in jeopardy by discovering so much in "Live Oak with Moss." He did not reserve these "sonnets" for the days of approaching death. Instead he broke up their loose narrative sequence and in the 1860 *Leaves of Grass* distributed them among poems that dealt with adhesiveness in a less intimate and perturbed way, in the manner of a social document. He changed the collective title to the symbolically cognate "Calamus," after the aromatic rush native to the Eastern and Southern states and also known as "sweet flag." "The recherché or ethereal sense of the term," he explained in 1867, "arises probably from the actual Calamus presenting the biggest & hardiest kind of spears of grass." But as early as 1855, in a passage celebrating "some of the spread of my body," he had made it plain that the primary features of calamus were not only its leaf and pine-tinged rootstalk but also its floral spike, phallic as the thrusting live oak haired with moss:

> Root of washed sweet-flag, timorous pond-snipe, nest of guarded
> duplicate eggs, it shall be you,
> Mixed tussled hay of head and beard and brawn it shall be you,
> Trickling sap of maple, fibre of manly wheat, it shall be you;
> Sun so generous it shall be you,
> Vapors lighting and shading my face it shall be you,
> You sweaty brooks and dews it shall be you,
> Winds whose soft-tickling genitals rub against me it shall be you,
> Broad muscular fields, branches of liveoak, loving lounger in my
> winding paths, it shall be you,
> Hands I have taken, face I have kissed, mortal I have ever touched,
> it shall be you.

For the rest of his life Whitman grappled with the self-doubts and renunciations of "Live Oak with Moss." With several younger men he was to know a certain love along with "sullen and suffering hours," hours of "sick, sick dread." But just as he had put himself in danger through poetry, through poetry he reconstituted himself and moved on to a new stage of composure and understanding. One evening late in the autumn of 1859 he called on the Prices, bringing with him the manuscript of a new poem that he told them was "about" a mockingbird and based on a real incident. At his urging,

Preacher Arnold and Abby Price read it aloud under the lamplight. Then he read it himself, and to their surprise—they thought of him as a demigod—he asked them for their criticisms, even though he seemed to be satisfied with what he had written. Helen Price remembered her introduction that evening to "Out of the Cradle Endlessly Rocking" as one of the high points of her life. A little later, across the ocean, a young Algernon Swinburne read this major new poem in the 1860 *Leaves of Grass* and called it "the most lovely and wonderful thing I have read for years and years . . . such beautiful skill and subtle power." (His own "Triumph of Time," evoking "the great sweet mother, Mother and lover of men, the sea," bore the impress of Whitman's elegy.)

The poet of "Out of the Cradle" again throws himself on the Paumanok sands of "Bardic Symbols." He is "a man—yet by these tears a little boy again" as he remembers the white arms of the breakers and the mockingbird's song of love, loss, and the transcending of loss.

He poured forth the meanings which I, of all men, know.

The outsetting bard is always to hear "the cries of unsatisfied love" and be the chanter of "pains" as well as "joys," of

. . . the fire, the sweet hell within,
The unknown want, the destiny of me.

13
Meteors

I.

"OUT OF THE CRADLE ENDLESSLY ROCKING" (then titled "A Child's Reminiscence") appeared at Christmastime 1859 in the *Saturday Press*, an urbane literary weekly entering upon its second year of sparkling but incurably penniless existence. "Our readers may, if they choose," said the editor's note, "consider as our Christmas or New Year's present to them, the curious warble by Walt Whitman . . . on our First Page." Within days the Cincinnati *Daily Commercial* rejected the gift out of hand as "unmixed and hopeless drivel" and described it as a disgrace to the *Saturday Press*, "the prince of literary weeklies, the *arbiter elegantiarum* of dramatic and poetic taste." In response the *Saturday Press* provided Whitman with a forum for an anonymous, distinctly truculent defense of "Out of the Cradle" and other "mystic leaves." "Walt Whitman's method in the construction of his songs," he declared, "is strictly the method of the Italian Opera," which on first hearing inevitably confounded listeners accustomed to "tunes, piano-noises, and the performances of the negro bands." He went on to say that *Leaves of Grass* has "not yet been really published at all" but soon would be—in a new edition "far, very far ahead" of the first and second in "quality, quantity, and in supple lyric exuberance . . . The market needs to-day to be supplied—the Great West especially—with copious thousands of copies."

The editor of the *Saturday Press*, Henry Clapp, had "stepped out from the crowd of hooters—was my friend: a much needed ally," Whitman was to say, "a pioneer, breaking ground before the public was ready to settle." "My dear Walt," Clapp wrote in March 1860, when the book was in press, "I can do a great deal for it. I meant to have done more last week." Apart from paid advertisements, between December 1859 and December 1860 Clapp published at least twenty-five items by or about Whitman, including reviews, commentary, controversy, imitations and parodies; he was party to a literary and domestic skirmish over *Leaves of Grass* conducted in four successive issues during June 1860. It was occasioned by a review that Clapp had solicited from one of Walt's fervid admirers, Juliette Hayward Beach of Albion, New York, a writer and copublisher, with her husband Calvin, of the Orleans County *Republican*. Calvin apparently anticipated or intercepted her article and sent in his own, which declared that Walt was a sexual predator, had the moral sensitivities of "a stock-breeder," and ought to kill himself. Clapp must have been drunk when this arrived in the mail—he printed it over Juliette's name on June 2 along with an editorial note congratulating himself for giving houseroom to "every variety of opinion" on a volatile topic. On the ninth, Clapp offered a "Correction"—"the article in our last issue . . . was written, not by her, but by Mr. Beach." On the sixteenth he published some panegyrics from a Philadelphia paper as a corrective to Beach's "lump of ——— you know what," as Whitman called it. Juliette's own article, this time signed "A Woman," finally appeared on the twenty-third. She hailed the "deep spiritual significance" of *Leaves of Grass* and predicted that it would inevitably become "the standard book of poems in the future of America." "God bless him," she said. "Walt Whitman on earth is immortal as well as beyond it." It is not known how the Beaches' marriage managed to weather this public squabble—"quite a stew," Whitman said. According to Ellen O'Connor he carried on a romance by mail with Juliette and addressed a tender poem to her, "Out of the Rolling Ocean the Crowd":

> . . . I salute the air, the ocean and the land,
> Every day at sundown for your dear sake my love.

"Walt is a genius," "*de facto* our poet laureate," a friendly newspaper editor announced. "Emerson has said so, Clapp says so." Clapp found in *Leaves of Grass* the radical boldness, social and artistic, that had been his touchstone since he visited Paris in his thirties and settled in New York to become king of literary bohemia. In the twilight vault of Pfaff's beer cellar under the Broadway pavement near Bleecker Street Clapp ruled over a court of clever people—his associate editor Thomas Bailey Aldrich ("wittiest man in seven centuries," Mark Twain was to say); Fitz-James O'Brien, the author of some remarkable short stories thought the equal of Poe's; George Arnold, poet and popular literary farceur; and the leading humorist of the day, Artemus Ward. "Brandy and soda," Clapp proposed when Ward showed him a telegraphed inquiry from a lecture agent, "What will you take for forty nights in California?" Whitman remembered the drama critic Edward G. P. Wilkins as "noble, slim, sickish, dressy, Frenchy," exquisitely attentive to his linen, cravat and gloves, outwardly little more than "a dude," but still as outspoken an admirer of *Leaves of Grass* as two less fashionable habitués of Pfaff's, the Polish patriot Count Adam Gurowski and John Swinton of the New York *Times* (William's brother and also Orson Fowler's son-in-law). "My beloved Walt," Swinton was to write, recalling his first sight of a copy of *Leaves of Grass* at a Brooklyn newsstand in 1855. "I got it, looked into it with wonder, and felt that there was something that touched the depths of my humanity. Since then you have grown before me, grown around me, and grown into me." (That letter had "sugar in it," Walt said.)

Bohemia's queen was the famous Charleston beauty Ada Clare, actress and writer, who had borne a child out of wedlock by the composer-piano virtuoso Louis Moreau Gottschalk and now boldly signed hotel and ship registers, "Miss Clare and Son." She was the New Woman—liberated in sex, expression, and parity with men—that Whitman celebrated in his poems. When she died in 1874 under horrible circumstances—of hydrophobia, from the bite of a lap dog in a theatrical agent's office—he was "inexpressibly shocked." "Poor, poor Ada Clare," he said, contemplating her "gay, easy, sunny, free, loose, but *not ungood* life." She was one reason he loved the South. Another was the New Orleans-born Adah Isaacs Menken, also a writer and actress and the heroine of celebrated off-stage adventures. When Walt first knew her at Pfaff's she was going through a legally inconclusive divorce from the first of her four husbands and a legally inconclusive marriage to the second, the American heavyweight titleholder known in and out of the ring as The Benicia Boy; as soon as their child was born the Boy denied they had ever been married.

She found a refuge from misery in her starring role in the Byronic melodrama *Mazeppa*. Wearing the merest G-string over flesh-tinted tights she rode off into the stage sky lashed to the back of a "fiery steed of Tartary." *Mazeppa* made her internationally famous as the "naked lady," "the most perfectly developed woman in the world." She was photographed with Alexandre Dumas *père* in a pose suggesting considerable intimacy and was reputed to be the morganatic bride of King Charles of Württemberg; she attempted a liaison with Swinburne but failed to earn the ten-pound reward that Dante Gabriel Rossetti offered if she got Swinburne into bed. In form and subject matter *Infelicia*, her volume of verse published shortly after she died in Paris in 1868, showed Whitman's liberating influence. Writing in the New York *Sunday Mirror* in 1860, she said he stood "centuries ahead of his contemporaries," a champion of "liberty and humanity" through whom a "Divine voice" spoke. She predicted that like Poe, another maligned writer "swimming against the current," Whitman would have "marble statues" erected in his honor.

"Supper at Pfaff's cellar, Broadway, 1860," noted one of Whitman's partisans, E. C. Stedman. Among the fourteen present were Whitman, Clapp, Arnold, O'Brien, Wilkins, Ada Clare, Aldrich and Artemus Ward. By 1877, Stedman counted, nine of the fourteen were dead—"No other list of names that I remember could show such a death roll." Clapp died in poverty, an alcoholic, after making an attempt to revive the *Saturday Press* in 1865. "This paper was stopped in 1860 for want of means," he announced. "It is now started again for the same reason." Within a period of two weeks before it went under for good, the *Saturday Press* published Whitman's "O Captain! My Captain!" and a dazzling story soon to become world famous as "The Celebrated Jumping Frog of Calaveras County." Not even one complete file of Clapp's brilliant paper survives. Sardonic to the end he datelined his occasional correspondence from the municipal drying-out ward on Blackwell's Island "My Cottage by the sea." Artemus Ward, George Arnold, and Ned Wilkins were in their early thirties when they died—they had been victims, eventually, of what Whitman called "a restless craving for mental excitement," of the desperate expenditures of energy and the unrelenting anxiety about subsistence that were among the harsher aspects of literary bohemia and made the inhabitants "bad husbands" and strangely ineffectual. "They won't hurt you," Ward told a newcomer at Pfaff's. "These are Bohemians. A Bohemian is an educated hoss-thief!"

It had been a doubtful proposition from the start whether bohemia as a way of life and art, an alternative to philistinism on the one side and an emerging genteel tradition on the other, could ever be naturalized in New York after being transplanted from Paris. So thought William Dean Howells, then a young literary postulant from Ohio (with a deliberate scorn for transappalachian niceties Clapp identified him as a "Hoosier"). When Howells recounted his recent pilgrimage to Concord and described himself and the revered Hawthorne as shy, Clapp said, "Oh, a couple of shysters." Clapp described Horace Greeley as "a self-made man that worships his creator," and a certain clergyman as awaiting "a vacancy in the Trinity." Clapp may have been mulling over his mistrust of middle-class society in general when he advised, "Never tell secrets to your relatives. Blood will tell." Howells was repelled by Clapp's flippancy and cynicism, his malign glitter and his contempt for New England culture. Uncomfortable in his presence, Howells was proud nonetheless to be one of his writers. "It was very nearly as well for one to be accepted by the *Press* as to be accepted by the *Atlantic*, and for the time there was no other literary comparison."

The night in August 1860 that Howells overcame his dread of Gomorrah and visited Pfaff's fragrant temple of tobacco smoke, lager beer, Rhine wine, wurst and sauerkraut, the main fact that lodged itself in his mind was the presence of Walt Whitman, in a rough flannel coat with baggy trousers, seated at his ease a little apart from the main table but clearly the object of a cult. For almost three years after he left the Brooklyn *Times* Whitman was one of the regulars at Pfaff's. "Don't you miss *Walt*," he asked his mother when this period in his life was over, "loafing around & carting himself off to New York, toward the latter part of every afternoon?" A friendly editor described him on his way to Pfaff's crossing over on the Fulton Ferry, gazing at the harbor traffic and the forests of masts, exchanging small talk with the deckhands. Perched on the box alongside the driver he rode the Broadway stage uptown to Bleecker Street, and helped collect the fares. He was so much a feature on the Broadway line that a Boston paper reported he was earning his living as a driver, just as Robert Burns had done as a ploughman.

The Pfaff's style of steady drinking and late suppers was not naturally Whitman's. Neither was the social and conversational style there, "cutting" and barbed, although he could not help being infected by it and later had to swear off smart talk along with hot rum punches. "Yes, Tom, I like your *tinkles:* I like them very well," he said, referring to Aldrich's book of poems, *The Bells,* published the same year as *Leaves of Grass.* Aldrich, in turn, thought of him as a charlatan; so did the drama critic William Winter—"little Willie Winter, miserable cuss!" as Whitman remembered him, "a dried up cadaverous schoolmaster"—who described *Leaves of Grass* as "odoriferous." "My own greatest pleasure at Pfaff's," Whitman recalled, "was to look on—to see, talk little, absorb. I never was a great discusser, anyway." He was comfortable not in center ring with Clapp but at one of the less conspicuous tables with a group of young men about town—easy in their manners, fairly well educated, middle or upper class—whom he banteringly named the Fred Gray Association. A doctor's son, Frederick Schiller Gray served as a general's aide-de-camp during the War and later became a doctor, as did Charles Russell; another member of the "Association," Hugo Fritsch, was the son of the Austrian consul; others were merchants, brokers, sportsmen. In 1863, when they had all been scattered by the War, Walt envisioned a time when they would all meet again, "allowing no interloper, & have our drinks & things, & resume the chain & consolidate & achieve a night better & mellower than ever."

Despite some qualifications, Whitman had found in that gloomy vault beneath the sidewalk a more *gemütlich* and inspiriting social base than Abby Price's Brooklyn parlor. His dealings with editors reflected a new self-regard and assertiveness. "The price is $40. Cash down on acceptance," he said when he submitted a poem to *Harper's* in January 1860. "Should my name be printed in the programme of contributors at any time it must not be lower down than third in the list. . . . I reserve the use of the piece in any collection of my poems I may publish in the future." Since the summer he had been working with his friends Thomas and Andrew Rome, who set new poems in type for him and pulled proof copies, and he was still planning to reissue *Leaves of Grass* himself when he received a letter, again addressed to him in care of Fowler and Wells, from a new publishing firm in Boston. Crusaders of a transcendentalist bent, the partners were at that moment riding the crest of their first and only success,

James Redpath's rushed-into-print tribute to the abolitionist martyr, Captain John Brown:

Boston Feb 10/60

Walt Whitman

Dr Sir.   We want to be the publishers of Walt. Whitman's poems—Leaves of Grass.—When the book was first issued we were clerks in the establishment we now own. We read the book with profit and pleasure. It is a true poem and writ by a *true* man.

When a man dares to speak his thought in this day of refinement —so called—it is difficult to find his mates to act amen to it. Now *we* want to be known as the publishers of Walt. Whitman's books, and put our name as such under his, on title-pages.—If you will allow it we can and will put your books into good form, and style attractive to the eye; we can and will sell a large number of copies; we have great facilities by and through numberless Agents in selling. We can dispose of more books than most publishing houses (we do not "puff" here but speak *truth*).

We are young men. We "celebrate" ourselves by acts. Try us. You can do us good. We can do you good—pecuniarily.

Now Sir, if you wish to make acquaintance with us, and accept us as your publishers, we will offer to either buy the stereo type plates of Leaves of Grass, or pay you for the use of them, in addition to regular copy right.

Are you writing other poems? Are they ready for the press? Will you let us read them? Will you write us? Please give us your residence.

Yours Fraternally
Thayer & Eldridge

"It is quite curious, all this should spring up so suddenly, aint it[?]" Walt remarked to Jeff about this "first proposition" and the publishing agreement that it led to. By Thursday March 15 he was in Boston to begin seeing the Thayer and Eldridge edition of his work through the press. On Saturday Emerson called at Whitman's rented room downtown, greeted him with great courtesy, and among the other hospitalities offered that day registered him for guest reading privileges at the Boston Athenaeum. Before their late midday dinner they walked for two hours crossing and recrossing the Common under the bare elms along the Beacon Street slope.

II

Willingly or unwillingly Emerson had stood godfather to *Leaves of Grass* and had a certain stake in its growth; as they walked along the Common he urged Whitman to reconsider some of his new poems. It was not "Calamus" that troubled him. A long time back Emerson had had a crush on a fellow undergraduate at Harvard, Martin Gay, nicknamed "Cool" by their classmates, and wrote ardent poetry about him as well as a fantasy laced with sexual symbolism. But that episode had since become layered-over, and Emerson apparently found Whitman's celebrations of the love of comrades as unexceptionable as a later generation found Housman's *A Shropshire Lad*. (Whitman too possessed something that appeared on no phrenologist's chart, a "very large" bump of denial.) Instead of "Calamus," Emerson cited such provocations to public complacency as the poem "To a Common Prostitute"—

> Be composed—be at ease with me—I am Walt Whitman, liberal and
>   lusty as Nature,
> Not till the sun excludes you, do I exclude you,

—and numerous passages in "Children of Adam." The times and the taste of the times were not ready, he argued, talking "the finest talk that was ever talked," as Whitman recalled, and marshaling his points as if they were an army corps advancing. The mere mention of nakedness and the limbs of the body was taboo. Sexuality, especially the sexuality of women, was an unholy secret, to be kept, not flaunted, as Whitman insisted upon doing. Just to hint at masturbation was unthinkable, and yet here was Whitman's

> . . . young man that wakes, deep at night, his hot hand seeking to
>   repress what would master him—the strange half-welcome
>   pangs, visions, sweats,
> The pulse pounding through palms and trembling encircling fingers
>   —the young man all colored, red, ashamed, angry.

A daring metonymy, that last clause, and yet by any standards these lines were intolerable, provided that anyone was willing to admit to knowing what they were about in the first place. How would an educated reader, man or woman, already put off by Whitman's lawless meters and elastic morals, respond to "stalwart loins," "loveflesh swelling and deliciously aching," "limitless limpid jets of love hot and enormous," "phallic thumb of love," "bellies pressed and glued together with love"?

"Emerson was not a man to be scared or shocked . . . by the small-fry moralities, the miniature vices," Whitman said. The objections Emerson raised were in the end neither moral nor aesthetic; they were purely prudential. In practical, commercial terms, meaning the sales and unimpeded circulation of the new book, there was a limit to how far Whitman could exercise the "free and brave thought" and "the courage of treatment" Emerson had saluted in his famous letter. That limit was set by the public, or at any rate by their watchdogs, and for the sake of *Leaves of Grass* in 1860 and the predictable future, Emerson concluded, the objectionable passages must be excised, a small enough concession, considering the larger work that was at stake. "But would there be as good a book left?" Whitman asked. Emerson thought this over briefly. "I did not say as good a book," he answered. "I said a good book."

"If I had cut sex out," Whitman reflected years later, "I might just as well have cut everything out"—sex was the root of roots, the life beneath the life, and without "Children of Adam" the entire structure of *Leaves of Grass* would come down about his ears. Whitman's heterosexual poems often ranted and postured, and they had their share of camp, but in the aggregate they strove for the candor, simplicity and joy unashamed of Adam in the Garden. "The dirtiest book in all the world is the expurgated book," Whitman told Traubel. "Expurgation is apology—yes, surrender—yes, an admission that something or other was wrong. Emerson said expurgate—I said no, no. . . . I have not lived to regret my Emerson no." As they finished walking the unpaved paths below the State House, Whitman felt "down in my soul the clear and unmistakeable conviction to disobey all, and pursue my own way." He told Emerson that *Leaves of Grass* would have to stand or fall as it was, and with this settled, they went to the American House in Hanover Square and had "a bully dinner."

Even the bohemian Henry Clapp favored the side of prudence. "I think you would have done well to follow Mr. Emerson's advice," he told Walt, and in the *Saturday Press* he conceded that *Leaves of*

Grass "does not lack passages which should never have been published at all." W. W. Thayer and Charles W. Eldridge, the young Boston publishers, had no such hesitations, "have not asked me at all what I was going to put into the book," Walt told Abby Price after he had been away for two weeks, "just took me to the stereotype foundry, and [gave] orders to follow my directions." He spent about three hours a day correcting proof and also exercising much of the authority of a publisher in matters of typography, decorations, paper, presswork, and binding. "Thayer & Eldridge . . . think every thing I do is the right thing."

"It is quite 'odd,' of course," Walt said about the physical appearance of the new *Leaves of Grass,* a thick octavo volume of 456 pages bound in orange cloth blind-stamped with symbolic devices repeated in the text as tailpieces: the western hemisphere of the globe—Whitman's "New World"—surmounting a swash of clouds; a rising sun with nine spokes of light; a pointing hand with a butterfly—symbol of the soul, resurrection, metamorphosis, and eternal life—perched on the index finger.* As before and in subsequent editions, the title page omits the author's name; in Whitman's distinctive manner it gives the date of publication as "Year 85 of The States (1860–61)." The uncaptioned frontispiece portrait, by a New York friend, Charles Hine, has little of the casualness and arrogance of 1855. The poet wears a Byronic collar with a flowing tie and looks like Victor Hugo, Garibaldi, or an opera singer, and although the face has been softened and bloated by the engraver the picture still gives an

---

* The same symbolic butterfly appears on the backstrip of *Leaves of Grass* in 1884, a year after Whitman sat for a studio photograph (used as frontispiece in 1889) that showed him with a butterfly apparently perched on his right forefinger. "I've always had the knack of attracting birds and butterflies and other wild critters," Whitman said about this picture to William Roscoe Thayer. "They know that I like 'em and won't hurt 'em and so they come." Thayer had wondered what a summer butterfly was doing inside a photographer's studio so cold that Whitman was wearing a heavy sweater. In all probability, as Esther Shephard showed in 1938, Whitman was holding an object that turned up in Harned's collection of Whitman memorabilia at the Library of Congress, "a small cardboard butterfly with a loop of fine wire attached, by means of which it could be fastened to a finger." Printed on the blue, red, green and yellow wings of Whitman's cardboard butterfly are lines by the hymnologist John Mason Neale, author of "Jerusalem the Golden" and "Good King Wenceslas." (William Roscoe Thayer, "Personal Recollections of Walt Whitman," *Scribner's Magazine,* June 1919, p. 685; Esther Shephard, *Walt Whitman's Pose* [New York, 1938], pp. 250–52.)

impression of buffalo strength. Perhaps "the best of all," Whitman
said about Hine's original. "I was in full bloom then: weighed two
hundred and ten pounds. . . . I was in the best of health: not a thing
was amiss: I was like Carlyle's man, who, asked the state of
his system, exclaimed: 'System? system? what have I to do with
systems?' "

Its prose prefaces discarded, *Leaves of Grass* at last stood on its own
"with no other matter but poems," as Whitman had promised Sarah
Tyndale in 1857, "no letters to or from Emerson—no notices, or
any thing of that sort." For the first time it had organic unity and
canonical finality as a theory of art and a sort of whole duty of man
for the nineteenth century and after. Some of the earlier poems had
been revised. "Song of Myself," untitled in 1855 and "Poem of Walt
Whitman, an American" in 1856, was now simply "Walt Whitman."
The "Sun-Down Poem" of 1856 takes on its final and memorable
title, "Crossing Brooklyn Ferry." There are 124 new poems, including "Out of the Cradle Endlessly Rocking" (now "A Word Out of
the Sea") and three major clusters, "Chants Democratic," "Enfans
d'Adam," and "Calamus." The book opens with an important new
poem, "Proto-Leaf" (later, "Starting from Paumanok") in which
Whitman celebrates his birth and antecedents, his program, and his
themes—democracy, love, comradeship, natural religion, personality. He is the chanter of "the Many in One":

> Take my leaves America!
> Make welcome for them everywhere, for they are your own
>   offspring . . .
> O now I triumph—and you shall also . . .

In "So Long!", the closing poem of 1860 and of every subsequent
edition, Whitman, like Osiris, announces the end of one life cycle
and the beginning of a posthumous one:

> It appears to me I am dying,

he says.

> My songs cease—I abandon them,
> From behind the screen where I hid, I advance personally.

251

This is no book,
Who touches this, touches a man,
(Is it night? Are we here alone?)
It is I you hold, and who holds you,
I spring from the pages into your arms—decease calls me forth.

O how your fingers drowse me!
Your breath falls around me like dew—your pulse lulls the tympans
       of my ears,
I feel immerged from head to foot,
Delicious—enough.

And so *Leaves of Grass* was being "really published" for the first time. "Altogether, Jeff," Walt wrote in May, shortly before the first finished copies were ready at the bindery, "I am very, very much satisfied that the thing, in the permanent form it now is, looks as well and reads as well (to my own notion) as I anticipated—because a good deal, after all, was an experiment—and now I am satisfied." His slough was well behind him. "I feel as if things had taken a turn with me, at last."

He was planning to come home to Brooklyn for a while after the book was produced and then go off on a tour of New England—"partly business and partly for edification"—and a visit to his sister Hannah in Burlington. Meanwhile, he lived in a lodginghouse for two dollars a week and took his meals at a restaurant—"7 cents for a cup of coffee, and 19 cts for a beefsteak," he complained to Jeff, *"and me so fond of coffee and beefsteak."* He liked Boston far more than he had anticipated and found the Yankees friendly, generous, and intelligent.

The city was a center of abolitionism and high principles, but it was also conformist in culture, manners and dress, cramped by *"respectability,"* "squeezed into the stereotype mould." "Everybody here is so like everybody else," he told Abby Price, "and I am Walt Whitman!—Yankee curiosity and cuteness, for once, is thoroughly stumped, confounded, petrified, made desperate." He enjoyed the "immense sensation" that he created when, with his lounging gait and rough clothes, he walked the Common, or Washington Street, the city's Broadway, where Thayer and Eldridge had their offices, or solemn State Street, where he admired the Doric United States Custom House—"one of the noblest pieces of Com[mercial] architecture in the world." He must have been the most unaccountable visitor that ever entered the solemn premises of the Boston Athenaeum.

Several Sundays Whitman went to morning services at the Seamen's Bethel, a Methodist chapel down by the harbor, to hear the celebrated sailor-preacher Father Taylor. Emerson had compared Taylor with Demosthenes, Shakespeare and Burns—"He shows us what a man can do." In *American Notes* Dickens wrote at length about Taylor, who had served ten years and more before the mast, and whose "imagery was all drawn from the sea, and from the incidents of a seaman's life." Taylor is Father Mapple in *Moby-Dick*. For Whitman, the sixty-seven-year-old chaplain was the only "essentially perfect orator" he had ever heard, Elias Hicks, Daniel Webster and Henry Clay not excepted. With a Bible under his arm Taylor paced his quarterdeck of a pulpit exhorting his crew to bend their shoulders to the capstan and weigh anchor for heaven. "When Father Taylor preach'd or pray'd," Whitman said, thinking of his own ambitions as a poet speaking the language of daily life, "the rhetoric and art, the mere words, (which usually play such a big part) seem'd altogether to disappear, and the *live feeling* advanced upon you and seiz'd you with a power before unknown." Like Elias Hicks, Taylor had tenderness and passion along with "a curious remorseless firmness, as of some surgeon operating on a belov'd patient."

Walt was much missed at Pfaff's that spring, as he heard from Clapp and the others. They awaited an open letter from him reporting on his progress in Boston. He could have told them he had found another phalanx of partisans there. Thayer and Eldridge, his first "real" publishers, idolized him and counted themselves among those "men and women who *love* thee and hold thy spirit close by their own." Walt told Jeff that his publishers were sure that *Leaves of Grass* would prove "a valuable investment, increasing by months and years, not going off in a rocket way, (like 'Uncle Tom's Cabin')," a quixotic comparison on Eldridge's part that had the effect of both calming and overexciting his author. In addition to an elegantly turned-out book, which they advertised as "*a specimen of beautiful and honest workmanship*, beyond anything of its price ever yet printed . . . in the world," they distributed, gratis, a 64-page promotional brochure of reviews and criticisms of *Leaves of Grass*, including Whitman's unsigned panegyrics. At times even this author felt that Thayer and Eldridge were going too far. He read one specimen of hypomanic advertising copy, offered to revise it, took it back to his room, and put in in the fire. By mid-June the first printing of one thousand copies was nearly gone, a second was at the binder's, and Thayer and Eldridge were shaping new marketing plans despite what they described as "considerable opposition among the trade . . . partly born of prejudice and partly of cowardice." Disregarding these and other storm warnings in the conduct of their business, they continued to believe that they could create for *Leaves of Grass* "an overwhelming demand among the mass public." Toward the end of the year, with their business only a few months away from bankruptcy, they announced a new volume of Whitman's poems "in preparation," *Banner at Day-Break*.

In 1855–56 the poet and abolitionist novelist John Townsend Trowbridge had discovered *Leaves of Grass*. It was as bold as "nature itself," he decided, the work of "a sort of Emerson run wild," but he had his doubts, too: why did this poetry have to be so formless and obscure, and at times so coarse? When he heard from a mutual friend on Washington Street that its author was reading proof in the stereotype foundry around the corner, he expected to meet a mid-century Socrates or King Solomon, and he was disappointed. He found Whitman in a dingy office in the company of a sickly-looking boy from his lodginghouse—"I am trying to cheer him up and strengthen him with my magnetism." About rereading his own work in proof he said, "I am astonished to find myself capable of feeling so much." But for the most part Whitman was "the quietest of men," scarcely forthcoming or interested in making an impression. He agreed to spend Sunday at Trowbridge's house on Prospect Hill in Somerville, and this time he opened up, talking freely about himself and his early life, his friendships with "the common people" and the aspirations that smoldered within him for so long.

"The book he knew best was the Bible," Trowbridge noted, "the prophetical parts of which stirred in him a vague desire to be the bard or prophet of his own time and country." Finally Emerson brought him to "a boil." Trowbridge came away from this spellbinding narrative, one of Whitman's variant versions of history, with a picture that stayed with him: the thirty-five-year-old carpenter holding a sandwich in one hand and in the other a volume of Emerson that revealed to him "his greatness and his destiny." Never a Whitman idolator, however, Trowbridge had no hesitation about teasing him. Preparing a salad for their dinner, Trowbridge was doing what the critics would soon be doing, "Cutting up *Leaves of Grass.*" In the waning afternoon, when Whitman said it was time for him to be getting back to Boston, someone tried to cover the face of the clock. "Put *Leaves of Grass* there," Trowbridge said. "Nobody can see through that." He noticed that his visitor enjoyed any allusion to his poems, serious or jocular.

Trowbridge was to be Whitman's lifelong friend and admirer, like Charley Eldridge and like Eldridge's most dependable author, James Redpath, who in addition to his John Brown biography published two other "anti-slavery works" with the firm during 1860. "I love you, Walt!" Redpath wrote in June, after Walt returned to Brooklyn. "A Conquering Brigade will ere long march to the music of your barbaric yawp." The eventual leader of the brigade, and the most important figure in Whitman's later public career, was yet another house author, the twenty-eight-year-old William Douglas O'Connor. "My dear, dear friend," Whitman was to write of him, "and staunch (probably my staunchest) literary believer and champion from the first." A poet turned short-story writer, O'Connor had just been dismissed from his editorial job on the *Saturday Evening Post* in Philadelphia; like Whitman, he had been enticed back to his native Boston by Charley Eldridge, who offered him twenty dollars a week for six months to write a polemical novel about the fugitive-slave laws (with the exception of one literary book on their list, *Leaves of Grass*, Thayer and Eldridge were movement publishers). With Harriet Beecher Stowe always at the back of his mind, Eldridge held out the characteristic promise that O'Connor's novel, *Harrington: A Story of True Love*, published in November, would sell at least 25,000 copies and earn a great deal of money all around.

"As I saw and knew him then," Whitman wrote about their first meetings in Boston during the spring of 1860, O'Connor "was a gallant, handsome, gay-hearted, fine-voiced, glowing-eyed man; lithe-moving on his feet, of healthy and magnetic atmosphere and presence, and the most welcome company in the world. He was a thorough-going anti-slavery believer, speaker, and writer, (doctrinaire,) and though I took a fancy to him from the first, I remember I fear'd his ardent abolitionism—was afraid it would probably keep us apart." They came to the issues of race and slavery with such opposed understandings that it was difficult at times to believe they were dealing with the same social realities.

Walt noted that although there were fewer blacks in Boston than in New York or Philadelphia, they were treated with what seemed to him great liberality. They worked side by side with whites at their jobs, he said, mentioning in his notebook a black compositor in a printing office, a black clerk employed at the State House, and a black lawyer from Chelsea named Anderson, "quite smart and just as big as the best of them." Blacks were served at public eating places in Boston and "Nobody minds it," he said, adding, "I am too much a citizen of the world to have the least compunction." As depicted in O'Connor's novel, the black people of Boston were "shut out of the mechanic occupations; shut out of commerce; shut out of the professions," excluded from omnibuses, theaters, schools, churches, "decent dwellings" and "decent graveyards"—in short, from everything except "the gallows and the jail." O'Connor believed with Emerson that the execution of John Brown made "the gallows glorious like the Cross." Whitman, too, acknowledged a martyrdom but did not allow it "to spoil my supper," as he remarked to Traubel. "I see martyrdoms wherever I go . . . Why should I go off emotionally half-cocked only about the ostentatious cases?" Northern abolitionists and Southern fire-eaters had more in common than they thought: they were all "quite insane."

In 1860 O'Connor did not share Whitman's forebodings about these and other issues that were to stand between them. The Christmas before he came to Boston he read "Out of the Cradle" in the *Saturday Press* and exclaimed, "What astonishing beauty, what reach of spiritual sight—what depth of feeling." Now he found "health and happiness" merely in being near "the great Walt." "He is so large & strong—so pure, proud, & tender, with such an ineffable *bon-hommie* & wholesome sweetness of presence: all the young men & women are in love with him."

III

Fire, smoke, and thunder from cannon in New York harbor saluted the arrival on June 16 of an American warship bringing diplomat princes of Japan. Bareheaded, impassive as bronze statues, they rode in open barouches in a Broadway pageant and submitted to the stares of "million footed Manhattan unpent," Whitman wrote. In one of his new poems, he had described the bard of *Leaves of Grass* looking westward toward Asia and mankind's ancient home:

Inquiring, tireless, seeking that yet unfound,
I, a child, very old, over waves toward the house of maternity, the
  land of migrations, look afar,
Look off the shores of my Western sea—having arrived at last where
  I am—the circle almost circled.

Now he merged himself in seas of bystanders and celebrated these
exotic visitors as more than envoys come to exchange ratifications of
a commercial treaty opening imperial ports to traders from the
young republic half a world away. The Japanese diplomats were
"lesson-giving princes," and their eastward passage was as symbolic
as Columbus' westward passage. The harbor salutes, the cheering
crowds, the Broadway buildings festooned with pennants and bunt-
ing marked the completion of a spiritual rondure.

. . . the orb is enclosed,
The ring is circled, the journey is done,

Whitman wrote in "The Errand-Bearers," printed in the New York
Times on June 27.

On the twenty-eighth another "wonder," Isambard Kingdom Bru-
nel's mammoth steamship, *Great Eastern*, "swam up my bay." Half
a million people watched the floating city—five times larger than
any vessel yet launched, a triumph of seagoing luxury and engineering hubris—arrive on its maiden voyage from Southampton and tie
up at its North River pier at Bank Street; berthed, it stretched for
nearly three city blocks. On October 11 the Prince of Wales, first
royalty to visit New York, the future King Edward VII, rode up
Broadway from Bowling Green in an open carriage drawn by six
champing horses. Whitman addressed him in a poem.

There in the crowds stood I, and singled you out with attachment.

The ball in the Prince's honor at the Academy of Music was the
nobbiest social event in the city's history, and for a while, like the
manias for the Japanese envoys and the *Great Eastern*, Prince-mania
reigned until the inevitable reaction set in. George Templeton
Strong was positive that "by Monday next, the remotest allusion to
His Royal Highness will act like ipecac."

On November 15 a meteor was sighted in the day sky over New

York. "Omens, Auguries and Portents Dire," said the *Times* headline, playing on traditional associations with wars and disasters. Whitman was to commemorate 1859–60 as "Year of Meteors," "year all mottled with evil and good—year of forebodings."

What am I myself but one of your meteors?

After the brilliant promise of the spring his affairs had taken a steep downward turn along with those of his allies. "Just now I am in a state of disrepair even in respect to getting out another issue of the S.P.," Henry Clapp told him, "and all for want of a paltry two or three hundred dollars." On Walt's advice, Thayer and Eldridge advanced Clapp enough to tide him over, and in the belief they could make the *Saturday Press* "pay," even in a time of "literary flunkeyism," they offered to assume financial control. Before the year was out Clapp's valiant journal suspended publication, and Thayer and Eldridge themselves went bankrupt. They were forced to turn over their stock (including the plates of *Leaves of Grass*) to Horace Wentworth, a Boston publisher Thayer considered "an illiterate man" and a "bitter and relentless enemy." Although the partners had promised to sell *Leaves of Grass* to "the mass public" and do its author some good, "pecuniarily," it remained a rogue book that the critics attacked and that earned for Whitman only about $250 in royalties. *Banner at Day-Break*, the bravely titled new book that Thayer and Eldridge had announced in June, entered a limbo from which it emerged, as *Drum-Taps*, after five years of war.

By Whitman's reckoning, "Year of Meteors," the last peacetime year, was set in its course in December 1859, when John Brown, "an old man, tall, with white hair," mounted the scaffold in Virginia. It ended in November 1860, when Abraham Lincoln won the presidency.

The American poet-hero of the 1855 *Leaves of Grass* preface prefigured the archangel that Lincoln was to become in Whitman's imagination. Like Lincoln, this bard spoke for the common people and for his country as a union, "a teeming nation of nations." He was "the equable man," "the equalizer of his age and land." His spirit was marked by largeness, simplicity, candor and generosity. In time of peace he spoke "the spirit of peace. . . . In war he is the most deadly force of the war." (When the war came Whitman served as if he had already heard Lincoln's call "to bind up the nation's wounds; to care for him who shall have borne the battle.") The "I" of "Song of Myself" has the sad and brooding quality that Whitman associated with the martyr-president:

> I am the man, I suffer'd, I was there . . .
> Agonies are one of my changes of garments . . .
> Behold, I do not give lectures or a little charity,
> When I give I give myself.

But the same "I" also displays Lincoln's shrewd, homely humor:

> Walt you contain enough, why don't you let it out then?
> I do not say these things for a dollar or to fill up the time while I
>   wait for a boat . . .

In his 1856 political tract, "The Eighteenth Presidency!" Whitman said that he would be "much pleased to see some heroic, shrewd, fully-informed, healthy-bodied, middle-aged, beard-faced American blacksmith or boatman come down from the West across the Alleghanies, and walk into the Presidency, dressed in a clean suit of working attire, and with the tan all over his face, breast, and arms." Whitman stopped short of mentioning "honest Abe" and "the rail-splitter," but he called for his Lincolnesque candidate, "the Redeemer President of These States," to come from "the real West, the log hut, the clearing, the woods, the prairie, the hillside." Two years before he first mentioned Lincoln by name—in a brief newspaper item about the debates with Stephen Douglas—Whitman had begun to shape a legend. *

---

* In the words of Stephen B. Oates, Lincoln's most acute and evenhanded modern biographer,

> The truth was that Lincoln felt embarrassed about his log-cabin origins and never liked to talk about them. . . . he had worked all his adult life to overcome the limitations of his frontier background, to make himself into a literate and professional man who commanded the respect of his colleagues. So if he ever discussed his childhood or his parents, said William Herndon, Lincoln's law partner, "it was with great reluctance and significant reserve. There was something about his origin he never cared to dwell on." (Stephen B. Oates, *With Malice Toward None: The Life of Abraham Lincoln* [New York: New American Library, 1978], p. 4.)

With Lincoln soon to take the oath of office, Whitman made notes for a "Brochure" that was apparently intended for the same purpose as "The Eighteenth Presidency!"—

Two characters as
of a Dialogue
between A.
L____n and
W. Whitman
—as in ? a dream
? or better
Lessons for a
President elect
—Dialogues between W. W.
and "President elect"

The "dream" yielded in February 1861 to Whitman's first sight of Abraham Lincoln. General Scott and Senator Seward were warning of assassination plots and a rebel takeover of Washington; despite the whistle-stop speeches, the bands and banners and cheering crowds along the way, Lincoln's twelve-day journey from Springfield to the inaugural platform at the Capitol was cautious, even furtive. Opposition papers in New York City, a nest of Copperheads, called him a baboon and a yokel. Whitman was certain "many an assassin's knife and pistol lurk'd in hip or breast-pocket there, ready, as soon as break and riot came." On the afternoon of the nineteenth Lincoln arrived by train from Albany and drove with his party to the Astor House in a line of shabby hacks. From the top of a Broadway omnibus that had been stopped with all other traffic, Whitman watched him step out on the sidewalk, stretch his arms and legs, and scan the vast crowd of thirty or forty thousand people who, by some tacit agreement to avoid provocations of any sort, preserved "a sulky, unbroken silence."

"I had, I say, a capital view of it all, and especially of Mr. Lincoln, his look and gait—his perfect composure and coolness—his unusual and uncouth height, his dress of complete black, stovepipe hat push'd back on the head, dark-brown complexion, seam'd and wrinkled yet canny-looking face, black, bushy head of hair, disproportionately long neck, and his hands held behind him as he stood observing the people. He look'd with curiosity upon that immense sea of faces, and the sea of faces return'd the look with similar curiosity." After another relieving stretch or two, Lincoln turned and disappeared through the broad entrance of the Astor House, "and the dumb-show ended." "As I sat on the top of my omnibus, and had a good view of him, the thought, dim and inchoate then, has since come out clear enough, that four sorts of genius, four mighty and primal hands, will be needed to the complete limning of this man's future portrait—the eyes and brains and finger-touch of Plutarch and Eschylus and Michel Angelo, assisted by Rabelais."

George Templeton Strong heard the first news of the bombardment of Fort Sumter late in the evening of April 12—"I can hardly hope that the rebels have been so foolish and thoughtless as to take the initiative in civil war and bring matters to a crisis." Toward midnight Whitman was walking down Broadway after attending a performance of Verdi's *A Masked Ball* at the Academy of Music when he heard the newsboys crying their extras. He bought a paper and read it under the blaze of gaslights outside the Metropolitan Hotel. Years later, probably with Verdi's opera in mind, he was to say that the war had not been "a quadrille in a ball-room." It had turned the entire country, North and South, into "one vast central hospital." But in April 1861, like Strong and most Unionists, he looked on the upstart rebellion in South Carolina with disbelief and scorn. One government official went on record as predicting the whole thing would blow over in sixty days. Whitman noticed that volunteers being mustered in at the Brooklyn armory "were all provided with pieces of rope, conspicuously tied to their musket-barrels, with which to bring back each man a prisoner from the audacious South, to be led in a noose, on our men's early and triumphant return!" The quadrille ended, the "soft opera-music changed" for good, "the real war" began, on July 21, when Beauregard, Johnston, and Stonewall Jackson routed the Union army at Bull Run.

IV

"The city seems to have gone suddenly wild and crazy," Strong wrote on April 20. A quarter of a million New Yorkers turned out for a rally in Union Square honoring Major Robert Anderson, the hero of Fort Sumter. George Whitman, not usually given to impulsive acts, put his cabinetmaker's tools in the safekeeping of his employer and signed up for one hundred days service as a militia private. "The Women and children make a regular practice of saying as we pass them hurrah for Jeff Davis," he was soon writing from camp near Baltimore. "Mother you need not wory about me at all as I am not in want of anything and I dont believe we shal see any fighting at all." His one-hundred–day hitch became four years. By the time he was mustered out he had fought in twenty-one engagements or sieges, spent five months in Confederate military prisons, and seen most of his comrades killed. "His preservation and return alive seem a miracle," said his brother Walt, a superheated Union patriot from the start. He once got into a scuffle at Pfaff's with George Arnold who had proposed the toast, "Success to Southern Arms!" (This was apparently meant in the spirit of the burlesque war correspondence Arnold was writing under the pseudonym "McArone.") But Walt at forty-two, over-age for the ranks and without any discernible qualifications to be an officer, had little desire to go for a soldier.* "I had my temptations," he recalled, "but they were not strong enough to tempt. I could never think of myself as firing a gun or drawing a sword on another man."

When enlistment fever swept New York after Sumter, Walt vowed to put himself on a new footing.

> Thursday April 18, '61.
> I have this hour, this day, resolved to inaugurate for myself a pure, perfect, sweet, cleanblooded robust body by ignoring all drinks but water and pure milk—and all fat meats, late suppers—a great body —a purged, cleansed, spiritualized, invigorated body.

But this hydropathic discipline was at least as literary as it was patriotic. "So far, so well," he wrote when he turned forty-two, "but the most and the best of the Poem I perceive remains unwritten, and is the work of my life yet to be done. The paths to the house are made—but where is the house itself?" The summer of Bull Run he took his customary vacation trip to Greenport. He baited his line with fiddler crabs and hauled in blackfish from the dock; he sailed to Montauk, ran along the beach, feasted on sea-bass chowder and

* Whitman reported to Emerson from Washington in January 1863 that "the Army (I noticed it first in camp, and the same here among the wounded) is *very young*—and far more American than we supposed—ages range mainly from 20 to 30—a light sprinkling of men older—and a bigger sprinkling of young lads of 17 and 18."

stewed pullet, and slept in a furled sail. He once told Kennedy that he had stopped going to Pfaff's after his scuffle with George Arnold, but he remained a fixture there during the first twenty months of the war, even though the temple of wurst and lager now had a darker symbolism:

> —The vault at Pfaff's where the drinkers and laughers meet to eat
> and drink and carouse
> While on the walk immediately overhead pass the myriad feet of
> Broadway
> As the dead in their graves are underfoot hidden
> And the living pass over them . . .

"Walt Whitman is at Pfaff's almost every night," John Burroughs noted in October 1862. "He lives in Brooklyn, is unmarried, and 'manages,' Clapp says, to earn 6 or 7 dollars per week writing for the papers. He wrote a number of articles for the 'Leader' some time ago, on the Hospitals. . . . I do not like to believe that he can write in any other style than that of 'Leaves of Grass.' "

At Pfaff's during the first September of the war Walt read aloud from the manuscript of a new poem that was about to be published, almost simultaneously, in the Boston *Evening Transcript*, the New York *Leader*, and *Harper's Weekly*.

> Beat! beat! drums!—blow! bugles! blow!
> Through the windows—through doors—burst like a ruthless force,
> Into the solemn church, and scatter the congregation,
> Into the school where the scholar is studying;
> Leave not the bridegroom quiet—no happiness must he have now
> with his bride,
> Nor the peaceful farmer any peace, ploughing his field or gathering
> his grain,
> So fierce you whirr and pound you drums—so shrill you bugles
> blow. . . .

But his other poems on similar or related timely themes met with less success at the hands of the editors. James Russell Lowell at the *Atlantic* turned down three for a reason that, as stated, struck Whitman as "a bit odd." "We could not possibly use [them]," Lowell said less than six months after Sumter, "before their interest,—which is of the present,—would have passed." "Years that whirl I know not whither," reads one verse fragment dealing with 1861 and 1862, a time when his granite foothold in purpose gave way to quicksand.

Schemes, politics fail—all is shaken—all gives way
Nothing is sure.

The affirmation that follows this had a melodramatic ring:

Only the theme I sing, the great Soul,
One's-self, that must never be shaken—that out of all is sure,
Out of failures, wars, deaths—what at last but One's self is sure?
With the Soul I defy you quicksand years, slipping from under my
      feet.

The irrepressible Poet of America who never had to put his name on his title pages was now to be found listed in the Brooklyn directory as "copyist," soon to be his formal occupation in wartime Washington. He earned his six or seven dollars a week as the anonymous or pseudonymous author of potboiling articles, including a twenty-five–part history of Brooklyn, much of it filler.

The *Leader* articles that Burroughs mentioned show Whitman in the role of loafer-observer recording images of the city (the series title is "City Photographs"). He describes the Bowery's mix of Germans and Jews, circus people, sports and rowdies; the auction halls, carpet shops, restaurants and beer halls; the cheap hotels where the prudent guest sleeps with his wallet under the pillow. The shooting galleries now offer prospective soldiers free instruction by "an accomplished professor." The Bowery was more pungent and idiomatic than the fashionable avenues. "Things are in their working-day clothes, more democratic, with a broader, jauntier swing, and in a more direct contact with vulgar life." But it was in the wards of New-York Hospital, then off Broadway at Pearl Street, that Whitman found vulgar life reduced to its barest terms of survival. He also found there his wartime vocation—hospital visitor, nurse, "wound-dresser."

Arous'd and angry, I'd thought to beat the alarum, and urge
      relentless war,

But soon my fingers fail'd me, my face droop'd and I resign'd
     myself,
To sit by the wounded and soothe them, or silently watch the dead.

The novelist Anthony Trollope, one of several distinguished visitors to New-York Hospital around this time, fainted during his tour;
this happened frequently. "Amputations are going on—the atten-
dants are dressing wounds," Whitman was to write from the Washington hospitals. "As you pass by, you must be on your guard
where you look." What sustained him, along with the surgeon's
"remorseless firmness" of will that he admired in Father Taylor's
preaching, was a curious dreamlike remoteness, a fractured consciousness that separated the "impassive hand" holding bandages,
water and sponges from the "burning flame" in his heart. Once
again, as in "The Sleepers," he seemed to be wandering all night
in his vision, dreaming in his dream all the dreams of the other
dreamers. Now, "in silence, in dreams' projections," he wrote in
"The Wound-Dresser," he saw himself threading his way through
suffering:

From the stump of the arm, the amputated hand,
I undo the clotted lint, remove the slough, wash off the matter and
     blood,
Back on his pillow the soldier bends with curv'd neck and side-
     falling head,
His eyes are closed, his face is pale, he dares not look on the bloody
     stump,
And has not yet looked on it.

The New-York Hospital staff gave him the freedom of the wards,
the offices and examining rooms, the pathological museum with its
appalling specimens of tumors and hypertrophied limbs. He was
present, he said with professional aplomb, at "several very fine operations"—a cystotomy for a bladder stone bigger than the end joint
of his thumb, an amputation, routine procedure then for limb
wounds and injuries.

What is removed drops horribly in a pail.

Before the chloroform sponge did its work more than one patient saw a bulky man with an iron-gray beard standing a little to one side of the operating table.*

By the spring of 1862 one wing of New-York Hospital had already been taken over by the military. But for a year or so before then Walt had been coming to the wards to see sick and injured stage-driver friends, members of that "strange, quick-eyed, and wondrous race" whose nicknames he recited like Homer's catalogue of captains and contingents—Broadway Jack, Dressmaker, Balky Bill, Old Elephant, Tippy, Pop Rice, Yellow Joe. One of the house officers, Dr. D. B. St. John Roosa, said that he and the other doctors "always wondered" why Walt was interested in "the class of men whom he visited." They questioned him over off-duty beers at Pfaff's. He told the doctors little more than that his heart went out to poor devils who had to work outside in all weathers, and besides there was much he had learned from them. He was more willing to talk about his poems, and he gave Roosa a copy of *Leaves of Grass*. "I must confess that I did not understand them then," Roosa recalled many years later, "any more than I understand the character of the man who wrote them."

"There is a lady come from time to time," Walt reported from the hospital. "She brings illustrated and other papers, books of stories, little comforts in the way of eating and drinking, shirts, gowns, handkerchiefs, &c. I dare not mention her name, but she is beautiful. . . . She is clearly averse to the eclat of good works, and sometimes, to avoid show, sends her gifts by a servant." It may have been this dark lady of the wards who, two weeks earlier, had her servant

---

* Amputation was to become "the trade-mark of Civil War surgery. . . . More arms and legs were chopped off in this war than in any other conflict in which the country has ever been engaged. According to Federal records, three out of four operations were amputations, and there is good reason to believe the same figures obtained in the Confederacy. At Gettysburg, for an entire week, from dawn to twilight, some surgeons did nothing but cut off arms and legs. . . . For what it is worth, legend has it that younger soldiers often saved their limbs by hiding a pistol under a pillow and drawing it out at the opportune time." As a hospital visitor Whitman intervened on a number of occasions; a paragraph in the New York *Tribune* in 1880 quotes a grateful veteran of the Union Army—"This is the leg that man saved for me." (Stewart Brooks, *Civil War Medicine* [Springfield, Ill., 1966], p. 97; the *Tribune* item is from Richard Maurice Bucke, M.D., *Walt Whitman* [Philadelphia, 1883], p. 37.)

deliver a letter to Walt "At Pfaff's Restaurant, BroadWay, New York." Beyond her letter, signed "Ellen Eyre," she remains unidentified. She cited a "fancy I had long nourished for you" and represented herself as a Dumas heroine in a world of assignations and disguises.

> My social position enjoins precaution & mystery, and perhaps the enjoyment of my friends society is heightened while in yielding to its fascination I preserve my incognito, yet mystery lends an ineffable charm to love and when a woman is bent upon the gratification of her inclinations—She is pardonable if she still spreads the veil of decorum over her actions. . . . I trust you will think well enough of me soon to renew the pleasure you afforded me last P.M. and I therefore write to remind you that there is a sensible head as well as a sympathetic heart, both of which would gladly evolve wit & warmth for your direction & comfort—You have already my whereabouts & my home —It shall only depend upon you to make them yours and me the happiest of women.
>
> I am always
Yours Sincerely
Ellen Eyre.

According to one conflation of things known and things conjectured, Walt first met Ellen Eyre, now married, when she was Miss Ellen Grey of Brooklyn, an actress he saw onstage at the Bowery Theatre in 1857 and whose photograph—identified as that of "a young N. Y. actress," and "an old sweetheart of mine"—hung over the mantelpiece at Mickle Street. But in his written record, at any rate, Ellen Eyre makes her first appearance by name in her letter of March 25, 1862, and her last three and a half months later in a notebook entry, memorandum of an encounter with a Fifth Avenue stage driver, another probable link between her and the hospital wards:

> *Frank Sweeney* (July 8 '62) 5th Ave. Brown face, large features, black moustache (is the one I told the whole story to about Ellen Eyre)— talks very little.

The barest facts about Ellen Eyre, not to mention "the whole story," tail off into nothingness.

At the end of September, Walt spent an evening at Pfaff's with Fred Gray, home on a two-day furlough after fighting at Antietam. "He gave me a fearful account of the battlefield," he noted. For a few hours on September 17, with George's 51st New York Regiment leading the attack, McClellan had had Lee on the run but then drew back, the worst blunder of the war to date. By the time the cannon finished their red business at Antietam the Shenandoah Valley echoed with the screams of twenty thousand Union and Confederate wounded; a long, bloody stalemate lay ahead. On December 13, another blunderer, General Ambrose Burnside, led the Army of the Potomac in a suicidal charge on the Confederate entrenchments at Fredericksburg. George's regiment advanced in formation over a narrow plain so completely enfiladed, said an enemy gunner, that "a chicken could not live in that field when we open on it." Walt said that the Union disaster at Fredericksburg was "the most complete piece of mismanagement perhaps ever yet known in the earth's wars."

George's name, garbled as "First Lieutenant G. W. Whitmore," appeared in the *Tribune* list of regimental casualties on the sixteenth. Walt set out immediately for the front, had his money stolen while changing trains at Philadelphia, arrived in Washington without a dime for food or carfare. For a time of "the greatest suffering I ever experienced in my life," he hunted through the hospitals for George, "walking all day and night, unable to ride, trying to get information, trying to get access to big people, &c—I could not get the least clue to anything." Two men he had met in Boston in the spring of 1860 came to his aid. O'Connor, now clerk of the Light-House Board in Washington, and Charles Eldridge, assistant to the Army Paymaster, lent him money and got him a military pass to travel to Falmouth, Virginia, where George's regiment had regrouped. One of the first sights that greeted him outside the improvised field hospital there was a heap, large enough to fill a horse cart, of amputated limbs, "cut, bloody, black and blue, swelled and sickening." But he finally caught up with George, who was not only alive but well, probably the luckiest of the ten thousand Union soldiers wounded at Fredericksburg; he had been cut in the cheek by a shell fragment. "[R]emember your galliant Son is a Capting," George wrote to his mother after Walt found him (he had been promoted on the eve of the battle). "You cant imagine how sorry I was to hear how worried you have been about me, and all the while I was as well as ever, so you see how foolish it is to frett." But she and Jeff remained so hysterically fearful that Walt, normally realistic about the chances of George's surviving the war (they were at best 75 per cent), went out of his way to assure them that "to be in the army is a mixture of danger and *security* in this war which few realize—they think exclusively of the danger."

Walt shared his brother's tent and mess for more than a week. Living so close to the front, to the dressing stations and the hospital tents pitched on the frozen ground, the fresh barrel-stave markers in the burial field, the vexed Rappahannock, and the ruins of Fredericksburg, he saw "what well men and sick men and mangled men endure." At Falmouth he wrote the prose draft of a *Drum-Taps* poem.

> *Sight at daybreak*—in camp in front of the hospital tent on a stretcher, (three dead men lying,) each with a blanket spread over him—I lift up one and look at the young man's face, calm and yellow,—'tis strange!
> (Young man: I think this face of yours the face of my dead Christ!)

The living suffered but also shared an astonishingly tender communion without pledge or demand, a loving intimacy of the sort he wanted to celebrate in "Calamus." Being among the men seemed to promise him a radical way of simplifying his own existence, a degree of remission. "I can be satisfied and happy henceforward if I can get one meal a day, and know that mother and all are in good health." On December 28 he said goodbye to George and went back to Washington, planning to stay there for a few weeks at least. He told Emerson the next day his "New York stagnation" had ended "for good."

14

"America, brought to hospital in her fair youth"

I

WHEN FORT SUMTER FELL, Federal troops were rushed from the North to relieve Washington and were billeted in the Capitol. They ate bread baked in army ovens that had been set up in vaults under the western terrace and staged mock sessions in the Senate and House chambers. By 1863, when Whitman settled in Washington, the Capitol had been returned to its original function and given an opulence that was Medicean, unrepublican, or downright depraved, depending on the viewer. The great triple dome was nearly finished after seven years of construction and dominated the skyline for miles, focusing the main effects of the entire structure, "its serenity, its *aplomb*," Whitman said. The interiors were particularly splendid at night, as the 37th Congress wound up its business under a glowing glass-paneled ceiling and poured out into the heroic halls. The Congress itself Whitman found less splendid—"much gab, great fear of public opinion, plenty of low business talent, but no masterful man." Outside the Capitol, from the surrounding eminence of park, cultivated trees, and statuary he could make out the distant campfires of fortifications ringing the most heavily defended city in the world, the North's major entrepot for troops and matériel and the prize most coveted by the Confederacy. A desultory Southern settlement—a "rude colony," Henry Adams called it, with "unfinished Greek temples for workrooms, and sloughs for roads"—had become both the functional and the symbolic proving place of Union.

Day and night these roads were traveled by trains of army wagons, sometimes a hundred and more to a convoy. Herds of cattle passed along the same dusty and rutted thoroughfares on their way to pens hard by the Washington Monument, then only a stub of masonry with the dignity of a distillery smokestack. Bound for the front in July 1863—Lee had swept into Pennsylvania and was threatening to cut off the capital—veteran cavalrymen, sunburned, unshaven, wearing weathered blue uniforms, rattled past 14th and L, where William and Nelly O'Connor had found a room for Whitman. From the corner he saw the open barouche, escorted by mounted soldiers with drawn sabers, that at day's end carried Abraham Lincoln from the White House, poisoned by summer exhalations from the Potomac flats, to the purer air of a cottage on the outskirts. Midway through his first term, Lincoln was far from being universally admired. "Everything he does reminds me of an old lady," Jeff wrote to Walt. "I don't know what effect it is going to have on the war," George said about the Emancipation Proclamation, regarded by administration critics as evidence of Lincoln's dictatorial ambitions, "but one thing is certain, he has got to lick the south before he can free the niggers." Instead of licking the South, Lincoln as commander in chief had so far been responsible for a chain of blunders culminating in a bloody stalemate. Still, Whitman mused when he saw Lincoln passing in the street, "Who can see that man without losing all wish to be sharp upon him personally? Who can say he has not a good soul?" A few months earlier Lincoln's face had reminded him of "a hoosier Michel Angelo, so awful ugly it becomes beautiful, with its strange mouth, its deep cut, cris-cross lines, and its doughnut complexion. . . . he has shown, I sometimes think, an almost supernatural tact in keeping the ship afloat at all, with head steady, not only not going down, and now certain not to, but with proud and resolute spirit, and flag flying in sight of the world, menacing and high as ever." He had already recognized in Lincoln the archetypal Captain who was to lie "fallen cold and dead" on the deck. At the White House, chatting with the writer John Hay, Lincoln's assistant private secretary and military aide, Whitman again studied the President from a distance. "Saw Mr. Lincoln standing, talking with a gentleman, apparently a dear friend. His face & manner have an expression & are inexpressibly sweet—one hand on his friend's shoulder, the other holds his hand. I love the President personally." The great captain, with whom Whitman apparently never exchanged a word or a handshake, was a comrade who solved the problems of freedom through affection—

Those who love each other shall be invincible

—and also a subject for an idealized self-portrait.

> I should say the invisible foundations and vertebra of his character, more than any man's in history, were mystical, abstract, moral and spiritual. . . . a man of indomitable firmness (even obstinacy) on rare occasions, involving great points; but he was generally very easy, flexible, tolerant, almost slouchy, respecting minor matters. . . . the only thing like passion or infatuation in the man was the passion for the Union of These States.

Armory Square Hospital, built on the modern pavilion plan in the summer of 1862, was an exception among Washington's forty or fifty military hospitals, most of which had been converted in haste from other functions. They held as many as seventy thousand sick and wounded, a number roughly equal to the city's peacetime population. Overflow casualties were housed in the Capitol, in churches, taverns, and schools, in the Georgetown prison and General Lee's Alexandria mansion. Whitman found them lying between rows of glass display cases in the Patent Office, "noblest of Washington buildings." This Greek Revival shrine to American ingenuity was normally an exhibition hall for models representing "every kind of utensil, machine, or invention, it ever enter'd into the mind of man to conceive." In the opening days of the war a Rhode Island regiment had been billeted there. Now it was a hospital, "a curious scene, especially at night when lit up. The glass cases, the beds, the forms lying there, the gallery above, and the marble pavement under foot —the suffering and the fortitude to bear it in various degrees— occasionally, from some, the groan that could not be repress'd."

In this city of makeshifts the same vaulted and pillared halls were to be the scene of Abraham Lincoln's Second Inaugural Ball. "I have been up to look at the dance and supper-rooms," Whitman was to write in 1865, "and I could not help thinking, what a different scene they presented to my view a while since, fill'd with a crowded mass of the worst wounded of the war, brought in from second Bull Run, Antietam, and Fredericksburgh. To-night, beautiful women, perfumes, the violins' sweetness, the polka and the waltz; then the amputation, the blue face, the groan, the glassy eye of the dying, the clotted rag, the odor of wounds and blood."

Life in the wartime Federal City peaked to a "mad, wild, hellish" intensity. Tides of office seekers, profiteers and promoters, voyeurs, zealots, do-gooders, quacks, religious enthusiasts, prostitutes, grieving wives and relatives, swindlers, scamperers from ruined reputations and sinking ships drove up the price of food and drink ("38 cts for beer," Whitman noted with disbelief) and made accommodations scarce. Skulkers and deserters made it "pokerish" to walk at night in the vicinity of Armory Square Hospital and the adjacent Smithsonian castle; Whitman's landlord at L Street protected the front entrance against intruders with seven locks and a big bulldog. More than New Orleans in the victorious rattle and vivacity of 1848, more than Manhattan, and despite the frightful suffering in its hospitals, Washington seemed to Whitman a city of romance, of things beginning. He said he had been drawn there by "a profound conviction of necessity, affinity."

"I fetch up here in harsh and superb plight—wretchedly poor, excellent well, (my only torment, family matters)," he wrote to Emerson after coming back from Falmouth, "realizing that it is necessary for me to fall for the time in the wise old way, to push my fortune, to be brazen, and get employment, and have an income." Eldridge hired him as a part-time copyist in the Army Paymaster's office; through John Swinton he sold four articles to the New York Times in 1863, among them a long report on the Washington hospitals, "The Great Army of the Sick." But in Whitman's plans copying for hourly wages and hacking in the press were merely ways of tiding him over until he found a government clerkship. He asked Emerson to use his influence with three of the most powerful men in the land, Senator Charles Sumner of Massachusetts, Secretary of State William Seward, and Secretary of the Treasury Salmon Chase (who expected to succeed Lincoln in the White House after the next election).

"I was pulling eminent wires in those days," Whitman recalled. Perhaps he had forgotten that for all its wisdom and brazenness, his lobbying for employment was in the end frustrated by his own naïveté and barely subintentional miscues. His strategy of applying "on literary grounds, not political," as he explained it to Emerson, invited grotesque connections between the earnest applicant and the hero of *Leaves of Grass;* not even the office of President could accommodate "a kosmos." Sumner, who struck him as "a sort of gelding— no good," offered vague promises and counsels of patience, then passed him on to another "big bug" Senator, Preston King of New York, who at least came right out with it. "Why, how can I do this thing, or any other thing for you—how do I know but you are a secessionist—you look for all the world, like an old Southern planter —a regular Carolina or Virginia planter." It was not only Walt's beard and ruddy face, his big soft-brimmed hat and country clothes that added up to this impression. When he got started on his New Orleans adventure, the Southern social virtues, and the Confederate wounded he met in the hospitals he even sounded "secesh." King bucked him to the Army Quartermaster General, Montgomery Meigs, and there that particular line of influence came to a dead halt, although Walt still managed to congratulate himself on "getting better and better acquainted with office-hunting wisdom, and Washington peculiarities generally."

Emerson had been dubious about the venture, suggesting that if Whitman had set his mind on living in Washington—"least attractive (to me) of cities"—he would perhaps do better in journalism than in government. But he recommended him nonetheless in terms that leavened the enthusiasm of 1855 with a note of warning to patrons in the corridors of power. "Permit me to say that he is known to me as a man of strong original genius," he wrote on January 10,

> combining, with marked eccentricities, great powers & valuable traits of character: a self-relying, large-hearted man, much beloved by his friends; entirely patriotic & benevolent in his theory, tastes, & practice. If his writings are in certain points open to criticism, they yet show extraordinary power, & are more deeply American, democratic, & in the interest of political liberty, than those of any other poet. He is indeed a child of the people, & their champion.
>
> A man of his talents & dispositions will quickly make himself useful, and, if the Government has work that he can do, I think it may easily find, that it has called to its side more valuable aid than it bargained for.

For some reason Whitman never used his entree to Seward, and he held on to a letter to Chase that Emerson had given him for almost a year, until the end of 1863, when his friend John Townsend Trowbridge came to Washington to write a campaign biography of Chase. A guest in the Secretary's mansion, after breakfast one day Trowbridge handed the letter to Chase, who read it, uttered a few commonplaces about wishing to oblige him and Mr. Emerson, and then came to the point: he wanted to have nothing to do with the man who had written that "very bad book" and was still, despite a penitential and possibly even exemplary year of service to the sick and wounded, "a decidedly disreputable person." Hoping to save everyone concerned from embarrassment, Trowbridge tried to withdraw the letter but discovered that Secretary Chase was an autograph collector. "I have nothing of Emerson's in his handwriting," he said, "and I shall be glad to keep this." He kept it for a month and a half before surrendering it to the Treasury files with the endorsement, "Clerkship Walt Whitman Applicant New York: Recommended by R. W. Emerson." "I should probably have had no difficulty in securing the appointment," Trowbridge reflected, "if I had withheld Emerson's letter, and called my friend simply Mr. Whitman, or Mr. Walter Whitman, without mentioning Leaves of Grass."

"He is just the meanest & biggest kind of a shyster," Whitman remarked about Chase. But there were more immediate ways of accounting for the fact that it was to take two years of politicking, mostly by others on his behalf, before he finally landed a clerkship, in the Interior Department, and why he had cared little about his lack of success until then. "I feel so engrossed with my soldiers," he wrote to Jeff in March 1863, "I do not devote that attention to my office-hunting, which is needed for success." In January he had been appointed a Delegate of the Christian Commission, a wartime agency of the YMCAs, and became, as he signed himself inside the cover of a notebook, "Walt Whitman—Soldiers' Missionary." His commission listed some of his unpaid duties: "distributing stores where needed, in hospitals and camps; circulating good reading material amongst soldiers and sailors; visiting the sick and wounded, to instruct, comfort, and cheer them, and aid them in correspondence with their friends at home; aiding Surgeons on the battlefield and elsewhere in the care and conveyance of the wounded to hospitals."

A year after he received his commission Whitman told a "pretty high" Army officer, further identified only as an admirer of *Leaves of Grass*, that he had "a great desire to be present at a first class battle." The officer took him aside, and, while declining to elaborate, assured him his wish might be gratified in a matter of weeks. Early in February 1864 he was passed through army lines to Culpeper, Virginia, half a mile from the Union perimeter. The town had already changed hands three or four times; there were reports now of an advancing rebel force. "We were all ready to skedaddle from here last night," he wrote, "horses harnessed in all directions, & traps packed up . . . but orders came during the night to stay for the present, there was no danger." He had come down to Culpeper too early by several months for Grant's face-off with Lee in the nearby Wilderness salient and missed his last chance to experience at first hand the bloody trials of valor he imagined in the battle vignettes of "Song of Myself." The transforming imagination, the tireless "I," had to feed on the combat experiences of soldier-patients from every state in the Union and Confederacy.

"There comes that odious Walt Whitman to talk evil and unbelief to my boys," a nurse at Armory Square Hospital complained in a letter to her husband. "I think I would rather see the Evil One himself." Redpath reported that even Emerson, for all his fame and influence, was unable to round up New Englanders willing to finance Walt's modest distributions of fruit, preserves, pickles, ice cream, candy, cookies, wine and brandy, chewing and smoking tobacco, handkerchiefs, shirts, socks, and underwear, reading and writing materials, postage stamps, and small change. "There is a prejudice agst you here among the 'fine' ladies and gentlemen of the transcendental School," Redpath wrote from Boston. "It is believed that you are not ashamed of your reproductive organs." Walt managed to raise money for his hospital work from friends in Brooklyn, New York, and elsewhere, but there was never enough "to do the good I would like to do—& the work grows upon me," he told his mother. "I would like to inaugurate a plan by which I could raise means on my own hook." He revived, but soon abandoned as usual, a perennial scheme of giving lectures and readings for money; this time his notes for an oration to be given in the cities of the North dealt with

The Dead in this War,
    there they lie, strewing the fields & woods of the south—
The Virginia peninsula, Malvern Hill & Fair Oaks
    the banks of the Chickahominy

.   .   .   .

The bloody terraces of Fredericksburgh—
    Antietam Bridge—the grisly ravines of Manassas . . .

For all his money problems, by the end of the war Whitman figured
he had made over six hundred hospital visits and tours, often lasting
for several days and nights, and in some degree had ministered to
nearly a hundred thousand of the sick and wounded of both sides.

"Mother, when you or Jeff writes again, tell me if my papers &
MSS are all right," Walt said in March 1863. "I should be very sorry
indeed if they got scattered or used up or any thing—*especially* the
copy of Leaves of Grass covered in blue paper, and the little MS
book 'Drum Taps' . . . I want them all carefully kept." In May he
had a long talk about *Drum-Taps*, by title, with a new acquaintance,
Elijah Allen, who kept an Army and Navy store in Washington and
also had a special interest in literary things—he was a close friend of
John Burroughs and was soon to marry the popular poet, Elizabeth
Akers, known then and after only as the author of one poem, "Rock
Me to Sleep." "He told me some of his plans and what he intends to
'celebrate,' as he terms it," Allen said. By November, when Walt
made a trip home and retrieved his manuscripts, the project had
taken on a new urgency. "I must bring out Drum Taps. I *must* be
continually bringing out poems—now is the hey day."

Two years were to pass before he finally published *Drum-Taps*,
and during that time another project closer to his heart than office-
hunting had also taken second place to his soldiers. As soon as he
arrived in Washington he began to work on a prose book about
America "brought to hospital in her fair youth," as he told Emerson,
"brought and deposited here in this great, whited sepulchre." He
wrote his memoranda at the scene—in the wards, by bedsides—in
soiled, creased little notebooks that he made by folding and pinning
a couple of sheets of paper. By October 1863, as he told Redpath,
he thought he had enough material to bring out this book "*immediately.*" It was to be "of the time, worthy the time—something considerably more than mere hospital sketches." He planned to bring
home to the people the need to reform not only the Army Medical

Department but the Army as a whole, especially its "feudal" system of officering.*

> Talk with Ben in Ward A about tyrannous and unnecessary exposure of the soldiers [he noted], how many officers there are who dare not go into engagements nor even out on picket with their own men, for fear of their lives from their own men—the 8th N Y Cav Col Davis (killed afterward) who . . . made the poor sick men (sick with diarrhea) dismount & mount 13 times to make them do it in a military style—I have not seen a single officer that seemed to know American men.

But the soul and body trials of "masculine young manhood" that he witnessed in the hospitals dwarfed indignation, baffled understanding and description, made conventional piety blasphemous. "It pleas'd him very much," Walt said after he read passages from the New Testament to a soldier who was dying. "The tears were in his eyes—he asked me if I 'enjoyed religion'—I said probably not my dear, in the way you mean." They kissed. Month after month such encounters opened "a new world somehow to me, giving closer insights, new things, exploring deeper mines than any yet, showing our humanity." Twelve years had to pass before he was ready to publish *Memoranda During the War*, privately and in an edition of perhaps one hundred copies; by then he was an invalid. The "interior history" of the war "will never be written," he said, "perhaps must not and should not be." That history had been too passionate, too incredible and sacred, to be violated by telling. "The real war will never get in the books."

"Something considerably more than mere hospital sketches," Whitman had said when he described his plans to Redpath. Specifically he was thinking of Louisa May Alcott's popular *Hospital Sketches*, which Redpath published during the summer of 1863. Her

---

* Whitman returned to this subject in *Democratic Vistas*.

> The whole present system of the officering and personnel of the army and navy of these States, and the spirit and letter of their trebly-aristocratic rules and regulations, is a monstrous exotic, a nuisance and revolt, and belong here just as much as orders of nobility, or the Pope's council of cardinals. I say if the present theory of our army and navy is sensible and true, then the rest of America is an unmitigated fraud. [*Prose Works*, 1892, II, pp. 389–90.]

candid narrative of a month's service as a nurse in Washington—she was invalided home with typhoid fever—depicted practices that in almost every respect, including lethal overdosing with the emetic calomel, violated Florence Nightingale's first injunction, "Do the sick no harm." Whitman too found repeated instances of callousness, neglect and incompetence. "No thorough previous preparation, no system, no foresight, no genius. Always plenty of stores, no doubt, but always miles away; never where they are needed, and never the proper application." Lacking practiced doctors, a rudimentary ambulance corps, and even a general hospital, the Federals, one historian says, "entered the war with medical capabilities below those of Imperial Rome."

For a quarter of a century a doddering veteran of the War of 1812 had served as Surgeon General; when he died in May 1861 he was succeeded by another relic of 1812, who had to be removed for incompetence after less than a year. Until then, men had been inducted without much regard to their health or fitness for service, casually fed and clothed, and housed in camps where open sewers and overflowing latrines helped account for the fact that during the first year of the fighting a third of the army was on sick call. The wounded sometimes lay for days where they fell before being loaded like cordwood in supply wagons and hauled over rough roads to primary stations. A few years before Lister proved the value of antiseptic surgery, doctors in blood-stained coats cut and sawed with dirty instruments, moistened sutures with saliva, plied the needle with infected fingers, and washed their hands only when they became smelly or sticky; "surgical fevers"—osteomyelitis, erysipelas, gangrene, and pyemia—were rampant. Survivors of field surgery were packed into dilapidated buildings, where, if not altogether neglected, they were cared for by other soldiers—convalescents, invalids, prisoners, undesirables, and "the ineffective under arms"—who had been pressed into a disagreeable service and were either too resentful not to do harm or too feeble to do good.

The situation improved toward the end of the war. Dorothea Dix, first Superintendent of Female Nurses of the Army, recruited competent, mature women (plain and over thirty, she insisted), but she was herself "very queer and arbitrary," Alcott said, and after a series of wrangles over hospital administration was relieved of much of her authority. Nursing the sick and wounded was no longer entrusted to soldiers and romantic adventurers, but it was only grudgingly recognized as a profession for women (the country did not have graduate nurses until the 1870s) and never recognized as a profession for men, even though men made up eighty percent of the nurses on both sides of the war. Redpath was only half joking when he told Whitman that the Transcendentalist ladies and gentlemen believed "eunuchs only are fit for nurses." All this was another instance of the gender stereotypy Whitman resisted with as much passion as he did official heartlessness and sanctimony. Too many of his fellow Delegates of the Christian Commission seemed to busy themselves with distributing an appalling total of thirty-nine million pages of pious tracts and lecturing the legless on the evils of dancing. "You ought to see the way the men as they lie helpless in bed turn away their faces from the sight of these Agents, Chaplains, &c. (*hirelings* as Elias Hicks would call them—they seem to me always a set of foxes & wolves)."

"In my visits to the hospitals," he recalled, "I found it was in the simple matter of Personal Presence, and emanating ordinary cheer and magnetism, that I succeeded and help'd more than by medical nursing or delicacies, or gifts of money, or anything else." After work at the paymaster's office he bathed, rested, and put on fresh clothes—a dark wine-colored suit, army boots with black morocco tops, a broad felt hat adorned with a black-and-gold cord with acorns. He wore a necktie now. "You can imagine I cut quite a swell." A sprig or flower in his buttonhole, his haversack of gifts slung over his shoulder, he moved at will past guards, doctors and nurses, and came to the wards as if to "a festival," Burroughs said. He looked like a rich old sea captain, he was so red-faced and patriarchal-looking and big.

He played games of Twenty Questions, got the soldiers involved in general conversations, wrote letters for them, and, as if he were riding the Broadway stages or walking the beach of Coney Island, he declaimed passages from Shakespeare, Scott, and the like. For the time being he had suspended, even concealed, his identity as Walt Whitman the poet, although, when a soldier found out who he was and wanted to learn more, Walt hunted up one of his newspaper articles or, on occasion, read aloud from *Leaves of Grass*. "Please send me some of your Poems, your choise ones," an ex-soldier asked him in 1871, "for I always enjoyed them so much when you read them to me in old Ward A. I never shall forget what pains you took to help pass away our weary hours. our Heavenly Father will reward you for it."

At first, not reckoning the eventual cost, he appeared to be one of the beneficiaries of these visits. "I am very happy," he told Redpath in October 1863. "I was never so beloved. I am running over with health, fat, red & sunburnt in face &c. I tell thee I am just the one to go [to] our sick boys." They clung to him, put their arms around his neck, drew his face down, and he was enriched "personally, egotistically, in unprecedented ways"—"It is delicious to be the object of so much love & reliance." "In Armery Square you come in every evening," a soldier wrote. "I remember of your kissing me."

> Many a soldier's loving arms about this neck have cross'd and rested,
> Many a soldier's kiss dwells on these bearded lips.

The soldiers were like "my own children or younger brothers," companions of his trips to Peconic Bay under summer skies.

There were hints, though, of further reaches of arousal in the way the wound-dresser and noncombatant fantasized about battle—

> the mad, determin'd tussle of the armies, in all their separate large and little squads . . . each steep'd from crown to toe in desperate, mortal purports . . . the conflict, hand-to-hand—the many conflicts in the dark, those shadowy-tangled, flashing moonbeam'd woods— the writhing groups and squads . . . the indescribable mix . . . the devils fully rous'd in human hearts.

He felt an electric thrill in nearness and touch: "I always feel drawn toward the men and like their personal contact when we are crowded close together, so frequently these days in the street cars." Even after five hours of self-imposed duty in the wards, as if he had come from a lovers' tryst he walked out into the sweet and clear night and marveled at everything he saw. The President's House, patrolled by sentries in blue overcoats, gleamed spectral white under a "voluptuous" and "moist" half-moon. Until long after midnight he wandered along Pennsylvania Avenue toward the Patent Office. "The sky, the planets, the constellations all so bright, so calm, so expressively silent, so soothing after those Hospital scenes." Those scenes were terrible, but they were also beautiful, "a link, a bridge, a connection," as he suggested in trial lines in 1863:

> The Soul, reaching throwing out for love,
> As the spider, from some little promontory, throwing out filament
>   after filament, tirelessly out of itself, that one at least may
>   catch and form a link, a bridge, a connection
> O I saw one passing alone, saying hardly a word—yet full of love I
>   detected him, by certain signs
> O eyes wishfully turning! O silent eyes!

At times he felt ashamed of being so well and whole and buffalo-like. He tried to imagine himself one of the wounded gasping for breath, crazed out of his head with pain and fever, the chloroform sponge pressed to his face as the surgeon readied the knife and saw. This was in part an exercise in empathy, in emulating heroic impassiveness. He told Emerson that the sculptor Horatio Stone, now a Union Army contract surgeon who had treated frightful casualties of Bull Run, Antietam and Fredericksburg, could not recall "one single case of a man's meeting the approach of death, whether sudden or slow, with fear or trembling—but always of these young men meeting their death with steady composure, and often with curious readiness." Implausible as it was, Walt cited Stone's version several times: he had to believe it for his own survival. The war became "just the same old story," he said in May 1864, "poor suffering young men, great swarms of them come up here, now, every day, all battered & bloody—there have 4000 arrived here this morning, & 1500 yesterday—the journey from the field till they get aboard the boats at Bell Plain is horrible."

Instead of glories Whitman had horrors previously unimaginable strung like beads on his smallest sights and hearings. "A burning flame" in his heart, the poet prayed for the misericord as a love gift:

> Come sweet death! be persuaded O beautiful death!
> In mercy come quickly.

But the wound-dresser, writing his memoranda by the deathbed, breathing septic air whose foulness the tobacco he handed out could never begin to neutralize, forced himself into composure and readiness, matter-of-factness, a delicate distancing of his emotions.

June 18th.—In one of the hospitals I find Thomas Haley, company M, 4th New York cavalry—a regular Irish boy, a fine specimen of youthful physical manliness—shot through the lungs—inevitably dying—came over to this country from Ireland to enlist—has not a single friend or acquaintance here—is sleeping soundly at this moment, (but it is the sleep of death)—has a bullet-hole straight through the lung. I saw Tom when first brought here, three days since, and didn't suppose he could live twelve hours—(yet he looks well enough in the face to a casual observer.) He lies there with his frame exposed above the waist, all naked, for coolness, a fine built man, the tan not yet bleach'd from his cheeks and neck. It is useless to talk to him, as with his sad hurt, and the stimulants they give him, and the utter strangeness of every object, face, furniture, &c., the poor fellow, even when awake, is like some frighten'd, shy animal. Much of the time he sleeps, or half sleeps. (Sometimes I thought he knew more than he show'd.) I often come and sit by him in perfect silence; he will breathe for ten minutes as softly and evenly as a young babe asleep. Poor youth, so handsome, athletic, with profuse beautiful shining hair. One time as I sat looking at him while he lay asleep, he suddenly, without the least start, awaken'd, open'd his eyes, gave me a long steady look, turning his face very slightly to gaze easier—one long, clear, silent look—a slight sigh—then turn'd back and went into his doze again. Little he knew, poor death-stricken boy, the heart of the stranger that hover'd near.

After a time came "welcome oblivion, painlessness, death." A white bandage was bound around and under the jaw, the pillows were removed, "the limpsy head falls down, the arms are softly placed by the side, all composed, all still,—and the broad white sheet is thrown over everything."

It was only after the guns too were all still that Whitman permitted himself to keen over "the dead, the dead, the dead—*our* dead," more than half a million, Union and Confederate. Now they inhabited a vast landscape, and in mourning them and the violations of their sanctity of sepulture, Whitman became Osiris again. The great cycle of *Leaves of Grass* had renewed the dead. The nation was now "saturated, perfumed with their impalpable ashes' exhalation in Nature's chemistry distill'd, and shall be so forever, in every grain of wheat and ear of corn, and every flower that grows, and every breath we draw."

II

At Armory Square Hospital early in 1863 Whitman met Lewy Brown, a twenty-year-old Maryland soldier wounded in the leg at Rappahannock Station. "A most affectionate fellow," he noted in his pocket diary, "very fond of having me come and sit by him." The following January, after complications set in, Lewy's left leg was amputated five inches below the knee. Walt was present at the operation and sat up several nights at the bedside until things slowly took a turn for the better. Lewy began looking forward to being a civilian again and going to school; he was going to learn bookkeeping as a trade and raise his writing above bare literacy. "My darling boy," Walt reassured him (he also caressed him verbally as "my dear son," "my darling," "my darling comrade"), "when you write to me, you must write without ceremony, I like to hear every little thing about yourself & your affairs—you need never care how you write to me, Lewy, if you will only—I never think about literary perfection in letters either, it is the *man* & the *feeling*." Walt had become his father, mother and brother, sponged him and fed him, held him and kissed him ("a long kiss, half a minute long") and gave him homely advice. There is little evidence that Lewy and similarly dependent younger men found anything excessive in this, anything that raised doubts about their heterosexual integrity or his. Will Wallace, a hospital steward who addressed Walt as "the Prince of Bohemians" and signed himself "Your protegee," tried to entice him to Nashville with the promise of "five young ladies who act in the capacity of nurses—i e, *one of* them is French, young and beautiful to set your eyes upon. Can you not visit us and note for yourself?" Walt replied that he was just then recovering from the "deplorable" effects of an affair with a "frenchy" of his own. Wallace commiserated. "You are not alone. I had to dismiss mine to save the reputation of the Hospital and your humble servant."

Like Walt, who to the end was not sure that he understood his own meanings, his soldiers in this pre-Freudian age were as naïve in their self-awareness as they were generous in spirit; he remembered their "strange spiritual sweetness," their "unworldliness, disinterestedness, and animal purity."* "We all loved each other more than we supposed," he said about the young men at Pfaff's. Now he said about his soldiers, "I believe no men ever loved each other as I & some of these poor wounded, sick & dying men love each other," and Lewy Brown echoed this—"There is many a soldier now that never thinks of you but with emotions of the greatest gratitude. . . . I never think of you but it makes my heart glad to think I have bin permitted to know one so good." After his discharge, Lewy worked in Washington for the Provost General and then the Treasury Department. Walt saw him from time to time, calmly, but with a certain ache nonetheless, for their old closeness and intensity, their interlocking needs, the bare-bone simplicities of wartime comradeship, were gone for good and not much missed by Lewy, who was well again and moving on to new stages of intimacy in his 83-year life span. Whitman experienced loss even when his soldiers recovered, built ties to families, farms and jobs, sent him their news and pictures, and named their children after him. On at least one occasion Walt's sense of loss was as sharp as it had been in the predictive conflicts and bereavements of "Live Oak with Moss."

Around the beginning of April 1863, Sergeant Thomas P. Sawyer, a Massachusetts soldier Walt met through Lewy Brown, left Washington to rejoin his regiment. As Sawyer explained in a note to Lewy, he had forgotten his "Prommice" to come by Walt's room to

* The idioms and familiar practices of the period have to be understood accordingly and not bent to the present, as these two passages suggest.

John Burroughs, who was unquestionably "straight," writes as follows in 1863–64. "I have been much with Walt. Have even slept with him. I love him very much. . . . He loves everything and everybody. I saw a soldier the other day stop on the street and kiss him. He kisses me as if I were a girl. . . . He bathed today while I was there—such a handsome body, and such delicate, rosy flesh I never saw before. I told him he looked good enough to eat."

From an interview with people in Huntington who remembered Whitman from his *Long Islander* days there: "We inquired whether Walt was a gay lad among the lassies of the village—a beau in the rustic society of his day—and both received the same reply: 'Not in the least.' 'He seemed to hate women,' said one of them—a hard, and, I am sure, quite too strong expression, but one which forcibly shows how alien even to his hot blood of twenty summers were all effeminate longings." (Clara Barrus, *Whitman and Burroughs, Comrades* [Boston, 1931], pp. 13, 17; Daniel G. Brinton and Horace L. Traubel, "A Visit to West Hills," *Walt Whitman Fellowship Papers*, Philadelphia, December 1894.)

pick up a gift bundle of clothes—a blue shirt, a pair of drawers, some socks. "I came away so soon that it sliped my mind and I am very sorry for it, tell him that I shall write to him my self in a few days, give him my love and best wishes for ever." Walt reproached him mildly—"I should often have thought now Tom may be wearing around his body something from *me*." Tom did not understand with what emotions "old wooly-neck," as Walt called himself, had invested common articles available at Allen's Army and Navy store. On April 21, around the time he had claimed he was involved with his "frenchy," Walt sent Tom a rambling letter that ended with a plea.

> Dear comrade, you must not forget me, for I never shall you. My love you have in life or death forever. I don't know how you feel about it, but it is the wish of my heart to have your friendship, and also that if you should come safe out of this war, we should come together again in some place where we could make our living, and be true comrades and never be separated while life lasts—and take Lew Brown too, and never separate from him. Or if things are not to be —if you get these lines, my dear, darling comrade, and any thing should go wrong, so that we do not meet again, here on earth, it seems to me, (the way I feel now,) that my soul could never be entirely happy, even in the world to come without you, dear comrade. And if it is God's will, I hope we shall yet meet, as I say, if you feel as I do about it—and if [it] is destined that we shall not, you have my love none the less, whatever should keep you from me, no matter how many years. God bless you, Tom, and preserve you through the perils of the fight.
>
> Good bye, my darling comrade, my dear darling brother, for so I will call you, and wish you to call me the same.

In a sentence that he deleted from his draft letter Walt acknowledged, "What I have written is pretty strong talk, I suppose, but I mean exactly what I say." Less articulate than Lewy, Tom had someone else help him compose and then copy out a reply that could just as well have dealt with a proposition involving cast-iron stoves. "I fully reciprocate your friendship as expressed in your letter and it will afford me great pleasure to meet you after the war will have terminated or sooner if circumstances will permit." (Nearly a year later he finally wrote his first letter to Walt in his own hand—"I hope you will forgive me and in the future I will do better and I

hope we may meet again in this world.") Meanwhile Walt had persisted, as if determined to have his heart broken. "I do not expect
you to return for me the same degree of love I have for you," he told
Tom at the end of May. In August he said, "Dear brother, how I
should like to see you. . . . I cant understand why you have ceased
to correspond with me." In September he tried again. Early in November he appealed through Lewy Brown. "Lew, when you write
to Tom Sawyer you know what to say from me—he is the one I love
in my heart, & always shall till death & afterwards too." A final,
piteous appeal on November 20: "I do not know why you do not
write to me. Do you wish to shake me off? That I cannot believe."
By then Walt was winding up a tender friendship with another
Armory Square soldier. "Walt, you will be a second Father to me,
won't you?" asked Elijah Douglass Fox—"I never before met with a
man that I could love as I do you." "I cannot bear the thought of
being separated from you," Walt answered after Fox had gone home
to his wife in Michigan—"the blessing of God on you by night &
day, my darling boy." It was only after the war was over that Walt
found in Peter Doyle, paroled Confederate soldier, the heart's companion he had been looking for all the while.

III

"The O'Connor home was my home," Whitman recalled. "They
were beyond all others—William, Nelly—my understanders, my
lovers: they more than any others. I was nearer to them than any
others—oh! much nearer. A man's family is the people who love
him—the people who comprehend him." They gave him a home
when he first arrived in Washington, arranged for him to live in their
rooming house, insisted he take all his meals at their table. Along
with their five-year-old daughter he was the center of their lives at a
time when other centers were failing them. In O'Connor's postwar
story, "The Carpenter," Whitman appears as a Christ-like "gray
redeemer" and "lover of soldiers"—"I walk the hospitals"—who
heals the wounds of a war-riven family and tells them, "Better than
all is love. Love is better than all."
Nelly was slight, sharp-featured, plain, "rather intellectual than
physical," Walt chose to believe. Her husband was glowing-eyed,
vivid, magnetic, "superbly free and defiant" in bearing, irresistible

as an advocate. Before they married in 1856 she had been active in the women's rights movement and worked on William Lloyd Garrison's unequivocating abolitionist weekly, *The Liberator;* she and O'Connor, both New Englanders, shared a passion for radical causes. When Whitman became a member of their household circle in 1863 they were mourning the death of an infant son; the loss accelerated a drifting apart that ended in a separation nine years later. Like Charley Eldridge, Whitman often wondered whether O'Connor "showed her sufficient consideration." Perhaps O'Connor's zealotry, pardonable when enlisted in a good cause, was evidence of a fundamental vacancy of self. He suffered from spells of depression and withdrawal that Nelly feared "would develop into an insanity." He ate his breakfast in silence, left the house in silence, and often did not return until after midnight, having worked in his office at the Light-House Board and then walked about the city alone. Perhaps he saw other women.

Nelly invested her emotions in Walt. She responded to him physically, to his bulk and vigor and rosy freshness. When he came out of a snowstorm one evening he reminded her of the spirit of Christmas—he brought with him a bottle of Scotch, a lemon, and some lump sugar, the makings of hot toddies and an evening of laughter. She liked to hear him singing in his room while he dressed after a bath and to feel the heat his hands left on the outside of the water pitcher he filled at the corner pump. "I have missed you terribly every minute of the time," she wrote after he went home to Brooklyn for a visit. "I think I never in my life felt so wholly blue and unhappy about any one's going away as I did, and have since, about your going. . . . Ah! Walt, I don't believe other people need you as much as we do. I am *sure* they don't need you as much as *I* do." Her avowals to Walt, her husband's best friend, became more overt and in time even desperate. "I always know that you know that I love you all the time," she wrote in 1870:

> Even though we should never meet again, my feeling could never change, and I am sure that you know it as well as I do. I do flatter myself too, that you care for me—not as I love you, because you are great and strong, and more sufficient unto yourself than any woman can be. Besides you have the great outflow of your pen which saves you from the need of personal love as one feels it who has no such resource. . . . It is only when I am away from you that I am con-

scious of how deeply you have influenced my life, my thoughts, my feelings, my views—*myself*. In fact, in every way, you seem to have permeated my whole being. . . . You must not neglect the golden opportunity of letting me love you and see you all that is possible. I think that I must have been very good at some time to have deserved such a blessing.

After O'Connor died in 1889 she told Walt, "I have had several most *vivid* dreams of you, so distinct that all the next day I felt as if I had been with you; and I wonder whether my 'astral body' went to you, or yours came to me." She offered to move into Mickle Street, "keep house for me," he said, "go into alliance, get spliced," but he dismissed the idea as "impossible, or at least unlikely." If something had ever been possible between them, the time for it had passed long ago. He had managed always to keep her at arm's length, in the early years in Washington scarcely distinguishing between her and O'Connor in the affection they competed to offer him. "I liked her," he recalled, and he left it at that. He had told Nelly several times that he did not envy other men their wives, only their children, and that he had been accustomed to his freedom for so long it would be "a great mistake" if he were ever to marry. Of course, he added, everything might have been different "if I had been caught young." All his life, with men as well as with women, his mother being the lone exception, he was either on the giving or the receiving end of a one-way traffic in love. He was not self-sufficient, as Nelly believed, nor did his writing "save" him from "the need of personal love," but perhaps his life had to be partial in order for his work to be whole.

In the summer of 1863, after the O'Connors' landlord decided to put the house up at auction, they moved to other quarters; in October Walt rented a third-story back room on Sixth Street, near Pennsylvania Avenue. He practiced a simplicity there that combined Brooklyn and Walden Pond—he was reading Thoreau then—with a style he associated with students and artists in Montparnasse. When he came to Walt's tenement for breakfast, Trowbridge, who had spent the night in Secretary Chase's grand house on the corner diagonally opposite, was at first overwhelmed by the contrast. Newspapers were piled on a trunk and cheap pine table, boots lay about on the floor, the bed was unmade—like Alcott when he visited

Walt in Brooklyn, Trowbridge could not help noticing that "the thing which should have been under the bed unfortunately wasn't." Still only half dressed at ten o'clock, Walt sliced a baker's loaf with his pocket knife, put the slices on a pointed stick, and toasted them over a little sheet-iron stove. He offered a lump of butter in a brown-paper wrapper that doubled as their common plate, brewed tea in a covered tin mug, and spooned out sugar from a paper sack. When breakfast was over, the butter plate went into the fire, like the shingles he used for his dinner chop or bit of beefsteak.

Sundays Whitman went to the O'Connors' for roast beef, lima beans, and stewed tomatoes. He remembered these regular dinners as a "compensating joy of my Washington life" and frequently shared them with Charley Eldridge, the Ohio poet and journalist John J. Piatt, and Assistant Attorney General J. Hubley Ashton, who was to help him find a government clerkship. Among other guests were his former linguistics coach, William Swinton, who served as a war correspondent until he was caught eavesdropping on Grant and nearly put before a firing squad, and the hot-tempered Polish intellectual and revolutionist Count Adam Gurowski. A veteran of the Harvard faculty, Pfaff's restaurant, and Horace Greeley's *Tribune*, Gurowski was "a maniac," according to O'Connor, "a madman with lucid intervals." Whitman found him entertaining and exotic—he was the brother-in-law of a Bourbon princess and had lost an eye in a duel—but "very crazy" all the same. The count's *Diary*, which provoked a libel action when the first volume came out in 1862 and cost him his job as confidential adviser to Secretary Seward, suggested that practically everyone in wartime Washington, the President included, was either a coward or an intriguer. Among the few he praised were Grant, Secretary of War Stanton, and Whitman, "the incarnation of a genuine American original genius"—"Walt alone in his heart and in his mind has a shrine for the nameless, for the heroic people."

O'Connor's convictions, like Gurowski's, were free of moderating restraints; in his binary way he had only two positions: for or against. "William is in the best sense an orator—is eminently passionate, pictorial, electric," said Whitman, whose style tended to be tempered and ruminative. "I'd rather hear O'Connor argue for what I consider wrong than hear most people argue for what I think right: he has charm, color, vigor; he possesses himself of the field; he pierces you to the vitals and you thank him for doing it." O'Connor was a convert to the heady theories of Miss Delia Salter Bacon, author of *The Philosophy of the Plays of Shakespeare Unfolded*, a 582-page study that she published two years before her recent death within the precincts of the Hartford Retreat for the insane. Whitman attended mildly and noncommittally as O'Connor railed against the fools and knaves who for two and a half centuries had been crediting the immortal works of Francis Bacon to a "fat peasant" and "third-rate play-actor" from Stratford-on-Avon. But when issues of politics, social justice, and the war were raised the two went at each other like bulls—neighbors and the policeman on the beat banged on the front door to stop what sounded like disorderly conduct. It seemed to Nelly that one day something would be said during these "terrible combats" to destroy a friendship.

O'Connor regarded slavery as the worst abomination in all human history—the Civil War was Armageddon; the Children of Light must win at any cost. "My opinion is *to stop the war now*," Whitman argued in 1863. He had seen enough of Armageddon in the hospitals to decide it was "about nine hundred and ninety-nine parts diarrhea to one part glory: the people who like the wars should be compelled to fight the wars." "In comparison with this slaughter," he told O'Connor, "I don't care for the niggers"—slavery *was* a crying sin but it was not the *only* crying sin in the universe. "I never knew him to have a friend among the negroes while he was in Washington," Eldridge recalled. He was as outraged as O'Connor by Whitman's inexplicable (as it appeared to them) streak of social copperheadism. Hoping to implant other views, in July 1863 Eldridge and his chief, Army Paymaster Major Lyman Hapgood, brought Whitman along to Analostan Island, off Georgetown, when the First Regiment, U. S. Colored Troops, fell in to collect their pay. "They are manly enough, bright enough, look as if they had the soldier-stuff in them," Whitman said, noting about a dozen George Washingtons in the ranks and a sprinkling of Horace Greeleys and Alfred Tennysons. "Occasionally, but not often, there are some thoroughly African physiognomies, very black in color, large protruding lips, low forehead, etc. But I have to say that I do not see one utterly revolting face."

The following spring five black regiments marched in review with the rest of Burnside's army—"It looked funny to see the President standing with his hat off to them just the same as the rest." They fought bravely, even Whitman was to acknowledge, but he continued to believe that blacks in general were genetically and psychologically unfitted for "amalgamation." "Ethiopia" had saluted and served the flag but was "Ethiopia" still. The victorious North, with its four million newly liberated citizens, was in the same bind as "the man that won the elephant in a raffle." O'Connor forgave as mere differences what he would have considered unforgivable moral lapses in another person. He was coming to believe that the author of *Leaves of Grass* nevertheless stood with Aeschylus, Rabelais, Victor Hugo, and "William Shakespeare."

From time to time Whitman sent affectionate letters to his boys at Pfaff's saying that despite the scattering of the war they were enshrined for good "in the portrait-gallery of my mind & heart"; if he could, he'd come back to New York just to drink a few hot rum punches with them. "I was always between two loves at that time," he said to Traubel years later; he had reread the letters and was wiping the tears away with his coatsleeve. "I wanted to be in New York, I had to be in Washington: I was never in the one place but I was restless for the other: my heart was distracted." In 1863 the choice was not so difficult as he remembered.

That July, a mob of laborers protesting the wartime draft laws—in particular the provision exempting anyone able to pay the government $300 or hire a substitute—precipitated the bloodiest riots in New York's violent history. "Its almost enough to make a fellow ashamed of being a Yorker," George Whitman wrote from camp near Covington, Kentucky. "I could hardly believe, that a thing of that kind would be alowed to get such headway in the City of New York. . . . I would have went into that fight with just as good a heart, as if they had belonged to the rebel army." Walt reported from Washington that hotheads there were all for sending up gunboats to shell "radical" and "anti-slavery" Manhattan into line. "I remain silent, partly amused, partly scornful," he said. "The Town is taken by its rats," wrote Herman Melville, "—ship rats and rats of the wharves." After three days of sacking, looting, lynching, and a thousand fatalities, the rioters were dispersed by troops that had to be detached from Meade's force at Gettysburg.

As for Jeff's being drafted, Walt was certain that financially and in other ways it would mean "the downfall almost of our whole family." The Whitmans managed to raise the statutory three hundred dollars by borrowing and by skimping on expenses in a household that already seemed to be subsisting mainly on tomatoes and cucumbers for dinner. In letters from home Walt read charges and countercharges of miserliness and extravagance. "Mother, I hope you will live better," he wrote after one barrage of recriminations. "Jeff tells me you & Jess & Ed live on poor stuff, you are so economical. . . . get a steak occasionally, won't you?" George, who was sending his army pay home to his mother, said the same— "don't be afraid to use the money for there is plenty more where that came from."

But money was only one of their problems. Hannah was sick, depressed, and battling with Charley Heyde—there was talk of sending Walt to Burlington to rescue her and bring her home. Jesse was now as helpless as Eddy, but more troublesome. He was no longer able to hold a job, awoke in moods of violence, vomited his meals, and between sick spells was good only for rocking his niece's cradle hour after hour in a sort of edgy catatonia. His friends, if not yet his mother, whom he sometimes menaced with a chair, had decided he was insane. Jesse had already worried ten years off her life, said Jeff, who believed that the root of Jesse's troubles was syphilis, now advanced, keepsake from an "Irish whore," and wanted him put away for good along with Eddy, "the most infernal lazy and the most ugly human being I have ever met."

Andrew, thirty-six, dying of tuberculosis and alcoholism, had put himself in the hands of a "celebrated Italian Doctor"—"infernal son of a bitch," Jeff called him—who was demanding the piratical sum of $180 in advance to treat him in his Brooklyn hydropathy establishment. Meanwhile, Andrew's hard-drinking wife Nancy neglected their two children and was pregnant again, "the lazeyest and dirtiest woman i ever want to see," Louisa Whitman wrote after seeing where they lived: "o walt how poverty stricken every thing looked, it made me feel bad all night and so dirty every thing." "Mother, you must just resign yourself to things that occur," he told her. As balm for these and other afflictions—rheumatism, a rented house so cramped that the family gathered in the basement, feuds with their tenants—he and George, separately, held out the prospect of a little place they planned to buy for her some day soon, half an acre or so somewhere out on Long Island, where she would have nothing to do but feed the chickens, bake pumpkin pies, and play with her grandchildren when they came visiting.

"Dear Walt, do come home if only for a short time," Jeff wrote on October 15. "And unless you come home quite soon you certainly will never see Andrew alive." Walt put off the trip for over two weeks, ostensibly so he could vote the Union ticket in Brooklyn on Election Day, November 3, and help rout the copperhead candidates —"about as great a victory for us," he told Lewy Brown a few days later, "as if we had flaxed General Lee himself, & all his men." It may have been the discipline he acquired in the hospitals that enabled him to remain comparatively detached from family affairs at Portland Avenue, even though he knew Andrew was bound for the next world and the others were much as he had been led to believe, his mother excepted. He made her a mirror of his determination not to be infected by the surrounding despair—"Mother is very well & active & cheerful," he told Nelly O'Connor, and despite her frugality, which he was seeing at first hand now, he said that she would gladly "give the last mouthful in the house to any union soldier that needed it." There was no reason for him to reject any of the pleasures of "this land of wealth & plenty" so far from the front that the war hardly seemed to be going on: Verdi, Bellini and Donizetti at the Academy of Music, the theater, late supper parties, store windows along Broadway, the splendid view from the pilot's deck of the Fulton Street ferry. His old paper, the *Eagle*, ran what his mother called "a very good little peice" that paid tribute to him as a prominent Brooklynite who was now rendering heroic services among the sick, wounded and dying.

He said goodbye and left for Washington on December 1. The accounts various members of his family sent him immediately after Andrew's death two days later have a Victorian amplitude of valetudinary detail. Andrew asked to be taken to his mother's house to die, but "nancy made a great adue and said you shant have him he belongs to me." His mother and the others came to Nancy's house to wait with him—"The poor boy seemed to think that that would take nearly all the horror of it away." His last night Nancy went to bed drunk, and "when she came out in the morning she brought such a smell that Jeffy got sick." After twenty-four hours dying Andrew "turned his head and looked at your and georges pictures for some time and then shut his eyes god grant i may never witness another."

Jesse saw the body laid out in George's frock coat and vest and "took on very much and looked a little strange." When he came

home, he attacked his three-year-old niece after some trivial provo-
cation, uttered "a terrible oath," and threatened her mother. "He
looked just like a madman," Mattie told Walt, "and what he would
have done if your mother had not interfered the Lord only knows. I
still thought I would not let him see I was affraid and I told him he
better try it if he dare to when he flew at me again and said he did
not mean to hurt me but now he Be D—— if he wouldn't knock my
brains out such a D—— fool as I was hadn't right to live. I managed
to get out of the basement, but it was a long time before I could get
upstairs." "Had I been home," Jeff said, "so help me God i would
have shot him dead on the spot. . . . I wish to God he was ready to
put along side of Andrew. There would be but few tears shed on my
part I can tell you." A year later Walt had Jesse committed to the
Kings County Lunatic Asylum; by then George was a prisoner of
war and Nancy, who had given birth (her child was subsequently
run over and killed by a brewery wagon), was a prostitute. Such, in
part, were the short and simple annals of Whitman's ravaged family.

"I did not go on to Andrew's funeral, (I suppose it was yesterday)," he wrote to George on December 6, "but I am very very sorry
now that I did not stay while I was at home." Nine days later he
sounded the same uncharacteristic note of remorse. "Mother, I think
about you all more than ever—& poor Andrew, I often think about
him." The next time he was home, he said, he would not "go off
gallivanting" but spend the time quietly with her. When he turned
forty-five in May 1864, after a lifetime of independence and health
he was not only "homesick, something new for me," but on the
verge of physical collapse. He was so weak when he came home
again, on June 22, that nearly three weeks passed before he was able
to go outdoors for a carriage ride with Jeff. When he returned to
Washington it was "in the character of a man not entirely well," "not
so unconsciously hearty as before."

IV

Symptoms suggesting severe hypertension (and perhaps mercury
poisoning, from overdoses of calomel) signaled Whitman's collapse:
depressions, insomnia, night sweats and night terrors, spells of dizziness, faintness and trembling, terrible headaches, photophobia,
sinusitis and sore throat, deafness, buzzing and humming in the

ears. He told Traubel once that his troubles started in the summer of 1863, when he cut his hand while assisting at an amputation; the cut became infected, angry red lines ran up his arm to his shoulder. But he had felt warning signs before this accident, and a few weeks after it he said he was "first rate in health . . . my hand has entirely healed." Doctors in Washington cautioned him against "hospital fever" and "hospital fatigue" and said he was spending too much time breathing the effluvia of gangrene and dysentery; in the end, following their diagnosis, his system was penetrated by a "virus" or "the malaria." Whitman considered himself as direct a casualty of the hospitals as some soldiers who would have had a better chance of recovery if they had been left on the battlefield. His case was "tenacious, peculiar and somewhat baffling." He sensed that its origins were not exclusively physical.

"I have seen all the horrors of soldier's life," he said, hinting at the dynamics of survivor guilt, "& not been kept up by its excitement —it is awful to see so much, & not be able to relieve it." Never before had his chronically objectless affections been "so thoroughly and (so far) permanently absorbed, to the very roots, as by these huge swarms of dear, wounded, sick, dying boys—I get very much attached." But nursing, socially the most approved although instinctually not the most gratifying channel for a grand passion, proved to be a dangerous occupation. The perfect health Whitman was so proud of broke in the hospitals along with a delicate structure of denial and sublimation. Love became irreversibly linked with disease, mutilation, death, absence, further reaches of the sterile shoreline he glimpsed before the war:

> Me and mine, loose windrows, little corpses,
> Froth, snowy white and bubbles,
> (See, from my dead lips the ooze exuding at last,
> See, the prismatic colors glistening and rolling,)
> Tufts of straw, sands, fragments . . .

Each soldier was another Sawyer. For thirteen months Whitman watched as Oscar Cunningham, a casualty of Chancellorsville, wasted away at Armory Square. "When he was brought here I thought he ought to have been taken to a sculptor to model for an emblematic figure of the west, he was such a handsome giant over 6 feet high, with a great head of brown yellow shining hair thick &

longish, & a manly noble manner & talk." Cunningham's death on June 5, 1864, came as "a blessed relief," but by then the hospitals had filled up and overflowed again, this time with casualties of the Wilderness campaign. "Many of the amputations have to be done over again—one new feature is that many of the poor afflicted young men are crazy, every ward has some in it that are wandering—they have suffered too much . . . I sometimes wish I was out of it." After he came home to Brooklyn on the twenty-second, he was out of it for eight of the last ten months of the war.

On September 30, at the end of a month of Union victories at Atlanta and in the Shenandoah, George Whitman, who had led a charmed life for three and a half years, was captured in combat. Aside from two letters received soon after he was taken, until January Walt did not know whether he had survived the "indescribably horrible" conditions inside the Confederate stockades and deadlines (26,000 Union prisoners died there). During the months of waiting and semimourning he raised his spirits by looking ahead to a revised, postwar edition of *Leaves of Grass*. Two days before Christmas he finished an "Introduction" that he marked in a bold hand, *"Good— & must be used."* With an economy and directness new to his public prose the opening sentences justified his entire work and program.

> I claim that in literature, I have judged and felt every thing from an American point of view which is no local standard, for America to me, includes humanity and is the universal. America (I have said to myself) demands one Song, at any rate, that is bold, modern, and all-surrounding as she is herself.

Christmas day was cold, leaden, and damp. Toward noon, George's trunk, shipped from regimental headquarters, arrived at Portland Avenue. It stood in the basement room until evening, when Walt and the others at last felt up to opening it. "One could not help feeling depressed." Inside were George's dress uniform, his officer's sash, and other articles of clothing, his revolver, some books and souvenirs, the company roster, a little case of photographs of his comrades ("several of them I knew as killed in battle"), and his war diary, for the most part a dry list of places, dates, engagements, and distances but, nonetheless, for his brother, "a perfect poem of the war." George's luck remained intact, although he came near dying of pneumonia. In February, having survived the hardships and deprivations of Libby Prison, he was released in a general exchange. "I arrived here from the Hotel de Libby," he wrote from Annapolis on the twenty-fourth, "and if ever a poor devil was glad to get in a Christian Country it was me."

Meanwhile, Walt's angling for a government job finally produced results. Through O'Connor, Ashton, and William Tod Otto, Assistant Secretary of the Interior, he managed to get an appointment, from January 1, 1865, as a clerk at $1,200 a year. He was assigned to the Interior Department's Office of Indian Affairs, located in the basement of the Patent Office. In the same building where he had visited overflow casualties and was soon to see the preparations for Lincoln's Inaugural Ball, he now copied out reports and bids and stood within touching distance of Cheyenne, Navajo and Apache chiefs wearing ceremonial paint, necklaces of bears' claws, fringed buckskins, scarlet blankets, and headdresses of eagles' feathers and buffalo skulls; diplomatic war parties from tribes in the West and Northwest squatted or leaned against the anteroom walls while they waited to present to the Indian Commissioner, William P. Dole, their terms for annuities, supplies and treaty lands. Occasionally Walt visited the Indians at their hotels and, according to a bit of self-publicity he prepared for the Washington press, had himself announced to their interpreter—"The poet-chief has come to shake hands. . . . The poet-chief says we are really all the same man and brethren together, at last, however different our places, and dress and language." The Indians acknowledged these sentiments with an approving chorus of *Ugh*'s. Whitman understood from the start that his clerkship was "a good and easy berth," as O'Connor assured him, "leaving you time to attend to the soldiers, to your poems, &c., in a word, what Archimedes wanted, a place on which to rest the lever." After two months he took three weeks of home leave; in May he was routinely promoted to a higher job grade. "I take things very easy," he reported to Jeff. "The rule is to come at 9 and go at 4—but I don't come at 9, and only stay till 4 when I want." By his characteristic allusion to Archimedes and his lever O'Connor had meant to suggest that the author of *Leaves of Grass* and the forthcoming *Drum-Taps* needed only "a place to stand" in order to "move the world."

During the last spring of the war Whitman listened to a strangely mingled music of fifes, cornets, snares, and the muffled drums that cadence dead marches. His feelings had been as transformed as the title *Drum-Taps*, first signifying a reveille tattoo for the martial spirit, then "taps" in its late Civil War and modern sense—lights out, last post, a farewell to earth, sounded on the bugle. "What are taps?" he asked in his old age when his memory was failing. "As I guess at it now it is a military good-night—a sort of last ceremony before turning in—the final message of the drums before sleep." He had almost forgotten that at the beginning of the war "Manhattan drum-taps" had summoned young men to fall in and arm and that he had seen himself as a sort of drummer beating "the alarum" and urging "relentless war." But the music he heard at war's end he had already sounded in 1855:

> I play not marches for accepted victors only, I play marches for
>   conquer'd and slain persons.
>
> Have you heard that it was good to gain the day?
> I also say it is good to fall, battles are lost in the same spirit in which
>   they are won.

Charles Sumner, who had also beat the alarum and urged relentless war against the slaveholders, pointed to an apotheosis of nationhood—the States were now United for good, "one and indivisible, with a new consciousness of national life." In the flush of victory James Russell Lowell said, "Every man feels himself a part, sensitive and sympathetic, of this vast organism, a partner in its life or death." Whitman saluted Freedom and Union, "Victress on the peaks," but offered her only "psalms of the dead" instead of "mastery's rapturous verse." But even as he mourned the 500,000 and more fallen on both sides, he too recognized a gain. "Before I went down to the Field, and among the Hospitals, I had my hours of doubt about These States; but not since," he wrote. "And curious as it may seem, the War, to me, *proved* Humanity, and proved America and the Modern." Draft laws and draft riots aside, it had been essentially a volunteer army, "the unnamed, unknown rank and file," that fought the war to its conclusion and thereby justified the principle of popular democracy "beyond the proudest claims and wildest hopes of its enthusiasts."

Whitman's war—"the war of attempted Secession"—had not been about slavery at all, never about slavery, he was to say over and over again, but about democracy and union, organic principles of personality as well as politics, preconditions of his psychic wholeness and the validity of *Leaves of Grass*. "The chief thing was to stick together." Democracy married "perfect individualism" with "the idea of the aggregate," "the great word Solidarity." Its civil wars were fought on internal battlefields as well. "What is any Nation, after all—and what is a human being—but a struggle between conflicting, paradoxical, opposing elements—and they themselves and their most violent contests, important parts of that One Identity, and of its development?" Like the nation "proved" by the war, his evolving life work reflected an evolving consciousness of self. Given the Whitman analogy of psyches and polities, Lincoln's call for "a just, and a lasting peace, among ourselves, and with all nations," could be heard as a call for the poet to resume the building of what he described to O'Connor early in 1865 as "a gigantic embryo or skeleton of Personality, fit for the West, for native models." As he said at the end of his life, the book he had been writing and rewriting over the course of nearly four decades "could not possibly have emerged or been fashion'd or completed, from any other era than the latter half of the Nineteenth Century, nor any other land than democratic America, and from the absolute triumph of the National Union Arms."

On April 1, eight days before the war ended, Whitman contracted with Peter Eckler of New York for paper, plates, and presswork on 500 copies of *Drum-Taps*. On April 17, two days after Lincoln died, Whitman made a stop-press insertion of a short poem of mourning, "Hush'd Be the Camps To-day." On or about May 1, when printed sheets were due at the bindery, Whitman decided that without a major poem about Lincoln *Drum-Taps* was an anachronism. After two years of postponements he postponed *Drum-Taps* again, distributed to friends the few copies that had been bound, put the sheets in storage, and began writing a group of new poems. Among them was "When Lilacs Last in the Dooryard Bloom'd," "the most sweet and sonorous nocturn ever chanted in the church of the world," Swinburne was to say. Lincoln's murder, "the crowning crime of the Rebellion," as Whitman called it in a letter to the *Armory Square Hospital Gazette*, was also the crowning challenge to the poet.

A great storm had followed each battle of the war—Whitman wondered if some subtle and pervasive sympathy had been at work in nature. When he came back to Washington in January 1865, to take up his duties at the Indian Bureau the sulky, leaden heaviness of the winter weather was broken night after night by luminous blue skies. "The Western star, Venus, in the earlier hours of the evening, has never been so large, so clear. . . . The star was wonderful, the moon like a young mother. . . . I heard, slow and clear, the deliberate notes of a bugle come up out of the silence." The Western star, the music coming up out of the silence like the liquid caroling of the hermit thrush, and the early lilacs of that memorable spring were to be the chief symbols in Whitman's dirge over "the sweetest, wisest soul of all my days and lands," the hero to whom he had joined his own life. On Inauguration Day, March 4, rain and hail struck the Capitol like a volley of grapeshot. When the President came out on the portico to take the oath of office and deliver his address the air suddenly turned sweet and clear and the sun came out—"a curious little white cloud, the only one in that part of the sky, appear'd like a hovering bird, right over him." Visibly ill and worn out, Lincoln spoke of "this terrible war" as a judgment visited upon both sides for the sin of slavery; now that the war was nearly done the next work was "to bind up the nation's wounds." "With malice toward none; with charity for all"—Whitman's word was "Reconciliation":

Word over all, beautiful as the sky,
Beautiful that war and all its deeds of carnage must in time be
      utterly lost,
That the hands of the sisters Death and Night incessantly softly
      wash again, and ever again, this soil'd world;
For my enemy is dead, a man divine as myself is dead,
I look where he lies white-faced and still in the coffin—I draw near,
Bend down and touch lightly with my lips the white face in the
      coffin.

That evening, as he stood in the White House grounds, Whitman was suddenly swept along in the surge of people pouring in to attend the public reception in the East Room. "Fine music from the Marine band, off in a side place. I saw Mr. Lincoln, drest all in black, with white gloves and a claw-hammer coat, receiving, as if in duty bound, shaking hands, looking very disconsolate, and as if he would give anything to be somewhere else." Whitman was on leave in Brooklyn when the church bells rang out on April 9 for the surrender at Appomattox Courthouse. Around 7:30 the morning of the fifteenth they began tolling for Abraham Lincoln. Walt and his mother read the papers in silence over their untouched breakfast, and then he crossed over to Manhattan and walked up Broadway past shuttered stores hung with black. Toward noon the sky darkened and people huddled in doorways to escape the steady rain. "Black clouds driving overhead," he wrote in his notebook. "Lincoln's death—black, black, black—as you look toward the sky—long broad black like great serpents."

> Appear'd the cloud, appear'd the long black trail,
> And I knew death, its thought, and the sacred knowledge of death.

Under favoring May skies in Washington, Whitman watched the massed brigades of the Union Army, an almost unbroken line of 200,000 soldiers in two days with many more still to come, pass in review before the new President, Andrew Johnson, an ordinary-looking man dressed in black. Major George Whitman marched in the line with the 51st New York Regiment. A few days later, having traveled more than 20,000 miles across eighteen states since the beginning of the war, he marched with his comrades again, this time across the Long Bridge from Arlington and past the Capitol to the Baltimore and Ohio station, bound for civilian life and the arts of peace. Walt saw the train bend round a curve and go into the distance—the men clustered on the roofs "like bees," agents of work, wealth and community.

15

Good Gray Poet

I

A MONTH BEFORE HE WAS KILLED, Abraham Lincoln appointed a new Secretary of the Interior, Senator James Harlan of Iowa, a political ally, family friend, and prominent Methodist layman (soon to be lampooned by Mark Twain as "the Rev. Orson Balaam . . . great Injun pacificator and land dealer"). It took Harlan no time at all to decide that the Interior Department was "a sort of Augean stable." Wherever he looked he found affronts to the standards of prudence and rectitude he had enforced in earlier commands as president of Iowa Wesleyan University and professor of the mental and moral sciences. On May 30 he issued a ukase to his deputies:

> You will please report to me as early as practicable the names and positions in your Bureau of all employees whom you know to have entertained disloyal sentiments toward the Government of the United States since the Bombardment of Fort Sumter.
>
> 2d All such persons as have not been known to entertain loyal sentiments, and who have affiliated with those who were known to be disloyal.
>
> 3d All such persons as are not necessary for the transaction of the public business, or who are inefficient.
>
> 4″ All such persons, as disregard in their conduct, habits and associations the rules of decorum & propriety prescribed by a Christian Civilization.

The head of Whitman's Indian Bureau, William P. Dole, barely troubled to hide his disgust. None of his workers was disloyal, tainted, or superfluous, he told Secretary Harlan. "Doubtless some of them could be more efficient but I am not now prepared to discriminate. . . . Nor am I aware that there are any persons connected with the Office here, whose conduct does not come within the rules of decorum & propriety prescribed by a Christian Civilization." Before Harlan was finished with his housecleaning, Dole had been purged along with the Superintendent of the Census, about eighty clerks, and, according to O'Connor, all the women in the department "on the ground that their presence there might be injurious to . . . the 'morals' of the men." Harlan issued the most far-reaching of his pink slips on June 30:

> The services of Walter Whitman of New York as a clerk in the Indian Office will be dispensed with from and after this date.

The general purge at Interior had already kicked up a fair amount of commotion, but when O'Connor heard the news about Whitman he stormed into Ashton's office. He had no interest in the other victims; for him, Whitman's case was unique and involved a messianic pattern of gospel, persecution and passion. By the time O'Connor was well into his stock of historical parallels Ashton too knew for a certainty that Harlan was of the blood of the Spanish Inquisitors. When Ashton confronted him the next morning, the Secretary freely admitted what was at issue: a book, containing outrageous and offensive passages, that (by one account) was now displayed on a table in his office. It was the copy of *Leaves of Grass*, covered in blue paper and containing corrections and new material for a fourth edition, that Whitman had been keeping in his desk drawer along with other personal articles. "It's no use, Mr. Ashton," Harlan said, "I will not have the author of that book in this Department. No, if the President of the United States should order his reinstatement, I would resign sooner than I would put him back." But at least he agreed not to blacklist Whitman, who had been out of a job for less than twenty-four hours when Ashton emerged from the meeting and had him transferred to the Attorney General's office.

"The meanest feature of it all was not his dismissal of me," Whitman was to say, "but his rooting in my desk in the dead of night looking for evidence against me. What instinct ever drove him to my desk? He must have had some intimation from some one that I was what I was." (It may have been Whitman who laid the trail by making a welcoming gift to the new Secretary of a copy of the canceled *Drum-Taps.*) More than twenty years later, when Whitman found Harlan's dismissal notice and related papers in the archive at Mickle Street and gave them to Traubel for safekeeping, he was ostentatiously mild in his comments, as if even at the moment the axe fell he had managed

> . . . to be self-balanced for contingencies,
> To confront night, storms, hunger, ridicule, accidents, rebuffs, as
>   the trees and animals do.

"Don't ever assail Harlan as if he was a scoundrel," he said to Traubel. "He was only a fool: there was only a dim light in his noddle: he had to steer by that light: what else could he do?" And he added with a laugh, "I have always had a latent sneaking admiration for his cowardly despicable act." For the first time in his life he had been able to rely on a few passionate allies—"understanders" and "avowers"—to defend his cause and virtually relieve him of the need to take any public action on his own; he had only to supply O'Connor with some autobiographical and literary notes, and O'Connor would go into battle damning the torpedoes. Still, the dismissal crystallized in his mind a ten-year pattern that he willfully, but sometimes obsessively, distorted and then regarded with bitter gratification. The "equable man" of 1855 now favored and even welcomed the role of prophet mocked and dishonored in his own country. "*Here* the enemy have the ground mostly to themselves," he told Jeff.

Three weeks after the dismissal—and by coincidence, ten years to the day since Emerson first greeted the new poet—O'Connor finished drafting a fifteen-page letter of protest to Harlan. He cited Whitman's hospital service as evidence of "probity, patriotism, and spotless personal character" but put the case almost exclusively "on literary grounds." *Leaves of Grass* was unique in world literature, the brief ran: it celebrated an integral modern personality in all its natural acts and appetites; it was imbued with the spirit of democracy, "entirely Western and new, yet cosmopolitan, friendly and religious"; it was an "epic of the stirring events of the day" and was soon to include a series of poems "descriptive and expressive of the late war." ("War itself he does not celebrate," Whitman said in his notes for O'Connor, adding that "W.W. also comprehends in the plan of his poem, a series of pieces, which shall be the expression of the religious or spiritual nature of man.") More than ever before, O'Connor argued, more than "the entire mass of the rest of the poets now living," Whitman deserved his government's respect, support and protection. Had he been willing to admit parallels, he could have cited official positions held by Washington Irving and Hawthorne and more recently by William Dean Howells and Bret Harte. The year after Whitman was fired Herman Melville became a deputy inspector of customs.

O'Connor's letter, which according to plan was to be signed by Ashton on the letterhead of the Attorney General's office, was never sent, it being clearly foolhardy for a subordinate in one department to call down the head of another in an official communication. Besides, Harlan's victim was better off than ever in his new job and was to enjoy a conspicuous degree of "distinguished consideration" under seven attorneys general. No, O'Connor decided, the issues were too principled to be dissipated in bureaucratic feuding. The unsent letter was the germ of a 46-page pamphlet that he wrote during the summer and published at his own expense early in 1866. The Bad Gray Poet—stigmatized by "the enemy" for having no morals, no manners, and no place in literature or the Interior Department—became, in the brilliant title of O'Connor's pamphlet, "The Good Gray Poet": sage, martyr, redeemer.

At the age of forty-six, Whitman settled contentedly into a job "well suited to a lazy, elderly, literary gentleman." He was allowed to take a month's leave in the fall, when *Drum-Taps* was published —if he had wanted to stay in New York longer he could have hired a substitute and made a small profit on the transaction. He had the privilege of buying books for his own use and charging them to the departmental library; he read them at his leisure in a comfortable, well-lighted office that looked out across the Potomac to the Arlington hills. In contrast with his dealings with Harlan, now when he sent a copy of *Leaves of Grass* along with "best esteem & love" to the Attorney General, he received in return a Christmas present of "a beautiful knife, a real Rogers' steel."

Elizabeth Akers, the author of "Rock Me to Sleep" ("Make me a child again just for tonight!"), disapproved of him in every respect, and his friendship with Elijah Allen had trailed off. But through Allen he had met an admirer of some years' standing, the young nature writer John Burroughs, then a clerk at the Treasury Department. He came almost daily for breakfasts or dinners with Burroughs and his wife, Ursula, in their little brick house behind the Capitol, on the site of one of the present Senate office buildings—in Burroughs' time the tract also accommodated a potato patch and a cow. "If that is not the face of a poet, then it is the face of a god," Burroughs said soon after he first met Whitman in 1863; three years later he was writing a biographical study, *Notes on Walt Whitman as Poet and Person*. "He reminds one of the first men, the beginners," Burroughs wrote, "has a primitive, outdoor look—not so much from being in the open air as from the texture and quality of his make—a look as of the earth, the sea, or the mountains." But for Burroughs, this same force of raw nature also possessed an enormous gentleness and affection. "There is something indescribable in his look, in his eye—as in that of the mother of many children." In turn, Whitman responded to a sensibility as pastoral as Burroughs' beloved Catskills and to qualities of proportion and quiet self-sufficiency that were missing from O'Connor's makeup. While O'Connor worked away on his fiery tract, Burroughs, who in the summer of 1865 had just come back from a woodland vacation, was thinking and talking mainly about birds, in particular, the gray-brown hermit thrush. He claimed that even Audubon, who had ignited his lifelong passion for ornithology, had not got this one quite right. The hermit thrush's clear, flutelike, deliberate song—Burroughs rendered it in print as "O spheral, spheral! . . . O holy, holy!"—was "the finest sound in nature," "perhaps more of an evening than a morning hymn . . . the voice of that calm, sweet solemnity one attains to in his best moments." In mid-September, Burroughs noted that Whitman had been "deeply interested in what I tell him of the Hermit Thrush, and he says he has largely used the information I have given him in one of his principal poems."

"Sings oftener after sundown . . . is very secluded . . . likes shaded, dark places," Whitman wrote in one of his improvised notebooks. "His song is a hymn . . . in swamps—is very shy . . . never sings near the farm houses—never in the settlement—is the bird of the solemn primal woods & of Nature pure & holy." That summer, with a sustained inspiration and sureness of word and design he had not known since "Out of the Cradle Endlessly Rocking," he wrote his great elegy for Abraham Lincoln:

When lilacs last in the dooryard bloom'd,
And the great star early droop'd in the western sky in the night,
I mourn'd, and yet shall mourn with ever-returning spring.

"Retrievements out of the night," memories of the dead President fused with the western star Whitman had marveled at the winter skies; the bugle notes he heard coming up out of the night silence and sounding "Lights Out" fused with the voice of the hermit thrush.

Solitary the thrush,
The hermit withdrawn to himself, avoiding the settlements,
Sings by himself a song.

Song of the bleeding throat . . .

In a critical essay published in 1866, Burroughs said that the rhythms and harmonies of "Lilacs" as well as its method ("a constant interplay—a turning and re-turning of images and sentiments") could best be understood through "the analogy of music." Swamp-wild like the hermit thrush's, Whitman's music also derived from opera and oratorio. "Art-singing and Heart-singing," as he distinguished them twenty years earlier, had become synonymous. Like Milton's "Lycidas," Shelley's "Adonais," and other great occasional poems, Whitman's farewell to Abraham Lincoln, "the sweetest, wisest soul of all my days and lands," transcends its occasion—Lincoln is never mentioned in it either by name or by office. But "Lilacs" is also an unconscious farewell to the creative powers of an "elderly, literary gentleman" who had said he expected to "range along the high plateau of my life & capacity for a few years now, & then swiftly descend." With the hermit thrush's carol, Whitman again came to terms

. . . with the knowledge of death as walking one side of me,
And the thought of death close-walking the other side of me.

When he placed on Lincoln's coffin his symbolic sprig of lilac in flower, "every leaf a miracle," he looked ahead to his own tomb in Harleigh Cemetery.

"Drum-Taps has none of the perturbations of Leaves of Grass," he told O'Connor. It was "more perfect as a work of art" and better "adjusted in all its proportions," displayed greater "control" and was stripped of "verbal superfluity":

> But I am perhaps mainly satisfied with Drum-Taps because it delivers my ambition of the task that has haunted me, namely, to express in a poem (& in the way I like, which is not at all by directly stating it) the pending action of this *Time & Land we swim in,* with all their large conflicting fluctuations of despair & hope, the shiftings, masses, & the whirl & deafening din, (yet over all, as by invisible hand, a definite purport & ideal)—with the unprecedented anguish of wounded & suffering, the beautiful young men, in wholesale death & agony, everything sometimes as if in blood color, & dripping blood.

Drum-Taps, a counterpart to Melville's *Battle Pieces,* served this purpose brilliantly, but at some cost to Whitman's art. During the war that strained his emotions and health to the breaking point he became a more biddable poet, more accommodating in his pursuit of acceptance, willing to risk less. The rhymed, metrically regular, and in other respects thoroughly conventional "O Captain! My Captain!", written within a month or two of "Lilacs," became his only poem to make the anthologies while he lived. "Damn My Captain. . . . I'm almost sorry I ever wrote the poem," he complained to Horace Traubel. The best he could say for it was, "It had certain emotional immediate reasons for being," among them his early glimpsing of Lincoln as an archangel Captain and also the widely circulated newspaper report that the night before he was shot Lincoln dreamed about a ship entering harbor under full sail.* But in its Tennysonian sonority and sweetness of diction even the great

---

* "He had had that very dream before every great national success," George Templeton Strong noted a week after the assassination, "and he was certain he should hear of some great piece of news within forty-eight hours. A poet could make something of that." The poet may have found some clues in *Moby-Dick,* where Starbuck pleads with the doomed Ahab, "Oh, my Captain! my Captain! noble soul! grand old heart! . . . How cheerily, how hilariously, O my Captain, would we bowl on our way to see old Nantucket again." (Strong, *Diary,* II, 691; *Moby-Dick,* [repr. N.Y., 1943], pp. 581, 605–6.)

"Lilacs" shares with "O Captain" and other poems in *Drum-Taps* a denaturing tendency, signs of retreat from the idiomatic boldness and emotional directness of Whitman's earlier work. Trowbridge felt that the "stock 'poetical' touches" Whitman had taken such care to write out of *Leaves of Grass* were now being deliberately written into *Drum-Taps*, for example, in the manuscript lines,

. . . lo, in these hours supreme,
No poem proud, I chanting bring to thee.

"Why do you say 'poem proud'?" Trowbridge asked. "You never would have said that in the first Leaves of Grass." "I think you're right," Whitman said tractably enough. But Trowbridge found the lines standing just as they were, inversions and archaisms intact, when *Drum-Taps* with its appended *Sequel* was finally published at the end of October 1865.

O'Connor was primed to argue publicly that the new book alone earned for its author a place "among the chief poets of the world." In November the New York *Times* declined his review, a reverse that along with others suggested to him that Whitman had again been left naked to his enemies. The New York publishing house that Whitman had contracted with to distribute *Drum-Taps*, did next to nothing for it. In the November issue of the *Round Table*, an influential weekly devoted to literature, society and art, William Dean Howells said that in the point of decency, at any rate, *Drum-Taps* was an improvement over "the preponderant beastliness" of *Leaves of Grass*, but so long as Whitman chose "to stop at mere consciousness, he cannot be called a true poet." "Quite put out," as Louisa Whitman reported, Tom Rome, who had printed *Leaves of Grass* in 1855, showed her "a long piece with flourishes," unsigned, in the November 16 *Nation*. More severe even than Howells' review, it dismissed *Drum-Taps* as "the effort of an essentially prosaic mind to lift itself, by a prolonged muscular effort, into poetry. . . . We find nothing but flashy imitations of ideas. We find art, measure, grace, sense sneered at on almost every page, and nothing positive given us in their stead." The writer concluded with a Flaubertian homily for the prose-bound bard. "You must be *possessed*, and you must strive to possess your possession. If in your striving you break into divine eloquence, then you are a poet. If the idea which possesses you is the idea of your country's greatness, then you are a national poet; and not otherwise."

Thirty-eight years later, with a sense of "deep and damning disgrace," Henry James confessed to having written this "little atrocity . . . perpetrated . . . in the gross impudence of youth." He had come since to regard Whitman as the greatest American poet. Edith Wharton, hearing James read "Lilacs"—"his voice filled the hushed room like an organ adagio"—found "a new proof of the way in which, above a certain level, the most divergent intelligences walk together like gods." In conscious emulation of "dear old Walt" with his oranges and peppermints, during World War I James was a hospital visitor and distributed little loving gifts to the soldiers. Earlier he had written an appreciation of Walt's posthumously published letters to Peter Doyle, "a young laboring man" who served in the Confederate Army before he was captured, paroled, and employed as a conductor on the Washington and Georgetown street railway. "There is not even by accident a line with a hint of style— it is all flat, familiar, affectionate, illiterate colloquy," James said about the letters. "The beauty of the natural is, here, the beauty of the particular nature, the man's own overflow in the deadly dry setting, the personal passion, the love of life plucked like a flower in a desert of innocent unconscious ugliness." (The novelist's brother, William, was also moved by the suffusions of Whitman's "inner joy.") But "the most charming passage in the volume," according to Henry, was Peter Doyle's account of his first meeting with Whitman. This probably took place toward the end of 1865.

II

We felt to each other at once [Doyle said]. The night was very stormy—he had been over to see Burroughs before he came down to take the car—the storm was awful. Walt had his blanket—it was thrown round his shoulders—he seemed like an old sea-captain. He was the only passenger, it was a lonely night, so I thought I would go and talk with him. Something in me made me do it and something in him drew me that way. He used to say there was something in me had the same effect on him. Anyway, I went into the car. We were familiar at once—I put my hand on his knee—we understood. He did not get out at the end of the trip—in fact went all the way back with me.

After that they often rode together on the long route along Pennsylvania Avenue from Georgetown past the White House and the Capitol to the Navy Yard on the Anacostia. Burroughs describes Whitman leaning against the dashboard by Doyle's side, "evidently his intimate friend" and assisting passengers or signaling the driver to stop and go. At the end of the last run of the night they had a drink or two in a saloon near the carbarns. Pete said, "Like as not I would go to sleep—lay my head on my hands on the table. Walt would stay there, wait, watch, keep me undisturbed—would wake me up when the hour of closing came." They communed in this "desert of innocent, unconscious ugliness" like Bloom and Stephen Dedalus in the cabmen's shelter in *Ulysses* and Nathanael West's own "Peter Doyle" holding hands with Miss Lonelyhearts under the table at Delahanty's speakeasy. Walt had imagined the scene in a poem he had written five years before they met.

> One flitting glimpse, caught through an interstice,
> Of a crowd of workmen and drivers in a bar-room, around the stove,
>   late of a winter night—And I unremarked, seated in a
>   corner;
> Of a youth who loves me, and whom I love, silently approaching,
>   and seating himself near, that he may hold me by the hand;
> A long while, amid the noises of coming and going—of drinking and
>   oath and smutty jest,
> There we two, content, happy in being together, speaking little,
>   perhaps not a word.

No longer "a man not entirely well," as he had said early in 1865, Whitman now boasted of being "fearfully well—indeed so red & fat people stop in the street and gaze at me." He led Peter Doyle, twenty-eight years younger, on long tramps around Washington, sometimes to Alexandria and back, with Pete protesting unavailingly, "I won't go a step further." He was always "whistling or singing," Pete said. "We would talk of ordinary matters. He would recite poetry, especially Shakespeare—he would hum airs or shout in the woods. . . . He never seemed to tire." They wore sprays of stephanotis in their jackets when they posed together in a photographer's studio. In one picture Pete looks gravely at the camera and stands like a dutiful son with his hand on his father's shoulder. In another they face each other, Pete with an embarrassed smile. "What do I look like there? Is it seriosity?" Whitman asked when he showed the second picture to cronies at Mickle Street. "Fondness," one of them suggested, "and Doyle should be a girl." "No—don't be too hard," Whitman said with a laugh. "That is my rebel friend, you know . . . a great big hearty full-blooded everyday divinely generous working man: a hail fellow well met—a little too fond of his beer, now and then, and of the women." In age, background, and taste Doyle's otherness from Walt, more pronounced even than Sergeant Thomas Sawyer's, amounted almost to a difference of gender. Whitman's ancestors, protestants in politics and religion, had lived in America for two centuries; he had once inveighed against "Catholics and ignorant Irish." His rebel friend was an Irish-born Catholic; like his father, a blacksmith, and his brothers, policemen and laborers, he was almost illiterate when Walt met him and began to tutor him in spelling, arithmetic and geography. "Walt knew all about the stars. He was eloquent when he talked about them," Pete said. Nonetheless, as Walt reminded him, he fell asleep, "your head on my shoulder like a chunk of wood," during one of these discourses, "an awful compliment to my lecturing powers." Walt could easily forgive this sort of lapse. "When I heard the learn'd astronomer," he wrote in *Drum-Taps*,

> I became tired and sick,
> Till rising and gliding out I wander'd off by myself,
> In the mystical moist night-air, and from time to time,
> Look'd up in perfect silence at the stars.

Pete's apparent indifference to his poetry was harder to accept. Pete lost the manuscript of *Drum-Taps* given him as a gift—"I did not appreciate it as I should now." In "your judgment," Walt chided him three years after they met, *Leaves of Grass* is "a great mass of crazy talk & hard words, all tangled up without sense or meaning."

Mainly objectless in his affections until now, Whitman extended himself with Peter Doyle farther than he had with any other man and at greater risk to his psychic safety. The simplest shared experience—sitting on the bulkhead door of Bacon's grocery on 7th

Street and eating watermelon off his clasp knife—he invested with
an overflow of love. He sent bouquets of flowers and tender notes.
"Good night, Pete—Good night, my darling son—here is a kiss for
you, dear boy—on the paper here—a good long one."

> I wish you were with me the few hours past [he wrote from the beach
> at Coney Island]. I have just had a splendid swim & souse in the surf
> —the waves are slowly rolling in, with a hoarse roar that is music to
> my ears . . . here around me, as I sit, it is nothing but barren sand
> —but I don't know how long I could sit here, to that soothing, rum-
> bling murmuring of the waves—& then the salt breeze.

When the occasion demanded he rebuked Pete like a father for
"growling and complaining," self-pity, groundless fears, fits of
brooding. "A little too fond . . . of the women," as Walt said, in the
summer of 1869 Pete had a skin disease on his face that both of them
believed might be a symptom of syphilis. He threatened to kill himself—he was eternally damned already for sins of the flesh. "I
was unspeakably shocked and repelled by that talk & proposition of
yours," Walt wrote to him from Brooklyn. He apologized for having
spoken so sternly the night before he left.

> It seemed indeed to me, (for I will talk out plain to you, dearest
> comrade,) that the one I loved, and who had always been so manly
> & sensible, was gone, & a fool & intentional murderer stood in his
> place. . . . My darling, if you are not well when I come back I will
> get a good room or two in some quiet place, (or out of Washington,
> perhaps in Baltimore,) and we will live together, & devote ourselves
> to the job of curing you, & rooting the cursed thing out entirely, &
> making you stronger & healthier than ever. I have had this in my
> mind before, but never broached it to you.

The rash turned out to be barber's itch, stubborn and painful but
without implications for the afterlife. "I want to hear about the face,"
Walt wrote eleven days later. When he came back to Washington he
went on living alone in rooming houses. Pete stayed where he was,
with his widowed mother. He was not so hearty and stable as Walt
believed him to be, but he was agreeably dependent and the stronger
for it—he became "Pete the Great."

Doyle once said that he knew about a woman in Washington who
had been Walt's mistress. He may have recollected a message he

passed on to Walt in 1868 from a workman named Jimmy Sorrill—
"the most thing that he don't understand is that young Lady that
said you make such a good bed fellow." "Dear Jimmy," Walt replied,
"You may not understand it, what that lady said about the bedfellow
business, but it's all right and regular—besides, I guess you understand it well enough." At times Walt went out of his way to suggest
that his affections took in not only the gratified lady along with other
"female women, some of them young & jolly" who flirted with him
—"I am quite a lady's man again in my old days"—but also the New
York pilots and drivers he exchanged kisses with and Pete's friends
in Washington: "Dave and all the rest of the rail road boys," "Tom
Hasset on No. 7," "Harry on No. 11," "Johnny Lee, my dear darling boy, I love him truly." Pete did not fully comprehend at all the
intensity and direction of the love Walt bestowed on him alone.

"I don't know what I should do if I hadn't you to think of and look
forward to," Walt said three years after he met Pete. He had entered
a time of "incessant enormous abnormal perturbation," as he described it in his notebook. In "Calamus," once again, he had already
anticipated such a time:

Hours continuing long, sore and heavy-hearted;
Hours of the dusk, when I withdraw to a lonesome and
            unfrequented spot, seating myself, leaning my face in my
            hands;
Hours sleepless, deep in the night, when I go forth, speeding swiftly
            the country roads, or through the city streets, or pacing
            miles and miles, stifling plaintive cries;
Hours discouraged, distracted—for the one I cannot content myself
            without, soon I saw him content himself without me;
Hours when I am forgotten, (O weeks and months are passing, but I
            believe I am never to forget!)
Sullen and suffering hours! (I am ashamed—but it is useless—I am
            what I am;)
Hours of my torment—I wonder if other men ever have the like, out
            of the like feelings?

Now he was tormented by the thought that Pete would not accept, much less return, the most defused expressions of love. Despite
the restraints put upon it, this love threatened to go beyond what
was infinitely compelling in fantasy and longing but still had to be

deferred; like Moses, he could not cross the river. "Depress the adhesive nature," he commanded himself. "It is in excess—making life a torment . . . diseased feverish disproportionate adhesiveness." Whitman recorded this crisis in two notebook entries. His underscorings are in purple ink, as are the figures "16" and "16.4," in schoolboy alphanumeric code, "P" and "PD." In three instances Whitman changed "him" to "her," but the dotted I of "him" is still faintly visible.

Remember where I am most weak, & most lacking. Yet always preserve a kind spirit and demeanor to 16. But pursue her no more.

. . .

July 15—1870—

To give up absolutely & for good, from this present hour, this feverish, fluctuating, useless undignified pursuit of 16.4—too long (much too long) persevered in—so humiliating—It must come at last & had better come now—(It cannot possibly be a success).
Let there from this hour be no faltering, no getting [word erased] at all henceforth, (not once, under any circumstances)—avoid seeing her, or meeting her, or any talk or explanations—or any meeting, whatever, from this hour forth, for life

July 15 '70

Twelve days later Whitman went home on leave. "We parted there, you know, at the corner of 7th st. Tuesday night. Pete, there was something in that hour from 10 to 11 oclock (parting though it was) that has left me pleasure & comfort for good—I never dreamed you made so much of having me with you, nor that you could feel so downcast at losing me. I foolishly thought it was all on the other side." But what Pete was able to give him in the way of returned affection could never be enough—Pete was like America itself which could never absorb the author of *Leaves of Grass* "as affectionately as he has absorbed it." Walt vowed to live "a more Serene Calm philosophic life."

III

The blue paperbound *Leaves of Grass* that Harlan cited as his grounds for firing Whitman was the "embryon" of the first postwar edition. When he gave the blue book to Traubel in 1890 Whitman told him, "This gives a glimpse into the workshop." All but 34 of its 456 pages show some sort of revision, ranging from punctuation and single-word corrections to wholesale deletions and additions, copious notes in ink and three colors of pencil, interleavings, and folded inserts. "With a kind of ruthlessness," a textual scholar says, "at times a frenzy," Whitman reviewed his work almost as if he were about to publish it for the first time. He reshaped, tightened and clarified individual poems, rearranged them in sequence and by group, rejected forty, shortened others, and eliminated some passages of a sort that Emerson compared with inventories. At times he flirts with genteel, conventional language, as Trowbridge had seen, and flattens out colloquialisms. "Life is a suck and a sell" becomes "life is a hollow game," which Longfellow could have written in mournful numbers. For every good reason he leaves "Song of Myself" relatively untouched, but he also leaves untouched even such descents into his worst manner as

O hymen! O hymenee!
Why do you tantalize me thus?

He deletes what may be a reference to anal intercourse,

Thruster holding me tight and that I hold tight!
We hurt each other as the bridegroom and the bride hurt each other.

But so far from trying to mute the pervading sexuality of *Leaves of Grass*, over O'Connor's objections he changes the line

City of my walks and joys!

to read

City of orgies, walks and joys,

and he titles the previously untitled poem "City of Orgies."

"Very well then I contradict myself": as he promised, Whitman's blue book gives a glimpse of the self-contradictory poet at work, dedicated, rigorous, unassuming, messianic, self-imitative, self-indulgent, at times tone-deaf to his own music. For all the work that went into it, the new edition remained transitional in design and massed effect—unfinished, perhaps unfinishable. He had submerged his vocation in hospital service but without losing sight of the old purpose, to be "a master after my own kind." Like a job printer preparing an estimate, inside the front cover of the blue book he calculates the relative lengths of the Bible, *The Iliad*, *The Aeneid*, Dante's *Inferno*, *Paradise Lost*, and *Leaves of Grass* (183,500 words, including *Drum-Taps*). The work-in-progress that had grown, changed, and aged just as he had was to be the American epic (Gertrude Stein might have called it *Everybody's Autobiography*) and Book of Common Poetry. "A few little silly fans languidly moved by shrunken fingers"—contemporary verse-writing, as he characterized it for O'Connor, was sentimental, depressed, enervated, tradition-bound, anachronistic—it needed to be "entirely recreated." "My ambition is to give something to our literature which will be our own, with neither foreign spirit, nor imagery nor form, but adapted to our case, grown out of our associations, boldly portraying the West, strengthening and intensifying the national soul, and finding the entire foundations of its birth and growth in our own country."

In August 1866 Whitman took a month's leave from the Attorney General's office and came to New York to read proof on the fourth edition of "that *unkillable* work." His mother, "pretty well for an old woman of 72," was now living in cramped quarters out near Brownsville. He visited her every day but he stayed with Abby and Helen Price on East 55th Street in Manhattan,

Proud and passionate city—mettlesome, mad, extravagant city,

as he had written in *Drum-Taps*. The Broadway and Fifth Avenue stage drivers greeted him with "renewed rapture." Riding with them by the hour it seemed to him that an inexhaustible panorama of fashionably dressed shoppers, visitors from abroad, tall façades of marble and iron, the press of traffic was exhibiting itself for the delight of "a great loafer like me." He took long rambles in Central Park, miraculously transformed over the past ten years from a wasteland of rocks and shanties to a vast democratic breathing-place stretching from the city's northern outskirt at 59th Street to the suburb of Harlem. For Whitman's taste, Olmsted and Vaux's cunningly variegated landscape of meers, ponds, meadows, romantic wilds, and winding paths was like the willfully intricate design of an ingrain carpet; the surrounding stone walls were contrary to "the spirit" and "visible fact" of a public park. Fifteen miles of perfect roads and bridle paths mainly attracted "the carriage-riding classes," "the full oceanic tide of New York's wealth and 'gentility.' " Still, Central Park satisfied him—it represented at least a trial marriage of art and enlightened enterprise, nature and the life of the city.

"The weather is perfect here," Whitman told Burroughs, "& if it wasn't for the worriment of the book, I should be as happy as a clam at high water, as they say down on old Long Island." The printers he worked with on Beekman Street were good fellows and willing enough, but they had trouble setting his irregular lines and kept making "ridiculous errors"—"It is my constant dread that the book will be disfigured." And this new edition, he said years later, had a continuing history of "grief." "Price $3," he wrote from Washington in October 1866—he was answering one of the infrequent inquiries that came in. "I publish & sell it myself—sending it from here by mail." He supposed this was going to be a temporary arrangement only while he hunted for a publisher, meanwhile ignoring charges of infringement brought by the owner of the old Thayer and Eldridge plates. A New York publisher made him an offer, but he rejected it because it was contingent on his leaving out lines thought to be objectionable. This was apparently the only offer he had the luxury of rejecting. After consulting "with several eminent men," he was informed by a Washington firm, "we deem it injudicious to commit ourselves."

Trowbridge met the same resistance when he tried to place the book in Boston. He told O'Connor that no publisher there had the sense or the courage to take on a book with such a conspicuous "seminal element." For a while during the spring of 1867 George Carleton of New York, an aggressive and successful publisher, appeared to be a candidate, but even O'Connor could not overcome the firm's eventual, "Pecksniffian" reluctance. Within a period of about a month Carleton (who later termed himself "the prize ass of the nineteenth century") had the distinction of turning down both *Leaves of Grass* and Mark Twain's first book. "So our Shakespeare goes without a publisher," O'Connor said in May 1867. Five months later Whitman's bindery in New York went into bankruptcy. "I received a portion of the books remaining," said Whitman. "The most of them were lost."

The Good Gray Poet, published in January 1866, was the major exception to a bleak pattern. In his freehand style, O'Connor misportrayed Whitman as "a protector of fugitive slaves" before the war, and during it a patriot eager "to get his name on the enrollment lists, that he might stand his chance for martial service." He introduces a little vignette of Abraham Lincoln gazing at the poet through a window in the East Room of the White House and saying, with a significant emphasis, "Well, *he* looks like a Man!"* Despite other characteristic extravagances, O'Connor levitated the issue of Whitman's dismissal—Harlan's pink slip became nothing less than a universal affront to the Word. "God grant that not in vain upon this outrage do I invoke the judgment of the mighty spirit of literature, and the fires of every honest heart!" he said in his peroration; he called on scholars, writers, editors, men of good will everywhere to make common cause with him.

Early in 1866 complimentary copies went out to fifty eminent men, among them Victor Hugo, John Stuart Mill, Cardinal Newman, Matthew Arnold, Emerson, and Senator Sumner. "I still think it is the most brilliant and vigorous effort I know of in controversial literature," the celebrated orator Wendell Phillips said on second reading. "It is one of those essays struck out in the heart of a great emergency which survive the occasion." Emerson was in the course of executing a slow retrograde maneuver away from Whitman's poetry and apparently did not respond in writing. Matthew Arnold, one of the few who did, offered a caution. "As to the general question of Mr. Walt Whitman's poetical achievement," he told

---

* O'Connor's source for this appealing but apocryphal tale was Whitman, who in turn had taken it in good faith from a letter sent him by an admirer in New York. The writer appears to have adapted the story from Goethe, who claimed that Napoleon said to him, "Indeed, you are a *Man*." (John J. McAleer, "Whitman and Goethe: More on the 'Van Rensellaer' Letter." *Walt Whitman Review*, VI, No. 4 [Dec. 1960], pp. 83–85.)

35

36

Whitman sent this picture of himself to Anne Gilchrist (below) in England. "I fed my heart with sweet hopes," she wrote to him, "strengthened it with looking into the eyes of thy picture. O surely in the ineffable tenderness of thy look speaks the yearning of thy man-soul towards my woman-soul."

No. 150

Office Christian Commission,

No. 13 Bank Street.

Philadelphia, Jany 20th 1863

To Officers of the Army and Navy of the United States, and others:

The **CHRISTIAN COMMISSION,** organized by a Convention of the Young Men's Christian Associations of the loyal States, to promote the spiritual and temporal welfare and improvement of the men of the Army and Navy, acting under the approbation and commendation of the President, the Secretaries of the Army and the Navy, and of the Generals in command, have appointed

Walt Whitman of Brooklyn N.Y.,

A Delegate, to act in accordance with instructions furnished herewith, under direction of the proper officers, in furtherance of the objects of the Christian Commission.

His services will be rendered in behalf of the Christian Commission, without remuneration from, or expense to, the Government.

His work will be that of distributing stores where needed, in hospitals and camps; circulating good reading matter amongst soldiers and sailors; visiting the sick and wounded, to instruct, comfort and cheer them, and aid them in correspondence with their friends at home; aiding Surgeons on the battle-field and elsewhere in the care and conveyance of the wounded to hospitals; helping Chaplains in their ministrations and influence for the good of the men under their care; and addressing soldiers and sailors, individually and collectively, in explanation of the work of the Christian Commission and its Delegates, and for their personal instruction and benefit, temporal and eternal.

All possible facilities, and all due courtesies, are asked for him, in the proper pursuance of any or all of these duties.

Geo, H. Stuart

Chairman Christian Commission.

37

Above, Whitman's commission as "Soldiers' Missionary." William Douglas O'Connor and his wife, Ellen, gave Whitman a home when he settled in wartime Washington.

38

39

40

A wartime tintype of Whitman's soldier brother, George. Below, one of Whitman's letters home.

a week to you, regular — but I will write soon to Jeff a good long letter — I have wanted to for some time, but have been much occupied. Dear brother, I wish you to say to Probasco & all the other young men on the Works, I send them my love & best thanks — never as they came more acceptable than the little fund they forwarded me, the last week, — Our wounded, from Hooker's battles, are worse wounded & more of them than any battle of the war & indeed (we have lost from 15,000 to 20,000) any I may say of modern times — besides, the weather has been very hot here, very bad for new wounds. Yet the rebellion has lost worse & more, — the more I find out about it the more I think they, the confederates, have rec'd an irreparable harm & loss in Virginia. — I should not be surprised to see them (either voluntarily or by force) leaving Virginia, — I don't see how on earth they can stay there — I think Hooker is already reaching after them again — I do not give up Hooker yet. Dear mother I should like to hear from Han, you, Han — I send my best love to Sister Mat & all. Good bye dearest mother. Walt.

Washington, Wednesday forenoon. May 13th 1863. Dearest mother. I am late with my letter this week — my poor, poor boys occupy my time very much — I go every day, & some times nights — I believe I mentioned a young man with a bad wound in the leg, had to have it propt up, & an attendant all the while dripping water on, — I was in hopes he would get through with it, but a few days ago he took a sudden bad turn, & died about 3 o'clock the same afternoon — it was horrible — he was of good family, & his name was John Elliott of Cumberland Valley, Bedford Co. Penn. — I felt very bad about it — I have wrote to his father — have not rec'd any answer yet — no friend nor any of his folks was here, the surgeons put off amputating the leg, he was so exhausted, but at last it was, imperating nec. essy to amputate — mother. I am

42

43

Above (42), Ward K, Armory Square Hospital, Washington; (43), hospital tents behind Douglas Hospital, Washington.

44

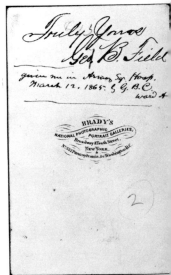

Visiting card photograph presented to Whitman by one of his soldier patients.

45

Whitman at about forty-five, photographed in Washington by Alexander Gardner. Whitman wrote letters to the families of sick and wounded soldiers. Soldiers who remembered him gratefully sent him photos and news of themselves after the war.

47

Washington
June 10, 1865.

Mr. & Mrs. Pratt:

As I am visiting your son Alfred occasionally, to cheer him up in his sickness in hospital, I thought you might like a few words, though from a stranger, yet a friend to your boy. I was there last night, and sat a while by the bed, as usual, & he showed me the letter he had just received from home. He wrote to you yesterday. He has had diarrhea pretty bad, but is now improved & goes about the hospital — but as the weather is pretty hot & powerful in the midst of the day, I advised him not to go out doors much at present. What he wants most is rest, and a chance to get his strength again. I expect he will

46

We are having very hot weather here, & it is dry & dusty — The City is alive with soldiers from both the Army of the Potomac & the Western Armies, brought here by Sherman. There have been some great Reviews here, as you have seen in the papers — & thousands of soldiers are going home every day.

You must write to Alfred often, as it cheers up a boy sick & away from home. Write all about domestic & farm incidents, and as cheerful as may be. Direct to him, in Ward C. Armory Square Hospital, Washington, D.C. Should any thing occur, I will write you again, but I feel confident he will continue doing well. For the present farewell.

Walt Whitman
Washington
D.C.

Washington D.C. 1865 — Walt Whitman & his rebel soldier friend Pete Doyle

48

With Peter Doyle, to whom he wrote a series of familiar, un-literary letters.

Brooklyn,
September 3, 1869.
Dear Pete,
I thought I would write you a letter to-day, as you would be anxious to hear. I rec'd your letter of Aug. 24. & it was a great comfort to me. I have read it several times since — Dear Pete, I hope every thing is going on favorably with you. I think about you every day & every night I do hope you are in good spirits & health. I want to hear about the face. I suppose you are working on the road.
There is nothing new or special in my affairs There is all kinds of fun & sport here, by day & night — & lots of theatres & amusements in full blast. I have not been to any of them — have not been to see any of my particular women friends though sent for, (the papers here have noticed my arrival) — have not been down to the sea-shore as I intended — In fact my jaunt this time has been a failure — Better luck next time. —— — Now Pete, dear, loving boy, I don't want you to worry about me — I shall come along all right. — As it is, I have a good square appetite most of the time yet good nights' sleep — & look about the same as usual, (which is, of course lovely & fascinating beyond description) Tell Johnny Lee I send him my love, & hope he is well & hearty. I think of him daily. I sent him a letter sometime ago, which I suppose he rec'd about Aug. 26 & showed you — but I have not had a word from him. Send him this letter to read, as he will wish to hear about me. God bless you dear Pete, dear loving comrade & Farewell till next time, my darling boy.
Walt.

49

51

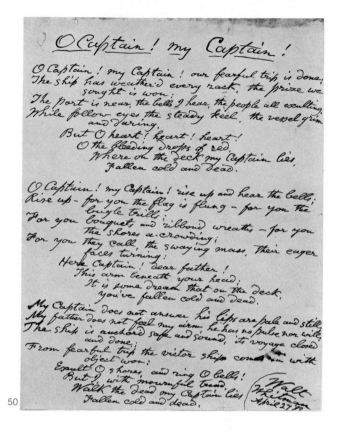

O Captain! my Captain!

O Captain! my Captain! our fearful trip is done,
The ship has weather'd every rack, the prize we
    sought is won;
The port is near, the bells I hear, the people all exulting,
While follow eyes the steady keel, the vessel grim
    and daring,
        But O heart! heart! heart!
            O the bleeding drops of red,
                Where on the deck my Captain lies,
                    Fallen cold and dead.

O Captain! my Captain! rise up and hear the bells;
Rise up—for you the flag is flung—for you the
    bugle trills,
For you bouquets and ribbon'd wreaths—for you
    the shores a-crowding;
For you they call, the swaying mass, their eager
    faces turning;
        Here Captain! dear father!
            This arm beneath your head;
                It is some dream that on the deck,
                    You've fallen cold and dead.

My Captain does not answer, his lips are pale and still,
My father does not feel my arm, he has no pulse nor will,
The ship is anchor'd safe and sound, its voyage closed
    and done;
From fearful trip the victor ship comes in with
    object won;
        Exult O shores, and ring O bells!
            But I, with mournful tread,
                Walk the deck my Captain lies,
                    Fallen cold and dead.

Walt
Whitman
April 27 [?]

50

A fair copy made by Whitman of his most popular poem. He described the picture of Lincoln as "the most satisfactory . . . I have ever seen (and I have seen hundreds of different ones)—looks just like I saw him last on the balcony of the National Hotel." The Lincoln photo and the photo of Whitman (below) at the end of the Civil War are both by Mathew Brady.

52

Machinery Hall, Centennial
Exhibition of 1876, Philadelphia.

53

Whitman in his buggy, with
Bill Duckett, 1885.

54

55

Camden: With one of his nurses, Warren Fritzinger. Whitman lived in a two-story house on Mickle Street. He worked and slept in the upstairs front room.

56

57

58

English admirers: John Addington Symonds (above) and Edward Carpenter (at right).

Whitman appeared on a cigar box label although he did not smoke.

59

60

61 62

As photographed by George C. Cox in 1887 and caricatured by Max Beerbohm in 1904. Beerbohm's title is "Walt Whitman inciting the Bird of Freedom to soar."

63

The Whitman fellowship (or "college") of Bolton, England, owned a lock of Whitman's hair.

64

Disciples: Horace Traubel and Dr. Richard Maurice Bucke shown in his study.

65

Whitman in 1883, a studio
portrait. The butterfly was
probably cardboard and wire.

67

66

Harry Stafford, around 1876.

69

Portrait of Walt Whitman, 1888, by the painter Thomas Eakins, who also took these photographs in 1891.

68

70

71

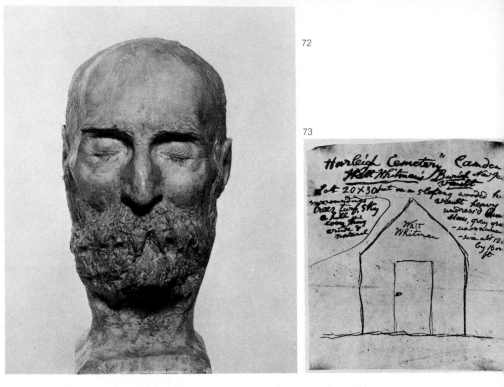

72

73

Death mask by Thomas Eakins and Samuel Murray. Whitman supplied the rough design of his tomb in Harleigh Cemetery, Camden.

74

O'Connor, "I add that while you think it is his highest merit that he is so unlike anyone else, to me this seems to be his demerit; no one can afford in literature to trade merely on his own bottom and to take no account of what other ages and nations have acquired: a great original literature America will never get in this way." America had a long way to go, Arnold suggested, before becoming "an independent intellectual power" instead of "an intellectual colony of Europe." Despite cheers even from Henry Clapp, who usually scoffed at exercises in hero-making, *The Good Gray Poet* never lived up to O'Connor's hopes: that it would do for freedom of expression what *Common Sense* did for independence and *Uncle Tom's Cabin* did for emancipation. But it set in motion a campaign to win respectability and international stature for Whitman. "It seems as if things were going to brighten up about 'Leaves of Grass,' " Whitman said. "I rather think it is going to be republished in England."

Henry Raymond, owner and editor of the New York *Times*, was no admirer of *Leaves of Grass*, having found in it, as he told O'Connor, "sundry nastinesses which will & *ought* to keep it out of libraries and parlors." But as polemics went, he thought *The Good Gray Poet* "the most brilliant monograph in our literature," and after balancing one work against the other he agreed to see a review by O'Connor of Whitman's new edition. "Don't make it too long," Raymond said. O'Connor responded with a six-thousand-word review that filled four columns of the *Times* on December 2, 1866. It drew an indignant letter to the editor from Charley Heyde in Burlington, Vermont, identifying himself as Walt's brother-in-law. *Leaves of Grass* and its author were Charley's favorite subjects and he considered himself an authority. On other occasions he charged that Walt knew as much about love as a maggot and that Hannah—"disorderly," a slave to "the lower animal instincts," devoid of "moral sense or principle"—was just a "practical version" of an "offensively vulgar book." By now almost hardened to Charley's "bedbuggy" antics, Walt dismissed the letter as the work of a malevolent but harmless pest—"the puppy." Raymond decided that Charley was "either crazy or a fool" and was sufficiently impressed by more favorable letters that came in to consider making O'Connor an offer to join the regular *Times* staff. O'Connor "grows stronger & stronger, & fiercer

& fiercer in his championship of 'Leaves of Grass,' " Walt said when the review was published. "No one can say a word against it, in his presence, without a storm." O'Connor had already joined forces with Whitman's other granitic supporter in Washington, John Burroughs.

"You must come with Walt and see us," O'Connor said in January 1866 after receiving Burroughs' letter of "sincere praise" for *The Good Gray Poet*. "I never force an acquaintance or friendship, believing it an uncanny thing to do, but let it grow itself—and you must help to grow this one." It grew so well that for a while, until their wives had a falling out, O'Connor rented rooms in the Burroughs house on Capitol Hill. During 1866, with help from O'Connor and Whitman, Burroughs wrote his first book, *Notes on Walt Whitman as Poet and Person*. After the *Atlantic* rejected the final chapter, a discussion of *Drum-Taps*, O'Connor took charge and promoted it at the *Galaxy*, a New York magazine that had quickly established itself as the *Atlantic*'s chief rival and closest counterpart. "I doubt whether the article will be accepted," Whitman predicted, and he was right at first. But O'Connor persisted, telling the *Galaxy* editors that *Leaves of Grass*, scorned by some New York literati, was nevertheless an established work with a sizable American and foreign readership. According to O'Connor, Burroughs' article, published in the *Galaxy* at the beginning of December, was the first discussion of Whitman's poetry to reveal "real critical power and insight, and a proper reverence." The following summer O'Connor published a fervid summary of the Burroughs biography in the *Times*. Raymond asked, "Don't you think the *Times* has done its share for the present in the apotheosis?"

Moncure Conway, once Emerson's legate to Whitman, took up the role of agent of apotheosis for England. He had spent the war years there, staying on afterward as pastor of an ultraliberal Congregational church in Islington and unofficial publicist for American culture. Enthusiastic rather than prudent (as Mark Twain was to discover when *Tom Sawyer* came out in England), Conway composed some highly colored recollections of his visits to Brooklyn. He quoted attractively from *Leaves of Grass*, but he also pictured its author as a heroic primitive who brought "priapism" and "the slop-bucket" into the drawing room. Like O'Connor, who called it "a frightful mess," Whitman was dumfounded by Conway's clumsy tribute in the *Fortnightly Review*, "about as impudent as it was friendly—quite a mixture of good & bad," a romance if not a collection of lies. With an English edition of his book still in the offing, as he believed, he laid down an official line that for reasons of "expediency" as well as truth exiled the wild man of Conway's account. In its place was a literary gentleman who could have passed muster at Windsor Castle.

> Personally the author of Leaves of Grass is in no sense or sort whatever the "rough," the "eccentric," "vagabond" or queer person, that the commentators, (always bound for the intensest possible sensational statement,) persist in making him. He has moved, & moves still, along the path of his life's happenings & fortunes, as they befall or have befallen him, with entire serenity & decorum, never defiant even to the conventions, always bodily sweet & fresh, dressed plainly & cleanly, a gait & demeanor of antique simplicity, cheerful & smiling. . . . All really refined persons, and the women more than the men, take to Walt Whitman. The most delicate & even conventional lady only needs to know him to love him.

At the end of April 1867 Conway arranged a strategy meeting in London. Present were two long-standing admirers of *Leaves of Grass*, Swinburne and the critic William Michael Rossetti, and also the publisher John Camden Hotten, an enterprising but shady operator, interested in Americana, avant-garde literature and erotica (of which he had a notable collection). They agreed that under the recently reinforced statute regulating obscene or pornographic matter, which put the burden of proof on the defendant, *Leaves of Grass* could probably not be published in England except in expurgated or abridged form. Both alternatives were unthinkable, as far as Whitman was concerned: but he disregarded the warning from Conway, went on preparing printer's copy for a complete edition, and drafted, for O'Connor's signature, a special introduction for British readers. Conway too continued to hope that "the volume with O'C.'s introduction shall come out just as it is," but he had begun to resign himself to the possibility that "it will in the end have to be done at our own expense." Rossetti's article, "Walt Whitman's Poems," in the July 6 *Chronicle*, a London weekly, suddenly made these prospects seem brighter than they were, for he argued persuasively that *Leaves of Grass* was "the largest poetic work of our period," the creation of a "very original and extraordinary genius." Presented with this endorsement by a prominent literary man, a founder of the Pre-Raphaelite group and brother of the poets Dante Gabriel and

Christina Rossetti, the American press responded in an obedient way to a reputation coming back through customs stamped "Made in England." "The article has had its effects here," Burroughs noted. *"The Round Table* copied the conclusion of it, and completely reversed its verdict of a year ago. *The Nation, Times,* etc., copied also; and now *The Citizen* appears with the article entire. We shall circulate it well. Our cause gains fast. The leaven is working and no mistake." The editor of the *Galaxy* was now soliciting contributions by Whitman, and over the next five years, at rates set by him, published four poems, the greater part of his long essay *Democratic Vistas,* and a number of laudatory references to their author, including Swinburne's "one of the great geniuses of our time."

"My feeling and attitude . . . are simply passive ones," Whitman said in November after he learned Hotten and Rossetti were going ahead with "a mere selection" from *Leaves of Grass.* ("With all the fussing and fretting I never got a complete edition . . . done in England," he was to say to Traubel. "I was always fishing for a full invite but was never more than conditionally received.") As he tactfully spelled it out for Whitman, Rossetti's policy was to put the textual integrity of *Leaves of Grass* as a whole second to that of its component poems. He included only those he entirely admired, entirely omitted those with words or passages that might offend "modern squeamishness," and declared that "if any blockhead chooses to call my Selection 'an expurgated edition,' that lie shall be on his own head, not mine." Only Whitman's 1855 prose preface, the importance of which Rossetti was among the first to recognize, was to be bowdlerized to the extent of softening or omitting some ten references to "father stuff," "venereal sores," "nipples," and the like. "I have no objection to his substituting other words," Whitman informed Conway, "leaving it all to his own tact, &c." Rossetti's editorial policy was just then compatible with his own inclination to make himself attractive to "all really refined persons."

Just a year or so earlier, when a publisher in New York made him an offer for *Leaves of Grass* that was contingent on a few deletions, Whitman refused with almost religious earnestness—"I dare not do it." Now, for the sake of an English beachhead and possibly in time "a full invite," he was willing to do what he had refused even Emerson when they walked in Boston Common. When Hotten published his bobtailed collection in February 1868 Whitman consoled himself at first with the rationalization that the book represented merely one editor's taste and not *Leaves of Grass* at all. But he soon saw through this—he called Rossetti's selection a "horrible dismemberment of my book." Even in the relative calm of his old age he became remorseful when the subject came up. "Rossetti said expurgate and I yielded," he was to say. "Rossetti was honest, I was honest—we both made a mistake."

So far from earning money for him, Whitman's new book cost him three dollars in duties when his author's copies cleared customs, and for a long while the closest he came to "a full invite" for *Leaves of Grass* was a pirated edition, with a mutilated text and a forged American imprint, that Hotten brought out. But the publication of his selected poems coincided with a dramatic upturn in his reputation abroad. He provided a Danish critic, translator of *Democratic Vistas*, with a list of "substantial facts": in America, in respect to both "literary recognition & wordly prosperity," he remained "under a heavy & depressing cloud"; editors, reviewers, booksellers, and literary persons "are quite generally banded against this new man (myself)"; he had "been ignominiously ejected from a moderate government employment at Washington by special order of a Cabinet officer, for the sole & avowed reason" that he was the author of *Leaves of Grass*. "Meanwhile, abroad, my book & myself have had a welcome quite dazzling." He was already a world poet, the subject of appreciative articles in Europe and Scandinavia. Turgenev turned his hand to some Russian translations—he was living in exile in France, where Whitman was soon to be regarded as a sort of literary parent by Laforgue, Rimbaud, Francis Vielé-Griffin, and other Symbolist writers. James Russell Lowell acknowledged a considerable Whitman vogue among foreign intellectuals but preferred to attribute this to the fact that they read him in Rossetti's edition, which omitted "dreary and tedious catalogues and the grossest of the physiological passages." Rossetti's edition was a turning point in the spiritual life of Richard Maurice Bucke, then beginning his medical practice in Canada. The Poet Laureate wrote Whitman flattering letters and hoped "that if you visit England, you will grant me the pleasure of receiving and entertaining you under my own roof." The distinguished critic and scholar, Professor Edward Dowden of Trinity College, Dublin, paid tribute in the *Westminster Review* to "The Poetry of Democracy: Walt Whitman." Swinburne, then at the height of his passion for Whitman (later to be repudiated along with Baudelaire and Whistler), addressed a poem "To Walt Whitman in America"—

> Send but a song oversea for us,
>   Heart of their hearts who are free,
> Heart of their singer, to be for us
>   More than our singing can be.

Three years earlier, in *William Blake: A Critical Essay* (1868), Swinburne had rhapsodized about Whitman's affinities with Blake, the one neglected in the United States, the other forgotten in England since his death in 1827, both simultaneous discoveries of Rossetti and his circle (a prominent member was Blake's first modern biographer, Alexander Gilchrist). The "points of contact and sides of likeness," Swinburne said, were "so many and so grave, as to afford some ground of reason to those who preach the transition of souls." John Swinton was so captivated by the resemblances that he claimed he was able to pass off lines from Blake as coming from *Leaves of Grass*—this was not hard to do with Blake's "Energy is the only life, and is from the Body. . . . Energy is Eternal Delight." Swinton "asked me pointedly whether I had not met with Blake's productions in my youth," Whitman reported. "Quite funny, isn't it?" He rejected but could not escape the connection and found his poems being cross-promoted with two other titles on Hotten's list, Swinburne's study of Blake and a color facsimile of *The Marriage of Heaven and Hell.**

---

* A manuscript note written at the time shows Whitman trying to make the best of this situation.

> Of William Blake & Walt Whitman Both are mystics, extatics but the difference between them is this—and a vast difference it is: Blake's visions grow to be the rule, displace the normal condition, fill the field, spurn this visible, objective life, & seat the subjective spirit on an absolute throne, wilful & uncontrolled. But Whitman, though he occasionaly prances off, takes flight with an abandon & capriciousness of step or wing, and a rapidity & whirling power, which quite dizzy the reader in his first attempts to follow, always holds the mastery over himself, &, even in his most intoxicated lunges or pirouettes, never once loses control, or even equilibrium. To the pe[rfect] sense, it is evident that he goes off because he permits himself to do so, while ever the director, or direct'g principle sits coolly at hand, able to stop the

The widow of Blake's biographer, Anne Gilchrist, experienced "a new birth of the soul" when she read Whitman for the first time in 1869. "There is nothing in him I shall ever let go my hold of," she told Rossetti, who had helped her finish the Blake book after her husband's death. Now, at her request, he lent her a complete *Leaves of Grass* and encouraged her to write an article that was pointedly titled "An Englishwoman's Estimate of Walt Whitman" when it came out in a Boston monthly in May 1870. "I know that poetry must do one of two things," she said,

> —either own this man as equal with her highest, completest manifestors, or stand aside, and admit that there is some thing come into the world nobler, diviner than herself, one that is free of the universe, and can tell its secrets as none before. . . . Happy America, that he should be her son! One sees, indeed, that only a young giant of a nation could produce this kind of greatness, so full of the ardor, the elasticity, the inexhaustible vigor and freshness, the joyousness, the audacity of youth.

As an answer to the charges of grossness and impropriety, Anne Gilchrist's article—which welcomed Whitman's "perfectly fearless, candid, ennobling treatment of the life of the body"—was all the more significant because its author was a woman of evident character, intellect, and culture. Of all the appreciations yet written, Rossetti said, hers was "the fullest, farthest, and most eloquent," a crowning event in the rehabilitation of *Leaves of Grass*.

"That Lady seems to understand you better than any one did before," Louisa Whitman told Walt, "as if she could see right

---

wild teetotum & reduce it to order, at any a moment. In Walt Whitman, escapades of this sort are the exceptions. The main character of his poetry is the normal, the universal, the simple, the eternal platform of the best manly & womanly qualities.

Despite Swinton's conjectures, Whitman apparently had no special knowledge of Blake prior to 1868; ten years later he made a fleeting reference to the Englishman's "half-mad vision"; and the sole example of any direct "influence" is the design of Whitman's tomb which, according to Anne Gilchrist's daughter Grace, he adapted from a Blake engraving. (*Faint Clews & Indirections, p.* 53; *Prose Works,* 1892, II, p. 670; Grace Gilchrist, "Chats with Walt Whitman," *Temple Bar Magazine* [London], CXIII, February 1898, pp. 211–12.)

through you." Rossetti too recognized that the pervading sentiments of Anne Gilchrist's "Estimate" were more than simply literary, and he persuaded her to publish it anonymously, so as to protect her reputation and the feelings of her children. "I do not even know her name," Whitman said to Helen Price—he had to use Rossetti as his intermediary when, without reckoning how they might be received, he sent *"the lady"* his books and several photographs in gratitude for "such an emphatic and smiling *Well done* from the heart & conscience of a true wife & mother," as he told Rossetti. "I had hitherto received no eulogium so magnificent." He was nearly alone in his failure to understand or at least acknowledge her drift. "O dear Walt," she was soon to write, "did you not feel in every word the breath of a woman's love?" After ten years of dutiful but passionless marriage and as many of widowhood, at the age of forty-two Anne Gilchrist fell in love. "Try me for this life . . . I am yet young enough to bear thee children, my darling, if God should so bless me. And would yield my life for this cause with serene joy if it were so appointed, if that were the price for thy having a 'perfect child.' " Only her duty to an aged mother, whose sole support she was, kept her from sailing for America right away to claim Whitman as her husband.

16

Passages

I

WHITMAN HAD ALREADY RECEIVED his share of declarations, delicate and otherwise, when Anne Gilchrist began writing love letters to him. In 1860 a total stranger, Susan Garnet Smith of Hartford, informed him that after reading *Leaves of Grass* she felt "a mysterious delicious thrill!" and decided it was her destiny to bear him "a noble beautiful perfect manchild."

> My womb is clean and pure. It is ready for thy child, my love. Angels guard the vestibule until thou comest to deposit our and the world's precious treasure. . . . Our boy, my love! Do you not already love him? He must be begotten on a mountain top, in the open air.

He wrote "? insane asylum" on the envelope of her letter, but admitted that if Susan was "insane" so were "Song of Myself" and "Children of Adam." Like a number of other women (and men) who responded to his poems and had their lives changed as a result, she was in part the victim of an innocent literal understanding. She took him at his word as phallic mystagogue:

> I pour the stuff to start sons and daughters fit for these States, I
>   press with slow rude muscle,
> I brace myself effectually, I listen to no entreaties,
> I dare not withdraw till I deposit what has so long accumulated
>   within me.

During the war he told Charley Eldridge he expected to "range along the high plateau of my life & capacity for a few years now, & then swiftly descend." By 1870 his hair had mainly gone from gray to white. He had trouble getting about, could no longer write or read without glasses, and, as in 1864, just before his collapse, he suffered increasingly from "heat prostration," dizziness, faintness, and other symptoms either of severe hypertension (his conspicuously florid complexion was consistent with this) or of a chronic disease of the whole man, mind and body (Victorian physicians called it "hypochondria"). A woman in Washington told him he looked like her idea of the patriarch Abraham; he had aged so fast it was hard to believe he had not been quite forty-six when the war ended and was now fifty-one, only three years older than the pleasure-loving Ulysses Grant. Susan Garnet Smith had faded into the scumbled past along with Juliette Beach of Albion, New York, the mysterious Ellen Eyre, Henry Clapp's willing beauties, and the young lady who sized up Walt as a good bedfellow. But he continued to exert the same personal magnetism. "I used to get love letters galore, those days," he recalled, "—perfumed letters." Nelly O'Connor he would have with him always. A passenger on Peter Doyle's streetcar gave Walt a rose when she alighted at her stop. A friend of hers visiting Washington rode with him several times in the car, studied his face with affection, but hesitated to speak to him. She finally spoke to Pete, who said that the ancient-looking man who regularly stood beside him on the Georgetown-Navy Yard run was the author of *Leaves of Grass*. She read it and drew from it "health, freshness, and aroma" along with a sense that life held "grander possibilities" than she had ever suspected. "I need make no apology for this note. You will not misunderstand it," she wrote. "I go to my home in Harrisburg, Pennsylvania, tomorrow. I may never again chance to see you, but you will believe, nevertheless, that I wish for you—and teach others to do the same—a long earth life of usefulness, and an eternity of *appreciation* and renown." "What do you think of that?" he remarked some twenty years later. "It's better than getting medals from a king or pensions from Congress."

Anne Gilchrist was different from the others, broader and stronger in her nature, more analytic and intellectual, with a clear scientific bent, but also more passionate, forthright and exigent. Her letters to Walt, whom she did not meet face to face until 1876, were as charged with emotion as the ones he wrote when on home leave in Brooklyn, missing Pete all the time—"My darling son, we will very soon be together again. . . . love to you, baby." She could not know she was offering what Walt could not accept or give in return, but she was true to her feelings, and her letters have a dignity that survived even the least diplomatic of his evasions. She was "a sort of human miracle to me," he was to say, "so profoundly considerate, intuitional, knowing." He respected her for being an archetypal "true, full-grown woman," self-sustaining, passionate, maternal, cerebral, an intimate of the Rossettis, Tennyson and the Carlyles. When she began her correspondence with Walt she had just recovered from a year-long illness—several times she came near dying and lay unable to move or speak. According to Rossetti, she was "not so capable as she used to be of continuous mental or bodily strain." And so it was possible that she was also the beguiling invalid of Victorian tradition, suffering from postconvalescent neurasthenia and a baffled premenopausal surge. Whitman knew that he owed her a special degree of considerateness along with a forthrightness equal to her own.

Anne had been twice reborn, once in the summer of 1869, when she discovered his poems and learned for the first time "what love meant . . . what life meant," and again during her illness, when she "looked death very close in the face." Walt's gift of a copy of *Leaves of Grass*, sent to her via Rossetti in appreciation of her "English-woman's Estimate," arrived with "no word for me alone," and she was so disappointed that for weeks she could not open it. "I was so sure you would speak, would send me some sign: that I was to wait —wait. So I fed my heart with sweet hopes: strengthened it with looking into the eyes of thy picture. O surely in the ineffable tenderness of thy look speaks the yearning of thy man-soul toward my woman-soul?" At last she decided that time had become too precious to be sacrificed to propriety. Early in September 1871, more than two years after her first rebirth, she went out into a field in Surrey, openly declared her love in a long letter, and felt "relieved, joyful, buoyant once more." "It is not happiness I plead with God for," she wrote, "—it is the very life of my Soul, my love is its life. Dear Walt. It is a sweet & precious thing this love—it clings so close, so close to the Soul and Body, all so tenderly dear, so beautiful, so sacred; it yearns with such passion to soothe and comfort & fill thee with sweet tender joy; it aspires as grandly, as gloriously as thy own soul, soft & tender to nestle and caress. If God were to say to me—

see—'he that you love you shall not be given to in this life—he is going to set sail on the unknown sea—will you go with him?'— never yet has bride sprung into her husbands arms with the joy I would take thy hand & spring from the shore." Seven weeks later, still waiting for an answer, she declared herself again. "Love thee day & night:—last thoughts, first thoughts. . . . My Soul has staked all upon it."

Walt's first letter to her was guarded and deliberate:

Washington City, U. S. : November 3, 1871.

DEAR FRIEND,

I have been waiting quite a long while for time & the right mood to answer your letter in a spirit as serious as its own, & in the same unmitigated trust & affection. But more daily work than ever has fallen upon me to do the current season, & though I am well & contented, my best moods seem to shun me. I wished to give to it a day, a sort of Sabbath or holy day apart to itself, under serene & propitious influences—confident that I could then write you a letter which would do you good, & me too. But I must at least show, without further delay, that I am not insensible to your love. I too send you my love. And do you feel no disappointment because I now write but briefly. My book is my best letter, my response, my truest explanation of all. In it I have put my body & spirit. You understand this better & fuller & clearer than any one else. And I too fully & clearly understand the loving & womanly letter it has evoked. Enough that there surely exists between us so beautiful & delicate a relation, accepted by both of us with joy.

WALT WHITMAN

She told him the word "enough" in his last sentence had been "like a blow on the breast to me." Still, she believed she had not been rejected, only deferred. "You might not be able to give me your great love yet," she answered. "But I can wait." She entered a "long long novitiate," as she called it, that ended with her death fourteen years later.

At the beginning of 1872 she sent him two pictures of herself, one taken in her early twenties and the other just before her breakdown —she was a large woman with a remarkably expressive face and dark, full, intense eyes. She had begun to hope that he would visit England and was "restless, anxious, impatient . . . above all, longing, longing so for you to come—to come & see if you feel happy beside me." Without fully knowing what he was doing, he allowed his hunger for recognition to trap him into teasing her hopes. "Did I tell you that I had received letters from Tennyson, & that he cordially invites me to visit him? Sometimes I dream of journeying to Old England, on such a visit—& then of seeing you & your children—but it is a dream only." The Poet Laureate's flattering hospitality was part of a grand ovation some of Whitman's friends told him to expect in England, and he was tempted to go, but he said he heard an inner voice warning him, "*Stay where you are, Walt Whitman.*" (Indirectly, through Burroughs, he also heard a voice of warning from Rossetti, who said he was not well enough known in England for a reading tour, something even Tennyson, Browning and Swinburne had not attempted.) Given all the circumstances, Anne Gilchrist included, it would have been a rash trip to make, and besides, as between England and America, *Leaves of Grass* was a "this side book," he was to say, and had to be guarded "against all counter-inspirations."

It was only after exchanging letters for half a year that Whitman finally brought himself to address the crux of Anne Gilchrist's mis-apprehensions. "Dear friend," he wrote in the postscript to an oth-erwise circumstantial account of family affairs and travel plans, "let me warn you somewhat about myself—and yourself also. You must not construct such an unauthorized and imaginary ideal Figure and call it W. W. and so devotedly invest your loving nature in it. The actual W. W. is a very plain personage, and entirely unworthy such devotion." This was a shrewd but overdelayed retreat from his first statement to her about *Leaves of Grass*, "In it I have put my body & spirit." But she was reluctant to accept his warning, firmly as he had put it, and continued to believe what she wanted to believe. Even at the end of her life, when she had finally given up all hope of marry-ing him, she still felt that his poems were "his actual presence" and caused "each reader to feel that he himself or herself has an actual relationship to him." Like Peter Doyle, "the actual W. W." remained the pursued and unrequiting party, and by the same rough symme-try he and Anne lived passional lives in abeyance. She yearned for the child she would never have by him, but, following his own open road to generativity, he was delivered of "triplets," he said: the fifth edition of *Leaves of Grass* ("my eldest daughter") and two further candidates for the future, "Passage to India," new poems celebrating voyages of "the unseen Soul," and *Democratic Vistas*, the work of an extraordinarily penetrating and original social philosopher and a major contribution to American prose literature. "All goes 'as well as could be expected' with me," he told O'Connor. "That's the phrase you know in parturition cases."

II

After the Northern and Southern guns had been silent for a few years, thoughtful Americans began to wonder if as much had not been lost as gained. Something precious had surely vanished from the shared life—simplicity, humane scale and tempo, mutuality, trust. Perhaps these critics were emotionally exhausted and saw mirages of Eden in a past that had not been edenic at all. Still, it seemed that each day of the postwar era brought fresh news of "public scandal, private fraud" in "the Land of Broken Promise," said James Russell Lowell. Swindlers, boodlers, speculators, suborners, the Ku Klux Klan, and the Tweed Ring were in the saddle and riding democracy down. There was a question about whether constitutional principles or merely party politics were at issue, but nonetheless a President of the United States, Andrew Johnson, stood charged in impeachment proceedings before the Senate with "high crimes and misdemeanors." His successor, Ulysses Grant—Whitman described him in 1868 as "good, worthy, non-demonstrative, average-representing"—inaugurated eight years of historic neglect and corruption in government. The great warrior's campaign slogan, "Let us have peace," turned out to mean, "Let us look the other way." "The progress of evolution from President Washington to President Grant," said Henry Adams, "was alone evidence enough to upset Darwin." "The present era of incredible rottenness is not Democratic, it is not Republican, it is *national*," Mark Twain said. "The Gilded Age," as he dubbed that era, worshiped "Gold and Greenbacks and Stock—father, son, and the ghost of same."

Stifled, O days! O lands! in every public and private corruption,

Whitman wrote,

334

Smothered in thievery, impotence, shamelessness, mountain-high;
Brazen effrontery, scheming, rolling like the ocean's waves around
and upon you, O my days! my lands!

Of the moralists and critics and artists who lashed the times Whitman, in *Democratic Vistas*, was perhaps the most savagely and unflinchingly thoroughgoing because he was the most profoundly engaged. His psychic wholeness and the validity of his life work were at stake, just as they had been during the darkest days of the war, when not one European government wished the Union to survive. Now, in addition to the daily tidings of public and private corruption, Whitman again listened to voices from across the ocean arguing that democracy was the low politics and low culture of Philistines and the mindless mass. Carlyle's word was *Schwärmerei*, which he rendered freely as " 'the Gathering of Men in Swarms,' and what prodigies they are in the habit of doing and believing, when thrown into that miraculous condition." Matthew Arnold, author of *Culture and Anarchy*, was another croaker. He "was not in the abstract sense a damned fool," Whitman was to say, "but with respect to the modern—to America—he was the damndest of damned fools—a total ignoramus—knew nothing at all." Arnold's brand of "culture" was almost as hard to take as his "anarchy."

But if Arnold was just "one of the dudes of literature," Carlyle could not be dismissed so easily. No one could beat him for pure "cussedness," Whitman said—Carlyle was "kinky." No one since Isaiah had voiced so much unrelieved bitterness with the secular world. "Never was there less of a flunkey or temporizer. Never had political progressivism a foe it could more heartily respect." Carlyle's most recent polemic, "Shooting Niagara," published in Horace Greeley's *Tribune* during August 1867, was a finger in the eye of just about every American of liberal inclinations. Carlyle said that extending the vote to the English working class, as mandated by Disraeli's Reform Bill, merely assured a fresh supply of "blockheadism, gullibility, bribeability, amenability to beer and balderdash, by way of amending the woes we have had from our previous supplies of that bad article." By allowing an electoral head count to become "the Divine Court of Appeal on every question and interest of mankind" (a principle Americans were about to reaffirm in the Fourteenth and Fifteenth Amendments to the Constitution), England was headed over Niagara Falls in a barrel, in emulation of its former colony. In what Carlyle regarded as an apocalyptic demonstration of *Schwärmerei*, half a million Northerners and Southerners lost their lives fighting a civil war for the empty purpose of emancipating "three million absurd Blacks." Carlyle had managed to reduce Union, progress, freedom—"the good old cause," Whitman called it—to "Settlement of the Nigger Question."

"Such a comic-painful hullabaloo and vituperative cat-squalling as this . . . I never yet encountered," Whitman said about "Shooting Niagara." But he set to work right away on "a counterblast or rejoinder" that he titled "Democracy" when it appeared in the *Galaxy* for December 1867. It was the first of three linked essays that made up *Democratic Vistas*, the 84-page pamphlet that he published privately with the title-page dateline, "Washington D. C. 1871." "I will not gloss over the appalling dangers of universal suffrage in the United States," Whitman wrote. "In fact, it is to admit and face these dangers I am writing." Nearly forty years earlier Carlyle had described the ills of English society as "foul elephantine leprosy," "gangrene," and a "fatal paralysis" spreading inward from the extremities, "as if towards the heart itself." Now Whitman claimed that American society was "canker'd, crude, superstitious, and rotten" and employing the same rhetoric of pathology, developed his own bleak and savage analysis.

I say we had best look our times and lands searchingly in the face, like a physician diagnosing some deep disease. Never was there, perhaps, more hollowness of heart than at present, and here in the United States. Genuine belief seems to have left us. The underlying principles of the States are not honestly believ'd in, (for all this hectic glow, and these melodramatic screamings,) nor is humanity itself believ'd in. What penetrating eye does not everywhere see through the mask? The spectacle is appalling. We live in an atmosphere of hypocrisy throughout. . . . The depravity of the business classes of our country is not less than has been supposed, but infinitely greater. The official services of America, national, state, and municipal, in all their branches and departments, except the judiciary, are saturated in corruption, bribery, falsehood, mal-administration; and the judiciary is tainted. The great cities reek with respectable as much as non-respectable robbery and scoundrelism. . . . The best class we show, is but a mob of fashionably dress'd speculators and vulgarians. . . . I say that our New World democracy, however great a success in uplifting the masses out of their sloughs, in materialistic development, products, and in a certain highly-deceptive superficial popular intellectuality, is, so far, an almost complete failure in its social aspects, and in really grand religious, moral, literary, and esthetic results. In vain do we march with unprecedented strides to empire so colossal, outvying the antique, beyond Alexander's, beyond the proudest sway of Rome. In vain have we annex'd Texas, California, Alaska, and reach north for Canada and south for Cuba. It is as if we were somehow being endow'd with a vast and more and more thoroughly-appointed body, and then left with little or no soul.

"I had no idea he was so conservative," one of Whitman's admirers said after reading these and further reflections on material progress, "infidelism," and a secular culture of "the mean flat average . . . the common calibre." Whitman's first patriotic reaction against "Shooting Niagara" had yielded to his recognition that "I had more than once been in the like mood," and he sent Carlyle a copy of *Democratic Vistas* with "true respects & love." They agreed on the diseases of modern society—their differences had to do with whether these diseases were terminal. In Whitman's view, America was as yet unformed, unrealized: its failures were transitional, growing pains; even its blunders were discoveries. When he looked ahead to the second centennial of the republic and beyond he parted company not only with Carlyle but with Mark Twain, Henry James, Adams, Howells, writers whose dominant spirit was nostalgic, elegiac or detached.

Whitman's indictment of the present was his baseline for the future. He believed that America, for all its troubles, alone possessed the prerequisites for a great moral and religious civilization. By assuring "freedom to the free," as Lincoln had said, America remained "the last, best hope of earth." "We have frequently printed the word Democracy," Whitman wrote. "Yet I cannot too often repeat that it is a word the real gist of which still sleeps. . . . It is a great word, whose history, I suppose, remains unwritten, because that history has yet to be enacted." Democracy was both a psychological and a political absolute. Its history was to be enacted through "Personalism," Whitman's term for the complex, fertile interplay of individual identity and the social aggregate, and through "Literature," democracy's "Soul" and "sole reliance." The priests had departed, their function absorbed by "races of orbic bards"—"sweet democratic despots of the west"—making icons for a new trinity: political freedom, science and natural religion.

Coming out of Whitman's darkest nights and deepest imperatives, *Democratic Vistas* was at once the least personal but the most powerful of his prose exercises in self-justification. Its resolutions fostered a remarkable radiance and openness of spirit, despite griefs and illnesses. "What is life but an experiment? and mortality but an exercise? with reference to results beyond. And so shall my poems be," he wrote on his fifty-third birthday. "I ventured from the beginning, my own way, taking chances—and would keep on venturing."

"Passage to India," another of the "triplets" of 1870–71, was the verse counterpart of *Democratic Vistas;* it was also the last of Whitman's major poems on the grand scale and, as he described it, the culminating statement of all his lurking religious meanings, of his faith in "the unfolding of cosmic purposes" through evolution. But it was also intended to be the beginning of an entirely new and separate book of poems. "After chanting in *Leaves of Grass* the songs of the Body and Existence," he now planned "a further, equally needed volume exhibiting the problem and paradox of the same ardent and fully appointed Personality entering the sphere of the resistless gravitation of spiritual law." In his notebook he identified "the spinal Idea" of "Passage to India": "That the divine efforts of heroes, and their ideas, faithfully lived up to [,] will finally prevail, and be accomplished however long deferred." He compared his poem to the final scene of some ancient saga: "A farewell gathering on ship's deck and on shore . . . a starting out on unknown seas." His starting place was the world of materials and "the great achievements of the present": the Suez Canal, the Atlantic Cable, the American transcontinental railroad, and other recent engineering triumphs that promised to unite the peoples of the earth into a nation of nations. Like Columbus, like Tennyson's Ulysses sailing "beyond the sunset, and the baths of all the western stars," the hero-poet of "Passage to India" steers

> . . . for the deep waters only,
> Reckless O soul, exploring, I with thee, and thou with me,
> For we are bound where mariner has not yet dared to go,
> And we will risk the ship, ourselves and all.

"Every great problem," Whitman noted, "is *The Passage to India.*"
The material civilization of the nineteenth century, its deep diseases
cured, was to evolve into a grand spiritual civilization in which
"Nature and Man shall be disjoin'd and diffused no more." Again,
as in *Democratic Vistas*, the mission of literature was to be altogether
fulfilled:

> Finally shall come the poet worthy that name,
> The true son of God shall come singing his songs.

The perturbations that made his love for Peter Doyle a torment
yielded to a vision of universal brotherhood. "Urge" became the
explorations and arrivals of a "brave soul" sailing "the seas of God."

> All these hearts as of fretted children shall be sooth'd,
> All affection shall be fully responded to, the secret shall be told,
> All these separations and gaps shall be taken up and hook'd and
>   linked together,
> The whole earth, this cold, impassive, voiceless earth, shall be
>   completely justified.

III

In September 1871, at the invitation of the American Institute of
New York, Whitman read in public a long poem he had composed
for the opening of their annual industrial arts fair. He received a
one-hundred-dollar honorarium, his expenses, and a great deal of
attention. The following June he delivered the commencement poem
at Dartmouth. Measured against even his average, both poems were
too "orbic," too "bardic" in rhetoric, for their emotional and intellectual freight. But their quality was of less consequence to him than
their occasions, invigorating journeys of the ego into the world of
external event. In other ways as well his life was becoming freer,
more ample, and suggested the coming of a second spring. There
had been a love feast on the Potomac in May 1872, one of the last
happy gatherings of Whitman's Washington circle before it broke up
for good. William and Nelly O'Connor, John Burroughs, Whitman,
and a few others were the guests of Dr. Frank Baker, the Smithson-

ian's medical historian, on a canal boat that took them to High Island for a picnic. Baker's invitation bore the lines from *Leaves of Grass*,

Now I see the secret of the making of the best persons
Is to grow in the open air, and to eat and sleep with the earth.

During 1872 Whitman took four months of leave from his job to tend to literary business, travel, and spend time with his mother. She was nearly eighty, arthritic, and barely able to keep house for herself and Eddy. George had married and moved to Camden. Jeff was chief engineer of the water system in St. Louis. Jesse had died in 1870 at the Kings County Lunatic Asylum. "O Walt," she wrote when she heard he was dead, "aint it sad to think the poor soul hadent a friend near him in his last moments and to think he had a paupers grave. . . . if he has ever done so wrong he was my first born." Lonely and failing, she made a pet of Walt, her second born, whenever he came home. She cooked breakfast for him every morning—"grand" feasts of buckwheat cakes or broiled salmon with potatoes, homemade bread, and sweet butter. "My mammy makes the best coffee in the world," he told Pete. As if he were a child again at his mother's apron strings in West Hills he kept her company while she did her household chores, cooked and read the newspapers.

When he ran into the transatlantic celebrity Joaquin Miller on Fifth Avenue in July, they had enough in common for three hours of conversation. Like Whitman, the bard of the Sierras (who changed his first name from Cincinnatus to the more dashing Joaquin) had been taken up by Rossetti and his circle, but Miller had actually gone to London and made a great success there. More of a showman than a poet, he thrilled the drawing rooms with his frontiersman outfit of boots, chaps, red shirt and sombrero. "It helps sell the poems, you know, and it tickles the duchesses." Miller was "a natural prince," Whitman said admiringly, although something of a "*California Hamlet*, unhappy every where." His own press-agentry, like the plain gray suits he favored, was less theatrical than Miller's but wore better. Friendly editors printed the personal items and other unattributed copy that he sent them. Unfriendly editors at least recognized his controversy value. How else could it have been known so quickly and so generally that Tennyson had invited him to visit, that Swinburne ranked him with Victor Hugo, and that "it would astonish Longfellow and Lowell to travel in England and learn how highly Walt Whitman is regarded"? His caricature appeared in a series of "Men of the Times," and he puffed it for the Washington *Evening Star*. "It represents W. W. at full length, with characteristic easy attitude, immense beard, hand in pants pocket, enormous and open shirt collar, exaggerating all the points till they are funny, while the likeness is admirably preserved." (The "W. W." in itself was presumptive of fame.) The report of his death in a railroad accident in upstate New York became a publicity bonanza. He returned from his supposed grave, one paper said, looking "as well as could be expected for a man who has suffered from two columns of obituary notice." A number of other rectifications were published, but for a while, as Walt told Nelly O'Connor, he could not appear in public without giving at least a few people a start. Among his other anonymous and pseudonymous published writings was his "Walt Whitman in Europe," a long article that he sent in manuscript to the journalist Colonel Richard Hinton with instructions to "Sign this with your name at the conclusion, and send it *at once* to the *Kansas Magazine* with a note proposing it for their ensuing January [1873] number." Hinton, an old *Leaves of Grass* and *Good Gray Poet* partisan who was well remembered in Kansas as one of John Brown's Free Soil guerrillas, obliged, and so did the editors, who had already published two of Whitman's poems. Celebrity, as Whitman demonstrated in and by the article (which he also placed in at least two eastern papers), was reflexive, self-renewing:

> As certain as that the bodily presence of the subject of this sketch remains altogether in the United States, well known by appearance to the vision of thousand and tens of thousands, it is just as certain that the subtle shadow of him, his fame, has established himself in Europe, and is branching and radiating there in all directions in the most amazing manner. . . . This is Walt Whitman, author of certain books of poems and some prose also, about all of which there is a singularly wide difference of opinion.

By Whitman's count, "After All, Not to Create Only," his American Institute poem, was published in twelve of the seventeen New York and Brooklyn dailies. Roberts Brothers, a bona fide Boston publishing house then enjoying the success of Louisa May Alcott's *Little Women* and its sequels, issued it as a pamphlet, somewhat to his surprise. "My percentage &c. I leave to you to fix," he said gratefully. "That the papers have freely printed & criticized the piece will much help, as it awakes interest & curiosity, & many will want to have it in good form to keep." There was no reason for him to point out that, with the exception of the editorial material that he himself had either cued or supplied, most of the criticisms had been derisive.

Workmen were still sawing and hammering away and bolting down the exhibits when Whitman, wearing a gray suit with white vest and open-necked shirt, began his recital in a low, unemphatic voice; what was audible in the reading did not prove to be altogether intelligible.

> After all, not to create only, or found only,
> But to bring, perhaps from afar, what is already founded,
> To give it our own identity, average, limitless, free.

This delphic prospect opened, at times, on badlands of bathos and incongruity, although the *ensemble*, as Whitman might say, was absolutely distinctive. The muse of poetry was bidden to migrate from the Old World and take her place in Grant's America among the fixtures of the age of energy:

> By thud of machinery and shrill steam-whistle undismay'd,
> Bluff'd not a bit by drain-pipe, gasometers, artificial fertilizers,
> Smiling and pleas'd with palpable intent to stay,
> She's here, install'd amid the kitchen ware!

In the *Tribune*, Bayard Taylor, once a member of the friendly circle at Pfaff's, lampooned this latest effusion of "the Kosmos, yawping abroad." The Boston *Journal* called it a "dementation," the *Atlantic Monthly* a curious "catalogue" of American "emotions, inventions, and geographical sub-divisions." Congressman James Garfield, whom Walt frequently ran into along Pennsylvania Avenue, saluted him by raising his right arm and saying with a smile, "After all, not to create only." Still, when the Centennial came around in 1876 Whitman dusted off his dementation, gave it a timely title, "Song of the Exposition," and, without much success, tried to sell it to newspapers in New York, Chicago and London.

"I am to be *on exhibition*," he told John Burroughs about his commencement reading at Darmouth in June 1872, a "great occasion."

Flattered and excited by the prospect of appearing for the first time before a college audience, he sent out his customary publicity and advance texts. The graduating seniors who had invited him hoped that he would read or do something scandalous to discomfort the faculty. If they were disappointed, he was not. The trip north was a pleasure outing that took him again through the large unconscious American landscape he internalized so lovingly. He spent two leisurely days traveling through the farmlands of the Connecticut Valley to Hanover, where he read his poem in the college church on the afternoon of June 26. He was preceded on the commencement literary program by the Reverend Edward Everett Hale of Boston, who sixteen years earlier had praised the power and reality of *Leaves of Grass*. Whitman's offering, "As a Strong Bird on Pinions Free," the title poem of a small collection he brought out at the end of the summer, recapitulated familiar themes—democracy, the modern, the voyages and destinies of the soul—in a familiar manner. His press release described his verse as a series of *"ejaculations"* with the exhilarating effect of oxygen, but his performance at Dartmouth, although he told Pete that "all went off very well," was apparently lulling. His audience, polite if unimpressed by what they managed to hear, knew for sure the reading was over only when they saw the program chairman rise and shake hands with the poet. He enjoyed himself at the commencement concert that evening, waving his arms in applause and shouting, bravo!

After a night in the college pastor's house on the Hanover green, he rode the Vermont Central up the White River valley to Burlington to stay with his sister Hannah in her brick house on the edge of Lake Champlain. His visit either coincided with or brought on a brief truce in her life of warfare with Charley Heyde, the "skunk" and "leech" Walt believed to be the direct cause of all her miseries. Charley had no more desire to be with Walt than Walt with him; he virtually moved out of the house and into his studio downtown, where he went on painting unsellable pictures of Mount Mansfield and Camel's Hump and also, if Hannah's accusations had any basis, trying to seduce young women who came to him for art lessons. Hannah appeared to be better off than Walt had expected—*"every thing much better,"* he said pointedly—and she told her mother that his "comeing done me a great deal of good, he has promised to come again and I think he will, and he must stay longer." (They exchanged affectionate letters to the end of Walt's life but never saw each other again.) He spent a week with her, took the lake steamer to Ticonderoga, stayed over in Albany, and sailed home down the Hudson on July 4 "through a succession of splendid & magnificent thunderstorms (10 or 12 of them) alternated by spells of clearest sunlight."

In Washington that August he and O'Connor had what proved to be the last of their noisy debates. This time, as Nelly had been fearing for almost a decade, they went too far—nothing that was said could have been imaginable earlier or unsaid now. As on other occasions over the dinner table and in the parlor the ostensible topic was the black man and the vote. On this issue Whitman was as conservative as ever. The enfranchisement of voters without regard to race, color or previous condition of servitude, as the Fifteenth Amendment required, was another demonstration of the "appalling dangers" of universal suffrage. During the summer of 1872 the practical wisdom of the Amendment was about to be put to the test for the first time in a presidential election, with Grant's chief opponent, Horace Greeley, openly bidding for the black vote. Whitman may have been inflamed by newspaper reports and editorials about Greeley's candidacy. He charged into the argument with O'Connor more vigorously than usual (his well-publicized "Quaker mildness" was official, not organic) and, as Burroughs later understood, was "rather brutal and insulting." Nelly, who openly adored him, compromised herself by taking his side in the argument, and he may have been encouraged to make some rash reference to O'Connor's failings as a husband. (The precise progress of this terrible fracas can only be inferred—the three contestants were reluctant to discuss it later except in the most general way.) O'Connor apparently felt that he had been betrayed by both his wife and his best friend, and he responded with the same hot spirit that informed the pages of *The Good Gray Poet*. He left Nelly after that evening and did not move back under the same roof with her until about 1888, when he was dying of locomotor ataxia.

The day after the argument Walt put out his hand when he met O'Connor in the street. O'Connor merely bowed and walked on coldly. He continued to resist attempts at a reconciliation on Walt's part and that of friendly intermediaries like John Burroughs—he did not call even during Walt's grave illness that winter. "His heart and his home had been broken," a niece said, "and he was in no mood to forgive."

Perhaps the explosion was inevitable, given the tensions and personalities involved. All the same, in the space of an hour or less, Whitman lost his most ardent and effectual champion, and with the breakup of the O'Connor menage he lost his oldest domestic and psychological shelter in Washington. By the time winter came he lost two other such shelters, one when Burroughs went back to New York State and put the Capitol Hill house up for sale, and the other when Louisa Whitman broke up housekeeping in Brooklyn and moved in with George in Camden. Whitman's last ties to the Long Island of his birth, young manhood and literary vision were cut for good. In October he drew up a hasty will leaving everything he had in trust for Eddy (he amplified it the next year and listed printing plates, books out on consignment, accounts receivable, and a total of fifteen hundred dollars in savings-bank accounts). "Don't be alarmed —& don't laugh either," Walt said when he drew up the first will and sent it to George for safekeeping. "I just took a notion to-day that I would like to fix it so." He celebrated the open road and a life of experiment, but ever since the forced moves of his childhood, from one house to a shabbier, he had known loss to be another face of change. He was seeking to console himself as well when, shortly after she left Brooklyn, he said, "Mother, it is always disagreeable to make a great change, & especially for old folks." Until she died he held out the hope that she and Eddy would come to live with him in a house he planned to buy or build in Washington.

On January 18, 1873, the Atlantic Cable carried news of the death, in Torquay, England, of Edward Bulwer-Lytton, author of the popular catastrophe novel, *The Last Days of Pompeii.* The news reminded Whitman that Lytton, for all his addiction to "tinsel sentimentality" and upper-class snobberies, had been a gifted, satisfying storyteller some of whose many novels deserved to be remembered. (Whitman undoubtedly did not know that Lytton had dismissed *Leaves of Grass* as the work of "an impudent, blatant impostor.") On the twenty-third, a miserable day of rain and sleet in Washington, Whitman stayed late at his office in the Treasury building lying on a sofa by the fire and lazily reading Lytton's novel about ambition and success, *What Will He Do with It?* He felt faint after a while and put the book down; more than a year was to pass before he took it up again. At the Treasury door a concerned guard offered to escort him to his lodging around the corner on Fifteenth Street, but he went by himself, climbed the stairs to his fourth-floor room, and fell asleep. He woke in the middle of the night without sensation or movement on his left side. He was no better in the morning, becoming dizzy and nauseated when he tried to sit up. Dr. William Drinkard, a neighboring physician who was summoned, told him he had suffered a paralytic stroke.* "Had been simmering inside for six or seven years," Whitman noted, "—broke out during those times temporarily—and then went over. But now a serious attack beyond all cure."

Peter Doyle, Charley Eldridge, Nelly O'Connor, and John Burroughs, back in Washington briefly on a business visit, spelled each other as nurses. "Pete, do you remember . . . how you used to come to my solitary garret-room and make up my bed, and enliven me, and chat for an hour or so—or perhaps go out and get the medicines Dr. Drinkard had order'd for me—before you went on duty?" By the middle of February he was able to go out on the street for the first time since his stroke, but he needed someone on each side to hold him up. His faltering recovery was slowed and then reversed as he followed the terminal illness and death of "my dear, dear sister Martha," Jeff's wife. He was barely able to move ten steps without

---

* Drinkard, a Southern sympathizer who studied in Paris and London during the war, wrote up the case for the Philadelphia doctor who treated Whitman that summer.

On the 23rd of January last, Mr. Whitman previously in good health—was attacked with left hemiplegia, presenting all the symptoms of such conditions, though none of them very marked at the time. Speech was hardly appreciably impaired: facial distortion was slight, and deviation of tongue just perceptible: left upper extremity never wholly useless: left lower showing the paretic condition—more than any other part or organ. Constipation, slight at onset of attack, has required little attention subsequent. Under the influence of rest, and such incidental treatment as was demanded from time to time, his general condition has slowly improved: locomotive power having, however, been only imperfectly regained. His principal annoyance has been a recurrent headache, with tendency to nausea—never actually reaching the point. After subsidence of everything like active manifestations, I commenced cautiously, the use of induced current—with Gaiffe's battery, and continued it for a number of weeks, without apparent result, beyond a decided improvement in nutrition of the lower limb. (Drinkard to Dr. Matthew Grier, July 24, 1873, Trent Coll., Duke University Library; Charles E. Feinberg, "Walt Whitman and His Doctors," *Archives of Internal Medicine*, Vol. 114 [December 1964], p. 836.)

feeling sick, and in his depressed state he preferred to be alone most of the time, propped up in a rocking chair and looking out the window. By early May he again felt strong enough to work at the Treasury building a few hours at a time and to walk a few blocks, but this was the peak of his recovery.

"My head feels bad . . . i have such trembling spels," Louisa Whitman wrote to him around May 12. A few days later she added, "dont come till you can walk good and without injury to your getting fully recovered." He managed to get to Camden three days before her death on May 23, four months to the day since he had his stroke. He kept among his papers to the end a stained envelope which he had marked "Mother's last lines." Inside was a scrap of paper inscribed in a faltering hand, "dont mourn for me my beloved sons and daughters. farewell my dear beloved walter." To the end she singled him out as her favorite. He sat up by her coffin all night before the funeral and in the morning he was still sitting there, his head down, both hands clasped on his cane. Over and over again in a keening rhythm he lifted and brought it down on the floor with a thud. Mourners in the next room felt the floor shake. This death was "the great dark cloud of my life," he told his mother's old friend Abby Price, "the only stagggering, staying blow & trouble I have had—but *unspeakable*—my physical sickness, bad as it is, is nothing to it."

He returned to Washington briefly in June, arranged for a leave of absence, and left for Camden "in a very depressed condition," Charley Eldridge reported to Burroughs, "complaining more in regard to himself than I have ever heard him do since he got sick. . . . I begin to wonder whether Walt is going to recover, and I am very apprehensive of another attack. . . . He is a mere physical wreck to what he was" and in danger of turning "hypochondriacal," by which Burroughs meant chronically depressed and misanthropic. In the mental disordering of his grief, Whitman had lost himself as well as his mother. He regressed to a time far in the past and, apart from inevitable idealizations of the dead, he wiped his memory clean of the fact that Louisa was an old woman and that by his own choice he had lived away from her for the past ten years.

In reparation for the lost time he moved into her rooms in George's house and kept everything just as it had been before her death, even to the gray dress, his favorite, that hung in the wardrobe. He lived day and night "in her memory & atmosphere"—

"Every object of furniture, &c. is familiar & has an emotional history." He slept in her bed, lay against the pillow she made for him and used herself at the end, read at her table, sat in the mahogany armchair he gave her a few years before *Leaves of Grass* first came out. He wrote Nelly O'Connor "a perturbed sort of letter" that he thought should be torn up, but he sent it anyway—"I look long & long at my mother's miniature, & at my sister Mat's—I have very good one's of each—& O the wish if I could only be with them—." In August, when he took the ring from his finger and sent it to Anne Gilchrist as a friendship offering, he was feeling too empty, too recklessly absorbed in the thought of a "termination" other than recovery, to think of the effect upon her. "I feel the pressure of the ring that pressed your flesh & now will press mine so long as I draw breath," she answered. "Perhaps if my hand were in yours, dear Walt, you would get along faster."

By the end of the summer he started going over to Philadelphia on the ferry, but when he got back from these outings he felt depressed all over again and had spells of dizziness, mental confusion, and deadly weakness in his limbs. He complained that there was no one he cared to see in Camden and sat by himself for hours at a stretch, doing nothing. "I think it is best to face my situation—it is pretty serious," he told Peter Doyle. "I want you to be prepared, if anything should happen to me." He revised his will again and on at least two occasions destroyed in haste masses of letters and papers. He contributed his share and more to the smoking pyres that in his century marked trail's end for other authors who dreaded what the biographers might find after they were dead and gone.

By the end of 1873 his health and spirits had picked up a little and he was able to sell some prose and poetry to the magazines. "Prayer of Columbus," published in *Harper's New Monthly Magazine* in March 1874, returned to the themes of "Passage to India," but now the brave soul that had set out to sail the seas of God was "a battered, wreck'd old man . . . venting a heavy heart." "As I see it now," Whitman told Nelly O'Connor about the new poem, "I shouldn't wonder if I have unconsciously put a sort of autobiographical dash in it." Anne Gilchrist, signing herself "Your loving Annie," recognized the autobiographical parallels immediately—"You too have sailed over stormy seas to your goal—surrounded with mocking disbelievers—you too have paid the great price of health—our Columbus." A visit from Pete at the end of May came at a time "when

I was feeling almost at my worst." In June, almost a year and a half since his stroke, he was too feeble still to travel to Tufts College, where—a reminder of his better days at Dartmouth—he had been invited to deliver a commencement poem. In July, despite appeals to President Grant, he was discharged from his government clerkship and out of necessity began to face up to the prospect of being stranded for good in Camden, "a receiving vault." He spent $450 on a building lot on Royden Street and made arrangements to have his boxes sent on from Washington, but, as he told Burroughs, "All questions of *what I shall do* are to me so subordinate to the question of whether I shall soon or ever get well, (or partially well,) that I hardly entertain them seriously." In February 1875 he had another paralytic stroke, on his right side. "I was down, down, down that year," he later said. "I came out of it—God knows how."

17

Timber Creek

I

ALL OVER AMERICA, church bells pealing, the roar of artillery, and rocket bursts welcomed in 1876, a year of centennial mania undampened by Custer's debacle on the banks of the Little Bighorn and a presidential contest nearly decided at bayonet's point. During the first minutes of 1876 Camdenites were treated to an especially splendid show of sounds and lights coming across the Delaware River from Philadelphia, site of a great international centennial fair. Halls of glass and iron, one of them reputed to be the largest in the world, were going up on an enclosed tract of 450 acres in Fairmount Park. The fairgrounds were to be served by the Pennsylvania Railroad's special Centennial depot, designed to handle two trains a minute. President Grant and Emperor Dom Pedro of Brazil opened the exhibition on May 10. By November 10, when it closed, eight million visitors, the equivalent of a fifth of the national population, had passed through the turnstiles and marveled at how far the United States had come in just one hundred years toward fulfilling its destiny as the light of the world.

The real and symbolic heart of the Centennial Exhibition of 1876 was a forty-foot-high steam engine that supplied power to 8,000 presses, pumps, gins, mills and lathes in Machinery Hall. "It is in these things of iron and steel," said William Dean Howells, "that the national genius most freely speaks." Still, the sponsors of this visionary world of automation did not confine themselves to the materials and technologies of the age of energy. They invited Richard Wagner, then staging the *Ring des Nibelungen* complete for the first time at his Festspielhaus in Bayreuth, to compose a "Centennial March." At the opening ceremonies in Philadelphia his composition was received with attention, at any rate, and the reverence due anything so transitory and immaterial that had cost five thousand dollars in gold. The poet Sidney Lanier supplied the text of a cantata, "Centennial Meditation of Columbia," to Mendelssohnian strains by the Hartford organist Dudley Buck. John Greenleaf Whittier wrote the Centennial hymn after Longfellow, Bryant, Lowell and Holmes declined the honor. Painting and sculpture had a place at the fair as well, although the committee of acceptance looked askance at Thomas Eakins' masterpiece of naturalism in the tradition of Rembrandt, "Portrait of Professor Gross," and exiled it to a wall of the first-aid station. (Like Whitman, later his friend and subject, Eakins scorned the exotic, picturesque and overdressed.) As for Whitman, he had not been invited to contribute anything to the fair, even though he had just published a two-volume "Centennial Edition" of his work and in other ways had asserted claims on the role of Centennial Poet. That role was filled by his former admirer Bayard Taylor. "I do not seem to belong to great show events," Whitman later recalled with a mildness that belied his true feelings in 1876. He came to the fair as an ordinary paying visitor, was wheeled about for two and a half hours in a rolling chair, a popular innovation at Fairmount Park, and after the giantism, din and clutter he encountered in one pavilion after another, was entranced by the simplicities of the Japanese summer house and its garden of dwarf evergreens. He had fallen back on other plans for marking 1876. In January, from his obscure site on the Camden shore of the Delaware, he sent up a starshell of his own, and it burst in the skies of two continents.

The two-volume edition Whitman produced at a Camden print shop comprised a reissue of the 1871 *Leaves of Grass* and a "Melange" of his other writings, including *Democratic Vistas*, *Passage to India*, and a group of "Centennial Songs." He titled the second volume *Two Rivulets* (the "rivulets" stood for the dualities of prose and verse, the real and the ideal, politics and immortality) and said in his preface that he had put it together "at the eleventh hour, under grave illness." Printed from an awkward mix of existing plates and new typesetting, erratically paginated, *Two Rivulets* had a needy, make-shift, but unmistakably Whitman look. "Forgive me for not writing before. Much of the time I cannot write, from paralysis," he told an unidentified correspondent at the end of December 1875. "I publish & shall sell the volumes myself, for two good reasons. No established publisher in the country will print my books, & during the last three years of my illness & helplessness every one of the three successive book agents I have had in N. Y. has embezzled the proceeds."

At fifty-six, after twenty years as a professional author, Whitman was still his own publisher, his own production and sales manager and shipping clerk; now he had neither "book agents" nor Fowler and Wells. Unemployed and likely to remain so, he counted on the Centennial edition to stand between him and dependency on George. He offered his books at ten dollars the set, sent on application to the author in Camden and on receipt of price, post-office money order preferable. He was in effect a subscription publisher, but without door-to-door salesmen to drum up orders. He relied on word of mouth, random publicity, and the usual homemade reviews, one of which Whitelaw Reid ran in the New York *Tribune* in February 1876. By then Whitman's new edition and other expenses had left him with about six hundred dollars in savings, not enough to put up a "shanty" for his remaining years. He told an acquaintance, "I have come to the end of my rope, & am in fact ridiculously poor," and although this sounded like an appeal for charity, it became his official line, not to be gainsaid. Moncure Conway's well-intentioned denials that Whitman was "in distress or dependent upon his relatives" were denounced as "singularly *malapropos*" and "hurtful to my case." With varying degrees of fantasy and exaggeration, but always with a scintilla of fact, in his end-of-the-rope mood he saw himself as a victim of both conspiracy and neglect.

Several leading magazines—conspicuously the *Galaxy* and *Harper's*—had bought his work, but he preferred to believe that all of them were in the hands of either "fops," like Howells, or "old fogies," like Dr. Josiah Gilbert Holland of *Scribner's Monthly*. Holland called him a "wretched old fraud," "a pest and an abomination," and sent insulting rejection letters that rankled for years. When Bayard Taylor joined the *Tribune* editorial staff in March 1876 the paper ceased to be a reliable ally. Whitman had learned to expect little or nothing in the way of support from the great men of New England—Lowell, for example, "the chief of staff in that army of the devil," or Long-fellow, even though he paid Whitman "a sort of one-horse visit," polite but meaningless, when he was on his way to the Philadelphia Exposition. (Privately, Longfellow admired *Drum-Taps* but felt that whatever "true poetical power" Whitman had was "obscured by a total want of education and of delicacy of feelings.") Emerson was a category all to himself.

The Concord sage had never followed up his first letter of recognition with anything comparable. Whether he had "recanted," and, if he had, whether capriciously or under the influence of Whitman's "*deadly haters* in and around Boston," was an issue debated among the faithful with the same sectarian passion as the divinity of Christ or the doctrine of predestination. "Its importance is immensely overrated," Anne Gilchrist protested. "No man, however eminent, can make or mar another man's fame." Looking back to the way Whitman had used Emerson's 1855 letter as a passport and charter for *Leaves of Grass*, one could argue with her about short-term effects, at any rate. But the fact remained that if Emerson had not formally "recanted" he had certainly drawn away. His 1860 debate with Whitman under the elms in Boston Common crystallized his objections to *Leaves of Grass*. Ten years later the English intellectual James Bryce noted that Emerson had ceased to expect much from Whitman,

> whom he describes very amusingly. . . . Walt, by his account, must be not only a conceited but a rather affected creature, valuing himself on his roughness and shewing a contempt for the ordinary usages of good breeding. He has an immense estimate of his own performances, and does not desire criticism. He has had some sort of education, and read a good deal of poetry, so he is not quite so much a child of nature as might be expected.

From time to time Emerson's gibes were meant for Whitman to hear. "Tell Walt I am not satisfied, not satisfied," he said in 1871. "I expect—him—to make—the songs of the—nation—but he seems contented to—make the inventories." The following January Whitman and Burroughs heard him lecture on "Imagination and Poetry" and were disappointed. "He maintains the same attitude—draws on the same themes—as twenty-five years ago," Whitman complained about his former "Master," once the arch-rebel of American thought.

"It all seems to me quite attenuated," like tea made from brewed-out leaves. When they talked after the lecture, Burroughs was aware of a certain coolness to Whitman on Emerson's part. A few days later, seeing Emerson off at the depot in Washington, he found out what the trouble was. "He thought Walt's friends ought to quarrel a little more with him and insist on his being a little more tame and orderly —more mindful of the requirements of beauty, of art, of culture, etc.—all of which was very pitiful to me, and I wanted to tell him so. But the train started just then and I got off." Burroughs decided that Walt could get along nicely without such timid counsel, and Walt agreed. "I know what I am about better than Emerson does," he said, but he tempered this with some of his old admiration and gratitude—"I love to hear what the gods have to say." Emerson's enervated lecture (which Burroughs found remote from "the needs of the American people today") was a sign of the mental vacancy that had been coming on him for some time. By the time Anne Gilchrist paid him a visit in 1878 he could not remember the name of his best friend, Henry Thoreau, and asked her if the Walt Whitman whose photograph she showed him was an Englishman.

From Whitman's point of view Emerson had already been guilty of more reprehensible sins of omission. In 1874 he had finished putting together a poetry anthology, *Parnassus*, that was supposed to compete with Francis Turner Palgrave's enormously popular *Golden Treasury of the Best Songs and Lyrical Poems in the English Language*. Among the living Americans represented in Emerson's five hundred two-columned pages of selections were Longfellow, Lowell, Whittier and Bryant. This was as it should have been. He showed favor also to E. C. Stedman and a Wisconsin poet, long since forgotten, named Forceythe Willson, whose "genius" was "akin to Dante's." Perhaps predictably, there was nothing by Poe, whom Emerson had once dismissed as "the jingle man," or Melville, who was generally forgotten, or Emily Dickinson, who published only five poems before she died in 1886. But there was not so much as a single line in *Parnassus* from the book Emerson had called "the most extraordinary piece of wit and wisdom America has yet contributed." Maybe there was a glimmer of consolation in the report that while editing the anthology Emerson had been under the thumb of his daughter Edith, who hated Whitman. Still, it was humiliating beyond all account to be denied houseroom on this Parnassus, even by a doddering god.

In a Boston journal at the beginning of January 1876 Whitman read an attack calling his work nauseating drivel about armpit odors —the writer charged Rossetti and other English partisans with perpetrating a "really cruel hoax" on the reading public. On the eighteenth the Springfield (Massachusetts) *Republican*, a friendly paper, printed a well-intentioned denial of "loose talk" to the effect that Whitman was "a neglected martyr" now living "in want." His despair and loneliness fused at that moment with a shrewdly manipulative sense of occasion, a genius for publicity, that had never yet failed him. "Walt Whitman's Actual American Position," an unsigned article he wrote and placed in a Camden paper, the *West Jersey Press*, on January 26, was at the same time a cry out of the depths and a superb piece of advertising copy. He immediately sent clippings to Rossetti, Dowden and other supporters, with instructions to circulate them to magazines and newspapers. Given such impellence, a 1,300-word white paper issued from the provinces turned out to be the most widely circulated and commented-on of all Whitman's anonymous works.

"Whitman's poems in their public reception have fallen stillborn in this country," the article declared. "They have been met, and are met today, with the determined denial, disgust and scorn of orthodox American authors, publishers and editors, and, in a pecuniary and worldly sense, have certainly wrecked the life of their author." He reviewed the past twenty years: the "*howl* of criticism and the charge of obscenity" that first greeted *Leaves of Grass*, his steadfast indifference to popularity and profits, the long war service that planted "the seeds of the disease that now cripples him," his treatment at the hands of Secretary Harlan, and finally his "half-sick, half-well" subsistence in Camden. "Whitman has grown gray in battle. Little or no impression, (at least ostensibly,) seems to have been made. Still he stands alone." His life was composed of "deep shadows, streaked with just enough light to relieve them." He returned to his charges of persecution and neglect, including his omission from Emerson's anthology, and concluded with a pitch for the Centennial edition:

> We have now said enough to suggest the bleakness of the actual situation. But the poet himself is more resolute and persevering than ever. "Old, poor, and paralyzed," he has, for a twelvemonth past been occupying himself by preparing, largely with his own handi-

work, here in Camden, a small edition of his complete works in two volumes, which he himself now sells, partly "to keep the wolf from the door" in old age—and partly to give before he dies, as absolute expression as may be to his ideas.

Two weeks later the *Tribune*, as yet free of Bayard Taylor's eventually dominating influence, ran a summary and concluded that Whitman's situation was "black and desolate." A relative silence ensued. Then on March 11, in London, Rossetti printed excerpts in the *Athenaeum* along with a statement from Whitman that the *West Jersey Press* article, printed "with my consent," may even have understated "the *plain truth.*" In the *Daily News* two days later the Scottish poet and critic, Robert Buchanan, a Whitmanite since 1868, invoked parallels with Christ and Socrates and denounced America's mistreatment of its greatest poet, a "Golden Eagle . . . pursued by a crowd of prosperous rooks and crows" and condemned to "literary outlawry and official persecution." He proposed the formation of an English committee to come to Whitman's rescue by recruiting subscribers to the Centennial edition.

Buchanan's vividly intemperate outburst in the *Daily News* was duly flashed by cable to newspapers in the States, and it soon became evident that by defining his "actual position" Whitman had started a two-continent literary war. At issue was not only his alleged neglect and persecution but whether Centennial America had advanced sufficiently since its founding to be able to recognize and live with originality. According to one English line of argument, perhaps the chickenheartedness shown by the American literary establishment in its dealings with Whitman was just a sign of colonial culture. In rebuttal, Bayard Taylor, for one, argued that it was precisely Whitman's barbarism and formlessness that were likely to excite the "blasé," "decorous," and "overcloyed palates of a large class of English authors and readers." "We have enough, and more than enough, of unresolved elements in our American life," Taylor said, and we crave "the lost blessing of repose."

During the spring the domestic and transatlantic debate generated at least twenty-five articles, including further defenses of "the great Poet and Martyr" by Buchanan, counterattacks by Taylor, and an editorial in the (London) *Saturday Review* that dismissed *Leaves of Grass* as "garbage" and Buchanan's "Golden Eagle" simile as grotesquely misleading—Whitman was instead "a dirty bird . . .

shunned on account of its unclean habits." Whitman's spirits rose
along with the fierceness of the battle. He crowed to Rossetti,
"There is a small fury & much eructive spitting & sputtering already
among the 'literary coteries' here from Robt. Buchanan's lance-slash
at them anent of me." Friends rallied to the cause, just as they had
done ten years earlier after the Harlan firing. "It seems to me that
[his] countrymen should not allow him to suffer from penury in his
old age," John Swinton wrote in a letter to the New York *Herald*.
"His closing days should be cheered by those kindly memories,
which, I hope, are not to reach him wholly from Great Britain." By
the time Burroughs committed his forces in April with a long public
letter, Buchanan's "lance-slash" had become "an artillery and bayonet charge combined," Whitman said, like Pickett's gallant charge at
Gettysburg, only more successful. O'Connor, though still estranged
from both his wife and his old friend, put personal grievances aside
and joined the battle with more than three thousand words of polemic in the *Tribune*, "Walt Whitman: Is He Persecuted?" The answer to O'Connor's question was evident in the first paragraph,
which described Bayard Taylor's editorials as "a new kind of
dragon's teeth" breeding "the foul and copious abuse and insults
journals of every description in this country are not ashamed to offer
to a great genius, even when age, poverty, and illness have drawn
around him their sad sanctuary." O'Connor asked for Whitman
nothing more than "the candid effort at a fair interpretation of his
writings, which his admitted genius deserves."

Eventually there came what the *Atlantic* called "a lull in the Walt
Whitman controversy, which lately raged so fiercely in both hemispheres." When the smoke lifted, Whitman found that his position
in the United States as well as in England was far stronger than it
had been when 1876 opened, even though the issues of poverty and
neglect continued to be debated during the last sixteen years of his
life. E. C. Stedman's evenhanded appreciation in the November
1880 *Scribner's Monthly*, formerly enemy territory, was one of several
signs that a time had come when *Leaves of Grass* could be discussed
on its own merits and without reference to whether Whitman had
abused Emerson's confidence or worn red flannel shirts in polite
company or frequented dives and whorehouses or any of a hundred
other circumstances either immaterial or imagined.

Whitman had gained pretty nearly everything he might have
asked for—a way to exorcise depression and discharge despair; inner

equilibrium; public demonstrations of love and loyalty; international prominence; a more benign climate of appreciation; sales for his Centennial edition. Among the English subscribers were Ruskin, Lord Houghton, Edmund Gosse, Justin McCarthy, George Saintsbury, and G. H. Lewes, George Eliot's husband. Tennyson had heard that Whitman was "in great straits, almost starving" and sent five pounds as an outright gift. Dowden ordered six sets. In the States the sculptor John Quincy Adams Ward, one of the many prospects John Swinton lined up, ordered five sets. Whitman's book sales for 1876 came to $1552.83, not a great sum, considering that he bore all the costs of composition, printing and binding. But it was larger then he expected when he first announced the new edition, and in June he ordered a second printing. Ten years later, when the wolf was at the door again, substantially the same group of English subscribers sent "offerings" of almost two thousand dollars in cash gifts. Their money was welcome then, but not so welcome as it had been in 1876 when, Whitman said, "blessed gales from the British Islands . . . plucked me like a brand from the burning, and gave me life again. . . . I do not forget it, and shall not; and if I ever have a biographer I charge him to put it in the narrative."

As spring approached, the old physical complaints were still with him—gastric and liver troubles, dizziness, lameness—but there was a distinct upward trend in his spirits. The *West Jersey Press* affair had yielded what he called "deep medicines." The day after the article first appeared he felt well enough to give a public reading in aid of the other poor of Camden. He played by the hour with his infant nephew Walt, George and Louisa Whitman's only child, and he accepted with serenity the boy's death in the July heat wave. He sat by the coffin surrounded by the neighborhood children, fondling them and trying to explain that no one, not even grownups, understood what death was. He became sociable again and went over to Philadelphia often to take dinner and drink wine with friends. "I get out nearly every day," he wrote to Dowden, "but not far, & cannot walk from lameness—make much of the river here, the broad Delaware, crossing a great deal on the ferry, full of life & fun to me."

II

When he revised his will in 1873 Walt left his silver watch to Peter Doyle, "with my love." Since then, Pete, who had lost his streetcar job and was doing hazardous work as a brakeman on the Baltimore and Potomac Railroad, had been able to manage only an occasional visit to Camden. Their old intimacy waned. "I ought to have written you before," Walt said after several months of silence passed between them. "But I often, often think of you, boy, & let that make it up." There was no need for him to say so, but a new protégé, Harry Stafford, had taken Pete's place and would in time receive Walt's silver watch. Walt was as exigent with him as he had been with Pete. "How I wish you could come in now, even if but for an hour & take off your coat, & sit down on my lap . . . I want to see you, my darling son, & I can't wait any longer." They wrestled, and Walt, the semi-invalid, drew enough strength from the younger man to pin him to the floor, just as he had been able to outwalk Pete in the Washington days. When he traveled with Harry he introduced him as "my (adopted) son," "my nephew," "my young man," and explained that they were in the habit of sharing a room and a bed. Burroughs was annoyed to see them roughhousing together and cutting up "like two boys." "Great tribulation in the kitchen in the morning," he wrote in his journal after they had spent a few days with him at Esopus in the Catskills. "Can't get them up to breakfast in time. Walt takes Harry with him as a kind of foil or refuge from the intellectual bores."

When they met, Harry Stafford was eighteen and working as errand boy at the Camden print shop where Whitman saw *Two Rivulets* through the press. Harry responded gratefully to the attention and affection of a man nearly forty years his senior who was reputed to be a famous writer and was treated with deference by the printers and pressmen. Like other young men to whom Walt was drawn he was barely literate, still unformed in identity and direction. He was subject to "blue spells," fits of temper, impulsive acts, flights into fantasy, all of which were exacerbated by a relationship he was not able to understand and had to accept on faith—it made demands and awakened responses that were profoundly confusing as he made his passage into full manhood. In his more assuring role

359

of mentor rather than lover Walt tried to moderate these mood swings in line with the spirit of *Leaves of Grass,* as he interpreted that spirit for Harry. "It makes (tries to make) every fellow see himself, & see that he has got to work out his salvation himself—has got to pull the oars & hold the plow, or swing the axe himself—& that the real blessings of life are not the fictions generally supposed, but are real, & are mostly within reach of all—you chew on this."

After they had known each other for a month or two, Harry took him home to meet his parents. George and Susan Stafford were tenant farmers at Laurel Springs (or "White Horse"), a crossroads settlement twelve miles from Camden. Soon Walt was staying there for days and even weeks at a time. He was a paying guest, as he was at his brother's place at Camden. He was also an adopted member of the Stafford family and companion to Harry's six brothers and sisters. "I think he is the best man I ever knew," Susan Stafford told Whitman's English admirer, Edward Carpenter. Carpenter was moved by the ease and intimacy with which they dealt with one another. "Am with folks I love, & that love me," Whitman said. "Have had a real good old-fashion'd time, first-rate for me—It is a farm, every thing plain & plenty, & blazing wood fires—in the eating line, lots of chickens, eggs, fresh pork &c: (they kill a hog every two weeks)." Living with the Staffords, in a farmhouse surrounded by meadows, woods, a pond, and a little creek, was like going back to old times on Long Island. When he went on rambling drives to the fields or the marl pit or farm auctions in George Stafford's roomy old wagon he remembered rides with his grandfather Van Velsor at Cold Spring. Coming in to supper as grace was about to be said, he rested his hands affectionately on George's head before passing to his place at the table. *"If I had not known you*—if it hadn't been for you & our friendship & my going down there summers to the creek with you," he was to tell Harry, "I believe *I should not be a living man to-day*—I think & remember these things & they comfort me—& you, *my darling boy, are the central figure of them all."*

"I take an interest in the boy in the office, Harry Stafford—I know his father & mother," Walt had written to one of the Camden printers in April 1876. He could have been describing his own family at West Hills, his refusal to do farm work, his apprentice years.

There is a large family, very respectable American people—farmers, but only a hired farm—Mr. Stafford is in weak health—

I am anxious Harry should *learn the printer's trade thoroughly*—*I want him to learn to set type as fast as possible*—want you to give him a chance (less of the mere errands &c)—There is a good deal really in the boy, if he has a chance.

Don't say any thing about this note to him—or in fact to any one —just tear it up, & *keep the matter to yourself private.*

Less than a month later Harry quit his job, apparently hoping to find more exciting work at the Exposition grounds in Philadelphia. "I fear he is to much trouble to you all ready," Harry's mother apologized to Walt. "I hope Harry will ever be Greatfull to you fore all your kindness to him." Harry tried his restless hand after that at a series of positions, many of which Walt helped him find. He worked for the *West Jersey Press* and other papers, was a telegraph operator for the Camden and Atlantic Railroad, tried for appointments to the lighthouse and lifesaving services, and drifted to Canada, where he served as an attendant in Dr. Bucke's lunatic asylum until the "unearthly noises" of the inmates got him down. "H S and Eva Westcott married," Whitman wrote in his diary for June 25, 1884. The last of his sustained love affairs had modulated into friendship, like the others. He could not spend Thanksgiving with them, he wrote to Harry's wife that November, but "it would be a true comfort for me if it was so I could come in every few days, and you and Harry and I could be together—I am sure it would be good for me. . . . I appreciate your loving wishes & feelings, & send you mine the same, for both of you." And so he was alone again, without the "ridiculous little storms & squalls" that had given him pain. Harry too remembered that they had had "many rough times together." "Can you forgive me and take me back and love me the same," he once wrote. "I will try by the grace of God to do better. I cannot give you up, and it make me feel so bad to think how we have spent the last day or two; and all for my temper. I will have to *controol* it or it will send me to the states prison or some other bad place. Cant you take me back and love me the same."

Other men figured in these storms of jealousy and recrimination. Walt had again taken to writing down the names of drivers, conductors, ferrymen, delivery boys, and the like in whom he took an interest.

> John Williamson, tall, young . . .
> John McLaughlin, black eyed . . .
> Wm Stillé, young man formerly at Coley's grocery . . .
> Rob't McKelvey, Market st driver—young, blackeyed, affectionate

At Laurel Springs he met a twenty-five-year-old farmhand, Edward Cattell, whose name appears in a number of notebook and diary entries.

> the hour (night, June 19, '76, Ed & I,) at the front gate by the road saw E. C.
> Sept meetings with Ed C by the pond moonlit nights
> Ed Cattell with me

After they had known each other for about eight months Walt sent Ed an urgent letter from Camden.

> Do not call to see me any more at the Stafford family, & do not call there at all any more—Dont ask me why—I will explain to you when we meet. . . . There is nothing in it that I think I do wrong, nor am ashamed of, but I wish it kept entirely between you and me—&—I shall feel very much hurt & displeased if you don't keep the whole thing & the present letter entirely to yourself. Mr and Mrs Stafford are very near & kind to me, & have been & are like brother & sister to me—& as to Harry you know how I love him. Ed, you too have my unalterable love, & always shall have. I want you to come up here & see me.

He and Ed exchanged letters from time to time and continued to see each other, but not so frequently as before. "It seems an age Since i last met With you down at the pond and a lovely time We had of it to old man," Ed wrote. "I love you walt and Know that my love is returned to."

Meanwhile, Walt had been pressing Harry to accept a ring from him. In the conventions of the time it signified friendship, but in the evolving intensity of their relationship it signified a marriage as well, and Harry apparently drew back.

talk with H S & gave him r[ing] Sept 26 '76—(took r back)
Nov 1—Talk with H S in front room S[tevens] street [in Camden]—
gave him r again
Nov 25, 26, 27, 28—Down at White Horse—Memorable talk with
H S—settles the matter

A few weeks later, reconsidering the matter, Walt arrived at a crisis point, just as he had done with Peter Doyle, and he used the same characteristic word, "perturbation," to describe it. With Pete he had made a vow impossible to keep, to avoid "any talk or explanation— or any meeting, whatever, from this hour forth, for life." This time he seems to have found a calmer remedy. "Had serious inward rev'n & conv'n," he said in a fragmentary daybook entry for December 19, 1876. "Saw clearly what it really meant—very profound medi- tation on all—happy & satisfied at last about it—singularly so. . . . (that this may last now without any more perturbation)." Still, the memorable talks, the crises and brief resolutions, continued to occur during 1877, when Walt was seeing something of Ed Cattell.

the scene in the front room Ap. 29, with H
July 20th '77, in the room at White Horse "good bye"

Harry became dependent and forlorn. "You may say that I dont care for you," he wrote after spending a sleepless night waiting for Walt to come back to Camden, "but I do, I think of you all the time. . . . I want you to look over the past and I will do my best to-ward you in the future. You are all the true friend I have, and when I cannot have you I will go away some ware, I don't know where." During the fall, although they were seeing each other in Camden and at the farm, Harry continued to write agitated letters. "I wish you would put the ring on my finger again, it seems to me there is something that is wanting to compleete our friendship when I am with you. I have tride to studdy it out but cannot find out what it is. You know when you put it on ther was but one thing to part it from me and that was death."

Feb 11 [1878]—Monday—Harry here—put r on his hand again

And yet, as Harry had said, something remained wanting. Walt told him a few years later that there were still "many things, confidences, questions, candid *says* you would like to have with me, you have never yet broached—me the same."

Anne Gilchrist—"Your own loving Annie"—had also promised to wear Walt's ring so long as she drew breath. The year 1876 found her freed of the ties that had been holding her in England. Her mother was dead, her oldest son started in his career, her three younger children ready and eager for a new life. She believed her long wait, her novitiate, was finally ended.

> Do not think me too wilful or headstrong, but I have taken our tickets & we shall sail Aug 30 for Philadelphia [she wrote]. O I passionately believe there are years in store for us, years of tranquil, tender happiness—me making your outward life serene & sweet—you making my inward life so rich—me learning, growing, loving—we shedding benign influences round us out of our happiness and fulfilled life— hold on but a little longer for me, my Walt—I am straining every nerve to hasten the day. I have enough for us all (with the simple unpretending ways we both love best).

He did his tactful best to hide his alarm, thanked her for her "good & comforting letter," and made casual reference to their mutual friend Rossetti, the progress of the Centennial edition, and, of course, his health, which was now sufficiently improved—"perhaps a shade better"—to permit him at least to think about coming over to England to visit her and other friends. He was not able to sustain this easygoing tone for long. "I do not approve your American trans-settlement," he said, getting to the point at last, but then he veered away, warning her not about his positive disinclination to "get hitched" but about the crudeness and meagerness of the social existence she was likely to find in his country. "Don't do any thing toward such a move, nor resolve on it, nor indeed make any move at all in it, without further advice from me. If I should get well enough to voyage, we will talk about it yet in London." But he could not turn her. Coming to America, she countered, "has been my settled, steady purpose (resting on a deep, strong faith) ever since 1869. . . . I cannot wait any longer"—Walt had used these words with Harry Stafford. She had developed a touch of Centennial frenzy herself. She imagined the grand sights and sounds of the Exposition and worried—needlessly, as it turned out—that because of the millions of visitors to Philadelphia she might not be able to find a suitable place in which to live. She planned a long, perhaps permanent stay and was bringing over furniture, pictures, and books. On September 10 her intended husband made a brief entry in his daybook, "Mrs G & family arrived." In his private records she remained "Mrs G" for the nearly two years she spent in Philadelphia.

He began seeing her nearly every day, riding the red cars of the Market Street line from the ferry station out to her rented row house on North 22nd Street. By the fall he was a part-time resident there and occupied a bedroom ("a kind of prophet's chamber," Edward Carpenter noted) that was always kept ready for him. He entertained guests—George Whitman and Lou, Burroughs, Carpenter—as if in his own house. He had a little stove installed in his room, and he put in a supply of wood for the winter. In warm weather his bamboo rocking-chair was carried to the pavement, and he introduced the Gilchrists to the American custom of socializing out by the front stoop while the neighbors did the same. Anne's children thought of him as a sort of eminent uncle.* He took Herbert, her twenty-one-year-old son, with him when he went to Laurel Springs, although there were collisions with Harry, who claimed the boy insulted him. ("If I had been near enough to smacked him in the 'Jaw' I would have done it," Harry said after a scene at the supper table. "He will find out sometime [t]hat he is fooling with the wrong one.") All in all, Walt occupied much the same position in the Gilchrist and Stafford households, except that with Anne and her children he recited poetry, Tennyson's more often than his own, and he talked about literary matters, the poetry of Victor Hugo and Heine, the novels of Scott, George Eliot, Bulwer Lytton, and George Sand, the social

---

* Herbert was studying to be a painter. Walt wrote an unsigned notice, for a Camden paper, of the portrait the boy was doing at Timber Creek. "The painting, which is now well advanced and promises to be an excellent likeness, represents Mr. Whitman sitting in an easy chair under a favorite tree. It is hoped that the painting will be retained in the country." Herbert later settled at Centerport, Long Island, where he barely managed to support himself as a painter. The Gilchrists' visit to America left a trail of defeat for them. Beatrice pursued a career in medicine in the same way her mother pursued Walt and with somewhat comparable results. In 1877, when Beatrice was studying medicine in Philadelphia, Walt cautioned her against "sheer overwork, & too intense concentration . . . resulting in terrible brain troubles & general caving in." She committed suicide in 1881.

style of the Boston writers and their circle—"They are supercilious to everybody. Emerson is the only sweet one among them and he has been spoilt by them. Yes, it is a stifling atmosphere for him." As for Thoreau: "I do not think it was so much a love of woods, streams, and hills that made him live in the country, as a morbid dislike of humanity." He recalled his pleasure in hearing Italian operas and the voice of Marietta Alboni. George Sand's *Consuelo*, the heroine as opera singer, he preferred to any of Shakespeare's women, and he acted out the scene in which she was singled out for the beauty and earnestness of her music. "How often have I dwelt upon that passage," he said, thinking back to an early time in the foreground of *Leaves of Grass* when, in his solitary way, he had singled himself out to be the poet he became.

When Anne heard him singing in his room before breakfast she understood it to be "an outburst of pure emotional and physical *abandon* to the delight of living," and surely it was not his health that remained the barrier between them. "Never saw Walt look so handsome," Burroughs said after spending the night with him at the Gilchrists', "so new and fresh." Carpenter said he looked like a god. Anne's daughter Grace was struck by his "majestic presence" and compared him to a mountain in the noonday sun. But it soon became clear to Anne that this enormous vitality, casually shared with others, came from a source that would always remain closed to her and that in her lifetime she could never be more than his "dear friend." "I saw that Anne Gilchrist was suffering," Carpenter recalled. "I saw that Whitman was all *kindness*—kindness itself toward her; but at the same time that his relation to her did not go farther than that word would indicate." She may not have been able to point to the precise moment when she realized that her coming to America had been a mistake. "I do not feel as if I ought to stay," she told a friend in December 1877—she was recovering then from what she described as "a somewhat severe operation (under ether) to cure an injury received at the birth of one of my children which has always troubled me." As soon as the worst of her discomfort was over Walt came back to the house:

Oct 5 after three weeks absence visited Mrs G's—
Mrs G temporarily sitting up
Dec 10-to-30—fine spell of weather—out every day—evenings at

Mrs G's
Dec 25—Christmas—dinner at north 22 st

They exchanged affectionate letters and saw each other several times after the spring of 1878 when she moved out of her house—"It stands empty and forlorn now," she said—to spend a year moving from place to place in the Northeast.

June 9 [1879] the Gilchrists sail'd from N Y for Glasgow

Before she embarked they talked in private at a friend's apartment on Fifth Avenue; and whatever degree of desolation she felt she kept to herself. Perhaps she never understood Walt's meanings, never understood "Calamus" as passionately as she understood "Children of Adam," for she still believed it was all a matter of waiting. "I think of you continually," she wrote when she was again settled in England, "& know that somewhere & some-how we are to meet again, & that there is a tie of love between us that time & change & death itself cannot touch." Her faith was romantic and traditional, but in her characteristic way, as a Victorian intellectual she also derived it from evolutionary science. The world, the race, each single soul, she told Whitman—all were "surely going somewhere."

III

A grassy farm lane that narrowed to a footpath led from the Stafford house to a stream, a secluded pond, and high woods. Calamus and cattails grew at the water's edge beneath banks of brush and tree roots. Like Adam, in this wild garden that he called Timber Creek, Whitman, gaining back strength and spirit, looked at nature as if for the first time—"I never really saw the skies before"—and marveled at the timeless cycle of renewal he celebrated in *Leaves of Grass*. The brown earth quickened in early spring and ripened into the sensual stillness of summer:

The fervent heat, but so much more endurable in this pure air— the white and pink pond-blossoms, with great heart-shaped leaves; the glassy waters of the creek, the banks, with dense bushery, and the picturesque beeches and shade and turf; the tremulous, reedy call of some bird from recesses, breaking the warm, indolent, half-voluptuous silence; an occasional wasp, hornet, honey-bee or bumble (they hover near my hands or face, yet annoy me not, nor I them, as they appear to examine, find nothing, and away they go)—the vast space of the sky overhead so clear, and the buzzard up there sailing his slow whirl in majestic spirals and discs; just over the surface of the pond, two large slate-color'd dragon-flies, with wings of lace, circling and darting and occasionally balancing themselves quite still, their wings quivering all the time . . .

In wayward, spontaneous notes, set down on the spot, just as he had done in the hospitals, Whitman rendered the continuum of his perceptions and sensations, made loving roll calls of the names of trees, birds, flowers, and insects, distinguished Timber Creek's thousand small and separate sounds: the distant rustle of dry corn-stalks and the wings of migrating birds, the hum of wild bees, "the *flup* of a pike leaping out, and rippling the water," "the quawk of some pond duck—(the crickets and grasshoppers are mute in the noon heat, but I hear the song of the first cicadas)." He wrote seated on stumps and logs or in an old chair the boys hauled out to the creek for him. Once in a while he met them there when they came to dive and splash in the pond. A quarter of a century earlier a diary note of June 1876—"The swim of the boys, Ed., Ed. C. & Harry" —might have been the germ of a surpassingly delicate and daring poem:

> The beards of the young men glisten'd with wet, it ran from their
>   long hair,
> Little streams pass'd all over their bodies.
>
> An unseen hand also pass'd over their bodies,
> It descended tremblingly from their temples and ribs.

At Timber Creek he also remembered the deaths of young men. "Who is there to whom the theme does not come home?" He found "nothing gloomy or depressing in such cases—on the contrary, as reminiscences, I find them soothing, bracing, tonic."

Tenderly will I use you curling grass,
It may be you transpire from the breasts of young men,
It may be if I had known them I would have loved them.

Timber Creek was the imagined landscape of his poetry. He
found there other transparent summer mornings on the grass. He
revisited the budding grove of sexual identity that had been the
setting of "Calamus."

In paths untrodden,
In the growth by margins of pond-waters,
Escaped from the life that exhibits itself.

"Away from the clank of the world," like Virgil's passionate shep-
herd finding words for his love in the deep shade of beech trees, he
was free

To tell the secret of my nights and days,
To celebrate the need of comrades.

"The token of comrades" was, as it always had been for him, calamus with the aromatic spears and thrusting spadix.

. . . what I draw from the water by the pond-side, that I reserve,
I will give of it, but only to them that love as I myself am capable of
    loving.

"There come moods," he wrote by the pond, "when these clothes
of ours are not only too irksome to wear, but are themselves indecent." For several summers he performed a solitary "Adamic" ritual
in his garden. Off to one side of the creek was an abandoned marlpit
with a little spring running through the middle of it under some
willows. He stripped himself naked, dug his feet into the black mud
and rolled in it, rinsed away the mud, rasped his body with a stiff
brush until his skin turned scarlet, rinsed again in the spring. After
his mud and water bath he bathed in the sun and air, making slow
promenades on the turf and declaiming and singing—"vocalism"—
at the top of his voice. "I make the echoes ring, I tell you!" He toned
his muscles, borrowed "elastic fibre and clear sap," wrestling with

oak and hickory saplings, just as he wrestled with Harry Stafford and drew strength from him. As he hauled and pushed he took great draughts of fragrant air into his lungs. "After I wrestle with the tree awhile, I can feel its young sap and virtue welling up out of the ground and tingling through me from crown to toe, like health's wine. . . . I hold on boughs or slender trees caressingly there in the sun and shade, wrestle with their innocent stalwartness." In the changing light he drank in with his eyes their rugged trunks, their shadowed deltas, unexpected bulges and gnarls, as if trees were the bodies of strong lovers; he remembered that ancient peoples worshiped trees and believed them to be the progenitors of the human race. "One does not wonder at the old story fables, (indeed, why fables?) of people falling into love-sickness with trees, seiz'd extatic with the mystic realism of the resistless silent strength in them— *strength*, which after all is perhaps the last, completest, highest beauty." In the instinctual and healing forest he spent hours at a time alone and happy, away from restraints, artifice, "perfumes":

Houses and rooms are full of perfumes, the shelves are crowded
    with perfumes,
I breathe the fragrance myself and know it and like it,
The distillation would intoxicate me also, but I shall not let it.

The atmosphere is not a perfume, it has no taste of the distillation, it
    is odorless,
It is for my mouth forever, I am in love with it,
I will go to the bank by the wood and become undisguised and
    naked,
I am mad for it to be in contact with me.

"Somehow I seem'd to get identity with each and every thing around me, in its condition," he said at Timber Creek. "Nature was naked, and I was also." Earth, rocks, trees, and small living things were lessons in imperturbability, concreteness and strength. *"Being"* was superior to "the human trait of mere *seeming*," the human habit of "persistent strayings and sickly abstractions." Literature yielded to "Nature." Wherever he looked he found eloquent dumb miracles, each "enclosing the suggestion of everything else": a yellow poplar swarming with wild bees; mulleins by the chestnut fence, the knobs on their erect stalks bursting into clear yellow flower; a balloon of white butterflies floating and rolling in the air above a field of cab-

bages, malachite-green; a dark-winged hawk circling the pond—
"Once he came quite close over my head; I saw plainly his hook'd
bill and hard restless eyes."

"Pete, if you came to see me to-day," Whitman wrote in 1877,
after his second summer at Timber Creek, "you would almost think
you saw your old Walt of six years ago—I am all fat & red & tanned
. . . thankful to God to be as well & jolly as I am." He dragged his
left foot and leaned heavily on his stick, but he went out into the
world. In 1879, the year he turned sixty, he made a three-month
visit to New York, gave the first of what became his annual Lincoln
lectures, and traveled west to the Rockies. He found "wonders,
revelations I wouldn't have miss'd for my life, the great central area
2000 miles square, the Prairie States, *the real America,*" he wrote to
Anne Gilchrist, and he sent her a map of his travels, past and present. He spent the next summer in Canada, on the Great Lakes and
the St. Lawrence. In 1881 he came to Boston to lecture and read
proof on the seventh edition of *Leaves of Grass;* he revisited the Whitman and Van Velsor homesteads around West Hills.

Meanwhile, he had found a theme for a new book, the pond at
Timber Creek. The notes he made there are his *Walden.* As a chron-
icler of solitude the poet of million-footed Manhattan and the Broadway pavements stands with Thoreau and John Burroughs, but his
pond notes are also the record of a return from the void of breakdown to a new stage of integration, generative, hospitable to change
and experiment. At first he planned to publish this material—
"prose, free gossip mostly"—in a book of a hundred pages or so to
be called *Idle Days & Nights of a Half-Paralytic* or, among the three
dozen "suggested and rejected names for this volume," *Away from
Books—Away from Art, Only Mulleins and Bumble-Bees, Echoes of a Life
in the 19th Century in the New World,* and *Ducks and Drakes,* the last a
reference to the democratic, inexhaustibly diverting pastime of skip-
ping flat stones along the surface of quiet waters. "*Down in the Woods,
July 2d, 1882,*" obeying "a happy hour's command, which seems
curiously imperative," he decided to combine the pond notes with
his book about wound-dressing and the hospitals, *Memoranda During
the War.* He undid his bundles of manuscripts and clippings and
drew out material on his ancestors and his early years, travel notes,
descriptions of New York and Philadelphia, a lecture he had given

in 1877 on the 140th anniversary of Thomas Paine's birth, reconsiderations of Emerson, Carlyle and Poe, other writings seemingly too miscellaneous to belong together but reflecting in some decisive way the interiors of his life and century, "a strange, unloosen'd, wondrous time." All of this he put together, intending to "send out the most wayward, spontaneous, fragmentary book ever printed." This "melange" and "incongruous huddle" had the appearance of something that had happened instead of being made. He gave it the title *Specimen Days*, and yet, to his mind, the pond remained the central image of his new book. "Do you know what *ducks and drakes* are?" he asked O'Connor, once again his friend and confidant. "Well, S. D. is a rapid skimming over the pond-surface of my life, thoughts, experiences, that way—the real area altogether untouch'd, but the flat pebble making a few dips as it flies & flits along—enough at least to give some living touches and contact points—I was quite willing to make an immensely *negative* book."

But for all that it deliberately does not tell—about the birth of *Leaves of Grass*, for example—*Specimen Days* is a profoundly intimate book, written in a lean, unassuming prose that is in direct contrast with his earlier manner. By indirections, random links, discriminated occasions invoking "the costless average, divine, original concrete," Whitman suggests how immense creativity, perturbations, loneliness, the bustle of the cities and the suffering of the war had their own enclosing significance and were also paths to the stillness and health of Timber Creek. Almost alone among the major American writers, he achieved in his last years radiance, serenity and generosity of spirit. "A Discovery of Old Age.—Perhaps the best is always cumulative," he said in the final pages of *Specimen Days*. "I cannot divest my appetite of literature, yet I find myself eventually trying it all by Nature—*first premises* many call it, but really the crowning result of all." Having for the moment, at any rate, settled to his satisfaction the relative claims of his life and his art, Whitman was ready to take up residence at Mickle Street. From there he looked back to the cities of his youth—New York, Brooklyn, New Orleans, Washington. "They are my cities of romance. They are the cities of things begun—this is the city of things finished." An old man who never married and had no heart's companion now except his books, he rode contentedly at anchor on the waters of the past.

Notes

The notes that follow are keyed to the text by page number and catch phrase. Unless shown, place of publication for works cited is New York. Abbreviations used are:

AL	*American Literature*. Durham, N. C., 1929—.
Allen	Gay Wilson Allen, *The Solitary Singer: A Critical Biography of Walt Whitman*, 1967.
Aurora	Joseph Jay Rubin and Charles H. Brown, eds., *Walt Whitman of the New York "Aurora,"* State College, Pa., 1950.
Barrus	Clara Barrus, *Whitman and Burroughs, Comrades*, Boston, 1931.
Blue Book	Arthur Golden, ed., *Walt Whitman's Blue Book*, 2 vols, 1968.
Bowers	Fredson Bowers, ed., *Whitman's Manuscripts: "Leaves of Grass" (1860)*, Chicago, 1955.
Bucke (1883)	Richard M. Bucke, *Walt Whitman*, Philadelphia, 1883.
Calamus	Richard Maurice Bucke, M. D., ed., *Calamus: A Series of Letters Written . . . by Walt Whitman to . . . Peter Doyle*, Boston, 1897.
Champion	Jerome Loving, *Walt Whitman's Champion: William Douglas O'Connor*, College Station, Texas, 1978.
Child's Reminiscence	Thomas O. Mabbott and Rollo G. Silver, eds., *A Child's Reminiscence* by Walt Whitman, Seattle, Wash., 1930.
Corr.	Edwin Haviland Miller, ed., *The Correspondence*, 6 vols., 1961–1977, New York University Press edition of *The Collected Writings of Walt Whitman*.
CPW	*Complete Prose Works*, 1902.
CRE	Harold W. Blodgett and Sculley Bradley, eds., *Leaves of Grass*, "Comprehensive Reader's Edition," 1965, New York University Press edition of *The Collected Writings of Walt Whitman*.
CWL	Jerome M. Loving, ed., *Civil War Letters of George Washington Whitman*, Durham, N. C., 1975.
DBN	William White, ed., *Daybooks and Notebooks*, 3 vols., 1978, New York University Press edition of *The Collected Writings of Walt Whitman*.
Eagle	Thomas L. Brasher, *Whitman as Editor of the Brooklyn "Daily Eagle,"* Detroit, 1970.

EPF	Thomas L. Brasher, ed., *The Early Poems and the Fiction*, 1963, New York University Press edition of *The Collected Writings of Walt Whitman*.
FCI	Clarence Gohdes and Rollo G. Silver, eds., *Faint Clews & Indirections: Manuscripts of Walt Whitman and His Family*, Durham, N. C., 1949.
GF	Cleveland Rodgers and John Black, eds., *The Gathering of the Forces*, 2 vols., 1920.
Gilchrist	Thomas B. Harned, ed., *The Letters of Anne Gilchrist and Walt Whitman*, 1918.
Glicksberg	Charles I. Glicksberg, ed., *Walt Whitman and the Civil War*, Philadelphia, 1933.
Imprints	*"Leaves of Grass" Imprints*, Boston, 1860.
In Re	Horace Traubel, Richard Maurice Bucke, and Thomas Harned, eds., *In Re Walt Whitman*, Philadelphia, 1893.
ISL	Emory Holloway and Vernolian Schwarz, *I Sit and Look Out*, 1932.
LC	Manuscript Division, Library of Congress, Washington, D. C.
LG—1855	*Leaves of Grass*, Brooklyn, N. Y., 1855. (Facsimile edition, with an introduction by Clifton Joseph Furness, 1939.)
LG—1860	*Leaves of Grass*, Boston, 1860. (Facsimile edition, with an introduction by Roy Harvey Pearce, Ithaca, N. Y., 1961.)
LG—1876	*Leaves of Grass*, Camden, N. J., 1876.
Mattie	Randall H. Waldron, ed., *Mattie: The Letters of Martha Mitchell Whitman*, 1977.
MDW	*Memoranda During the War [&] Death of Abraham Lincoln*, Camden, N. J., 1875. (Facsimile edition with an introduction by Roy P. Basler, Bloomington, Ind., 1962.)
NF	Dr. Richard Maurice Bucke, ed., *Notes and Fragments*, London, Ontario, Canada, 1899.
Notebook—1855–56	Harold W. Blodgett, ed., *An 1855–56 Notebook toward the Second Edition of "Leaves of Grass,"* Carbondale, Ill., 1959.
NYD	Emory Holloway and Ralph Adimari, *New York Dissected*, 1936.
PMLA	*Publications of the Modern Language Association of America*, 1886—.
PW	Floyd Stovall, ed., *Prose Works, 1892*, 2 vols., 1963. New York University Press edition of *The Collected Writings of Walt Whitman*.
Rubin	Joseph Jay Rubin, *The Historic Whitman*, University Park, Pa., 1973.
Stovall	Floyd Stovall, *The Foreground of "Leaves of Grass,"* Charlottesville, Va., 1974.
UPP	Emory Holloway, ed., *The Uncollected Poetry and Prose of Walt Whitman*, 2 vols, Garden City, N. Y., 1921.
WWC	Horace Traubel, *With Walt Whitman in Camden*, 5 vols., 1906–1959). Vol. I, Boston, 1906; II, 1908; III, 1914; IV, Philadelphia, 1953; V, Carbondale, Ill., 1964.
WWR	*Walt Whitman Review*, Detroit, 1955—.

374

CHAPTER I (*pages 11–32*)

page 11
"Chilling atmosphere": *Corr.*, III, 69.
page 11
"Mother thought": *In Re*, 33.
page 11
"What are you up to": *WWC*, III, 538–39, and IV, 267.
page 12
Oscar Wilde: *Corr.*, III, 264; *WWC*, II, 288; Edwin Haviland Miller, "Amy H. Dowe and Walt Whitman," *WWR*, XIII, No. 3 (September 1967), 76.
page 12
Milnes: *In Re*, 36.
page 12
"I know I am restless": *CRE*, 322.
page 13
"Visitor in life": John Burroughs, *Whitman, A Study*, Boston, 1896, 27.
page 13
"He got offers": *In Re*, 33. For George Whitman's finances, see Jerome M. Loving, "The Estate of George Washington Whitman," *Bulletin of the Missouri Historical Society*, XXXI, January 1975, 105–10. For WW's finances, see *Corr.*, VI, xi–xxxvi.
page 14
"She can beat the devil": *WWC*, I, 332.
page 14
"Little old shanty": *Corr.*, III, 368.
page 14
Sued his estate: *CWL*, 32–33.
page 15
"Ram a needle": *WWC*, IV, 282–83.
page 15
"Great tender mother-man": Burroughs, quoted in Barrus, 339.
page 15
Young poet: Stuart Merrill, "Walt Whitman," *WWR*, III, No. 4 (December 1957), 55–57.
page 16
"I have little doubt": Burroughs, *Whitman, A Study*, Boston, 1896, 52–53.
page 16
The visual record: Gay Wilson Allen, "The Iconography of Walt Whitman," in Edwin Haviland Miller, ed., *The Ar-tistic Legacy of Walt Whitman*, 1970, 127–52.
page 16
Sartor Resartus: London, 1908, 17.
page 16
"I have just arrived": *WWC*, I, 457–58.
page 17
Lost for years: John Johnston and J. W. Wallace, *Visits to Walt Whitman . . .* London, 1917, 157. Emerson's letter is reproduced in facsimile in *WWC*, IV, following 152.
page 17
"I cannot be awake": *CRE*, 652.
page 17
"will be also a master": *CPW*, VI, 84.
page 17
"It is I you hold": *CRE*, 505.
page 17
"The character you give me": *Corr.*, III, 266.
page 17
"The actual W.W.": *Corr.*, II, 170.
page 17
"Reserve and sadness": Edward Carpenter, *Days with Walt Whitman*, 1906, 42–43.
page 18
"Trippers and askers": *CRE* 32.
page 18
Secret personality: *PW*, II, 555.
page 19
"I have twice": *Corr.*, II, 276.
page 19
Burning some old manuscripts: *WWC*, I, 35.
page 19
"Not so much of a mess": *WWC*, I, 155.
page 20
"The most wayward": *PW*, I, 1, 115–117.
page 20
"Here I sit gossiping": *PW*, II, 712.
page 20
"We are of the opinion": Oliver Stevens to Osgood & Co., *Corr.*, III, 267n.
page 20
"The list whole & several": *Corr.*, III, 270.
page 20
"*No book on earth*": *Corr.*, III, 284.

page 21
"After continued personal ambition":
PW, II, 714.
page 21
"I know very well": *PW*, II, 718.
page 22
"A thick-skinned beast": William Roscoe Thayer, "Personal Recollections of Walt Whitman," *Scribner's Magazine*, June 1919, 685.
page 22
"The messages": *CRE*, 717, 729.
page 22
"I have not gain'd": *PW*, II, 712.
page 22
"I don't know": *WWC*, III, 118.
page 22
Total income of $1,333: *Corr.*, VI, xvii.
page 22
Andrew Carnegie: Joseph O. Baylen and Robert B. Holland, "Whitman, W. T. Stead, and the *Pall Mall Gazette*," *AL*, XXXIII, No. 1 (March 1961), 70.
page 23
"A quart of water": *WWC*, I, 222.
page 23
"Let us be candid": [E. C. Stedman], "Walt Whitman," *Scribner's Monthly*, XXXI, November 1880, 47.
page 23
"Probably no more": *PW*, II, 713, 727, 730, 732.
page 24
"After the Supper and Talk": *CRE*, 536.
page 24
"Did not burn it afterwards": Richard B. Sewall, *The Life of Emily Dickinson*, 1974, II, 574.
page 24
"I do *not* expect": *Corr.*, IV, 66.
page 25
"Suit my wants and tastes": *Corr.*, IV, 102.
page 25
"It is a closed book": *WWC*, V, 355.
page 25
"Hot—hot": *DBN*, II, 362; Howard M. Cooper, *Historical Sketch of Camden, N. J.*, Camden, N. J., 1909, 62–63.
page 25
Gift of a horse and buggy: Thomas

Donaldson, *Walt Whitman, The Man*, 1896, 173–182.
page 25
As Whitman liked to believe: Lewis E. Weeks, Jr., "Did Whittier Really Burn Whitman's *Leaves of Grass?*" *WWR*, XXII, No. 1 (March 1976), 22–29.
page 25
Holmes: *Atlantic Monthly*, LXVI (September 1890), 388–89; Donaldson, 177; John B. Pickard, ed., *The Letters of John Greenleaf Whittier*, Cambridge, Mass., 1975, 507.
page 26
Whittier pointedly expressed: Pickard, III, 506–7.
page 26
"Solemn humbug": M. A. De Wolfe Howe, ed., *New Letters of James Russell Lowell*, 1932, 115–16.
page 26
"I never read his book": Thomas H. Johnson and Theodora Ward, eds., *The Letters of Emily Dickinson*, Cambridge, Mass., 1958, II, 404–5.
page 26
"Still living somewhere": "Socrates in Camden, With A Look Round," *The Academy* (London), Aug. 15, 1885.
page 27
Mark Twain: Donaldson, 180; *Camden's Compliment to Walt Whitman*, Camden, N. J., 1889, 64–65; *WWC*, V, 229; *Mark Twain's Speeches*, New York, 1923, 327; *WWC*, IV, 208; *Corr.*, III, 176; *PW*, II, 576–77.
page 27
Vagaries of literary fame: Jay B. Hubbell. *Who Are The Major American Writers?* Durham, N. C., 1972, 65–70.
page 28
Burroughs noted: Barrus, 256.
page 28
"I bought a good horse": *PW*, I, 287.
page 28
Bill Duckett: Duckett's notes on these outings are in Feinberg Coll., LC.
page 29
"My Captain again": *WWC*, III, 204, and IV, 392–93.
page 29
"Superficial yet profound": *Putnam's*

Monthly Magazine, VI, No. 33 (September 1855).

page 29
"Also in the audience": MDW, Introduction, 40.

page 30
Whitman described: WW's reading copy of the lecture is printed in MDW.

page 30
Merrill: see note for page 15 above ("Young poet").

page 31
"Death to the spirit": WWC, I, 62.

page 31
"Brighter and stronger": Barrus, 264.

page 31
Noted in his daybook: DBN, II, 425.

page 31
"So you see": Corr., IV, 166.

page 31
"More precious than gold": WWC, I, 238–40.

page 32
"Where are you, Pete?": WWC, I, 298.

page 32
Eddy Whitman: WWC, II, 66.

page 32
"He presses my hand": Clara Barrus, ed. The Heart of Burroughs' Journals, Boston, 1928, 152–53.

page 32
"For a song": Corr., IV, 208.

CHAPTER 2 (pages 33–54)

page 33
"This head": LG—1855, 29.

page 33
The proceedings: Corr., IV, 383, 390.

page 33
One celebrant: In Re, 315–16.

page 34
Horace Traubel: Peter Van Egmond, ed., Memoirs of Thomas B. Harned, Hartford, Conn., 1972, 26.

page 34
Elective son: WWC, I, 207, and IV, 186.

page 34
Richard Maurice Bucke: Man's Moral Nature, 1879; "Twenty-Five Years Ago," The Overland Monthly, I, No. 6 (June 1883), 553–60; Artem Lozynsky, Richard Maurice Bucke: Medical Mystic, Detroit, Mich., 1977; Artem Lozynsky, ed., The Letters of Dr. Richard Maurice Bucke to Walt Whitman, Detroit, 1977.

page 34
A Whitman Fellowship: The Bolton "college" is described in Johnston and Wallace, Visits; the "Men of Harlech" verses are in Corr., V, 230n.

page 34
William O'Connor: WWC, II, 114; Champion, passim; the Washington visit is recounted in WWC, IV, 452–63.

page 35
Kennedy: Barrus. 201; WWC, I, 166; Corr., V, 140n.

page 35
"He took off his coat": WWC, I, 323.

page 36
"I am satisfied": Lozynsky, Letters of Dr. Richard Maurice Burke . . . , 264.

page 37
"A thousand books": In Re, 311.

page 38
"A picture of the world": Bucke (1883), 178.

page 38
"My spirit": CRE, 384.

page 38
Bucke estimated: "Portraits of Walt Whitman," New England Magazine, XX, March 1899, 33–50; see also Allen, as cited in note for page 16 above ("The visual record").

page 38
"Out from behind": CRE, 381–2. I have used the LG—1876 reading of these lines, as discussed in Harold W. Blodgett, "Whitman and the Linton Portrait," WWR, IV, No. 3 (September 1958), 90–92.

page 39
Thomas Eakins: Lincoln Kirstein, "Walt Whitman and Thomas Eakins," Aperture, 1972; Henry B. Rule, "Walt Whitman and Thomas Eakins," The Texas Quarterly, XVII, No. 4 (Winter 1974), 7–57.

page 39
"Mysterious" photograph: *WWC*, IV, *passim*, and V, *passim*; *In Re*, 33.
page 40
"How do you like that": *WWC*, I, 276.
page 40
"So damned flamboyant": *WWC*, II, 225.
page 41
"I don't worship": *WWC*, IV, 142; Huneker is quoted in Larzer Ziff, *The American 1890s*, 1966, 14; Barrus, 287; *WWC*, I, xvi.
page 41
"Some day": *WWC*, II, 316, 360, 543.
page 42
Whitman insisted: *WWC*, II, 140, 364.
page 42
Hearty old scripture phrase: Bucke (1883), 23.
page 43
"I never knew": *Calamus*, 25.
page 43
"As for dissipation": *In Re*, 36.
page 43
"I have loved you": *WWC*, I, 49–50.
page 43
"That last paragraph": *WWC*, II, 425.
page 44
"In paths untrodden": *LG—1860*, 341–42.
page 45
Edward Carpenter: P. N. Furbank, *E. M. Forster*, 1978, I, 256–57; *WWC*, I, 160.
page 45
Edmund Gosse: Phyllis Grosskurth, *John Addington Symonds*, London, 1964, 280–81; *Corr.*, III, 384; *WWC*, I, 40.
page 45
Roden Noel: Grosskurth, 119; *Corr.*, II, 162*n*.
page 45
Stoker, Stoddard: *WWC*, IV, 180–6; *WWC*, IV, 267–68.
page 45
Charles William Dalmon: Dalmon to WW, Sept. 27, 1888 (Feinberg Coll., LC).
page 45
John Addington Symonds: *In Re*, 302; Harold Blodgett, *Walt Whitman in En-*

gland, Ithaca, N.Y., 1934, 60; Grosskurth, *passim*.
page 45
"I desire": Herbert M. Schneller and Robert L. Peters, eds., *The Letters of John Addington Symonds*, Detroit, Mich., 1968, II, 201–2.
page 46
"Perhaps I don't know": *WWC*, I, 76–77.
page 46
Downright exasperated: *Corr.*, V, 64.
page 46
"Things which have perplexed": *Corr.*, IV, 408*n*.
page 46
"In your conception": *Corr.*, V, 72*n*.
page 47
"Y'rs of Aug: 3d": *Corr.*, V, 72–73.
page 47
"It is obvious": Symonds, *Studies in Sexual Inversion*, repr. 1964, 186.
page 47
The consensus: Barrus, 337–38.
page 48
"I know little": quoted in Oral S. Coad, "Whitman as Parent," *Journal of the Rutgers University Library*, VII, No. 1 (December 1943), 31–32.
page 48
"My belief": Ellen O'Connor (Calder) to Edward Carpenter, Jan. 11, 1910, (Bayley Coll., Ohio Wesleyan University Library).
page 48
"Two deceased children": *Corr.*, V, 202–3.
page 49
"I asked him": Bucke Collection auction catalogue, Anderson Galleries, New York, 1936, Number 307.
page 49
"Sort of deposition": Traubel to Edward Carpenter, Dec. 27, 1901 (Bayley Coll., Ohio Wesleyan University Library).
page 49
"Whenever he gets": *WWC*, IV, 30.
page 50
"I do not complain": *Corr.*, V, 225; WW's transactions with the tomb builders are recorded in *DBN*, *passim*,

and in their letters to him (Feinberg Coll., LC).

page 50
"That such a man": quoted in R. A. Coleman, "Trowbridge and Whitman," *PMLA*, LXIII (March 1948), 269.

page 50
"Greatly rejoiced": *Corr.*, V, 265n.

page 50
"It is my intention": *Corr.*, V, 240; information from Irene A. Talarowski, Harleigh Cemetery, Nov. 18, 1974.

page 51
"Walt Whitman wishes": *Corr.*, V, 275n.

page 51
"Depress'd mounds": *PW*, I, 6.

page 52
"I bequeath": *CRE*, 89.

page 52
Stark, elemental, and secure: "In February 1974 Professor Patrick D. Hazard, of Beaver College, Glenside, Penna., raised $700 to rehabilitate the vault, waterproof it, clean the discolored marble, and repair the broken concrete. The money was given to Mayor Angelo J. Errchetti, of Camden, on April 3, which was proclaimed 'Walt Whitman Day.'" *The Long-Islander* (Huntington, N. Y.), June 13, 1974, Sect. iii, 5.

page 52
"Day by day": Traubel to Buxton Forman, Jan. 4, 1891 (Berg Coll., New York Public Library).

page 52
"Invisible breeze": *PW*, II, 674–75.

page 52
Now he lay: Elizabeth L. Keller, *Walt Whitman in Mickle Street*, 1921; Artem Lozynsky, "Whitman's Death Bed," *AL*, XLVII, No. 1 (May 1975), 270–73; Daniel Longaker, "The Last Sickness and Death of Walt Whitman," *In Re*, 393–411; Josiah C. Trent, M. D., "Walt Whitman—A Case History," *Surgery, Gynecology, and Obstetrics*, LXXXVII, No. 1 (July 1948), 113–21.

page 53
"I think of you": *Corr.*, V, 277n.

page 53
Last letter: *Corr.*, V, 277.

page 53
"Red letter day": Philadelphia *Evening Bulletin*, March 30, 1892.

page 53
Unusual service: Traubel, "At the Graveside of Walt Whitman," *In Re*, 437–52.

page 54
Here was Walt: *LG—1860*, 312.

CHAPTER 3 (*pages 55–73*)

page 55
"I remember": *FCI*, 46.

page 56
"Two or three-score": *PW*, I, 7.

page 56
"The Whitmans": Manuscript notes, Sept. 11–13, 1850, pub. Edward Grier, *The Long-Islander* (Huntington, N. Y.), Sept. 27, 1973.

page 57
"Poor Tom Paine": Moncure D. Conway, *The Life of Thomas Paine*, 1892, II, 422–23.

page 57
Frances Wright: Frances Trollope, *Domestic Manners of the Americans*, repr. 1949, 263; *A Few Days in Athens*, 1869, 13; *WWC*, II, 499–500.

page 58
"Quite innocent": Odell Shepard, ed., *The Journals of Bronson Alcott*, Boston, 1938, 143.

page 58
"Bear my testimony": *WWC*, I, 79–80.

page 58
Cobbett: *A Year's Residence in the United States of America* (1819), repr. Carbondale, Ill., 1964, 195–97.

page 58
"It is very hard": *WWC*, IV, 486, III, 450.

page 58
Once told Burroughs: Barrus, 254.

page 59
"First rate carpenter": *FCI*, 47.

page 59
Sydney Smith: in *Edinburgh Review*,

XXXIII (January–May, 1820), 79–80.

page 59

Emerson: "Historic Notes of Life and Letters in New England," in Mark Van Doren, ed., *The Portable Emerson*, 1946, 516.

page 60

Tocqueville: *Democracy in America*, 1945, II, 99.

page 60

"There was a child": *LG—1855*, 90.

page 60

"I merely stir": *LG—1855*, 32.

page 60

"Most profound theme": *PW*, I, 258.

page 61

"I sometimes think": *An American Primer*, Philadelphia, 1904, Foreword.

page 61

"Perfect writer": *DBN*, III, 742.

page 61

"Eluding, fluid, beautiful": *DBN*, III, 730, 733.

page 61

"I look": *CRE*, 428 and *PW*, I, 10.

page 61

Recurrent dream: *PW*, I, 138–39.

page 62

Jesse, unstable, violent: Katherine Molinoff, *Some Notes on Whitman's Family*, 1941.

page 62

"He was a very handsome": *PW*, II, 693.

page 62

"Memorable vehemence": Stovall, 19.

page 62

"What is yours": *CRE*, 255.

page 63

"Young and middle age": *DBN*, III, 658.

page 63

Louisa Whitman: *WWC*, II, 113, 214, 280; *DBN*, III, 658–59.

page 63

"Child who went forth": *CRE*, 247.

page 64

Huntington township: for Long Island, Brooklyn, and New York, see: Robert H. Albion, *The Rise of New York Port*, 1970; Richard M. Bayles, *Historical and Descriptive Sketches of Suffolk County*, 1874, repr. 1962; Ralph Foster Weld, *Brooklyn Village, 1816–1834*, 1938; Rufus Rockwell Wilson, *Historic Long Island*, 1902.

page 64

"The child": *UPP*, II, 292.

page 64

"Methodist elder": *WWC*, I, 256.

page 65

"We occupied": *PW*, I, 13.

page 65

"We moved": "Family Record" (Berg Coll., New York Public Library).

page 65

Marquis de Lafayette: his 1824–1825 tour of the U. S. is studied in Fred Somkin, *Unquiet Eagle: Memory and Desire in the Idea of American Freedom, 1815–1860*, Ithaca, N. Y., 1967. Among WW's many references to Lafayette's Brooklyn visit are: *UPP*, II, 2–3, 256–57, 284–85; *PW*, I, 13; *PW*, II, 733.

page 66

" 'Our city' ": *Aurora*, 19.

page 67

"Moved to Adams st.": "Family Record."

page 67

Joseph Lancaster: Carlyle discusses the Lancastrian system in *Signs of the Times* (1829); Barbara Finkelstein, "Pedagogy as Intrusion," *History of Childhood Quarterly*, II, No. 3 (Winter 1975), esp. 356–75; Florence B. Freedman, *Walt Whitman Looks at the Schools*, 1950, 3–24.

page 67

Most vivid recollection: *UPP*, II, 265–66 and *DBN*, III, 614–15.

page 68

"With music strong": *CRE*, 46.

page 68

"Blood of Christ": *PW* I, 13, and II, 645.

page 69

"Like a cross": *WWC*, II, 125.

page 69

"If there is": *PW*, II, 643.

page 70

"Time of 'Revivals' ": *UPP*, II, 293.

page 70

"She pretended": *In Re*, 38.

page 70
"I was never made": *WWC*, II, 19.
page 71
"Edward C.": *PW*, I, 13.
page 71
"Reduce the Leaves": *WWC*, I, 96.
page 71
"Men of moderate means": quoted in Weld, 48.
page 72
Aaron Burr: *WWC*, II, 98 and WW's manuscript essay "On Aaron Burr" (Feinberg Coll., LC).
page 72
John Jacob Astor: *UPP*, I, 218–19 and *PW*, I, 17–18.
page 72
"Moved to Henry St.": "Family Record."
page 72
"It must have been": Autobiographical note (Feinberg Coll., LC).
page 72
Cholera: J. S. Chambers, *The Conquest of Cholera*, 1938; Charles E. Rosenberg, *The Cholera Years*, Chicago, 1962.
page 73
"For various reasons": *EPF*, 316n.
page 73
"Moved from Liberty st.": "Family Record."
page 73
Andrew Jackson: *UPP*, I, 118.
page 73
"I remained": "Family Record."

CHAPTER 4 (*pages 74–94*)

page 74
William Hartshorne: William White, "A Tribute to William Hartshorne: Unrecorded Whitman," *AL*, XLII, No. 4 (January 1971), 554–58; *UPP*, II, 246–49, 294; *PW*, I, 14.
page 75
"The jour printer": *LG—1855*, 21.
page 75
Samuel E. Clement: Weld, *Brooklyn Village*, 168–69; *Long Island Star*, June 1, 1831, and October 24, 1832.

page 75
"A shroud": *CRE*, 427–28.
page 76
"Several gentlemen": *UPP*, II, 3–4.
page 76
"There's one reason": *WWC*, II, 125.
page 77
Alden Spooner: Weld, *Brooklyn Village*, 30–44.
page 77
Tocqueville: *Democracy in America*, I, 315, and II, 111.
page 78
"The fire": *CRE*, 252.
page 78
Meteor shower: *NF*, 51.
page 78
"Fat-cheeked boy": Rollo G. Silver, "Whitman in 1850: Three Uncollected Articles," *AL*, XIX, No. 4 (January 1948), 311–12.
page 78
"I can": *PW* II, 596–97; for the dating of Booth's performance, see Stovall, 64.
page 79
"O what is it": *CRE*, 384.
page 79
First time he ever wanted: Bliss Perry, *Walt Whitman*, Boston, 1906, 15; *PW*, I, 286–87.
page 80
"Fame's Vanity": *EPF*, 23–24.
page 81
"Nobody, I hope": *UPP*, I, 37.
page 81
Philip Hone: Allan Nevins, ed., *The Diary of Philip Hone*, 1927, I, 185–91.
page 82
"Long ago": *In Re*, 39.
page 82
"Unstable as water": *EPF*, 327.
page 82
The teacher's desk: Horace L. Traubel, "Walt Whitman, Schoolmaster: Notes of a Conversation with Charles A. Roe, 1894." *Walt Whitman Fellowship Papers* (Philadelphia), No. 14 (April 1895); Florence B. Freedman, *Walt Whitman Looks at the Schools*, 24–34.
page 83
Sick cow: T. O. Mabbott, "Walt Whitman Edits the *Sunday Times* July 1842–

June 1843," *AL*, XXXIX, No. 1 (March 1967), 101–2.

page 83
"Of all human beings": *UPP*, I, 44–45.

page 84
"Singular young man": *CPW*, VI, 135.

page 84
Benjamin Carman: Willis Steell, "Walt Whitman's Early Life on Long Island," *Munsey's Magazine*, XL, No. 4 (January 1909), 501; *In Re*, 35.

page 84
Roe said: Traubel, "Walt Whitman, Schoolmaster . . . ," as cited in note for page 82 above ("the teacher's desk").

page 85
"A class of beings": *UPP*, I, 37.

page 85
"Tho' always": *Corr.*, V, 73.

page 85
"Though a bachelor": *EPF*, 248.

page 85
"My Boys and Girls": *EPF*, 248–50; Stephen A. Black, *Whitman's Journeys into Chaos*, Princeton, N. J., 1975, 25–31, 180–82.

page 87
An angel: *EPF*, 78–79.

page 87
Archibald Dean: *EPF*, 327.

page 87
At Smithtown: Katherine Molinoff, *An Unpublished Whitman Manuscript: The Record Book of the Smithtown Debating Society*, 1941; Katherine Molinoff, *Whitman's Teaching at Smithtown, 1837–1838*, 1942.

page 88
Tocqueville: *Democracy in America*, I, 250.

page 88
The following August: see Bliss Perry, "Emerson's Most Famous Speech," in Carl Bode, ed., *Ralph Waldo Emerson, A Profile*, 1968, 52–65; Mark Van Doren, ed., *The Portable Emerson*, 1946, 23–46.

page 89
"To inflate the chest": *CRE*, 181.

page 89
The Long Islander: Rubin, 37–39.

page 89
Whitman later acknowledged: *ISL*, 38.

page 90
Two items: reprinted in *The Long Islander* (Huntington, N. Y.), May 29, 1963.

page 90
"Everything seem'd": *PW*, I, 287.

page 91
" 'Beach-parties' ": *EPF*, 320; *UPP*, I, 48–51; *PW*, I, 11.

page 91
"Aquatic loafer": *WWC*, II, 21.

page 91
Young men bathing: Paul Fussell, *The Great War and Modern Memory*, 1975, 303–7.

page 91
"Twenty-eight young men": *CRE*, 38–39.

page 92
"I felt myself": Herbert Bergman and William White, "Whitman's Lost 'Sun-Down Papers,' Nos. 1–3," *American Book Collector*, XX (January 1970), 17–20.

page 93
"Our future Lot": *EPF*, 28.

page 93
Sold the *Long Islander*: Herbert Bergman, "Walt Whitman as a Journalist, 1831–January, 1848," *Journalism Quarterly*, XLVIII (Summer 1971), 195–204; Rubin, 39.

page 93
"Came down to New York": *UPP*, II, 87.

page 94
"Winter of 1840": *UPP*, II, 87.

page 94
"Miss Clarissa Lyvere": *Corr.*, VI, 3.

page 94
"No Turning Back": *New York Times*, Aug. 14, 1842; reprinted in Mabbott (as cited in note for page 83 above).

CHAPTER 5 (*pages 95–113*)

page 95
"Mrs. Chipman's": *UPP*, II, 87–88.

page 95
"Mr. K.": *Aurora*, 23.
page 96
Frances Trollope: *Domestic Manners of the Americans*, repr. 1949, 283–85.
page 96
Henry Saunders: *EPF*, 324; Joseph Jay Rubin, "Whitman and the Boy-Forger," *AL*, X, No. 2 (May 1938), 214–15.
page 96
"Boarding houses": *EPF*, 236.
page 96
Whitman figured: *UPP*, II, 6 and *NYD*, 96.
page 96
"Not those": *CRE*, 126.
page 97
Spreadeagle peroration: *UPP*, I, 51.
page 97
"Heaven save the mark": *UPP*, I, 33*n*.
page 97
"Only come-day": *WWC*, I, 6.
page 97
John Fellows: *PW*, I, 140; Conway, *The Life of Thomas Paine*, II, 422–23.
page 98
"A monthly magazine": *UPP*, II, 15.
page 98
"My stories": *Corr.*, I, 26.
page 98
"Dickens' American Notes": quoted in Lawrence H. Houtchens, "Charles Dickens and International Copyright," *AL*, XIII, No. 1 (March 1941), 23–24.
page 99
Made his grievances known: Dickens' speech is quoted in John S. Whitley and Arnold Goldman, eds., *American Notes*, Baltimore, 1972, 302.
page 99
"I consider Mr. Dickens": *UPP*, I, 69–72.
page 99
"Shall Hawthorne": *UPP*, I, 121–23.
page 100
Margaret Fuller's challenge: New York *Tribune*, 1846.
page 100
A great debate: John Stafford, *The Literary Criticism of "Young Amer-*

ica," Berkeley, Calif., 1952; Adams, O'Sullivan, and Emerson are quoted in Jay B. Hubbell, *Who Are the Major American Writers?* Durham, N. C., 1972, 63–64.
page 101
Emerson's lecture: *Aurora*, 10, 105; Robert E. Spiller and Wallace E. Williams, eds., *The Early Lectures of Ralph Waldo Emerson*, Cambridge, Mass., 1972, III, 347–65.
page 101
"Pictures": *CRE*, 647.
page 102
"You will hardly know": *CRE*, 89.
page 102
Anson Herrick and John F. Ropes: *Aurora*, 1–11, 117.
page 102
Assailed Bishop John Hughes: *Aurora*, 57–83, 141–42.
page 103
"For the next two or three hours": *Aurora*, 44–45.
page 104
Conventional invective: *Aurora*, 13.
page 104
Claimed that he had dashed it off: *WWC*, I, 93.
page 105
"Mere boy": *EPF*, 148.
page 105
Leslie Fiedler: *Love and Death in the American Novel*, 1960, 260.
page 105
"Damned rot": *WWC*, I, 93.
page 105
George Whitman recalled: *In Re*, 39.
page 105
Self-reviews: Esther Shephard, "Walt Whitman's Whereabouts in the Winter of 1842–1843," *AL*, XXIX, No. 3 (November 1957), 289–96.
page 106
"Rather stylish": *In Re*, 34: Perry, *Walt Whitman*, 22–23.
page 106
"On one hand": *Broadway Journal*, May 31, 1845, 347; repr. Burton R. Pollin, " 'Delightful Sights,' A Possible Whitman Article . . . ," *WWR*, XV, No. 3 (September 1969), 180–87.

page 106
"Wasn't it brave": *Aurora*, 12.
page 107
"With sleeves rolled up": *Aurora*, 21.
page 107
"The butcher-boy": *CRE*, 39.
page 107
"The glories": *CRE*, 160.
page 107
"Mannahatta": *PW*, II, 683; *Workshop*, 61.

page 108
Thomas Low Nichols: quoted in Russell B. Nye, *Society and Culture in America, 1830–1860*, 1974, 3.
page 109
"Between seven and eight": *Aurora*, 26–27; *UPP*, I, 154–55.
page 109
"Agonies": *CRE*, 67.
page 109
"Fire last night": Allan Nevins and Milton Halsey Thomas, eds., *The Diary of George Templeton Strong*, 1952, I, 127.
page 110
"Actually set people to work": *Aurora*, 41.
page 110
"We like to walk": *GF*, II, 108.
page 111
Prevailing mode of euphemism: Ann Douglas, "Heaven Our Home . . . ," *American Quarterly*, XXVI, No. 5 (December, 1974), 506–11; Stanley French, "The Cemetery as Cultural Institution . . . ," *American Quarterly*, XXVI, No. 1 (March 1974), 37–59; Geoffrey Gorer, "The Pornography of Death," *Encounter*, October 1955, 49–52; Robert W. Habenstein and William M. Lamers, *The History of American Funeral Directing*, Milwaukee, Wis., 1955, 261–67, 431.
page 111
"Like iron-willed destiny": *UPP*, I, 168–69.
page 111
"It is a place": *GF*, II, 93–96.
page 112
"In whatever direction": *GF*, II, 113–17.

page 113
E. Porter Belden: *New York: Past, Present, and Future*, 1849, advertising supplement, 6–13; John A. Kouwenhoven. *The Columbia Historical Portrait of New York*, 1953, 194.
page 113
"Remember": Bucke (1883), 67.
page 113
"A great city": *Corr.*, IV, 299.

CHAPTER 6 (*pages 114–23*)

page 114
Literary celebrities: *PW*, I, 17 and II, 595; *GF*, II, 595.
page 114
James Russell Lowell: Esther Shephard, "Walt Whitman's Whereabouts in the Winter of 1842–1843," *AL*, XXIX, No. 3 (November 1957), 291; Charles Eliot Norton, ed., *Letters of James Russell Lowell*, Boston, 1894, I, 270–71.
page 114
"Dialogue": *UPP*, II, 15–16.
page 115
According to Poe: George E Woodberry and Edmund C. Stedman, eds., *The Works of Edgar A. Poe*, Chicago, 1894–1895, VIII, 81.
page 115
"Poe was very cordial": *PW*, I, 17.
page 115
"Did not enthuse me": *WWC*, I, 138–39.
page 116
"In a dream": *PW*, I, 232.
page 117
"From the surface": Edward Carpenter, *Days with Walt Whitman*, 1906, 72–73.
page 117
Whitman's stories: Stephen A. Black, *Whitman's Journeys into Chaos*, Princeton, N. J., 1975; Rohn Samuel Friedman, *The Process of Identity: Whitman's Critical Vocabulary*, Honors dissertation, Harvard, 1973; Chaviva M. Hosek, *Design in Walt Whitman*, Ph.D. dissertation, Harvard, 1973; Justin

Kaplan, "Nine Old Bones," *Atlantic Monthly*, May 1968, 60–64; Michael S. Reynolds, "Whitman's Early Prose and 'The Sleepers,' " *AL*, XLI, No. 3 (November 1969), 406–14.

page 118
"The dark hours": *UPP*, I, 149–51.

page 119
"Wild Frank's face": *EPF*, 63.

page 120
"An image of beautiful terror": *EPF*, 66–67.

page 121
Manuscript fragments: *NF*, 114–15, 122–23.

page 122
D. H. Lawrence: *Studies in Classic American Literature*, Garden City, N. Y., 177, 182–83.

page 122
"With the careless indifference": *EPF*, 92.

page 122
"Fresh, and wet": *EPF*, 91.

page 123
"The grave": *EPF*, 93.

page 123
"Lisped to me constantly": *LG—1880*, 277.

CHAPTER 7 (*pages 124–45*)

page 124
The *Star*: Emory Holloway, "More Light on Whitman," *The American Mercury*, January 1924, 183–89; also Florence B. Freedman, ed., *Walt Whitman Looks at the Schools*, 1950, 213–17.

page 125
Father's surrogate or regent: deeds, receipts, and similar documents are in LC or printed in Allen, 598–600, and Charles E. Feinberg, "A Whitman Collector Destroys a Whitman Myth," *Papers of the Bibliographical Society of America*, LII (1958), 73–92.

page 125
"Ode" by Whitman: *EPF*, 34.

page 126
"When the last": *GF*, I, 79–80.

pages 127
The *Eagle*: *PW*, I, 288; *Eagle*, 70; *UPP*, 118–21.

page 127
" 'In the twinkling of an eye' ": *GF*, II, 228.

page 128
Book reviewer: *UPP*, I, 126–37.

page 128
Coleridge: *UPP*, I, 131.

page 128
Goethe: *UPP*, I, 140.

page 129
Hone: Allan Nevins, ed., *The Diary of Philip Hone, 1828–1851*, 1927, II, 774.

page 129
Emerson: Mark Van Doren, ed., *The Portable Emerson*, 1946, 322.

page 129
Lowell: Norman Foerster, ed., *American Poetry and Prose*, Boston, 1934, 688–89.

page 129
"If our fame": Freedman, 215–16.

page 130
"Thoroughly chastised": *GF*, I, 240–42.

page 130
"Resolved": William White, "Walter Whitman: King's County Democratic Party Secretary," *WWR*, XVII, No. 3 (September 1971), 92–98.

page 130
"Daring, burrowing energies": *GF*, II, 121–26.

page 131
Wilmot: David M. Potter, *The Impending Crisis*, 1976, 21–23; Leon F. Litwack, *North of Slavery*, Chicago, 1961, 47.

page 131
Slaveowners: *WWC*, IV, 364; *FCI*, 43.

page 132
"Degraded, shiftless": *UPP*, II, 316–17.

page 132
"Nature has set": *ISL*, 90.

page 132
Uncle Tom's Cabin: Cambridge, Mass., 1962, 184.

page 132
"The fire of her race": *EPF*, 204.

page 132
"I am a curse": *NF*, 19.
page 133
"Poem of the black person": *NF*, 170.
page 133
"The British": *Aurora*, 126–27.
page 133
Their "ranting": *GF*, II, 191–93.
page 133
Hearing Emerson say: *WWC*, IV, 161.
page 133
Strong: *Diary*, II, 22.
page 134
"Set Down Your Feet": *GF*, I, 194.
page 135
Last Barnburner editorial: *GF*, I, 227–28.
page 135
Whitman's dismissal: *GF*, I, xxxii–xxxvi; Herbert Bergman, "Walt Whitman as Journalist," *Journalism Quarterly*, XLVIII (1971), 203–4.
page 135
Whitman's account: *PW*, I, 288.
page 136
"Made him an offer": *PW*, I, 288; *UPP*, II, 88.
page 136
At Cumberland: WW describes the trip to New Orleans in *UPP*, I, 181–90.
page 137
Jeff wrote: *Corr.*, I, 27–28.
page 138
"River fiends": *EPF*, 43.
page 138
Arrived in New Orleans: *PW*, II, 604–7; *UPP*, II, 77–78; W. K. Dart, "Walt Whitman in New Orleans," *Publications of the Louisiana Historical Society*, VII (1915), 97–112; Emory Holloway "Walt Whitman in New Orleans," *Yale Review*, V, October 1915, 166–83.
page 138
"See the dirt": *Corr.*, I, 29.
page 140
"Quick mettle": *CRE*, 473.
page 140
Safe arrival: *EPF*, 43.
page 140
"St. Mary's Market": *UPP*, I, 224.

page 141
Standing in the gaslight: *UPP*, I, 202–5.
page 141
"The Octoroon": *WWC*, II, 283.
page 142
Binns: *A Life of Walt Whitman*, London, 1905, 51.
page 142
"Once I pass'd": *CRE*, 109–10.
page 143
Discovered the manuscript: *UPP*, II, 102.
page 143
Holloway himself: in *Free and Lonesome Heart: The Secret of Walt Whitman*.
page 143
"I saw in Louisiana" *CRE*, 126–27.
page 144
"Keep well": *Corr.*, I, 33.
page 144
Jeff reported: *Corr.*, I, 27–36.
page 144
"Singular sort of coldness": *UPP*, II, 77–78; *FCI*, 57–58; *COP*, 607–10.
page 145
First editorial: Saturday, Sept. 9, 1848; the issue is reproduced in E. F. Frey, *Catalogue of . . . the Trent Collection*, Durham, N. C., 1945.

CHAPTER 8 (*pages 146–64*)

page 146
Water cure: secondary sources are: Grace Adams and Edward Hutter, *The Mad Forties*, 1952; Siegfried Giedion, *Mechanization Takes Command*, 1948, 660–81.
page 146
Graham: Giedion, 201–8
page 147
Nearly one hundred yards: Robert G. Albion, *The Rise of New York Port*, 1970, 55–56.
page 147
"I see through the broadcloth": *CRE*, 35, 111, 102.
page 148
Henry Adams: *Education*, Boston, 1961, 385.

page 148
Victorian pursuit of health: Bruce Haley, *The Healthy Body and Victorian Culture*, Cambridge, Mass., 1978.
page 148
Phrenology, or the science of mind: for general accounts, see: John D. Davies, *Phrenology: Fad and Science*, New Haven, Conn., 1955; Madeline B. Stern, *Heads and Headlines: The Phrenological Fowlers*, Norman, Okla, 1971. Whitman's connection with phrenology was first discussed at length in: Edward Hungerford, "Walt Whitman and His Chart of Bumps," *AL*, II, No. 4 (January 1931), 350–84. Among subsequent articles are: Harold Aspiz, "Educating the Kosmos," *American Quarterly*, XVIII (1966), 655–66; Arthur Wrobel, "Whitman and the Phrenologists," *PMLA*, LXXXIX, No. 1 (January 1974), 17–23.
page 149
His death on November 10: Charles Follen, *Funeral Oration . . . at the Burial of Gaspar Spurzheim, M. D.*, Boston, 1832.
page 149
Strong: *Diary*, I, 46–47.
page 149
Holmes: Hjalmar O. Lokensgard, "Oliver Wendell Holmes's 'Phrenological Character,' " *New England Quarterly*, XII, No. 4 (December 1940), 711–18.
page 149
Mark Twain: *Autobiography*, 1959, 64–65; *Life on the Mississippi*, Boston, 1883, 270.
page 149
"One of the choice places": *PW*, II, 697.
page 150
"Animal magnetism": O. S. Fowler, *Practical Phrenology*, 1844, 59; Myrth Jimmie Killingsworth, "Another Source for Whitman's Use of 'Electric,' " *WWR*, XXIII, No. 2 (September 1977), 129–32; Edmund Reiss, "Whitman's Debt to Animal Magnetism," *PMLA*, LXXVIII (March 1963), 80–88.

page 150
"Mine is no callous": *CRE*, 57, 109, 424, 432.
page 151
"Morality and talent": *NF*, 81
page 151
"I do not press": *CRE*, 53.
page 152
One of Whitman's short stories: *EPF*, 330.
page 152
"This man": Hungerford, "Walt Whitman and His Chart of Bumps," 363; *FCI*, 233–36.
page 153
"I know what Holmes said": *WWC*, I, 385.
page 153
"Something *furtive*": Edward Carpenter, *Days with Walt Whitman*, 1906, 42–43.
page 153
"In a little house": *CRE*, 642.
page 153
"Who is this": *CRE*, 644, 645, 649.
page 155
"In winter": *CRE*, 178.
page 155
"Tall, large, rough-looking man": *NYD*, 130.
page 156
"Not much to lose": Rubin, 213.
page 156
"I withdraw": Rubin, 222.
page 156
Went to Greenport: WW's travel letters to the New York *Sunday Dispatch* are reprinted in Rubin, 311–23.
page 157
"Trailing for blue-fish": *CRE*, 179.
page 157
"In *proportion*": Rubin, 323.
page 158
"You and I": Rubin, 337.
page 158
"It avails not": *CRE*, 180–81.
page 158
George recalled: *In Re*, 35, 37, 39.
page 159
"Voluminous" and "prolix": *Corr.*, V, 282–83.

page 159
"I plumped in": *The Long Islander* (Huntington, N. Y.), Sept. 27, 1973, 11, 14.
page 160
"I take the liberty": *Corr.*, I, 38.
page 160
Financing and building: see note for page 125 ("Father's surrogate or regent").
page 160
Agreement with Minard S. Scofield: Feinberg Coll., LC.
page 161
"Mr. Scofield owes WW": *FCI*, 49.
page 161
Burroughs doubted: Bliss Perry, *Walt Whitman*, Boston, 1906, 55–56.
page 161
Salesman and Traveller's Directory: Rubin, 268.
page 161
S. Knaebel: Feinberg Coll., LC.
page 161
"God, 'twas delicious": *EPF*, 38.
page 162
"Not as a Massachusetts man": *The Writings and Speeches of Daniel Webster*, 1903, X, 57–60.
page 163
"If thou art balked": *EPF*, 36–37.
page 163
"Here, now, is a specimen": *UPP*, I, 25n.
page 164
"Not a grave": *EPF*, 39–40.
page 164
Alcott: Odell Shepard, *Pedlar's Progress*, Boston, 1937, 278.

CHAPTER 9 (*pages 165–83*)

page 165
"Big strong days": *WWC*, II, 503.
page 165
"Close phalanx": *UPP*, I, 237.
page 165
Charles L. Heyde: Katherine Molinoff, *Some Notes on Whitman's Family*, 1941, 24–43; *FCI*, 213–32; *WWC*, II, 498–500; Jeff Whitman is quoted in *CWL*, 11.

page 166
Harrison (and Libbey): *WWC*, II, 506.
page 166
"I don't know where": *UPP*, I, 237–38.
page 168
Brown's studio: *WWC*, II, 502; *UPP*, I, 135.
page 168
"To the artist": *UPP*, I, 241–47.
page 169
"Make no quotations": *NF*, 56.
page 170
Dr. Henry Abbott: *NYD*, 30–40; *PW*, II, 696–97; Stovall, 162–63.
page 170
"My definitive *carte visite*": *PW*, II, 712.
page 171
"Uniform hieroglyphic": *CRE*, 34–35.
page 171
"Scented herbage": *CRE*, 113; Esther Shephard, "Possible Sources of Some of Whitman's Ideas and Symbols . . . ," *Modern Language Quarterly*, XIV, March 1953, 74.
page 172
In the Eagle: *GF*, II, 291
page 173
Richard Chase: *Walt Whitman Reconsidered*, 1955, 48.
page 173
Strange admixture: *CRE*, 52, 54, 60, 72, 85, 89.
page 173
Rejected Carlyle: *PW*, I, 258, 262; *Corr.*, III, 302.
page 174
Hot eloquence: *PW*, II, 551, 697.
page 174
Hale: *Corr.*, I, 39–40; Richard H. Sewell, "Walt Whitman, John P. Hale, and the Free Democracy . . . ." *New England Quarterly*, XXXIV, June, 1961, 239–42; Richard H. Sewell, *John P. Hale and the Politics of Abolition*, Cambridge, Mass., 1965.
page 175
Whitman's "musical passion": *PW*, I, 21; *PW*, II, 697; *UPP*, I, 104–106; Robert D. Faner, *Walt Whitman & Opera*, Carbondale, Ill., 1951.
page 176
"Agonized squalls": Thomas L.

Brasher, "Whitman's Conversion to Opera," *WWR*, IV, No. 4 (December 1958), 109–10.

page 177
"Her voice": *GF*, II, 351–52.

page 177
Strong: *Diary*, II, 19–20.

page 177
Whitman attended: Rollo G. Silver, "Whitman in 1850: Three Uncollected Articles," *AL*, XIX, No. 4 (January 1948), 303–5; *PW*, II, 697.

page 178
"Be simple": *UPP*, II, 63.

page 178
Bettini: *UPP*, I, 257.

page 178
Alboni: *PW*, I, 235.

page 178
"Now in a moment": *CRE*, 252–53.

page 179
"Talents of gold": Silver, 314–16.

page 179
Following his own advice: see note for page 125 (Father's surrogate).

page 179
"Always magnetic": *WWC*, V, 463.

page 179
"400 deaths": *DBN*, II, 348n.

page 180
Exhibition catalogue: Benjamin Silliman and C. R. Goodrich, *The World of Science, Art, and Industry Illustrated*, 1854, 24–26.

page 181
"New York, Great Exposition": *PW*, II, 681; *ISL*, 129–30.

page 181
"High rising tier": *CRE*, 200.

page 181
"To exalt the present": *CRE*, 202.

page 182
"They had immense qualities": *PW*, I, 18–19.

page 182
"He was a goodfellow": *LG—1855*, 66.

page 182
Archangels: *CRE*, 42, 86.

page 183
Sheet of manuscript: *NF*, 116, 120; Emory Holloway, ed., *Leaves of Grass:*

Inclusive Edition, Garden City, N. Y., 1946, 577–78.

CHAPTER 10 (pages *184–201*)

page 184
"We did not know": *In Re*, 35.

page 184
"Built in Skillman st.": "Family Record" (Berg Coll., New York Public Library).

page 184
"As in 'A Backward Glance' ": *PW*, II, 714; *MDW*, "Personal—Note"; *Corr.*, III, 307.

page 185
Trial lines and fragments: Notebook, *ca.* 1854–1855, LC.

page 186
Turned thirty-five: *NYD*, 1–2; *NF*, 86.

page 186
Pocket notebook: LC, partially published *UPP*, II, 63–76. This is one of the ten Whitman notebooks that vanished from the LC manuscript collection during World War II; a photostat remains.

page 187
"I celebrate": *LG—1855*, 13.

page 187
"Test of a poem": *UPP*, II, 75.

page 188
"I tramp": *LG—1855*, 51.

page 188
"I will take": *UPP*, II, 66–67.

page 188
Other fragments: *UPP*, II, 66–76.

page 189
"Speech is the twin": *LG—1855*, 31.

page 189
"A trance": *Workshop*, 21.

page 190
Elias Hicks: *Corr.*, IV, 164.

page 191
"Techniques of ecstasy": Mircea Eliade, *Shamanism*. Princeton, N. J., 1972. Some other general sources are: Richard Maurice Bucke, M. D., *Cosmic Consciousness*, 1901; Andrew M. Greeley and William C. McCready, "Are We a

Nation of Mystics?" *The New York Times Magazine*, Jan. 26, 1975, 15ff.; William James, *Varieties of Religious Experience*, 1902; Marghanita Laski, *Ecstasy*, 1968.

page 191
"A Persian Lesson": CRE, 353; Massud Farzan, "Whitman and Sufism," *AL*, XLVII, No. 4 (January 1976), 572–82.

page 191
"Do you see": *CRE*, 88.

page 191
"I believe in you": *LG—1855*, 15–16.

page 192
Swedenborg: *UPP*, II, 16–17; *WWC*, V, 376.

page 193
"I am a look": *CRE*, 694.

page 193
"The privacy of the night": *CRE*, 103.

page 193
"Urge and urge," etc.: *LG—1855*, 14, 13, 30, 71, 72.

page 195
"I think I could turn": *LG—1855*, 34.

page 195
Traffic with the poets: *NF*, 97, 113, 127.

page 195
"Be simple": *UPP*, II, 63.

page 195
Alexander Smith: *NF*, 127; *In Re*, 28–29.

page 196
"My Friend!": Smith, *A Life-Drama and Other Poems*, Boston, 1853, 24–25.

page 196
"The great poet": *CRE*, 716.

page 196
"The Americans": *CRE*, 709.

page 196
"An individual": *CRE*, 729.

page 197
Ivan Marki: *The Trial of the Poet*, 1976, 26.

page 197
"This is what": *CRE*, 714–15.

page 198
"At the moment": *WWC*, II, 311.

page 198
Registered the title: William White, "More about the 'Publication' of the first *Leaves of Grass*," *AL*, XXVIII, No. 4 (January 1957), 516–17.

page 198
795 copies: William White, "The First (1855) 'Leaves of Grass': How Many Copies?" *Papers of the Bibliographical Society of America*, LVII (1963), 353–55.

page 198
It was burned: *WWC*, I, 56, 92.

page 199
"We may infer": *NYD*, 154.

page 200
"What am I": *CRE*, 392.

page 200
"Felt very much to blame": Allen, 151.

page 201
"Confirmed resolution": Bucke (1883), 25–26.

page 201
"Great is death": *LG—1855*, 95.

page 201
"Perceives that the corpse": *LG—1855*, [iii].

CHAPTER 11 (*pages 202–22*)

page 202
"Do you take it": *LG—1855*, 25.

page 202
Emerson almost believed: Edmund Wilson, ed., *The Shock of Recognition*, Garden City, N. Y., 1947, 246–52; Ralph L. Rusk, *The Life of Ralph Waldo Emerson*, 1949, 372–73.

page 202
"Dear Sir": *Corr.*, I, 41.

page 203
"Toward no other American": Moncure D. Conway, "Walt Whitman," *The Fortnightly Review* (London), VI (1866), 538–39.

page 203
William Howitt: *Imprints*, 29.

page 203
Criterion: *Imprints*, 55.

page 204
Lucretia Mott: Frederick B. Tolles, "A Quaker Reaction to *Leaves of Grass*," *AL*, XIX, No. 2 (May 1947), 170–71.

page 204
"One cannot leave it about": Charles

Eliot Norton, *Letters*, Boston, 1913, I, 135.
page 204
"No, no": Charles Eliot Norton, ed., *Letters of James Russell Lowell*, Boston, 1894, I, 270–71.
page 204
Review of a different sort: *NYD*, 154–61.
page 205
Life Illustrated: James K. Wallace, "Whitman and *Life Illustrated*," *WWR*, XVII, No. 4 (December 1971), 135–38.
page 205
At Mickle Street: *WWC*, III, 125; *PW*, II, 774.
page 205
"We sometime since": *LG—1855*, xvi.
page 206
A small broadside: Feinberg Coll., LC.
page 206
"Make no puns": *Notebook—1855–56*, 7–8.
page 206
Casual acquaintances: *Notebook—1855–56*, 3, 9.
page 207
"Poem of passage": *Notebook—1855–56*, 5–7.
page 207
"I greet you": *Notebook—1855–56*, 11.
page 207
A Boston paper: *Imprints*, 7.
page 207
Vaunting essay: *CRE*, 730–39.
page 208
Bucke's information: Bucke (1883), 9.
page 208
Whitman himself: *WWC*, III, 116; Thomas Donaldson, *Walt Whitman, the Man*, 1896, 50.
page 208
Supplied friendly journals: *Imprints*, 49; *NYD*, 171.
page 208
Three anonymous reviews: *Imprints*, 7–13, 20–27, 38–41; *In Re*, 13, 27.
page 208
William Swinton: C. Carroll Hollis, "Whitman and William Swinton," *AL*, XXX, No. 4 (January 1959), 425–49.

page 209
"Walt, some people": *WWC*, III, 459–60.
page 210
Wrote him off: *FCI*, 28–29; *PW*, II, 517–18.
page 210
"It is of no importance": *Corr.*, IV, 69–70.
page 210
"According to your letter": *WWC*, IV, 152.
page 211
"So non-polite": *Corr.*, I, 42, 42n.
page 211
"That was very wrong": Wilson, 251; Rusk, 373; Carlos Baker, "The Road to Concord . . ." *Princeton University Library Chronicle*, IX (April 1946), 100–117.
page 211
J. P. Lesley: Eleanor M. Tilton, *"Leaves of Grass:* Four Letters to Emerson," *Harvard Library Bulletin*, XXVII, No. 3 (July 1979), 336–41.
page 212
First meeting: Emerson, Diary Notebook, Houghton Library, Harvard; Rusk, 374; *WWC*, II, 105–6, 130; Edward Carpenter, *Days with Walt Whitman*, 1908, 166–67.
page 212
"As you seemed much interested": Moncure D. Conway, *Autobiography*, 1904, I, 215–17.
page 213
"Not in the least boisterous": Samuel Longfellow to Edward Everett Hale, from Brooklyn, n.d.; courtesy of George Gloss, Brattle Book Shop, Boston; *WWC*, II, 502–3.
page 214
"O I could sing": *CRE*, 233.
page 215
In the White House: *Workshop*, 92–113.
page 216
Most successful literary couple: Milton E. Flower, *James Parton*, Durham, N. C., 1951; *NYD*, 146–54.
page 217
"Leaves of Grass": William White,

"Fanny Fern to Walt Whitman," *American Book Collector*, XI (May 1961), 8–9.
page 217
"My woman's voice": *NYD*, 162–65.
page 217
"I was not their kind": *WWC*, II, 502–3.
page 217
Bronson Alcott: Odell Shepard, ed., *The Journals of Bronson Alcott*, Boston, 1938, 286–94; Richard L. Herrnstadt, *The Letters of A. Bronson Alcott*, Ames, Iowa, 1969, 199–227.
page 218
Henry Thoreau: F. B. Sanborn, ed., *Familiar Letters of Henry David Thoreau*, Boston, 1906, 290–97.
page 218
Visited with his mother: *WWC*, I, 212–13.
page 220
"Arrogant, masculine": *LG—1860*, 141.
page 220
Describing the encounter: *Familiar Letters*, 295–96.
page 221
"A great city": *CRE*, 189.
page 221
Seemed to Walt: *WWC*, I, 212–13, 231, 285, 448; *Workshop*, 263.

CHAPTER 12 (*pages 223–40*)

page 223
Public teacher: *NF*, 57; *Notebook—1855–56*, 3, 10.
page 223
"Now we start hence": *LG—1860*, 190–91.
page 224
"In the forthcoming": *Corr.*, I, 44.
page 224
James Parton: Barrus, 177–78; Oral S. Coad, "Whitman *vs.* Parton," *Journal of the Rutgers University Library*, IV, No. 1 (December 1940), 108; *Corr.*, II, 89–90; *WWC*, III, 237–39.
page 225
"The majority of people": *ISL*, 53–54.
page 225
Daily Times: Corr., III, 385–86.

page 226
He figured in October: *ISL*, 74.
page 226
Strong: *Diary*, II, 366–67, 369.
page 226
"We must now": ISL, 170.
page 227
Cyrus Field: *ISL*, *159*; *Notebook—1855–56*, 15.
page 227
Walt once said: *WWC*, I, 249.
page 227
"A noiseless patient": *CRE*, 450.
page 227
"A promise, a preface": Bowers, 56.
page 227
"I, now": *LG—1860*, 8.
page 228
"Shall I make": *CRE*, 657.
page 228
Frederick Huene: *ISL*, 12–13.
page 228
"The Great Construction": *NF*, 57.
page 228
Emerson said: quoted in *LG—1860*, xix.
page 228
Trinitarian gospel: *CRE*, 742.
page 228
"I am not content": *CRE*, 684.
page 228
William Swinton: C. Carroll Hollis, "Whitman and William Swinton: A Co-operative Friendship," *AL*, XXX, No. 4 (January 1959), 425–49.
page 229
"A perfect writer": *DBN*, III, 742.
page 229
Certain words: *DBN*, III, 738.
page 229
Dictionary and phrase book: *DBN*, III, 664–727.
page 229
"Only a language experiment: *An American Primer*, Boston, 1904, viii–ix.
page 230
Paradise Lost: NF, 98–99.
page 230
Keats's poetry: *NF*, 109.
page 230
"Go study": *Notebook—1855–56*, 13.
page 230
He dines: *NF*, 126.

page 230
House of Mrs. Abby Price: Bucke
(1883), 26–30.
page 231
"Conversation with Mr. Arnold": *NF*,
114.
page 231
Reverend Dr. Elbert Porter: *Corr.*, I,
44–45.
page 232
Daily Times: UPP, II, 16–18.
page 232
"Saint this": *CRE*, 743.
page 232
"Institutional, official": *WWC*, I, 256.
page 232
Marked his birthday: *Workshop*, 34–35.
page 232
"Time to *stir*": Notebook, 1859, LC.
page 233
"Bardic Symbols": *LG—1860*, 195–99.
page 233
American young men: *DBN*, III, 740–
41.
page 234
"Affection shall solve": *LG—1860*, 349.
page 234
"Of two simple men": *LG—1860*, 372.
page 234
"Scented herbage": *LG—1860*, 342.
page 234
"Of him I love": *LG—1860*, 362.
page 235
"Among the men": *LG—1860*, 376.
page 235
"Flocks of ideas": *DBN*, III, 765.
page 236
Walt wrote: *PW*, II, 692–93; *Corr.*, V,
123.
page 236
Walt loved Mattie: *MDW*, "Personal—
Note"; *Corr.*, II, 240.
page 236
Cycle of twelve lyrics: the evolution
and arrangement of this cycle is exam-
ined authoritatively and at length in
Bowers.
page 237
"Uttering joyous leaves": *LG—1860*,
365.
page 237
"For the one I love": *LG—1860*, 358.

page 237
"I am indifferent": *LG—1860*, 355.
page 237
"Who was not proud": *LG—1860*, 356.
page 238
"For an athlete": *LG—1860*, 374.
page 238
"A woman waits": *LG—1860*, 302.
page 238
"Through you": *LG—1860*, 304.
page 239
"The recherché": *Corr.*, I, 347.
page 239
"Root of washed sweet-flag": *CRE*, 53–
54.
page 240
Helen Price remembered: Bucke
(1883), 29.
page 240
Swinburne: quoted in *CRE*, 247n.
page 240
"Out of the Cradle": *CRE*, 246–53.

CHAPTER 13 (*pages 241–69*)

page 241
"Our readers": *Child's Reminiscence*, [10].
page 241
Within days: *Imprints*, 57, 59.
page 241
Provided Whitman with a forum:
Child's Reminiscence, 19–21.
page 241
Henry Clapp: *WWC*, I, 236–38.
page 242
Juliette Hayward Beach: information
on the Beach family from Mrs. Katherine Billings, Albion, N. Y., to author, June 1, 1978; the articles by the
Beaches are quoted in Allen, 261–
62.
page 242
"Lump of——": *Corr.*, I, 55.
page 242
A romance by mail: *UPP*, I, lviiin.;
CRE, 106–7.
page 242
"Walt is a genius": *NYD*, 174.
page 243
Pfaff's beer cellar: W. L. Alden, "Some

Phases of Literary New York in the Sixties," *Putnam's Monthly*, III (1907–1908), 554–58; W. D. Howells, *Literary Friends and Acquaintance*, 1900; Albert Parry, *Garrets and Pretenders*, 1930; William Winter, *Old Friends*, 1909.

page 243
"My beloved Walt": *WWC*, I, 23–25.

page 243
"Poor, poor Ada Clare": *Corr.*, I, 285.

page 244
"Centuries ahead": Allen Lesser, *Enchanting Rebel*, 1947, 64–65.

page 244
E. C. Stedman: *Life and Letters . . .* 1910, 206–9.

page 244
"Restless craving": *ISL*, 67.

page 245
"Hoosier": Edwin H. Cady, ed., *W. D. Howells as Critic*, London, 1973, 12–15.

page 245
"Don't you miss": *Corr.*, I, 136.

page 246
"I like your *tinkles*": Charles E. Samuels, *Thomas Bailey Aldrich*, 1965, 37.

page 246
"My own greatest pleasure": Bucke (1883), 65.

page 246
"Allowing no interloper": *Corr.*, I, 126–27.

page 246
"Price is $40": *Corr.*, I, 47.

page 247
"We want to be": Bowers, xxxii.

page 247
"It is quite curious": *Corr.*, I, 51.

page 248
"Be composed": *LG—1860*, 399.

page 248
"Young man that wakes": *LG—1860*, 306.

page 249
"Emerson was not": *WWC*, III, 439–40; *PW*, I, 281–82.

page 249
"If I had cut sex out": *WWC*, I, 49, 56–57, 124, 151.

page 249
Even the bohemian: *WWC*, II, 375–76; *Child's Reminiscence*, 27.

page 250
Young Boston publishers: *Corr.*, I, 49–50, 51.

page 250
"It is quite 'odd' ": *Corr.*, I, 52.

page 251
"The best of all": *WWC*, IV, 378–79.

page 251
"The Many in One": *LG—1860*, 8, 22.

page 251
"So Long!": *LG—1860*, 454.

page 252
"Altogether, Jeff": *Corr.*, I, 53–54.

page 252
Meanwhile he lived: *Corr.*, I, 49–54.

page 253
Father Taylor: *PW*, II, 549–52.

page 253
"Valuable investment": *Corr.*, I, 52.

page 253
"A specimen": *Child's Reminiscence*, 29.

page 254
"Considerable opposition": *Corr.*, I, 48n.

page 254
John Townsend Trowbridge: "Reminiscences of Walt Whitman," *Altantic Monthly*, LXXXIX (February 1902), 163–166; Rufus A. Coleman, "Further Reminiscences of Walt Whitman," *Modern Language Notes*, LXIII (April 1948), 266–68; Coleman, "Trowbridge and Whitman," *PMLA*, LXIII (March 1948), 262–73.

page 255
"I love you, Walt!": *WWC*, III, 460.

page 255
"My dear, dear friend": *PW*, II, 689–91; *Champion*, 3–49.

page 256
They worked side by side: Boston Notebook, 1860, LC.

page 256
O'Connor's novel: *Champion*, 38.

page 256
"Spoil my supper": *WWC*, II, 486.

page 256
"What astonishing beauty": *Champion*, 41.

page 257
"Inquiring, tireless": *LG—1860*, 312.

page 257
"The orb is enclosed": *CRE*, 245.

page 257
George Templeton Strong: *Diary*, III, 45.

page 257
In a poem: "Year of Meteors," *CRE*, 238–39.

page 258
Henry Clapp: *WWC*, II, 376.

page 259
1856 political tract: *Workshop*, 93, 99.

page 260
"Two characters": Notebook, 1860–61, LC.

page 260
First sight of Abraham Lincoln: *PW*, II, 499–501

page 261
George Templeton Strong: *Diary*, III, 117–18.

page 261
Whitman noticed: *PW*, I, 26.

page 262
"The Women and children": *CWL*, 39–40.

page 262
"His preservation": Glicksberg, 89.

page 262
"I have this hour": Notebook, 1860–61, LC.

page 262
"So far, so well": *Workshop*, 135.

page 263
"The vault at Pfaff's": *CRE*, 660.

page 263
John Burroughs noted: Barrus, 2–3.

page 263
"Beat! beat!": *CRE*, 283.

page 263
James Russell Lowell: *WWC*, II, 213.

page 264
"Schemes, politics": Glicksberg, 125–26.

page 264
Leader articles: Glicksberg, 15–62.

page 264
"Arous'd and angry": *CRE*, 309.

page 265
"Amputations are going on": *MDW*, 18–19.

page 265
"From the stump": *CRE*, 310–11.

page 266
Dr. D. B. St. John Roosa: in Henry Stoddard's column, "World of Letters," *The Mail and Express* (New York), June 20, 1898; I thank Prof. Edwin Haviland Miller for the loan of a photocopy.

page 266
"There is a lady": Glicksberg, 42–43.

page 267
"My social position": Edwin Haviland Miller, "Walt Whitman and Ellen Eyre," *AL*, XXXIII, No. 1 (March 1961), 64–68.

page 267
One conflation: C. Carroll Hollis, "Whitman's 'Ellen Eyre,'" *WWR*, II, No. 3 (September 1956), 24–26.

page 267
"*Frank Sweeney*": New York City notebook, 1861–62, LC; reproduced in Esther Shephard, *Walt Whitman's Pose*, 1938, opp. 244.

page 268
Disaster at Fredericksburg: *Corr.*, I, 68.

page 268
"Walking all day": *Corr.*, I, 58.

page 268
"[R]emember your galliant son": *CWL*, 77.

page 269
Went out of his way: *Corr.*, I, 68.

page 269
"*Sight at daybreak*": Glicksberg, 79.

page 269
"I can be satisfied": *Corr.*, I, 61–62.

CHAPTER 14 (*pages 270–301*)

page 270
When Whitman settled: *UPP*, I, 31; *Corr.*, I, 82; *DBN*, III, 655–56. Useful sources for wartime Washington are: Thomas Froncek, ed., *The City of Washington*, 1977; Margaret Leech, *Reveille in Washington*, 1941.

page 271
"Everything he does": *Corr.*, I, 113n.

page 271
"I don't know": *CWL*, 71.

page 271
"Who can see": *Corr.*, I, 113.
page 271
"Hoosier Michel Angelo": *Corr.*, I, 82–83.
page 271
"Saw Mr. Lincoln": Glicksberg, 138.
page 272
"I should say": *PW*, *II*, 603–4.
page 272
Patent Office: *PW*, I, 39–40, 95, 296.
page 273
"A profound conviction": *WWC*, II, 26.
page 273
Wrote to Emerson: *Corr.*, I, 61.
page 273
"Pulling eminent wires": *WWC*, II, 414–15.
page 274
Preston King: *Corr.*, I, 74.
page 274
"Permit me to say": *Corr.*, I, 65–66.
page 275
John Townsend Trowbridge: "Reminiscences of Walt Whitman," *Atlantic Monthly*, LXXXIX (February 1902), 170–71. WW's manuscript memorandum of the Trowbridge-Chase interview is reproduced in Thomas Donaldson, *Walt Whitman, The Man*, 1896, 156; his comments on Chase and office hunting are in *Corr.*, I, 80 and II, 35.
page 275
"Walt Whitman—Soldier's Missionary": William White, "An Unpublished Notebook . . . ," *American Book Collector*, XII, January 1962, 8–13.
page 275
His commission: Feinberg Coll., LC; reproduced in *Specimen Days*, Boston, 1971, 15.
page 276
"First class battle": *Corr.*, I, 193, 196; *PW*, I, 69–71.
page 276
"That odious Walt Whitman": Harriet Ward Foote Hawley, quoted in Froncek, 219.
page 276
"There is a prejudice": *Corr.*, I, 12·*n.*

page 276
"To do the good": *Corr.*, I, 109.
page 277
"The Dead in this War": K. A. Preuschen, "Walt Whitman's Undelivered Oration . . . ," *Etudes Anglaises*, XXIV, No. 2 (1971), 147–51.
page 277
"Mother, when you": *Corr.*, I, 85–86.
page 277
Elijah Allen: Barrus, 5.
page 277
"I must bring out": *Corr.*, I, 85.
page 277
"Of the time": *Corr.*, I, 172.
page 278
"Talk with Ben": *Corr.*, I, 171*n.*
page 278
"It pleas'd him": *MDW*, 21.
page 278
"A new world": *Corr.*, I, 81.
page 278
"Interior history": *PW*, I, 115–18.
page 279
"No thorough previous preparation": *MDW*, 38. Invaluable background sources are: Stewart Brooks, *Civil War Medicine*, Springfield, Ill. 1966; Bessie Z. Jones, ed., *Hospital Sketches*, by Louisa May Alcott, Cambridge, Mass., 1960.
page 279
One historian: Brooks, 12.
page 280
Eighty per cent: Brooks, 51.
page 280
"You ought to see": *Corr.*, I, 110–11.
page 280
"In my visits": *MDW*, 18.
page 280
"Please send me": *Corr.*, I, 12.
page 281
"I am very happy": *Corr.*, I, 164; *Corr.*, I, 142; William Stansberry to WW, May 12, 1874, Trent Coll., Duke University; *CRE*, 311.
page 281
"Mad, determin'd tussle": *PW*, I, 47.
page 281
"The sky, the planets": *MDW*, 27.
page 282
Trial lines: *UPP*, II, 93.

page 282
He told Emerson: *Corr.*, I, 70.
page 282
"Same old story": *Corr.*, I, 227.
page 282
"Come sweet death": *CRE*, 310.
page 283
"*June 18th.*": *PW*, II, 49–50.
page 283
"Welcome oblivion": *PW*, II, 618.
page 283
"The dead, the dead": *PW*, I, 114–15.
page 284
Lewy Brown: *Corr.*, I, 91, 118*n*, 134.
page 284
Will Wallace: Roger Asselineau, "Walt Whitman, Child of Adam? . . . ," *Modern Language Quarterly*, X, No. 1 (March 1949), 91–95.
page 285
"We all loved": *Corr.*, I, 124, 145–46, 237*n*.
page 285
"Prommice": *Corr.*, I, 90*n*.
page 286
"Dear comrade": *Corr.*, I, 92–93; the deleted sentence is supplied in *Corr.*, I, 93*n*.
page 286
"I fully reciprocate": *Corr.*, I, 90*n*, 91*n*.
page 287
"I do not expect": *Corr.*, I, 106–7, 139, 181.
page 287
Elijah Douglass Fox: *Corr.*, I, 186–88.
page 287
"The O'Connor home": *WWC*, III, 525–26. Ellen M. [O'Connor] Calder, "Personal Recollections of Walt Whitman," *Atlantic Monthly*, XCIX (June 1907), 825–34; *Champion*, passim; Florence B. Freedman, "New Light on an Old Quarrel . . . ," *WWR*, XI, No. 2 (June 1965), 27–52.
page 288
"I have missed you": *Corr.*, I, 234*n*.
page 288
"I always know": Ellen O'Connor to WW, Nov. 30, 1870, LC.
page 289
"I have had several": Ellen O'Connor

to WW, July 3, 1889, Feinberg Coll., LC.
page 289
Move into Mickle Street: *WWC*, V, 366.
page 289
He had told Nelly: *UPP*, I, lix*n*.
page 289
Trowbridge: see note for page 275 ("John Townsend Trowbridge").
page 290
"The incarnation": Adam Gurowski, *Diary*, Washington, 1866, III, 127–28.
page 290
"William is in the best sense": *WWC*, I, 11.
page 291
"*Stop the war*": White, "An Unpublished Notebook," 12; *WWC*, III, 293; William Sloane Kennedy, *Reminiscences of Walt Whitman*, London, 1896, 34–35.
page 291
Eldridge recalled: Barrus, 335.
page 291
"They are manly enough": *PW*, II, 587–89; *Corr.*, I, 212, 273, 299, 323.
page 292
"Between two loves": *WWC*, III, 581–82.
page 292
"It's almost enough": *CWL*, 102.
page 292
"I remain silent": *Corr.*, I, 117.
page 293
"Mother, I hope": *Corr.*, I, 143–46.
page 293
Jesse's troubles: these and other troubles are mentioned *passim* in *Corr.*, I, *CWL*, *FCI*, and *Mattie*.
page 294
"Dear Walt": *Corr.*, I, 165*n*; *Corr.*, I, 176.
page 294
Andrew's death: *FCI*, 187–90; *Mattie*, 32–35.
page 295
"Had I been home": *Corr.*, I, 189*n*.
page 295
"I did not go on": *Corr.*, I, 189–90.
page 295
"Not entirely well": *Corr.*, I, 254.

page 296
"Their diagnosis": *Corr.*, I, 233, 234.
page 296
"I have seen": *Corr.*, I, 230.
page 296
"Permanently absorbed": *Corr.*, I, 77.
page 296
"Me and mine": *CRE*, 256.
page 296
Oscar Cunningham: *Corr.*, I, 218n, 231.
page 297
An "Introduction": *Workshop*, 127; *Blue Book*, 1968, I, xiv.
page 297
George's trunk: Manuscript Notes on George W. Whitman, Dec. 26, 1864, Yale University Library; George's Civil War Diary is printed in *CWL*, 137–60.
page 298
"I arrived here": *CWL*, 134.
page 298
Office of Indian Affairs: *PW*, II, 577–79; Dixon Wecter, "Walt Whitman as Civil Servant," *PMLA*, LVIII (December 1943), 1094–97.
page 298
"Good and easy berth": *WWC*, II, 402.
page 298
"I take things very easy": *Corr.*, I, 250.
page 299
"What are taps?": *WWC*, II, 144.
page 299
"I play not marches": *CRE*, 46.
page 299
Charles Sumner: Sumner and Lowell are quoted in R. B. Nye, *Society and Culture in America, 1830–1860*, 1974, 9–10.
page 299
Whitman saluted: *CRE*, 324; *MDW*, 59.
page 300
"The chief thing": *WWC*, I, 13; *MDW*, 65.
page 300
Contracted with Peter Eckler: the contract and related documents are in Feinberg Coll., LC; F. DeWolfe Miller, ed., *Walt Whitman's "Drum-Taps"* . . . Gainesville, Fla., 1959.
page 301
Swinburne: *CRE*, 328n.

page 301
"Crowning crime": Emory Holloway, "Whitman on the War's Finale," *Colophon*, I, part 1 (March 1930), [4].
page 301
"Western star": *PW*, I, 94–95.
page 301
"Reconciliation": *CRE*, 321.
page 302
"Black clouds": Glicksberg, 174–75.
page 302
"Appear'd the cloud": *CRE*, 334.
page 302
Watched the massed brigades: *PW*, I, 105; Manuscript Notes on George W. Whitman, July 27, 1865, Yale University Library.

CHAPTER 15 (*pages 303–28*)

page 303
"Augean stable": Barrus, 33–34; J. G. Randall and Richard N. Current, *Lincoln, The President*, 1955, 252, 278–79; *PW*, II, 611–12; Jerome M. Loving, "Whitman and Harlan: New Evidence," *AL*, XLVIII, No. 2 (May 1976), 219–21.
page 304
"The Services of Walter Whitman": *WWC*, III, 471.
page 304
The general purge: the documents and WW's comments on his dismissal are in *WWC*, III, 468–477; Barrus, 25–35; *Champion*, 56–75; F. DeWolfe Miller, "Before *The Good Gray Poet*," *Tennessee Studies in Literature*, III (1958), 89–98.
page 305
"To be self-balanced": *CRE*, 11.
page 305
"Here the enemy": *Corr.*, II, 158.
page 305
Fifteen-page letter: *Champion*, 149–56 (includes WW's notes).
page 306
Settled contentedly: *Corr.*, I, 303, 319; V, 289.
page 307
"The face of a poet": Clara Barrus, ed.,

The Heart of Burroughs' Journals. Boston, 1928, 69.

page 307
"O spheral": *Wake-Robin*, Boston, 1913, 51–52.

page 307
Burroughs noted: Barrus, 24.

page 307
"Sings oftener": Feinberg Coll., LC; William White, "An Unpublished Whitman Notebook for 'Lilacs,' " *Modern Language Quarterly*, XXIV (June 1963), 177–80.

page 308
"When Lilacs": *CRE*, 328, 330.

page 308
Critical essay: "Walt Whitman and his *Drum-Taps*," *Galaxy*, II (December 1866), 606–15.

page 308
"Range along the high plateau": *Corr.*, I, 185.

page 309
"Drum-Taps has none": *Corr.*, I, 246–47.

page 309
"Damn My Captain": *WWC*, II, 304, 333.

page 310
Trowbridge: "Reminiscences of Walt Whitman," *Atlantic Monthly*, LXXXIX (February 1902), 172–75; *CRE*, 324.

page 310
"Quite put out": Allen, 361.

page 311
Henry James: Allen, 578–79; F. O. Matthiessen, *The James Family*, 1961, 488–95.

page 311
Toward the end of 1865: largely on the evidence of *PW*, I, 111, and WW's inscription on a photograph of the two (Feinberg Coll., LC); Allen, 363.

page 311
"We felt to each other": *Calamus*, 23.

page 312
Burroughs describes: *Calamus*, 13.

page 312
"Like as not": *Calamus*, 25.

page 312
"One flitting glimpse": *LG—1860*, 371.

page 312
"Fearfully well": *Corr.*, I, 292.

page 312
"Whistling or singing": *Calamus*, 26–27.

page 313
"What do I look like": *WWC*, III, 542–43.

page 313
"Your head on my shoulder": *Corr.*, II, 103–4; *CRE*, 271.

page 313
"I did not appreciate": *Calamus*, 30.

page 313
In "your judgment": *Corr.*, II, 59.

page 314
Tender notes: *Corr.*, II, 47n, 83–86, 103–4, 128.

page 315
Jimmy Sorrill: *Corr.*, II, 51, 51n, 56n.

page 315
Went out of his way: *Corr.*, II, 52, 62, 88, 102–3.

page 315
"I don't know": *Corr.*, II, 47.

page 315
"Hours continuing long": *LG—1860*, 355.

page 316
"Depress the adhesive nature": *Notebook*, 1868–70, LC; Roger Asselineau, *The Evolution of Walt Whitman*, Cambridge, Mass., 1960, II, 187, 329.

page 316
"We parted": *Corr.*, II, 101.

page 317
"With a kind of ruthlessness": *Blue Book*, II, xli.

page 317
"O hymen": *LG—1860*, 313.

page 317
"Thruster holding me": *Blue Book*, I, 51.

page 317
"City of my walks": *Blue Book*, I, 363: *Corr.*, I, 284.

page 318
"A few little silly fans": *Corr.*, I, 287–88.

page 318
"Proud and passionate city": *CRE*, 294.

page 319
Central Park: *DBN*, I, 145; *PW*, I, 198–99.

page 319
"The weather is perfect": *Corr.*, V, 288.

page 319
"I publish & sell it": *Corr.*, V, 289.

page 320
"So our Shakespeare": R. A. Coleman, "Trowbridge and O'Connor . . . ," *AL*, XXIII, No. 3 (November 1951), 327.

page 320
"I received a portion": *WWC*, II, 257.

page 320
"God grant": *Champion*, 203.

page 320
Wendell Phillips: Florence B. Freedman, "New Light on an Old Quarrel . . . ," *WWR*, XI, No. 2 (June, 1965), 33.

page 320
Matthew Arnold: Bliss Perry, *Walt Whitman*, Boston, 1906, 177–79; *Champion*, 71–72.

page 321
"It seems as if": *Corr.*, I, 301.

page 321
Henry Raymond: Barrus, 35; Perry, *Walt Whitman*, 176–77.

page 321
Charley Heyde: *Corr.*, I, 303; *FCI*, 222–24.

page 321
"Grows stronger & stronger": *Corr.*, I, 300.

page 322
"You must come": Barrus, 35–36.

page 322
Galaxy: Edward F. Grier, "Walt Whitman, the *Galaxy*, and *Democratic Vistas*," *AL*, XXIII, No. 3 (November 1951), 332–50; Robert Scholnick, "Whitman and the Magazines: Some Documentary Evidence," *AL*, XLIV, No. 2 (May 1972), 222–46.

page 322
"About as impudent": *Corr.*, I, 297.

page 323
"Personally the author": *Corr.*, I, 348.

page 324
"The article has had": Grier, 335.

page 324
"My feeling": *Corr.*, I, 346; *WWC*, II, 419–20.

page 324
Spelled it out: *WWC*, III, 303–6.

page 324
"I have no objection": *Corr.*, I, 347.

page 325
"Horrible dismemberment": *Corr.*, II, 133.

page 325
"Rossetti said expurgate": *WWC*, I, 150–51.

page 325
"Substantial facts": *Corr.*, II, 150–53.

page 325
"If you visit England": *Corr.*, II, 125–26; the growth of WW's reputation abroad is detailed in: Harold Blodgett, *Walt Whitman Abroad*, Ithaca, N.Y., 1934; Gay Wilson Allen, *The New Walt Whitman Handbook*, 1975, 249–327.

page 326
John Swinton: *Corr.*, II, 48–49.

page 327
"Englishwoman's Estimate": *The Radical* (Boston, Mass.), May 1870.

page 327
"That lady": *Corr.*, II, 98*n*.

page 328
Helen Price: Bucke (1883), 30.

page 328
He sent *"the lady"*: *Corr.*, II, 91–92.

page 328
"O dear Walt": Gilchrist, 62, 66.

CHAPTER 16 (*pages 329–49*)

page 329
Susan Garnet Smith: *WWC*, IV, 312–13.

page 329
"I pour the stuff": *CRE*, 102–3.

page 330
Charley Eldridge: *Corr.*, I, 185.

page 330
A passenger: Mrs. Nellie Eyster, *WWC*, I, 34–35.

page 331
"A sort of human miracle": *WWC*, III, 376–77.

page 331
"I was so sure": Gilchrist, 63.

page 331
"It is not happiness": Gilchrist, 61.

page 332
Walt's first letter: *Corr.*, II, 140.

page 332
The word "enough": Gilchrist, 70.

page 332
"Restless, anxious": Gilchrist, 72.

page 333
"Did I tell you": *Corr.*, II, 164; *WWC*, II, 374, 443.

page 333
"Dear friend": *Corr.*, II, 170.

page 333
Delivered of "triplets": *Corr.*, II, 116.

page 334
"Good, worthy, non-demonstrative": *Corr.*, II, 15.

page 334
"Stifled, O days": *CRE*, 591.

page 335
"*Schwärmerei*": "Shooting Niagara: And After?" *Macmillan's Magazine* (London), August 1867.

page 335
Matthew Arnold: *WWC*, I, 45, 122–23, V, 481.

page 335
"Never was there less": *PW*, II, 257.

page 336
"Comic-painful hullabaloo": *PW*, II, 750; *Corr.*, I, 338, 342.

page 336
"I will not gloss over": *PW*, II, 363.

page 336
"I say we had best": *PW*, 369–70.

page 337
"I had no idea": Barrus, 49.

page 337
Sent Carlyle a copy: *Corr.*, II, 185.

page 337
"We have frequently printed": *PW*, II, 393.

page 338
"What is life": *PW*, II, 740.

page 338
"Cosmic purposes": *WWC*, I, 156–57.

page 338
"After chanting": *CRE*, 746.

page 338
In his notebook: Fredson Bowers, "The Earliest Manuscript of Whitman's 'Passage to India' and its Notebook," *Bulletin of The New York Public Library*, LXI, No. 7 (July 1957), 319–52.

page 338
"Farewell gathering": *CRE*, 745.

page 338
"For the deep waters": *CRE*, 421.

page 339
"Every great problem": Bowers, "The Earliest Manuscript . . . ," 349.

page 339
"Finally shall come": *CRE*, 415.

page 339
"All these hearts": *CRE*, 415.

page 339
A love feast: Barrus, 71–72.

page 340
"O Walt": Allen, 419.

page 340
"My mammy": *Corr.*, II, 169.

page 340
Joaquin Miller: *Corr.*, II, 182–83.

page 340
"Would astonish Longfellow": *WWC*, I, 328–29.

page 341
Caricature appeared: F. DeWolfe Miller, *The Sunday Star* (Washington, D. C.), July 30, 1961.

page 341
Report of his death: *Corr.*, II, 123; W. E. Martin, Jr., "Whitmania from the Boston *Journal*," *WWR*, XXIII, No. 2 (June 1977), 90–92.

page 341
"Walt Whitman in Europe": *Kansas Magazine*, II, No. 6 (December 1872), 499–502; *Corr.*, II, 30*n*, 157, 189, V, 289, 295.

page 341
"My percentage": *Corr.*, II, 139.

page 342
"After all": *CRE*, 195.

page 342
"By thud of machinery": *CRE*, 198.

page 342
Congressman James Garfield: *WWC*, I, 324; *Calamus*, 32.

page 342
"I am to be *on exhibition*": *Corr.*, II, 178; Harold W. Blodgett, "Walt Whitman's Dartmouth Visit," *Dartmouth Alumni Bulletin*, XXV (February 1933), 13–15; Bliss Perry, *Walt Whitman*, Boston, 1906, 203–10.

page 343
Stay with his sister Hannah: *Corr.*, II, 182; Hannah Heyde to Louisa Whitman, Nov. 16, 1872, LC; Katherine Molinoff, *Some Notes on Whitman's Family*, 1941, 36.

page 344
Last of their noisy debates: chief sources are listed in note for page 287 ("The O'Connor home"); also, Barrus, 96–100.

page 345
"Don't be alarmed": *Corr.*, II, 187.

page 345
"Mother, it is always": *Corr.*, II, 183; *Corr.*, II, 203, 208, 211.

page 345
Bulwer-Lytton: *WWC*, III, 221–22; Lytton's opinion of WW is quoted in Amy Cruse, *The Victorians and Their Reading*, Boston, 1962, 258.

page 345
He felt faint: Bucke (1883), 45–46.

page 346
"Had been simmering": *NF*, 147–48.

page 346
"Pete, do you remember": *PW*, II, 612.

page 347
"My head feels bad": Allen, 452.

page 347
"Mother's last lines": *WWC*, IV, 514.

page 347
Sat by her coffin: *Corr.*, II, 221n.

page 347
"Great dark cloud": *Corr.*, II, 241–42.

page 347
Charley Eldridge reported: Barrus, 83.

page 347
"In her memory": *Corr.*, II, 230, 235.

page 348
"Perturbed sort of letter": *Corr.*, II, 239–40.

page 348
Took the ring from his finger: *Corr.*, II, 235; Gilchrist, 96, 103.

page 348
"I think it is best": *Corr.*, II, 248.

page 348
"As I see it now": *Corr.*, II, 272.

page 348
"You too have sailed": Gilchrist, 108.

page 349
"All questions": *Corr.*, II, 313.

page 349
"I was down": *WWC*, II, 208.

CHAPTER 17 (*pages 350–72*)

page 350
Centennial mania: Dee Brown, *The Year of the Century: 1876*, 1966.

page 351
"I do not seem to belong": *WWC*, I, 325.

page 352
"Forgive me": *Corr.*, II, 345.

page 352
"I have come to the end of my rope": *Corr.*, II, 343.

page 352
Moncure Conway's: *Corr.*, III, 37–38, 38n.

page 353
Longfellow admired: James Bryce, Diary, Sept. 1, 1870, Bodleian Library, Oxford University.

page 353
"Immensely over-rated": Barrus, 220–21.

page 353
James Bryce: Diary, Sept. 5, 1870, Bodleian Library, Oxford University.

page 353
"Tell Walt": Clara Barrus, *Life and Letters of John Burroughs*, Boston, 1925, I, 144.

page 353
"Maintains the same attitude": *Corr.*, II, 155.

page 354
"He thought Walt's friends": Barrus, 65.

page 354
"I know what I am about": Clara Barrus, *Life and Letters of John Burroughs*, I, 144.

page 355
"Walt Whitman's Actual American Position": *Workshop*, 245–48; the debate provoked by this article is authoritatively detailed in *Champion*, 109–23, 204–16 and Robert Scholnick, "The Selling of the 'Author's Edition': Whitman, O'Connor, and the *West Jersey Press* Affair," *WWR*, XXIII, No. 1 (March 1977), 3–23.

page 357
Whitman's spirits rose: *Corr.*, III, 30, 38n, 39.

page 357
"Walt Whitman: Is He Persecuted?": reprinted in *Champion*, 204–16.

page 357
"Lull in the Walt Whitman controversy": *Atlantic Monthly*, December 1877, 749–51.

page 358
Book sales for 1876: *Corr.*, VI, xvii.

page 358
"Blessed gales": *PW*, II, 699–700.

page 358
Accepted with serenity: Bucke (1883), 55n.

page 358
"I get out": *Corr.*, III, 27.

page 359
"I ought to have written": *Corr.*, III, 67.

page 359
"How I wish": *Corr.*, III, 86–87.

page 359
"My (adopted) son": *Corr.*, III, 67–68.

page 359
Burroughs was annoyed": Barrus, 164.

page 360
"It makes (tried to make)": *Corr.*, III, 211.

page 360
George and Susan Stafford: supplementing WW's accounts of the Stafford household and farm are: Sculley Bradley, "Walt Whitman on Timber Creek," *AL*, V, No. 3 (November 1933), 237–46; Edward Carpenter, *Days with Walt Whitman*, 1906, 10–15; Walter Teller, "Speaking of Books: Whitman at Timber Creek," *New York Times Book Review*, April 10, 1966, 2, 31.

page 360
"Am with folks": *Corr.*, III, 107.

page 360
"*If I had not known*": *Corr.*, III, 215.

page 360
"I take an interest": *Corr.*, III, 37.

page 361
"I fear he is": *Corr.*, III, 41n.

page 361
Wrote in his diary: *DBN*, II, 337.

page 361
"Would be a true comfort": *Corr.*, III, 381–82.

page 361
"Can you forgive me": Harry Stafford to WW, May 1, 1877, Feinberg Coll., LC (amending text in *Corr.*, III, 5).

page 361
Names of drivers: *DBN*, I, 43, 88, 89.

page 362
Edward Cattell: *Corr.*, III, 76n; *DBN*, I, 42, 61.

page 362
Urgent letter: *Corr.*, III, 77.

page 362
"It seems an age": *Corr.*, III, 77n.

page 362
Pressing Harry to accept: *DBN*, I, 44, 48, 49.

page 363
Calmer remedy: *DBN*, I, 51.

page 363
Memorable talks: *DBN*, I, 54, 58.

page 363
"You may say": *Corr.*, III, 5.

page 363
"I wish you would put": *Corr.*, III, 6–7.

page 363
"Feb 11 [1878]": *DBN*, I, 85.

page 363
"Many things, confidences": *Corr.*, III, 264.

page 364
"Do not think me": Gilchrist, 139, 141.

page 364
He did his tactful best: *Corr.*, III, 30–31.

page 364
Coming to America: Gilchrist, 147, 149.

page 365
"Mrs G": *DBN*, I, 41.

page 365
"If I had been near": *Corr.*, III, 92n.

page 365
With Anne and her children: Grace Gilchrist, "Chats with Walt Whitman," *Temple Bar Magazine* (London), CXIII, February 1898, 200–212; Herbert Harlakenden Gilchrist, ed., *Anne Gilchrist, Her Life and Writings*, 1887, 227–43; *Workshop*, 262–63.

page 366
"Anne Gilchrist was suffering": Edward Carpenter, *Some Friends of Walt Whitman*, London, 1924, 8,

page 366
"I do not feel as if": *Corr.*, III, 97n.

page 366
Walt had come back: *DBN*, I, 65, 75, 76.

page 367
"June 9 [1879]": *DBN*, I, 145.

page 367
"I think of you continually": Gilchrist, 194.

page 367
The world, the race: *CRE*, 525.

page 367
Looked at nature: *PW*, I, 128, 133.

page 368
Rendered the continuum: *PW*, I, 128–29.

page 368
"The swim of the boys": *Corr.*, III, 76n.

page 368
"The beards of the young men": *CRE*, 38–39.

page 368
Deaths of young men: *PW*, I, 155; *CRE*, 34.

page 369
"In paths untrodden": *CRE*, 112–13.

page 369
"What I draw from the water": *CRE*, 118–19.

page 369
"There come moods": *PW*, I, 152.

page 370
"After I wrestle": *PW*, I, 143, 153.

page 370
"One does not wonder": *PW*, I, 131.

page 370
"Houses and rooms": *CRE*, 29.

page 370
"Somehow I seem'd": *PW*, I, 152.

page 371
"Once he came": *PW*, I, 163.

page 371
"Pete, if you came": *Corr.*, III, 96.

page 371
"Wonders, revelations": *Corr.*, III, 169.

page 371
"Suggested and rejected names": *PW*, I, 247–48.

page 372
"*Ducks and drakes*": *Corr.*, III, 315.

page 372
"Discovery of Old Age": *PW*, I, 277.

page 372
"I cannot divest my appetite": *PW*, I, 294.

page 372
"Cities of romance": *WWC*, II, 29.

Index

Index

ILLUSTRATION SOURCES